The Representation of Slavery in the Greek Novel

This volume offers the first comprehensive treatment of how the five canonical Greek novels represent slaves and slavery. In each novel, one or both elite protagonists are enslaved, and Owens explores the significance of the genre's regular social degradation of these members of the elite.

Reading the novels in the context of social attitudes and stereotypes about slaves, Owens argues for an ideological division within the genre: the earlier novelists, Xenophon of Ephesus and Chariton, challenge and undermine elite stereotypes; the three later novelists, Longus, Achilles Tatius, and Heliodorus, affirm them. The critique of elite thinking about slavery in Xenophon and Chariton opens the possibility that these earlier authors and their readers included literate ex-slaves. The interests and needs of these authors and their readers shaped the emerging genre and not only made the protagonists' slavery a key motif but also made slavery itself a theme that helped define the genre.

The Representation of Slavery in the Greek Novel will be of interest not only to students of the ancient novel but also to anyone working on slavery in the ancient world.

William M. Owens is Associate Professor of Classics at Ohio University in Athens, Ohio. His research focuses on the representation of social institutions, practices, and ideologies in ancient literature, in particular comedy and the novel.

Routledge Monographs in Classical Studies

Titles include:

The Bible, Homer, and the Search for Meaning in Ancient Myths
Why We Would Be Better Off With Homer's Gods
John Heath

Fantasy in Greek and Roman Literature
Graham Anderson

Piracy, Pillage, and Plunder in Antiquity
Appropriation and the Ancient World
Edited by Richard Evans and Martine de Marre

Romans at War
Soldiers, Citizens, and Society in the Roman Republic
Edited by Jeremy Armstrong and Michael P. Fronda

Discourse of Kingship in Classical Greece
Carol Atack

Emotional Trauma in Greece and Rome
Representations and Reactions
Edited by Andromache Karanika and Vassiliki Panoussi

The Representation of Slavery in the Greek Novel
Resistance and Appropriation
William M. Owens

Memories of Utopia
The Revision of Histories and Landscapes in Late Antiquity
Edited by Bronwen Neil and Kosta Simic

For more information on this series, visit: www.routledge.com/classicalstudies/
series/RMCS

The Representation of Slavery in the Greek Novel
Resistance and Appropriation

William M. Owens

LONDON AND NEW YORK

First published 2020 by Routledge

2 Park Square, Milton Park, Abingdon, Oxon OX14 4RN
605 Third Avenue, New York, NY 10017

Routledge is an imprint of the Taylor & Francis Group, an informa business

First issued in paperback 2022

Copyright © 2020 William M. Owens

The right of William M. Owens to be identified as author of this work has been asserted by him in accordance with sections 77 and 78 of the Copyright, Designs and Patents Act 1988.

All rights reserved. No part of this book may be reprinted or reproduced or utilised in any form or by any electronic, mechanical, or other means, now known or hereafter invented, including photocopying and recording, or in any information storage or retrieval system, without permission in writing from the publishers.

Notice:
Product or corporate names may be trademarks or registered trademarks, and are used only for identification and explanation without intent to infringe.

Publisher's Note

The publisher has gone to great lengths to ensure the quality of this reprint but points out that some imperfections in the original copies may be apparent.

British Library Cataloguing-in-Publication Data
A catalogue record for this book is available from the British Library

Library of Congress Cataloging-in-Publication Data
Names: Owens, William M., author.
Title: The representation of slavery in the Greek novel : resistance and appropriation / William M. Owens.
Other titles: Routledge monographs in classical studies.
Identifiers: LCCN 2019036082 (print) | LCCN 2019036083 (ebook) | ISBN 9780367348755 (hardback) | ISBN 9780429328558 (ebook)
Subjects: LCSH: Greek prose literature—History and criticism. | Slavery in literature.
Classification: LCC PA3257 .O94 2019 (print) | LCC PA3257 (ebook) | DDC 883.009/3582—dc23
LC record available at https://lccn.loc.gov/2019036082
LC ebook record available at https://lccn.loc.gov/2019036083

ISBN: 978-0-367-34875-5 (hbk)
ISBN: 978-1-03-233764-7 (pbk)
DOI: 10.4324/9780429328558

Typeset in Times New Roman
by Apex CoVantage, LLC

For Kay

Contents

Preface   viii

List of Abbreviations   x

Introduction: degradation and resistance   1

1   *Ephesiaca*: enslavement and folktale   27

2   *Callirhoe*: narratives of slavery explicit and implied, told and retold   56

3   Two novels about slavery   88

4   *Daphnis and Chloe*: slavery as nature and art   121

5   Slavery and literary play in *Leucippe and Clitophon*   151

6   *Aethiopica*: love and slavery, philosophy and the novel   185

Afterword: conclusions summarized and two points of speculation   214

Bibliography   223

Index   239

Preface

I became interested in the Greek novel through my reading in the history of Roman slavery. Keith Bradley, in *Slavery and Society at Rome* (1994), draws on evidence in the ancient novelists, both Greek and Roman, to try to reconstruct details regarding ancient slavery that might otherwise be lost to us; for example, aspects of the institution's everyday reality and its psychological impact on slaves. In using ancient fiction for historical evidence, Bradley assumed that the novels reflected their contemporary reality. Such an assumption cannot be straightforward. I was inspired to look more closely into the matter and to read the Greek novels for the first time. My initial search for historical information had to yield some ground to my admiration for these novels themselves, melodramatic tales of love and adventure and unlike anything I had read before in Greek literature. I found that not only did they offer a plausible representation of different aspects of ancient slavery, they also engaged with questions raised by slavery on an ideological level. In my reading, the Greek novels came to be about slavery as well as love. Thus, this book.

I have many others to thank. First, I wish to acknowledge my teachers at Cornell and Yale, Fred Ahl, George Goold, and Gordon Williams, although George and Gordon are not here to hear an expression of gratitude that they very much deserve. Research on the book benefited early from my participation in a National Endowment for the Humanities (NEH) summer seminar in Rome under the direction of Eleanor Leach and Eve D'Ambra, "Identity and Self-Representation in the Subcultures of Ancient Rome." I am most grateful to them both, although Ellie is not here to see the book she helped shape in its first stages. As the project developed, I read papers at meetings, regional, national, and international. The comments these papers received helped me better focus my thinking; I note, in particular, discussions with John Morgan and Stephen Trzaskoma. I also have benefited from the comments of Matthew Leigh and Amy Richlin, who read early drafts of selected chapters; David Konstan, who read even earlier drafts; John Bodel; Page duBois; Sara Forsdyke; Matthew Leigh; Denise McCoskey; Patrice Rankine; Roberta Stewart; Greg Thalmann; and Dan Tompkins. Special thanks are due to Ed Cueva and Rose MacLean, who read the penultimate draft and offered helpful criticism and bibliographical advice.

Preface ix

I also wish to thank my colleagues at Ohio University, with whom I have had numerous conversations about the book as it evolved: Jim Andrews; Neil Bernstein, who helpfully commented on an early draft; Steve Hays; Lynne Lancaster; and Ruth Palmer. I am especially grateful to Tom Carpenter, who read a draft of the whole, made many wise suggestions, and offered encouragement throughout the process.

I have dedicated this book to my wife, Kay Tousley, for her patience and support during the time of the project. She has lived with it from the start and heard the oral first draft of every idea.

* * *

An earlier version of the chapter on Chariton appears as "Callirhoe: A Therapeutic Slave Narrative," in *Slaves and Masters in the Ancient Novel*, edd., Stelios Panayotakis and Gareth Schmeling (Ancient Narrative Supplementum 23) Eelde: Barkhuis.

Translations throughout are my own except as noted otherwise. I have used the following texts for the five novels: Henderson 2009 for Xenophon of Ephesus and Longus; Goold 1995 for Chariton; Vilborg 1955 for Achilles Tatius; Rattenbury and Lumb 1960 (1935), 1960 (1938), and 1960 (1943) for Heliodorus.

Abbreviations

AN	*Ancient Narrative*
ANRW	*Aufstieg und Niedergang der römischen Welt*
CJ	*Classical Journal*
CP	*Classical Philology*
CQ	*Classical Quarterly*
GCN	*Groningen Colloquia on the Ancient Novel*
GRBS	*Greek, Roman and Byzantine Studies*
IAph2007	*Inscriptions of Aphrodisias 2007*
IG	*Inscriptiones Graecae*
JHS	*Journal of Hellenic Studies*
LSJ	*Liddell and Scott, Greek-English Lexicon*
OCD	*Oxford Classical Dictionary*
P&P	*Past & Present*
RE	*Real-Encyclopädie der klassichen Altertumswissenschaft*
RhM	*Rheinisches Museum für Philologie*
TAPA	*Transactions of the American Philological Association*
YCS	*Yale Classical Studies*
ZPE	*Zeitschrift für Papyrologie und Epigraphik*

Introduction
Degradation and resistance

A peculiar institution in a peculiar literary genre

In nineteenth-century America, the practitioners and defenders of slavery referred to it as the South's "peculiar institution," a term suggesting that slavery was an integral part of the southern states' economy and culture, a way of life that outsiders did not value or understand.[1] However, slavery can be thought of as peculiar in a different sense, in that its practice depends on a fundamental contradiction in which enslaved human beings are classified and treated as a form of property along with animals and even inanimate objects. In this context, slavery is peculiar in the sense of being strange because it challenges basic assumptions about what it means to be a human being. The present study argues that the depiction of slavery is of central importance in a literary genre that itself may be regarded as peculiar, the ancient Greek erotic novel. The five examples of this genre that survive in their entirety are melodramatic stories of love, adventure, and danger. A young man and woman of elite status meet; they fall in love and marry – or, at least, are headed in the direction of marriage. They go on a journey, they are separated, and they face all sorts of danger. Finally, the lovers are reunited, restored to freedom, and restored to their original status. They live, it seems, happily ever after. Slavery, however, is always among the dangers that one or both protagonists experience. The detail is peculiar in its cultural context: The ancient Greek and Roman elites believed that not only was it shameful to be a slave; it was also shameful even to have been a slave. What was the significance of the regular social degradation of the elite protagonists in this genre?

The motif in which noble characters are enslaved is known from the established genres of epic, tragedy, and comedy. Odysseus' faithful swineherd, Eumaios, was the son of a king; his nurse, Eurycleia, was also likely of noble origin.[2] Euripides' *Trojan Women* dramatized the enslavement of the noble Hecabe, Andromache, and Cassandra; his *Ion* featured a temple slave who was the son of an Athenian princess. The motif was frequent in comedy. Prior to the action of Menander's *Sikyonioi*, pirates had kidnapped Philoumene, the daughter of an Athenian citizen, and sold her as a slave in Caria. In Terence's *Eunuchus* (an adaptation of Menander's play) Chaerea rapes the slave girl Pamphila; the two are able to marry after it is

2 Introduction

revealed that Pamphila is actually an Athenian citizen who had been kidnapped as a child. Tyndarus, the hero of Plautus' *Captivi*, was born to a noble family in Aetolia but kidnapped while still an infant and sold as a slave in the neighboring city of Elis. However, the Greek novels were different. Eumaios was not a protagonist in the *Odyssey*. Neither did every tragedy feature an enslaved protagonist, an Andromache, nor did every comedy star a Tyndarus. In contrast, each of the five surviving Greek novels depicts the enslavement of one or both protagonists. This plot element gives the Greek novel its peculiarity, serving as a marker that distinguishes the genre from other forms.

The genre itself seems to be new, emerging in the first centuries BCE and CE. Five complete examples survive.[3] The consensus of scholarship has located the two earliest in the first century CE: Xenophon of Ephesus' (henceforth "Xenophon") *Ephesiaca* (or *The Ephesian Tale*)[4] and Chariton's *Callirhoe*.[5] Xenophon's protagonists, the noble Ephesian youths Habrocomes and Anthia, go on a voyage soon after they are married. Phoenician pirates capture and enslave them. They are reunited only toward the end of the novel. Chariton's protagonists, Chaereas and Callirhoe, husband and wife, were the scions of noble Syracusan families. They, too, are both enslaved, but in separate episodes. Callirhoe is sold across the sea to an agricultural estate outside Miletus; Chaereas is sold into slavery after he is captured while trying to find his wife.

Scholarly consensus places the publication of the other three novels in the second half of the second century CE and later: Longus' *Daphnis and Chloe*; Achilles Tatius' (henceforth "Achilles") *Leucippe and Clitophon*; Heliodorus' *Aethiopica* (or, *The Ethiopian Tale*). Longus' protagonists, the eponymous Daphnis and Chloe, were each born to wealthy families in the city of Mitylene on Lesbos. Both were exposed as infants. In Longus' novel, only the hero becomes a slave when he was rescued and raised by a family of enslaved herdsmen. The family that rescued and raised Chloe were humble but not slaves. Similarly, in *Leucippe and Clitophon*, only one of the lovers becomes a slave, in this case, the heroine, Leucippe, who is sold by pirates to an agricultural estate near Ephesus. Finally, in *Aethiopica*, both Theagenes and Charicleia are briefly enslaved to the wife of the Persian governor of Egypt.

A new genre thus emerged that, in contrast to established literary forms, regularly featured the enslavement of one or both protagonists. Was this motif related to the emergence of the genre itself? To answer this question, I read how each of the five novels represents slaves, both the enslaved protagonists and other enslaved characters, in the context of the normative thinking or ideology of the slave-owning elite, that is, how ancient slave-owners customarily thought about slaves and how they justified slavery. My reading led to two conclusions and a suggestion. The first conclusion is broad. Slavery figures as an important theme in each of the five surviving novels, either as an object of consideration in itself or as a metaphor for thinking about other relationships. The second conclusion is tied closely to the consideration of elite thinking about slavery. I discern an ideological divide within the genre. The two earlier novels (i.e., first century CE), *Ephesiaca* and *Callirhoe*, subvert the way the elite thought about slaves. The

Introduction 3

later novels (i.e., after 150 CE), *Daphnis and Chloe*, *Leucippe and Clitophon*, and *Aethiopica*, imply an ideological point of view more in conformity with this thinking. This ideological divide is reinforced by the representation of enslaved secondary characters. We might call them real slaves to distinguish them from the enslaved elite protagonists. In the earlier novels, real slaves act as confidants and allies of the enslaved protagonists in their struggle to survive slavery. In the later novels, some real slave characters pose a greater threat to the enslaved protagonists than their masters do.

Finally, a suggestion: In the subversive stance that they adopt toward elite thinking regarding slaves, Xenophon and Chariton rationalize and condone the behavior of their enslaved protagonists even when these characters act like stereotypically bad slaves: when they lie and deceive and even when they commit acts of violence.[6] Both Xenophon and Chariton depict these behaviors as necessary for their protagonists' survival in slavery; indeed, these behaviors contribute, directly or indirectly, to the protagonists' escape from slavery and restoration to elite status. In brief, Xenophon and Chariton seem to reward bad-slave behavior. At the same time, these authors have salted their sympathetic attitude toward this behavior (their endorsement of it?) with ambivalence and reservation. Xenophon, for example, takes pains to justify Anthia's killing of a man, her owner's surrogate, who was about to rape her; Chariton expresses unease when Callirhoe deceives her master and relinquishes her sexual fidelity in return for freedom. Sometimes the enslaved but elite protagonists register discomfort with their own bad-slave behavior. They may express shame about it, conceal it, or lie about it. Despite their apparent subversion of elite thinking, Xenophon and Chariton seem concerned to give the ideology its due, in some ways even to affirm it.

This contradictory subversion and affirmation, that is, this ambivalence toward normative elite thinking, suggested to me the possibility that Xenophon and Chariton could have been ex-slaves writing, in part, for ex-slave readers. These authors did not write exclusively for ex-slaves; rather, their novels may have had a peculiar appeal for such readers.[7] The ambivalent subversion and affirmation of elite thinking in these novels would seem to align with the perspective of literate ex-slaves who had themselves become slave-owners. As ex-slaves, such individuals would remember what they once had to do to survive. The memory of their previous life prepared them to understand and even to condone enslaved protagonists who were forced to act like slaves. As current slave-owners, on the other hand, these same readers were assimilating the habits and attitudes of other slave-owners. They would not now condone bad-slave behavior in their own slaves. Thus, as readers, these literate ex-slaves found narratives that reflected aspects of their own conflicted thinking about slavery in the ambivalence of *Ephesiaca* and *Callirhoe*.

An additional consideration: Xenophon and Chariton may have been among the experimenters in the genre as it was taking form in the first century CE. Their work may have helped establish the emerging genre with a narration of slavery that was marked by sympathy for slaves, albeit sympathy salted with

4   *Introduction*

reservation. The later novelists inherited the narration of the protagonists' enslavement as a generic marker for the novel, but their ideological stance reflects more conventional elite thinking about slaves and slavery. In other words, the later authors, Longus, Achilles, and Heliodorus, included the enslavement of the protagonists as a plot element that helped to establish the generic identity of their narratives. At the same time, they rejected the subversive ideas present in Xenophon and Chariton (or similar authors) that subverted conventional elite thinking. Thus, there are traces of an ideological debate within the genre.

In this regard, I would argue that the genre, at least as represented by the five surviving novels, reflects meaningful engagement with slavery itself. Thus, the present reading differs from readings that have seen slavery as merely one of a series of the protagonists' adventures[8] or as a metaphor of displacement in a world where the *polis* was no longer central to identity[9] or as a stage in religious[10] or social[11] initiation. In its focus on slavery, the present reading may be closer to a number of studies concerned with the novels' representation of the *realia* of social and economic conditions in general.[12] However, instead of focusing on social *realia* as a thing apart, I have tried to read the representation of slavery as an integral part of how each of the novels functions as a work of literature.[13] In this regard, I follow William Fitzgerald's brief and insightful *Slavery in the Roman Literary Imagination* that surveys the representation of slavery in a range of Latin genres.[14] In Fitzgerald's view, the literature that treats the complex master–slave relationship is ideological, reflecting the perspective of slave-owners,[15] but is, nonetheless, "preeminently the place where such complexities are expressed, exploited and managed."[16] Similarly, each of the five surviving novels represents, exploits, and manages the master–slave relationship in a manner that is complex and ideological, though the ideological perspective in Xenophon and Chariton may not be that of the slave-owner.

In the final chapter of his book, Fitzgerald considers the possibility that Apuleius preserved traces of a servile point of view in Lucius' transformation into an ass:

> Clearly Apuleius has contaminated the novelistic plot of deracination and restoration with the animal fable, and it is an intriguing possibility that this may be the one literary genre in the ancient world that preserves traces of a fiction produced by slaves.[17]

Fitzgerald contrasts Lucius' experience as an ass with that of the enslaved protagonists of the Greek novels, who seem not really to become slaves because they preserve their beauty and chastity. However, I shall argue that the psychic (and possibly physical) impact of slavery on the elite protagonists is significant, at least as far as Xenophon and Chariton are concerned. The eminent historian of Roman slavery Keith Bradley anticipated this point in referring to Chariton's *Callirhoe* in order to illustrate the psychological and emotional trauma endured by slaves who suffer geographic dislocation. Chariton's heroine had been taken

Introduction 5

captive from her home in Sicily, sold into slavery at Miletus in Asia Minor, and then taken yet farther east to the court of the Great King in Babylon. Bradley notes that Callirhoe had been able to endure everything so long as she could hear Greek spoken and could see the Mediterranean, a visible connection with Syracuse, her homeland. But when she crossed the Euphrates and entered the realm of the king, she despaired of ever returning.[18] In this episode, Bradley sees the possibility that a slave's perspective has been preserved, in particular how an ancient slave might have felt about a particular aspect of her enslavement.[19] Such a detail could reflect an elite author's empathetic appreciation of the way slaves thought and felt; I shall argue that it is also possible that Xenophon and Chariton drew on a tradition of thinking about what happens in slavery that had been produced by slaves themselves.

Elite constructions of the slave

In this section, I describe an important aspect of elite thinking about slaves, the idea that the slave was an inferior or defective person deserving of slavery. In the section after this, I examine a related phenomenon, the resistance of slaves to their owners' attempts to degrade them. The contest between masters and slaves involving degradation and resistance to degradation frames the social context in which I read the novels' representation of slaves and slavery.

The thinking that informed the slave-owning elite's construction of the stereotypical slave may be described as an assembly of social prejudices rather than as a coherent system of ideas.[20] Nonetheless, these prejudices offer an important perspective on understanding the mentality of ancient slave-owners. They constituted more than casual social attitudes. Codified into law and systematized in philosophic discourse, stereotypes about slaves helped to normalize and justify the regular practices of institutional slavery. In this respect, it is helpful to consider them in the context of Orlando Patterson's construction of slavery as a system of domination that aims at the metaphorical death of the slave, that is, slavery as a form of social death.[21] As a dominated individual, the slave is alienated from his or her birthright and whatever status attaches to that right. The slave, thus, possesses no honor and is, in Patterson's famous formulation, "socially dead." Indeed, the socially dead slave lives but as a degraded and submissive member of the master's family, a fit object for coercion and exploitation.

Social degradation figures both intellectually and practically in the functioning of a slave system. It helps slave-owners rationalize their power and compels slaves to submit, either in response to violence or through their own internalization of degradation. It is also useful to note that Patterson's emphasis on slavery as a system of domination rather than an economic system is of particular relevance to the novels, which represent less the economic and legal aspects of slavery and more the human perspective of the characters, in particular, the social interactions between masters and slaves centering around domination and resistance. Patterson drew his evidence from slave societies around the world and through history. Thus, it is not surprising that Greek and Roman

6 *Introduction*

slave-owners shared similar ideas about slavery because they faced similar practical challenges in controlling and exploiting their slaves. They also faced similar intellectual challenges in rationalizing their domination.[22] Consequently, the thinking of Greek and Roman slave owners shared significant overlap despite local differences in matters such as the composition of the slave population, the economic impact of slave labor, or the practice of manumission.[23] In the imperial period, that is, the period of the novel, these similarities were enhanced because the Greek and Roman elites saw themselves as heirs to a common intellectual and cultural tradition. Shared ideas about slaves were part of the shared inheritance of elite identity. For this reason, it is fair to consider the representation of slavery in the Greek novels in the context of the thinking of both the Greek and the Roman elites.

Greek and Roman elites constructed slaves as defective persons who were both their moral inferiors and their moral opposites. The slave was motivated by physical pleasure or pain. The owner, conceived as an idealized free person, was inspired by principles.[24] The slave was a liar; the free person told the truth. The slave was either a coward or a violent brute; the free man possessed manly courage, *aretē* or *virtus*. The female slave's assumed sexual impurity contrasted with the female citizen's innate sexual modesty, her *sōphrosynē* or *pudicitia*.[25] There was also a somatic contrast between master and slave. The slave's ugliness enhanced the physical attractiveness of the owner, who, at least in the ideal, embodied physical as well as moral excellence, the aristocratic concept of the *kaloskagathos*; the typical slave was his physical and moral opposite, an example of what Ingomar Weiler called inverted *kalokagathia*.[26] These oppositions contributed to a habit of thought that reflexively set master and slave against one another. The slave was his master's natural enemy; for the Romans the enmity was proverbial: *totidem hostes esse quot servos*.[27] Despite their power of domination, Greek and Roman slave-owners feared their slaves.[28]

The influence, if not pervasiveness, of denigrating slave stereotypes may be observed in a variety of Greek and Latin texts. I note here just a few examples. The duplicitous slave of comedy, both Greek and Roman, the familiar *servus callidus*, reflects the elite view that slaves were natural liars and deceivers.[29] Peter Hunt has argued that the ideological construction of the slave as a coward influenced Thucydides to marginalize the participation of slaves in combat.[30] The general prejudice that slaves were mentally and morally defective led Greek and Roman elites to see their slaves as incompetent and negligent workers. Xenophon's *Oeconomicus* and the Roman agricultural manuals emphasized that slave workers required close supervision.[31] Otherwise, slaves might work poorly or slowly or avoid work altogether. Slave-owners also constructed the slave as inclined to criminal action, an assumption frequently reflected in Roman jurisprudence.[32] The first target for a slave's criminality might be the master. In *De re rustica* (1.7), Columella warned that unsupervised slaves might steal or destroy their owner's property.

Paradoxically, the slave-owners' assembly of degrading stereotypes included a stereotype of a good slave, a slave who was obedient without compulsion, who

Introduction   7

was loyal and affectionate to the master, and who placed the master's needs above his own.[33] W. G. Thalmann has pointed out that even the good-slave stereotype was degrading because it denied an essential aspect of the slave's humanity, that is, the assertion of the self. An early literary representation of the type is found in Homer's portrait of Eumaios, Odysseus' loyal swineherd.[34] In *Odyssey* 14, when Odysseus is finally back in Ithaca but disguised as a beggar, Eumaios receives his long-lost master but does not recognize him. All the time Odysseus was away, the swineherd had done his job and remained faithful to the master's family. However, Eumaios was a "good slave" in his inner mentality as well as his outward behavior. He tells the beggar that he loves his master more than his own homeland and parents (14.138–44):

> For I shall not yet
> come upon another master so mild, wherever I go.
> Not even if I should return again to the home of my mother and father
> where I was born first and where they raised me.
> Nor do I still mourn them so much, though I am eager
> to see them with my eyes in my homeland.
> But I am seized by yearning for departed Odysseus.

Eumaios was, in fact, the son of a king but had been kidnapped by a slave nurse and sold to Odysseus' father, Laertes. Nonetheless, as a good slave, he lives not for himself but for his master and his master's family. He remembers his life before slavery, indicated here in his recollection of his parents and homeland, but subordinates this to his identity as Odysseus' slave: life before and after social death.[35] The impetus for the suppression of identity came, of course, not from the slave but from the master and was part of the process of enslavement described by Orlando Patterson in which the master strips the slave of his natal identity.[36] The suppression of natal identity aimed at the suppression of autonomous will. Thalmann speaks of a "denial of subjectivity." The stereotype of the good slave reflects how slave-owners thought of slaves in the ideal, that is, as individuals who had no right to possess an autonomous will or who may even have lacked one by nature.[37] Thus, the normative view denigrated even the ideal slave, the loyal and obedient slave, as an incomplete human being, one without an autonomous will.

These stereotypes pervaded elite thinking. Children of the elite began to learn, perhaps while even in the cradle, how to think about slaves, how to address them, how to respond to them, how to command them, and how to punish them. They learned how to test the real slave against the impossible standard of the ideal slave and to find the real slave wanting. In brief, they learned how to be masters. The ideology of the slave-owner, an anthology of socially transmitted prejudices, was both pragmatic and flexible to the point of self-contradiction, as any belief system that treats an autonomous human being as property would need to be. Nonetheless, the stereotypes found expression even in philosophical thought that sought, in a systematic fashion, to make the power of slave-owners acceptable.

8   *Introduction*

Philosophy offered two basic approaches, one represented by Aristotle's theory of the natural slave, the other by the Stoics and their notion of a deterministic cosmic order of which slavery was a part.[38] In brief, Aristotle sought to naturalize the individual slave as a slave; the Stoics sought to naturalize slavery as a system. Aristotle developed the theory of the natural slave in Book I of the *Politics*.[39] In his view, the relationship between master and slave belonged to a broader category of natural relationships between superior and inferior, the natural ruler and the naturally ruled: male and female, human and animal, the rational element of the soul and the emotional element, the soul and the body. Not only did these relationships of ruler and ruled exist by necessity, but they were also in the interests of the inferior to be ruled by the superior (1254^a 21–24): women by men, animals by humans, the emotions by the mind, the body by the soul. Those who differed from other men as all men differ from animals, or the body differs from the soul, were, according to Aristotle, slaves by nature, and it was likewise in their interest to be ruled by a master (1254^b 16–20).

The natural slave's inferiority was, first of all, a psychic inferiority, an inferiority of the soul, the *psychē*. As a human being, the natural slave took part in reason (κοινωνῶν λόγου), but only to the extent that he could perceive reason in another and allow himself to be guided by it. The natural slave did not possess reason himself (1254^b 20–25).[40] Earlier, Aristotle had defined the slave, like the domesticated animal, as a form of living property, an *empsychon ktēma* (1253^b 32), one of the tools necessary for a master to lead the good life. The utility of the slave thus resembled that of a domesticated animal. Both the animal and the enslaved person provided for the material necessities of life through physical labor (1254^b 25–26). In connection with the physical tasks given to the slave, Aristotle hypothesized a somatic difference between slave and free. It was the intention of nature, although this intention was often (πολλάκις) not realized, to make the bodies of slaves and free men different as well as their souls. The bodies of slaves were strong, suited to the labor slaves must perform; the bodies of free men were upright, suited to the life of a citizen (1254^b 27–32).

In contrast, the Stoic doctrine would appear to contest the elite construction of the legal slave as a degraded person. All human beings were kindred and possessed of rationality, or *logos*, the finest and most rarified form of matter. *Logos* was divine and providential and imposed order on the world. In Stoic teaching, divine and rational *logos* was present in every human soul. Seneca gave this notion expression in a famous letter (*Ep.* 47.10): "Be open to consider that the one you call a slave arose from the same beginnings as you; he has a right to live under the same sky. Like you he breathes, lives, and dies!" *Logos* implied that all human beings, even slaves, had the capacity for reason and a common share of divinity. The capacity for reason entailed a capacity for virtue. In the Stoic view, virtue was acquired through the proper exercise of the rational capacity of the soul. Slaves, too, could use reason to recognize and to act in accordance with the will of God and in harmony with Nature. This doctrine entailed consequences, at least theoretically, in the management of slaves. Masters were obliged to treat them, as human beings possessed of *logos*, humanely.

Introduction   9

Stoics held that legal slavery was an external condition over which one had no control, in itself neither good nor bad – in Stoic terminology, a moral indifferent, an *adiaphoron*. What mattered instead was moral slavery, metaphorical slavery of the soul to the passions. Thus, a slave could have the soul of a free man and his master have the soul of a slave; thus the Stoic paradox that only the wise man was free and that foolish men were slaves.[41] At the same time, while legal slavery was a moral indifferent, it was, nonetheless, a part of the natural order of things. The same *logos* that resided in the soul of every human being determined the order of the cosmos, making some men masters and other men slaves. The wise man accepted the inevitable and embraced whatever role he had been assigned: rich man, poor man, king, or slave. This determinism naturalized the legal slavery of any individual by making it part of the greater order. Virtue (and personal happiness) consisted of accommodating one's will to it.[42]

Although they rejected the Aristotelian notion that slaves were inferior by nature, Stoics, at least indirectly, reinforced the social belief in the inferiority of slaves. For universal human rationality and kinship did not imply that men had been created as equals. Individuals possessed greater or lesser shares of *logos*. There was a hierarchy of leaders and followers. Leaders, the wise, were few. The path of Stoic virtue was steep and difficult, requiring discipline, training, and will. If he were a Stoic, a slave-owner would have acknowledged that some of the few who were truly wise were legal slaves. In all likelihood, however, he would have accepted that most legal slaves were also moral slaves. The Stoic metaphor for vice, that is, "slavery of the soul," indicates the persistence of the normative prejudice.[43] Thus, the difference between the Aristotelian doctrine of the natural slave and the Stoic belief in universal human kinship amounted to a theoretical distinction without a practical difference in how most individual slaves were regarded in social terms.[44] Both systems naturalized the practice of slavery, either through the naturalization of the slave as a defective individual or through the naturalization of slavery itself as a constituent part of a deterministic cosmos.[45]

It will be relevant to my hypothesis that Xenophon and Chariton were themselves ex-slaves writing in part for ex-slave readers to note here that the Romans reapplied their degrading stereotypes, *mutatis mutandis*, to freedmen. No longer a slave, the freedman was no longer subject to physical coercion. He could not be sold again. He could form a legitimate family and bequeath property to his heirs. If the slave were dead socially, the freedman might even hope for some degree of respect and honor. Indeed, in the course of the extended political crisis that ended in the establishment of the principate, quite a few ex-slaves rose to prominence. The ex-slave teachers of literature, the *grammatici* who contributed so much to the study of Roman letters, had their counterparts in business, ex-slaves who had made themselves rich through trade, manufacturing, and agriculture, and in professions such as architecture and medicine.[46] Other freedmen had served their ex-masters, or *patroni*, as political agents during the period of the civil wars.[47] With the end of the republic and the establishment of the principate, freedmen

10 *Introduction*

continued to be active in political service. Ex-slaves belonging to the imperial family were employed as secretaries, agents, and administrators in the running of the empire. A few of these freedmen wielded great power, grew rich in government service, and were especially resented by an elite whose role in governance had been usurped by the emperors and their agents.[48]

However, even spectacularly successful ex-slaves were not free from legal and economic restrictions and social degradation. Manumission conferred citizenship but not complete freedom from the *patronus*. Roman freedmen were legally and socially tied to their ex-masters in a compulsory version of the patron–client relationship.[49] A freedman might be obligated under the legal terms of his manumission to continue to serve his ex-master, providing days of work, or *operae*, whose nature and number were specified at the time of manumission. The freedman also remained socially subordinate, owing his ex-master *obsequium*, a notion that combined respect, deference, and obedience. Patrons could subject their freedmen and freedwomen to verbal rebuke, even physical chastisement if it were not too severe.[50] In the view of Roman jurisprudence, the ex-slave retained "the stain of slavery" or *macula servitutis*, that is, the degradation of his former condition, and was thus disqualified from public magistracies.[51] The freedman could not really pretend to possess true honor. Manumission did not wash away the stain of slavery. The sons of ex-slaves were ordinarily free of the stigma. But elite prejudice against ex-slaves was strong, and even the freeborn sons of ex-slaves might be insulted for their connection to slavery if a pretext was needed for an attack. Thus, the first-century CE moralist and rhetorician Valerius Maximus expressed indignation at the son of a freedman from the previous century, who had had the audacity to attack Pompey the Great in court; he was someone who still bore the stench of his father's slavery (6.2.8, *servitutem paternam redolenti*).[52] Freedom from slavery did not confer freedom from the memory of social degradation for ex-slave authors and readers.

Resistance to exploitation and degradation

A significant number of Roman slaves resisted their owners' efforts to exploit and degrade them. They resisted in part through their actions.[53] Columella, the author of a first-century CE manual on the management of agricultural estates, *villae*, recommended that remote estates, which could not be closely supervised, be staffed by tenant farmers rather than a workforce of slaves headed by a slave foreman, or *vilicus*, because slaves were apt to cause a great deal of harm to the estate (*De re rustica*, 1.7.6):

> They hire out the oxen; they do a poor job feeding (*male pascunt*) these and the other herd animals. They do not put proper effort (*nec industrie*) into plowing and they claim that they have planted much more seed than they have sown. And they do not tend that which they have put in the ground so that it grows properly. And when they gathered it into the barn, during threshing they reduce the amount every day (*cotidie*) through fraud or

Introduction 11

negligence (*vel fraude vel neglegentia*). For both they themselves steal it and they do not guard it from other thieves; nor do they enter into the books what has been stored in a trustworthy manner.

The moralizing condemnation reflects the influence of elite stereotypes of the slave at several points. Slaves cannot be trusted to do a good job because of their mental and moral defects. However, we need not take Columella's judgment at face value. Comparative evidence drawn from American slavery suggests an alternative way of understanding why these Roman slaves were doing a poor job. In his autobiography, the nineteenth-century American ex-slave Frederick Douglass describes an incident from his enslavement on a farm belonging to Thomas Auld on Maryland's eastern shore. Douglass used to allow a horse to run off to a farm five miles away that belonged to Auld's father-in-law. He would then have to retrieve the horse. Auld would upbraid and even whip Douglass for what he saw as repeated negligence. Douglass, on the other hand, understood his own actions not as negligence but as calculation:

> My reason for this kind of carelessness, or carefulness, was, that I could always get something to eat when I went there. Master William Hamilton, my master's father-in-law, always gave his slaves enough to eat. I never left there hungry, no matter how great the need of my speedy return.[54]

If Auld had realized that his slave's actions were deliberate and calculated rather than careless, Douglass would have paid a higher price for that extra food. Instead, he turned Auld's stereotypical thinking about slaves to his own advantage even as he consciously rejected it.

It is important to note that Columella, the slave-owner, attributes motive to his slaves whereas Douglass, the ex-slave, speaks for himself and understands his actions as a form of resistance. Keith Bradley suggests that evidence such as this allows us to read the ancient elite text against the grain, in this case, to infer an act of resistance where Columella saw, yet again, evidence of criminality and incompetence. Thus, Columella reveals indirectly that such resistance may have been regular (*coditie*), communal, and present in many aspects of the work performed at the estate.[55]

Both in its careful calculation and in its typical forms the resistance of Roman slaves resembles the resistance of slaves and subjugated peoples in other systems of domination. Such resistance helped to mitigate some of the material aspects of exploitation, for example, through the theft of food or the avoidance of hard work; this resistance also offered the emotional satisfaction of a victory, however small, over the master. These acts of resistance also reinforced, in the mind of the slave-owner, his stereotypical perception of the slave. Slaves, of course, knew that their owners viewed them as degraded. The stereotype gave them cover for their actions. Such behavior was expected of them. At the same time, slaves did not necessarily accept what the owner thought about their characters. Our direct evidence from Roman slavery preserves what

12   *Introduction*

owners thought about the behavior of their slaves but not how the slaves themselves conceived of their actions and motivations. Comparative evidence, however, suggests ways in which we might reasonably infer the slaves' perspectives.[56]

For Douglass, letting the horse run off was not carelessness but carefulness. His act of resistance was thus underwritten by the way he thought about it. In other words, an act of resistance was accompanied by resistance in thought. James Scott, in *Domination and the Arts of Resistance*, provides a conceptual framework for understanding the difference between how people without power and people with power think about and characterize their dealings with one another.[57] Scott calls the expression of these points of view, respectively, the hidden transcript and the public transcript. Scott conceptualized the hidden transcript by drawing evidence from subordinated populations in a broad range of cultures and historical periods: Malay villagers, Russian serfs, Hindu untouchables, Eastern European dissidents, African American slaves, and others. These subordinated peoples produced their own discourse regarding power relations between themselves and those with power over them. The discourse of hidden transcripts was explicit and unmeasured. It expressed anger and the desire for justice or revenge; in the absence of justice, it might offer solace; it counseled powerless people to be cunning. This discourse reversed or, as Scott puts it, negated the oppressors' degrading construction of their character. What a slave-owner might regard as servile criminality was now perceived and legitimated as a form of resistance, necessary for the slave both spiritually and materially. Scott notes, for example, the comment of William Wells Brown, an African American slave abolitionist and novelist who escaped to the North in 1833:

> But I did not regard it [pilfering] as stealing then; I do not regard it as such now. I hold that a slave has a moral right to eat, drink, and wear all that he needs ... because it was the labor of my own hands.[58]

The hidden transcripts of subjected peoples are unfiltered, direct, and angry. The risk of expressing such views in public, in the face of the boss, the landlord, or the master, is considerable. Accordingly, hidden transcripts are hidden. In contrast, the accounts of power relations produced by those in power are public. These public transcripts justify existing power arrangements; they assign subjugated groups roles indicating both their inferiority and their acceptance of subjugation. Acceptance may be signaled, for example, in public displays of deference in word and gesture. However, the outward compliance of a subjugated group does not indicate their sincere endorsement of the public transcript. However, it is unusual for subjugated individuals to express unambiguous disagreement in public. Instead, as Scott notes, they tend to insinuate their views into public discourse in disguised form. Unlike the direct and unmediated hidden transcript, public expressions of ideas drawn from a hidden transcript tend to be disguised, ambiguous, or indirect. In the presence of their employers, landlords, or masters, subordinated persons might, for example, be slow to show deference or ambiguous in their tone or gesture. They might express and disguise

Introduction 13

their discontent in the form of muttering, anonymous gossip, euphemism, fables, and related modes of ambiguous and deniable speech.[59]

Scott characterizes creation and circulation of both the original hidden transcript and its camouflaged forms as the practice of infrapolitics, that is, "the veiled cultural struggle and political expression of subordinate groups who have ample reason to fear venturing their unguarded opinion."[60] It is reasonable to assume that ancient slaves, like other dominated peoples, practiced some form of infrapolitics. Greek and Roman authors have left an abundant record of their dealings with their slaves, from which it is possible to infer that their slaves acted against enslavement through regular and daily acts of resistance: the theft, pilfering, sabotage, and similar acts deplored by their owners.[61] The slaves must have explained and justified (at least to themselves) these acts of resistance through a form of intellectual resistance, their hidden transcripts. These transcripts not only justified particular resistance acts; they also expressed the desire for justice or revenge, offered solace, or counseled the need for cunning. They affirmed enslaved persons of their human worth and pushed back their masters' degrading construction of their character. Finally, evidence also suggests that ancient slaves, like other dominated peoples, disguised the ideas of their hidden transcripts and circulated them in public.

Hidden transcripts: insinuation, appropriation, and literary production

A dominated group might express their ideas in public in direct and unmuted form but only under exceptional circumstances. Diodorus Siculus' account of the First Sicilian Slave War preserves the memory of such an occasion.[62] The rebels, under their leader, Eunus, were besieging a city.[63] At one point, from outside the range of their enemies' weapons, Eunus and his men taunted the Roman defenders, declaring that they, the Romans, were the slaves running away from danger (δραπέτας τῶν κινδύνων), not the actual slaves in rebellion (34/35.2. 46). Eunus then staged, at some distance from the city, a performance of mimes for the benefit of those inside (μίμους δὲ ἐξ ἀποστάσεως τοῖς ἔνδον ἐπεδείκνυτο), in which the slaves dramatized why they were rebelling from their masters (δι' ὧν οἱ δοῦλοι τὰς ἀπὸ τῶν ἰδίων κυρίων ἀποστασίας ἐξεθεάτριζον), reproaching them for the arrogance and insolence that had led to their destruction (ὀνειδίζοντες αὐτῶν τὴν ὑπερηφανίαν καὶ τὴν ὑπερβολὴν τῆς εἰς τὸν ὄλεθρον προαγούσης ὕβρεως).

These grievances likely reflected some of Diodorus' own Stoically inspired critique of bad slave-owners.[64] However, the fact that the historian had a point to make about the treatment of slaves does not preclude the likelihood that the slaves had their own ideas about how they had been treated. Diodorus' account may preserve both the medium through which these ideas were expressed and some of their content. The medium was the popular dramatic form of the mime. This mime had three audiences and a different message for each. First, the rebels taunt the Roman defenders as cowards who run away from danger. The insult was double-barbed, taking on two stereotypes about bad slaves –

14 *Introduction*

that they are cowards and that they are runaways – and turning them back on the Romans. Slaves and slave-owners "those inside the city" (τοῖς ἔνδον) comprised the other audiences. The mime reproaches besieged slave-owners for their injustice and reaches out in solidarity to their slaves, encouraging them to join the rebellion. After all, the rebels had revolted against their own masters (τῶν ἰδίων κυρίων); so, too, could they. Elite sources tend to obscure the subjectivity of slaves, often attributing their motivations to servile wickedness. But in this episode, Diodorus suggests that the slaves were thinking for themselves and had articulated their own accounts of their actions. In brief, the rebel slaves did not just shout insults at their enemies. They reversed a degrading stereotype and turned it back on them. They protested against the injustice that justified their rebellion. They reached out to their fellow slaves in an expression of solidarity and hope. Finally, they enacted their ideas in a recognizable dramatic form, the mime.

Eunus and his fellow slaves were already in open rebellion, so it is not surprising that they gave open expression to the thoughts behind their rebellion. Otherwise, dominated peoples tend to disguise their protests before advancing them into public discourse. As Scott notes, "[t]he hidden transcript of many historically important subordinate groups is irrecoverable for all practical purposes. What is often available, however, is what they have been able to introduce in muted or veiled form into the public transcript."[65] Among the forms available to ancient slaves for taking this step were popular stories and legends, fables, and folktales. In some cases, the elites appropriated these stories that slaves told and put them to new uses, preserving, if only unintentionally, traces of their original protests.[66]

Leslie Kurke suggests that the anonymous first-century CE *Life of Aesop* reflects aspects of a servile hidden transcript, which has been insinuated into public discourse through the camouflage of anonymity and humor.[67] The text satirizes tensions and hostilities in master–slave relationships through stories featuring the legendary slave Aesop and his master, the philosopher Xanthus. In the *Life*, Aesop uses his verbal dexterity to escape hard work and punishment but, above all, to confound and show up his master. For example, when Xanthus orders him to prepare "lentil" for dinner, Aesop cooks one lentil bean (39); when Xanthus orders him to take food from a banquet and give it "to her who loves me," Aesop sows marital discord by giving the food to Xanthus' dog instead of his wife (44); when his master reneges on a promise to free Aesop, the slave avenges himself by seducing Xanthus' wife (75).[68]

Some stories slaves told one another featured resistance to slavery. Plutarch's notice that Spartacus wanted to ferry a part of his army to Sicily, "in order to rekindle the slave war there, which had been not long before extinguished and which needed little additional fuel" (*Crassus*, 549), may be evidence that Spartacus and his army told stories about the second slave rebellion on Sicily 30 years before. A legend about Drimacus, a maroon slave leader on the island of Chios, may have been preserved because slave-owners appropriated it and added their own content. The version preserved in Athenaeus' *Deipnosophistae* (*The Learned Banqueters*, 265d–266e) describes Drimacus as a noble and heroic

Introduction 15

slave who resisted the excesses of Chian slave-owners; at the same time, Drimacus worked out a *modus vivendi* with the slave-owners, agreeing to take in plunder only so much as the runaway slaves required. Sara Forsdyke suggests that Athenaeus' version of the story reflects a dialectical process in which a popular story came to serve as a means of accommodation between groups in conflict.[69]

Another possible example of elite appropriation is found in the best-known folktale from antiquity, "Cupid and Psyche," which Apuleius inserted in his novel *Metamorphoses*. Apuleius either adapted an existing folktale or created this story himself, borrowing traditional folktale materials – a beautiful princess, evil sisters, a taboo violated, the rendering of magical assistance – to create a tale that seems like a folktale, that is, an ersatz folktale.[70] In Apuleius, the tale represents a complex and learned allegory regarding the slavery of the soul to love. Nonetheless, in Venus' persecution of Psyche, her runaway slave (cf. 5.31, *Psychen illam fugitivam volaticam*), there may lurk behind the allegory a story about a real slave, exploited and abused by her owner. The framing of the tale as a story told by an old slave to a young girl newly captured and bound for enslavement may point to versions of such tales that signified in a context of slavery.[71] In either reading, however, slavery, real or metaphorical, figures as a key element of the tale.

The preceding examples illustrate how the process of insinuation from below combined with appropriation from above may have preserved elements of original servile protests and possibly their form as well: the popular story, legend, and folktale, all of them oral forms easily accessed by slaves.[72] The oral traditions associated with other dominated peoples provide parallels. Writing about social and class conflict in European folktales, folklorist Jack Zipes notes that these traditional stories "gave vent to the frustration of the common people and embodied their needs and wishes."[73] In his discussion of the rich folktale tradition of enslaved African Americans, Lawrence Levine argues that many of these tales had a didactic purpose for slaves trying to negotiate their way in a world that had hope but was dominated by "malevolence, injustice, and arbitrary judgment" and that had to be dealt with here and now.[74] The lessons the tales imparted included, among other things, the importance of family ties and children, the need to know one's place, and the need to keep one's mouth shut. These tales also celebrated servile cunning, featuring trickster figures such as Brer Rabbit and a human trickster, a slave known as John.[75] They also offered fantasies of revenge, as in the awful death that Brer Rabbit provided for Brer Wolf to stop the villain from eating his children.

In antiquity, however, the literary form most closely associated with slaves was the fable. The best-known fabulists were or had been slaves: the legendary Aesop and the historical Phaedrus, whom the title of his manuscript identified as a freedman of Augustus: *Phaedri Augusti liberti fabularum Aesopiarum*. In the prologue to the third book of his collection, Phaedrus asserts that slaves had even invented the fable (33–37):

> Now I'll briefly tell you why the genre was found(ed) (*cur sit inventum genus*) of the fable. Because dominated slaves (*servitus obnoxia*)

16 *Introduction*

did not dare say what they wanted to,
they translated their personal feelings into fables
and avoided getting caught by means of invented jests.

The fable was particularly suited to the conditions that slaves faced. The use of animal characters provided camouflage behind which they could keep their true thoughts and feelings hidden. As a result, fables that slaves first circulated in private could have already been disguised for insinuation into the public transcript.[76] The fable's brief and memorable stories facilitated transmission. Slaves without literary education could grasp the pointed moral. For example, in the "Fox and the Eagle," an eagle seized a fox's cubs and carried them off to feed her own young.[77] The fox pleaded with the eagle, nested high in a tree, to return her children – to no avail. The fox then grabbed a firebrand and threatened to burn down the tree, and the eagle relented to save her eaglets. Keith Bradley suggested that this fable could reflect the experience of slaves, who might, like the fox, be separated from their family members because of the actions of one more powerful. The fox's threat of violence may reflect the slave's own threat of retaliation or, as Bradley remarked (given the high cost slaves paid for direct acts of violence), a consoling fantasy of retaliation.[78] The moral that Phaedrus attaches to the start of the tale suggests how a slave may have responded to having her children taken away from her, consoling herself with the hope that she was not utterly powerless and reflecting on the need to be inventive were she to try to pay her master back (1–2): "No matter how mighty they are, those on high should fear the lowly, / because skill and learning have access to revenge (*vindicta docili quia patet sollertiae*)." Other scholars have read particular fables as encoding the desire for freedom, counseling the need to be distrustful of the master, or the need to deceive.[79]

Slaves were not the exclusive users of fable; still less did slaves "invent" the genre.[80] However, the skepticism of Edward Champlin goes too far in the opposite direction. Champlin has argued that Phaedrus was not really an ex-slave but adopted the Aesopian persona and genre to disguise his own elite critique of power and society in Augustan Rome.[81] Even if Champlin is correct, his argument concedes an association between the fable and slavery. In addition, it may be argued that by using the fable as a means of critiquing imperial power, an elite Phaedrus would be appropriating a practice of slaves, that is, using the fable to disguise his protest.[82]

Slaves shared the fable with nonslaves, including elites; nonetheless, they found in the genre an accessible form for the expression of their thoughts and feelings and a means of insinuating them into the public transcript. Kenneth Rothwell seems to strike the right balance:

> It would be a mistake, too, to assert that the fable, in its very nature or essence somehow was the property of the lower classes. In practice, there was a recurrent tendency for fables to be used by them, and Phaedrus' claim that fables were a form of servile protest cannot be discounted altogether. At the very least, it is telling that there were those in antiquity

Introduction   17

who thought Aesop created fables for slaves. More importantly, fables teach lessons that reflect the viewpoint of the downtrodden.[83]

Drawing on examples taken from elite authors such as Aeschylus, Hesiod, Homer, and Aristotle, Sara Forsdyke demonstrates how the same fable could have signified differently for slave-owners and slaves.[84] For example, Aeschylus' use (or appropriation?) of the fable concerning the man who reared a lion cub in his house (*Agamemnon* 717–736): At first, the cub charmed its owners and fawned on them for food, but as a grown lion, the animal exhibited its ferocious nature, turned on its owners, and devoured them. As Forsdyke notes, in Aeschylus the lion cub refers to Helen, who was at first attractive but ultimately destructive; the fable also reflects the tragedian's moral message that injustice begets injustice. Paris' abduction of Helen led to the destruction of Troy. However, in another context, the same fable could have been meaningful for slaves. Like the lion cub, slaves are taken from their homes and placed in a foreign home. Slaves fawn on the master for food and shelter. Given the chance, however, they may revert to their natural hostility. Forsdyke concludes, "As told among slaves this fable expresses both the awful necessity to please one's oppressor and the dream of wreaking bloody revenge."[85]

As a literary form adapted to the expression of servile perspectives and protests, the Roman adaptation of Greek New Comedy, the *fabula palliata*, is the genre most relevant to the Greek novels. Amy Richlin, in *Slave Theater in the Roman Republic*, locates the historical and social context for the *palliata* in the latter half of the third century BCE, a period of endless war and mass enslavements.[86] Theatrical troupes comprised of slaves and other low-status persons staged the *palliatae* for audiences that included enslaved and poor people as well as elites. In response to the view that the plays, as state-sponsored and -sanctioned productions, reflected elite concerns, Richlin argues that performers were able to insinuate into the *palliatae* their servile and lower-class protests through the camouflage that was natural to comedy and theater itself.[87] As Eduard Fraenkel observed, Plautus, in particular, expanded the role of the slave in Greek New Comedy, to create the clever slave of the *fabula palliata*. This *servus callidus* was the quintessential Plautine hero, a character who uses his cunning and verbal acumen to outwit and thwart his master and other adversaries, *servi callidi* such as Pseudolus, Tranio, and Chrysalus.[88] These comedies, Richlin argues, drew on ideas generated in hidden transcripts; they drew on the experience of the performers themselves and many in the audience whose lives had been turned on end during this period to engage with realities such as enslavement and degradation, hard work, physical punishment, sexual exploitation, and hunger. They also expressed the anger of the oppressed and their desire for revenge, for freedom, and for family.

* * *

Slaves made use of what was available to them to express their hidden transcripts: the mime, for example, and traditional narrative forms, especially the fable. In the case of the *fabula palliata*, Plautus and others from a servile or

18   *Introduction*

lower-class background even played a role in shaping the genre itself, transforming Greek New Comedy into a dramatic form in which they could express and insinuate their views before a diverse audience that included slave-owners as well as slaves.

Xenophon and Chariton may thus belong to a tradition of literary activity inspired by the slave's experience of enslavement. Some 250 years after Plautus expanded the role of the clever slave and insinuated ideas of servile protest into the *palliata*, the two novelists, drawing on ideas generated in part in hidden transcripts, exploited another emerging genre, the erotic novel, to tell a story focused around the experience of slavery that was in basic sympathy with the slave. As early experimenters in the novel, they may have helped to shape it, making the protagonist's slave experience a motif that marked the genre. It is possible that these authors were conscious of their attachment to this tradition. They not only reflect similar sympathy for slaves and criticism of slave-owners; they also have incorporated elements from the forms associated with servile protest into their narratives. Xenophon, for example, makes significant use of traditional folktales to narrate key moments in his protagonists' slave experience.[89] Xenophon and Chariton also feature the machinations of slaves reminiscent of the comic *servus callidus*. The affinity with comedy may be ideological as well as literary. In contrast, while the later novelists, Longus, Achilles, and Heliodorus, cast comic clever slaves among their characters and inserted fables and folktales into their narratives, they repurposed these elements to the service of elite ideology. Still, even here, in an ideologically hostile context, it is possible to see traces, however faint, of ideas that may have originated in servile hidden transcripts.

Plan of the book

Chapters 1, 2, 4, 5, and 6 offer readings of how each of the five surviving Greek novels has represented slavery. The order of these readings has been determined by the nature of each novel's representation in addition to chronology. Chapters 1 and 2 present readings of *Ephesiaca* and *Callirhoe* in the context of the dominant elite's view of slaves and slavery. I examine how Xenophon and Chariton developed distinct modes for critiquing elite views, including the philosophical versions of these views. Of these two, a consensus regards Chariton as the earlier writer; however, the sharp outlines of Xenophon's critique make him the better place to start. Chapter 3 focuses on the treatment of selected motifs, ideas, and formal aspects in these authors in the context of slavery and hidden transcripts. I argue that both Xenophon and Chariton, as well as some of their readers, were ex-slaves. I consider how ex-slave readers may have responded to aspects of their novels. However, ex-slaves were not the only readers of *Ephesiaca* and *Callirhoe*. The novel was a shared genre, as were fable, folktale, and Roman Comedy. This chapter also considers the reception of Xenophon and Chariton by freeborn elite readers.

The chapters on Longus, Achilles Tatius, and Heliodorus focus on how these authors adapted the representation of slavery to other ends. These authors

Introduction 19

rejected or ignored the critiques found in Xenophon and Chariton. I treat Longus before Achilles, the earlier author, because, as I argue in Chapter 4, the author of *Daphnis and Chloe* offers a philosophic defense of slavery itself that may be read as a broad response to the sort of criticism of the institution found in Xenophon and Chariton. Longus' justification of slavery sets the stage for the more selective engagement I found in Achilles and Heliodorus. Chapter 5, on *Leucippe and Clitophon*, discusses the representation of slavery in the context of the novel's first-person narrator, Clitophon. What he notices or does not notice about slaves is an important element in his characterization as a representative of the slave-owning elite. The enslavement of the heroine Leucippe and Clitophon's own quasi-enslavement are treated as occasions for literary play, rhetorical elaboration, and humor, not servile protest. Achilles' literary engagement with slavery in a literary context is extensive; what seems to be missing from his novel is an interest in slavery itself.

Chapter 6, on *Aethiopica*, discusses how slaves and slavery are associated with a carnal and debased form of *erōs* that is opposed to the idealized love of the protagonists Theagenes and Charicleia. Heliodorus' representation of slavery has been attuned to his complex narrative strategy. The Egyptian priest Calasiris, who tells almost a third of the story as an inserted first-person narrator, pays scant attention to slave characters. In contrast, Cnemon, another inset first-person narrator, tells a tale that features the wicked slave Thisbe as the central character. Finally, the external third-person narrator, whom we might call Heliodorus, relates the episode in which the protagonists are enslaved in a narration replete with evil and devious slave characters. In brief, these later authors may have usurped and transformed a genre that had been shaped in its beginnings in part by the experience of slavery. However, they abandoned the critical perspective toward slave-owners and slavery implied in earlier authors such as Xenophon and Chariton. Their reflection of a perspective closer to the norm of elite opinion may be evidence of an ideological debate within the genre. Nonetheless, the later authors ended up making their novels, to some extent, "about slavery" by rejecting the critique of the institution they found in authors such as Xenophon and Chariton.

There are no Chapters 7 and 8, on Petronius and Apuleius. There could be. The Roman novelists, no less than the Greek, were informed by imperial culture. The Roman authors, too, represented the mentality and concerns of slaves and ex-slaves. This aspect of the *Satyrica* and *Metamorphoses* has already earned the attention of scholars such as Paul Veyne, in his essay "Vie de Trimalcion," and John Bodel, in "Trimalchio's Underworld." Keith Bradley has explored the relevance of slavery to the transformation of Apuleius' protagonist in "Animalizing the Slave."[90] The present volume, at least, suggests that the Roman novelists' representation of slaves and slavery merits another look, now through the context of the treatment of this theme in the Greek novels, in particular, to consider whether the representation of slaves and ex-slaves in Petronius and Apuleius reflects a consciousness of the treatment of this theme in the Greek novels.[91] Our reading of Trimalchio may take on an additional level of complexity if we

20 *Introduction*

consider, for example, his reference to the sexual abuse he experienced as a 14-year-old boy (75, *ad delicias ipsimi annos quattuordecim fui*) in the context of the sexual threats experienced by the novel protagonists Habrocomes, Anthia, and Callirhoe. Trimalchio's permanent loss of *pudicitia* may be in deliberate contrast to the *sōphrosynē* of such characters.

Nonetheless, there are factors that weigh in favor of treating the representation of slavery in the Roman novel in a separate volume. Petronius raises complicated genre issues. The *Satyrica* may be an erotic novel, a parody of an erotic novel, a comic-picaresque novel, or a mixture of these and other genres. Apuleius' representation of slavery in *Metamorphoses* is conducted at several levels: Lucius *qua* ass as animalized slave, the many human slaves that Lucius encounters in the course of his misadventures, Psyche as the metaphorical slave of Venus in the Cupid and Psyche tale, Lucius' metaphorical slavery to Isis. There is a possibility that Apuleius has adapted servile perspectives from the pseudo-Lucian's *Lucius, or the Ass*. Lucius' metaphorical slavery to Isis in Book 11 may be read in the context of Christian notions of metaphorical slavery to God. Thus, it seems better to treat the representation of slaves in the Roman novels in a separate book.

Instead, I conclude with an afterword that contains two points of speculation: the possible significance for readers of servile origin of the presence of the western Mediterranean, specifically Magna Graecia, Sicily, and southern Italy, in the novels of Xenophon and Chariton and the negative critical reception of the genre in antiquity in the context of its association with slavery.

Notes

1 Thus, for example, in "Conventions of the Slave States," *The Winyaw Intelligencer* (a Georgetown, South Carolina newspaper), April 13, 1833: "the existence and increase of incendiary papers, at the North, avowedly aiming to abolish our peculiar institutions, uproot the long established usages of our country, and destroy the great source of our pecuniary prosperity and political existence."
2 On Eurycleia's nobility: Thalmann 1998, 74–76.
3 The so-called Big Five. Stephens and Winkler 1995 have collected, edited, translated, and provided commentaries for the fragments of the other novels, including *Ninos, Metiochos and Parthenope*, and Iamblichus' *Babylonica*.
4 Some argue that Xenophon's novel is an epitome of a longer work; see the following discussion, p. 27, nn. 3 and 4. Even if these critics are correct, it is possible to treat the epitomized text of *Ephesiaca* on its own terms as a coherent work.
5 Whitmarsh 2005a discusses the evidence for and the significance of the titles for each of the novels; for example, Ἐφεσιακά may be an abbreviation for a longer title such as "τὰ κατ᾽Ἀνθίαν καὶ Ἁβροκόμην Ἐφεσιακά." According to Whitmarsh, titles with the name of the heroine (or the names of both protagonists) emphasized the personal and erotic nature of the narrative, as opposed to titles based on a place name, which suggested the narrative's historiographical associations. I follow Whitmarsh on this point but have adopted titles of common usage.
6 See the next section, pp. 5–10, for a fuller discussion of the stereotype and other aspects of normative elite thinking.
7 The historical and cultural context of a complex cultural form has relevant but not unlimited explanatory power: cf. the remarks of Swain 1996, 112; Whitmarsh

Introduction 21

2011, 10–11. For this reason, it is better to regard the argument concerning ex-slave readers as a hypothesis rather than a conclusion.

8 Cf. Bakhtin 1981, 86–110, in whose view the protagonists' calamities, including slavery, constituted an "adventure-time" that was without meaningful consequence.

9 Perry 1967. Also, Hägg 1983; Reardon 1991; Konstan 1994.

10 Kerényi 1927; Merkelbach 1962.

11 Lalanne 2006; Whitmarsh 2011. Cf. Montiglio 2005, 221–261 for a discussion of wandering in the novel as a process of character growth and development or, in the case of Heliodorus' Charicleia, an allegory with Platonic overtones for the soul wandering in search of love (p. 241).

12 Bowie 1977, 91–96 observed that the novels offered a "convincing reflection" of the real world. In contrast, Treu 1989a emphasized the genre's tendency to distort rather than to reflect reality. Studies focusing on the social *realia* in the novels include Scarcella 1970, 1977, 2003; Saïd 1999. Egger 1990 (diss.) remarks not only on the significance of real slaves but also on the phenomenon of the enslaved protagonists; the novels offer a generally benign depiction of slavery that aligns with the ideological disposition of elite readers, who accepted slavery and sought entertainment, not ideological challenge (p. 301). Master–slave relations between the noble protagonists and their slaves are often close (pp. 94–118). Female slaves serve as the heroine's close confidante in several of the novels. For the heroine, the threat presented by slavery was always sexual (pp. 306–312).

13 Cf. the criticism of Scarcella's use of the novels as primary evidence for social and economic conditions in Saïd 1999, 84–85.

14 Fitzgerald 2000.

15 The literary tradition in general reflected the perspective of the slave owner; cf. the comments of Joshel 2011, 214; also, Tordoff in Akrigg and Tordoff 2013, 61–62 and Wiles 1988, on Greek comedy as legitimizing the slave-owner's power.

16 Fitzgerald 2000, 9. Other studies that consider these complexities: Croally 1994, 97–103 (Euripides' *Troades*); Thalmann 1996 (Plautus' *Captivi*) and 1998 (Homer); Bradley 2000 (Apuleius' *Metamorphoses*).

17 Fitzgerald 2000, 99. I discuss later the evidence and arguments for the preservation of servile protest in other genres, pp. 13–17.

18 Bradley 1994, 47–48. One might object that at this point in the action Callirhoe is no longer Dionysius' slave but his wife. Nonetheless, Bradley's empathetic reading points in the right direction. Callirhoe's separation from home began with her enslavement.

19 Bradley 1994, 9 defends the use of fiction for historical evidence, arguing that, "in their assumptions of what is plausible and credible in everyday life, as too in their depictions of psychological response to crisis, these narratives also reflect aspects of contemporary reality that can provide valuable historical information."

20 Wrenhaven 2012 discusses the stereotypes of slaves in literary texts and images of the classical period as a reflection of an ideology that aimed to disguise or naturalize the sources of the slave-owners' power.

21 Patterson's important and influential book, *Slavery and Social Death* (1982), shifted the emphasis of slavery studies from consideration of the legal and economic aspects of the institution, in which the slave was owned as an object of property, to consideration of slavery as a system of domination entailing the social degradation of the slave as a human being. Cf. Vlassopoulos 2011, on Greek slavery, who examines the shortcomings of the view that slavery was a system of ownership, attributing this view to the influence of Aristotle. In practice, argues Vlassopoulos, the Greek masters and slaves treated slavery as a system of dynamic and contested domination. Brown 2009, in a review article considering scholarship on Atlantic slavery, cautions that Patterson's concept of "social death" has, in some cases, obscured the reality of slavery as it was experienced by the enslaved, a reality that involved many forms of

22 *Introduction*

resistance; "social death" may describe what the slave-owner aimed to impose in the ideal more than the consciousness of the enslaved individual. For additional consideration of the limitations of Patterson's approach, Lewis 2017.

22 Cf. the rationale for the use of comparative evidence from African American slavery in Bradley 2011, 372 and the comment of Thalmann 1998, 17, on how individuals tend to behave in systems of domination: "Whatever its particular forms at different periods, the domination and exploitation of some human beings by others apparently gave rise to similar problems, which led in turn to certain typical responses and justification and rationalization on the part of the masters and of adaptation and survival on the part of those dominated."

23 Greek manumission practices, of course, differed significantly from Roman; cf. Youni 2008, 2010: manumission in the Greek city states was less subject to formal legal regulation than Roman manumission; manumission often took the form of fictive sale to a divinity who, in a sense, served as guarantor of the process rather than the law; Greek manumission did not confer citizenship, and the former slave received the rights of a resident alien or *metic*.

24 This ethical contrast is illustrated in Aristophanes' *Wealth* 187–193, when Chremylus and his slave, Carion, enumerate to the character Wealth the things that one may have enough of (the point being one can never have enough wealth). The master imagines a sufficiency of love, art, honor, bravery, ambition, and military command; the slave dreams of a sufficiency of bread, dessert, cake, figs, barley cakes, and lentil soup. Cf. Fitzgerald 2000, 26, on this dichotomy in Roman comedy: "Just as the desire of the enamored master finds its lower equivalent in the hunger of the slave, and the former's amatory torment in the latter's tortured back, so in other contexts the slave's street savvy provides a cut-price version of the sagacity of his masters."

25 On sexual exploitation of slaves (male as well as female): Bradley 1994, 49–51; from the evidence for later antiquity, Harper 2011, 281–325 argues that the sexual exploitation of female slaves was an integral part of a sexual economy in which citizen women possessed honor, but slave women did not. Green 2015 notes material and textual evidence for the role slaves played in sexual activity as a form of status display, either as witnesses to or participants. Also: Kolendo 1981; Perry 2014.

26 Weiler 2002 notes that inverted *kalokagathia* included nonelite citizens and foreigners as well as slaves. Cf. Aristotle's half-hearted attempt to include the somatic difference in his theory of the natural slave at *Politics* 1254[b] 27–32. Iconographic representation of slaves: Himmelmann 1971 surveys the plastic and graphic representation of slaves in the archaic and classical periods. During the latter period, one tradition indicated the status of slaves through scale and costume rather than the figure's physical attributes, which were subject to a similar process of idealization as masters; at the same time, a parallel tradition marked slaves through stereotyped postures and somatic distortions that Himmelmann has aligned (p. 35, n. 4) with the Aristotelian ideal of a somatically distinct natural slave. Zanker 1989, 64–69 includes the representation of slaves along with that of individuals whose bodies had been deformed by age, work, or nature in the context of an opposition to the ideal of *kalokagathia*. Schumacher 2001, 71–90 focuses on a tendency in Roman as well as Greek art to depict slaves as smaller relative to their owners and, in domestic scenes, on a different representational plane. Wrenhaven 2012, 75–89 surveys the conventions in classical Greek art that marked out the slave as an "other," at pp. 123–127, with particular reference to Boeotian nurse figurines.

27 Seneca, *Ep.* 45.7. Cf. Seneca *Ep.* 4.8; 18.4; 47.5; Dionysios of Halicarnassus 10.59.6; Augustine *Conf.* 9.8.

28 Parker 1989, 237–238 argued that fear of revolt motivated Plautine jokes about punished slaves and reminded the (free) audience of the power they held as masters. Also, Gamauf 2007 with an emphasis on legal evidence.

Introduction 23

29 On the *servus callidus*: McCarthy 2000, 26–27.
30 Hunt 1998; on the stereotype of the slave as a coward, 160–164.
31 *Oeconomicus*, 5.15; 7.35; 9.15; 11.19; cf. the discussion in Columella, *De re rustica*, 1.7.6, and the later discussion, pp. 10–11.
32 The construction of the slave as criminal in Roman law: Bradley 1990; on the contrasting moral construction of stealing by masters and slaves in American slavery: Lichtenstein 1988.
33 Wrenhaven 2012, 90–127 discusses the good-slave stereotype with particular reference to nurses and pedagogues.
34 Thalmann 1998, 84–100.
35 One cannot avoid the implication that Eumaios is a good slave because of his noble birth; in other words, he was not a real slave on some level. The paradox is replicated in Tyndarus, the good slave in Plautus' *Captivi*; cf. Thalmann 1996.
36 Patterson 1982, 5–8.
37 Thalmann 1998, 25–28.
38 Garnsey 1996 provides an excellent overview of popular and philosophical thought about slavery.
39 Pellegrin 1982 argues that Aristotle's theory of the natural slave functioned ideologically, to naturalize hereditary slavery; Smith 1983 reviews inconsistencies and contradictions in the theory and critiques the argument itself; Kraut 2002, 277–305 argues that Aristotle's justification of slavery made sense in the context of popular attitudes regarding slaves.
40 Kraut 2002, 290–295 connects the class of individuals with a defective capacity for reason with non-Greek peoples, especially from Asia, who were, in Aristotle's and the popular view, fit to be enslaved (cf. 1285a19–22).
41 Cf. Diogenes Laertius, 7.121–122: μόνον τ'ἐλεύθερον [τὸν σοφόν]· τοὺς δὲ φαύλους δούλους. In his discussion of the paradox, Cicero distinguishes between actual slavery and metaphorical slavery of the soul to vice (*Paradoxa Stoicorum*, 5.35): "All wicked men are slaves. Slaves! This sounds more paradoxical and remarkable than it really is. They are saying that those who have been made property of masters because of debt or law are not slaves (*non enim ita dicunt eos esse servos ut mancipia quae sunt dominorum facta nexu aut aliquo iure civili*). But if slavery should be, as it is, the obedience of a broken and abject mind that lacks its own judgment, who would deny that all men who are weak, lustful, and wicked are slaves (*omnes leves omnes cupidos omnes denique improbos*)?"
42 The doctrine of determinism had its roots in the Early Stoa. Zeno and Chrysippus used the analogy of a dog tied to a cart (cf. Hippolytus, *Refutation of All Heresies*, 1.21.2). The dog can accommodate his free will to necessity (ποιῶν καὶ τὸ αὐτεξούσιον μετὰ τῆς ἀνάγκης) and follow the cart willingly or unwilling. Either way, however, the dog will follow the cart.
43 On Seneca's use of this metaphor: Edwards 2009. Imagine a person who asserts that skin color has no bearing on whether a person is good or bad but then proposes to label all good people, regardless of their skin color, as "white" and to label all bad people, regardless of their skin color, as "black."
44 Manning 1989 argues that humanitarian potential in Stoic ideas played only a limited and indirect role in bettering the condition of slaves; when a conflict arose between humanitarian ideals and the material interest of the owner, the latter won out. In the analysis of Bradley 1994, 135–140, Stoics never seriously questioned the place of slavery in society despite the doctrine of human kinship; much of the concern expressed by Stoics about the treatment of slaves, he argues, was actually directed towards the spiritual health of the owner rather than the well-being of the slave.
45 Cf. Williams 1998, 12: "Seneca and his various associates can let the social world be unjust, because they can, in accordance with one or another of their fantasies, suppose

24 Introduction

that one can get out of it. Aristotle knew that one could not get out of it, and his fantasy had to be that however imperfect it was likely in practice to be, at least it was not structurally unjust – the world could not be such that the best development of some people necessarily involved the coercion of others against their nature."

46 The many and varied contributions of freedmen to the culture and society of the late republic and early empire are well known. Still useful are the surveys in Duff 1958, 103–125; Treggiari 1969, 87–161.

47 Treggiari 1969, 177–192.

48 Cf. Hopkins 1965, 12–26, whose analysis suggests that the increasing complexity and differentiation of Roman institutions offered nonelite individuals an opportunity to gain partial entry into the elite by distinguishing themselves in some area of achievement and acquiring wealth. Hopkins characterized this upward mobility as a form of "status dissonance," in which the assimilating elite freedman distinguished himself in terms of wealth and achievement but remained without a distinguished family. Weaver 1967, 3-20 discusses status dissonance within the *familia Caesaris*.

49 Mouritsen 2011, 36–65.

50 Ulpian, *Dig.* 47.10.11.7, would not deny a patron his right of mild chastisement (*levis coercitio*) or verbal rebuke (*convici non impudici dictio*) even in the case of a married freedwoman; on this passage, Perry 2011, 142–143.

51 Cf. *Codex*: 10.33.2, indicating that an ex-slave serving as aedile would "defile the honor of the council with the stain of his slavery" (*violatam servili macula curiae dignitatem*).

52 The occasion of indignation in this instance may have been Valerius Maximus' association with a probable member of Pompey the Great's family, a Sextus Pompey who was consul in 14 CE and later governor of Asia; see Mouritsen 2011, 268 on the passage.

53 On the resistance of Roman slaves, Bradley 1994, 107–131, 2011, 362–384. McKeown 2011, 153–175 discusses resistance among slaves in Greece with attention to the difficulty of interpreting the evidence.

54 Douglass 1845, 67.

55 However, even poorly supervised slaves were likely to have contained their actions within limits. Slaves on the undersupervised estate did what they thought they could get away with, be it stealing, working poorly, malingering, or committing acts of sabotage and vandalism. On the other hand, slaves would not, ordinarily, undertake actions that would elicit harsh counteractions. Resistance aimed to alleviate the material conditions of slavery and to enable the slaves to win tactical victories over the master. For this reason, measured acts of resistance were more common than open violence, attacks against the owner or his delegates, and, certainly, full-blown rebellion: cf. Bradley 1989, 14–15, who notes the conditions under which resistance might cross the line into rebellion.

56 Bradley 1994 notes that we can neither prove nor refute the notion that Roman slaves understood the nature of the system that oppressed them. However (p. 131), "it is undeniably true that throughout history there have been many slaves who have withstood the oppression inherent in their condition. The proof lies in the combination of their words and actions, which leave the issue beyond doubt. . . . In all fundamentals, however, in terms of authority, control and the manipulation of power, the social relationship between slave-owner and slave was precisely the same at Rome as in the slave societies of the New World; and an objective assessment of the deeds and actions of Roman slaves shows that they fall into precisely the same categories of resistance behaviour associated with slaves in those same societies. It follows that resistance had a structural, and elemental, place in the history of slavery at Rome."

57 Scott 1990.

58 Scott 1990, 165. On the hidden transcript as a means of negating the public transcript, see 111–118.

Introduction 25

59 Scott 1990, 136–182 on disguising public expressions of discontent. Cf. Hillard 2013 on graffiti as a means of expressing opposition to optimate rule in late Republican Rome.
60 Scott 1990, 184. On infrapolitics in general: 183–201.
61 Cf. Joshel 2011, 215.
62 Richlin 2014, 213–214 describes this incident as an occasion on which "the hidden transcript has broken out into plain sight."
63 The fragmentary character of the excerpt, from the epitome of Constantine Porphyrogenitos, has left the city and the date uncertain.
64 Cf. Sacks 1990, 144–145, who notes that Diodorus' principal source for the First Sicilian Slave War was an account of the event by the Stoic philosopher Posidonius. At the same time, Diodorus' censure of the slave owners does not imply approval of Eunus, whom he portrayed as the inverse of a good king, that is, a coward and a charlatan: cf. Morton 2013.
65 Scott 1990, 136–182 (quote, p. 138).
66 Cf. the discussion of elite engagement with popular culture in early modern Europe in Burke 1978.
67 Kurke 2011, 10–12.
68 Cf. Hopkins 1993, 19, who suggests that this text asked its elite readers at points "to side with the slave against the master."
69 Forsdyke 2012, 73–89.
70 See Schlam 1993 for a survey of opinion regarding the tale's origins.
71 Cf. Owens 2020 forthcoming.
72 Anderson 2000, 16–17 notes that it is often difficult to draw clear distinctions, both in genre and in content, among myth, legend, folktale, and fairytale.
73 See Zipes 1979 on class and social conflict in the European folktale; quotation, p. 6.
74 Levine 2007, 81–135; quotation. p. 134.
75 The Brer Rabbit stories also provide another notable instance of preservation through elite appropriation. Before the war, Joel Chandler Harris, a white southerner, had heard these stories from slaves. After the war, he adapted them for the readers of the *Atlanta Constitution*, inventing the character of Uncle Remus, a faithful retainer still living on the plantation, who told stories to his ex-masters' little boy. So framed, the Uncle Remus tales reasserted white dominance after slavery and served as a form of entertainment for white Americans that was suitable even for children. On Harris, Mixon 1990; on the reframed ideology of the tales, Flusche 1975.
76 For the view that particular fables encoded the perspective of ancient slaves, cf. Daube 1972, 52–59; Ste. Croix 1981, 444–445; Bradley 1987, 150–153; Rothwell 1994. duBois's 2003, 174–177 survey of views is recommended. Richlin 2017, 338–340 identifies parallels between the camouflaged servile protests in fables and the elusive doublespeak of Plautine slaves.
77 In Perry 1965, 222–225.
78 Bradley 1987, 152.
79 Cf. the interpretation of other fables in Daube 1972, 54–56; Bradley 1987, 150–153.
80 Rather than claiming that slaves founded the genre, in *cur sit inventum genus* Phaedrus could have meant that slaves found the fable as an apt form for expressing and disguising their feelings.
81 Champlin 2005. Champlin, however, is incorrect in assuming that Phaedrus' knowledge of law and literature rules out the possibility he had been a slave: cf. Richlin 2014, 200, n. 26; MacLean 2018, 97. Bloomer 1997, 79, notes multiple ways in which Phaedrus marks out a servile or libertine status for his authorial persona. duBois 2003, 186–187, argues that the fable reflects aristocratic essentialism: "Just as the wolf is always a wolf, so the aristocrat is always an aristocrat; just as the tortoise is always a tortoise, so the slave . . . is born, lives, and dies a slave, naturally, essentially

26 *Introduction*

servile as the fox is vulpine." This may be true of some fables in some contexts but not all fables in all contexts.

82 Cf. the argument of MacLean 2018, that aspects of freedman culture served aristocrats in the first century CE as examples of how to survive under autocracy.

83 Rothwell 1994, 234–235.

84 Forsdyke 2012, 59–73. Cf. Trenkner 1958, who traces the incorporation of the novella, which she defines as a particular type of popular tale, more realistic than fable, myth, and legend, into a range of genres during the Classical period, including historiography, tragedy, and comedy. Trenkner's focus, however, is on the formal aspects of these tales rather than on their ideological contexts.

85 Forsdyke 2012, 66–67.

86 Richlin 2017; see also Richlin 2014.

87 Cf. McCarthy 2000, who argues that slavery served as a metaphor expressing the citizen's subordination in a hierarchical society and a desire to rebel against one's superiors.

88 The Greek settings and characters who were notional Greeks provided an additional level of disguise: Greek masters, not Roman, were being criticized and mocked. Thus, Donatus' observation on Terence, *Eunuchus* 57, that slaves were allowed to be cleverer than their masters in the *palliatae*, a freedom that slaves in the comedies in Roman dress, the *fabulae togatae*, did not enjoy: *concessum est in palliata poetis comicis servos dominis sapientiores fingere, quod idem in togata non fere licet.*

89 Scobie 1983, 1–40 argues more broadly that traditional storytelling influenced the creation of the novel itself; Scobie 1979, 53–56 moots the possibility that traditional storytelling informed the composition of *Ephesiaca* and *Callirhoe*.

90 Veyne 1961; Bodel 1994; Bradley 2000. In Owens forthcoming, I consider the relevance of slavery to the Cupid and Psyche tale.

91 Cf. Heinze 1899, who treats the structure of the *Satyrica* as a send-up of the Greek novel. Henderson 2010 takes the question up again with an eye to a later date for *Satyrica*.

1 *Ephesiaca*
Enslavement and folktale

Introduction

Xenophon of Ephesus' *Ephesiaca* and Chariton's *Callirhoe* are the two earliest novels of the novels that survive. Evidence does not allow for chronological precision, but Xenophon may have written his novel sometime in the late first or early second century CE.[1] The novel concerns the adventures of Habrocomes and Anthia, both of noble families in Ephesus. They see each other at a festival and fall in love. They begin to waste away, but after their parents learn from an oracle the reason for their ailment, they are married. Soon after, in response to the same oracle, they set out on a voyage to Egypt. Disaster strikes when Phoenician pirates capture them and take them as slaves to pirate headquarters at Tyre in Phoenicia. As beautiful enslaved youths, Habrocomes and Anthia are vulnerable to sexual exploitation. They also must endure the ever-present threat, sometimes the reality, of punishment. Early on, they are separated and made to suffer the slavery separately. Anthia passes from owner to owner, each time having to fend off a potential rapist. Before they are reunited and regain their freedom, Habrocomes' and Anthia's experience of slavery will have constituted a considerable portion of the novel.

Xenophon's *Ephesiaca* is both the least studied and least admired of the surviving novels.[2] The perceived poor quality of *Ephesiaca* and the entry for its author in the *Suda* (an encyclopedia compiled at Byzantium in the tenth century CE) that the novel comprised 10 books prompted Erwin Rohde to speculate that the surviving text was an epitome of a longer, more coherent work.[3] The arguments in the ensuing debate are complex, and the epitome theory can neither be fully proved nor refuted. Nonetheless, it is legitimate to consider the present text, be it epitome or original, as coherent on its own terms.[4] As Aldo Tagliabue notes in an important reappraisal of the author, Xenophon was "in full artistic control of his novel."[5] Tagliabue demonstrates how Xenophon has constructed the development of the protagonists' love from its beginnings as sexual desire to a spiritual connection that will transcend death. As a novelist, however, Xenophon also made artistic choices that distinguish *Ephesiaca* from the other surviving novels: a plot driven by action with an emphasis on both linguistic and compositional repetition; intertextual references on a thematic, rather than a linguistic,

28   Ephesiaca

level to a limited number of well-known works, such as the *Odyssey* and the *Phaedrus*; a simplified moral vision of good versus bad that concludes in an unambiguous happy ending. These artistic choices have produced a work that in Tagliabue's view "leans" toward paraliterature, a simpler novel that intentionally avoided the complexity of narration, theme, and moral vision associated with a literary work.[6]

Xenophon's representation of his protagonists' slavery constitutes additional evidence of his artistic command. He contrasts, for example, Habrocomes' and Anthia's metaphorical enslavement to love with their experience as actual slaves and reflects this contrast in a modulation of the novel's literary affinity, associating slavery to love with love elegy and narrating the protagonists' actual slavery through folktale paradigms. In certain situations, the elite protagonists adopt behaviors stereotypically associated with bad slaves. Xenophon treats the protagonists' bad-slave behavior sympathetically while acknowledging elite sensibilities regarding slave behavior. A contrast with Habrocomes' old tutor, a good slave who perishes, suggests that the protagonists' bad-slave behavior was necessary for them to survive in slavery and to escape from it.

The author's portrayal of secondary characters points to sympathy for slaves in general, not just the protagonists. Xenophon depicts real slave characters, that is, characters who were not enslaved elites, as kind and humane. These real slaves offer the protagonists important sympathy, wise advice, and genuine assistance. Habrocomes and Anthia have a close relationship with their personal slave attendants, Leucon and Rhode, who are captured with them and who thus become their masters' fellow slaves. At the end of the novel, the protagonists refashion their lives after slavery with these characters, now the protagonists' fellow ex-slaves. Two other real slaves, Lampon and Clytus, show special sympathy for the heroine within the context of their limited agency. Lampon even saves Anthia's life. In contrast, not all but many of the protagonists' masters are cruel and unjust. They subject the protagonists to physical punishment and sexual coercion; they judge the enslaved protagonists unjustly and harshly because they are slaves. The paraliterary opposition of good and bad, noted by Tagliabue in the context of antagonists who would thwart Habrocomes and Anthia in the realization of their love, is also evident in the conflict between good slaves and bad masters.

Slavery to love: *servitium amoris*

Xenophon anticipates Habrocomes' and Anthia's enslavement when they meet at a festival and fall in love. The god Eros, incensed at handsome Habrocomes' disdain for all others, declared war and made the protagonist his war captive (1.3.2, αἰχμάλωτος). Habrocomes concedes defeat in a soliloquy, in which he laments that he is compelled to be a slave to a girl (1.4.1, νενίκημαι καὶ παρθένῳ δουλεύειν ἀναγκάζομαι). He is humiliated by his unmanliness and cowardice (1.4.2, ὦ πάντα ἄνανδρος ἐγὼ καὶ πονηρός).[7] For her part, Anthia feels shame at feelings unbecoming to a maiden (1.4.6). Both protagonists waste

Ephesiaca 29

away, loving one another from afar and keeping the cause of their suffering secret (1.5.1–4). Their suffering is physical as well as mental. Habrocomes loses his manly vigor (1.5.5, τὸ σῶμα πᾶν ἠφάνιστο). There is no explicit reference to Anthia becoming enslaved to love; however, she suffers the same symptoms. Her parents note that her beauty is fading (1.5.6, ὁρῶντες αὐτῆς τὸ μὲν κάλλος μαραινόμενον) with no clear cause. Xenophon has aligned the lovesickness of both protagonists with the motifs of elegiac slavery to love, *servitium amoris*: personal humiliation, mental anguish, and physical suffering.[8]

Other novel protagonists become slaves of love; however, Xenophon alone draws a contrast between his protagonists' metaphorical slavery and their looming nonmetaphorical enslavement.[9] The connection is signaled soon after Habrocomes and Anthia fall sick. Their worried parents consult the oracle of Apollo at Colophon, who assures them that things would work out but not before their children are forced to endure terrible suffering and dreadful labors (1.6.2, δεινὰ ... πάθη καὶ ἀνήνυτα ἔργα), including a journey from home across the sea (ὑπεὶρ ἅλα) and chains (δεσμὰ δὲ μοχθήσουσι).[10] The supernatural device of the oracle connects the protagonists' metaphorical slavery to their future actual enslavement, when they will endure the humiliation, mental anguish, and physical suffering associated with actual slavery: separation from one's home, hard labor, and constraint.[11] First, however, Habrocomes and Anthia marry and are able to relieve their suffering as "slaves" of love. For a while, they are happy. "Their whole life was a festival (1.10.2, ἑορτή τε ἦν ἅπας ὁ βίος αὐτοῖς) and everything was full of cheerful feasting. They also forgot what had been prophesied (ἤδη καὶ τῶν μεμαντευμένων λήθη)."

(Folk)tales of real slavery: learning to think like a slave

The protagonists' nonmetaphorical slavery begins when Phoenician pirates capture them on the way to Egypt and take them to Tyre. Xenophon frames the narration of his protagonists' experience as nonmetaphorical slaves through two folktale types. The motif associated with Habrocomes' slavery is familiar from the story of the Hebrew slave Joseph and the wife of the Egyptian Potiphar, his master (*Genesis* 39): A protagonist rejects a woman's advances. She then accuses him falsely. The protagonist is punished.[12] Xenophon uses the "Potiphar's wife" tale twice in his account of Habrocomes' slavery. When the protagonist is a slave at Tyre and Manto, his master's daughter, tries to force him to have sex with her. He rejects her and Manto falsely accuses him to her father, who then has Habrocomes tortured. Xenophon repeats the motif when Habrocomes is a slave in Egypt. Cyno, the wife of his new owner, also tries to seduce the hero. But in this case, the woman proposes, in addition, to kill her husband. After Cyno commits the murder, Habrocomes rejects her. Greek versions of the tale type feature aristocratic protagonists. Rejected by Bellerophon, Sthenoboea laid a false accusation against him to her husband Proteus. Phaedra condemned her stepson Hippolytus to his father, Theseus.[13] But in the *Genesis* version, Joseph was a slave in Egypt, like Habrocomes. Xenophon appears to follow a tradition in which the tale involved slavery.

30   Ephesiaca

The folktale involving Anthia is related to a type described by Thompson as the "Escape from an Undesired Suitor."[14] In this tale, a woman employs guile, craft, or even violence to defend her virtue. Xenophon offers six versions of the motif in shorter and longer forms. The heroine's slave status is clear or implied in five of the six iterations. These repetitions reflect not only Anthia's steadfast loyalty to her husband but also how her situation as a slave forced her to rely on various forms of guile and, in one desperate instance, violence.[15] Habrocomes also is changed by his experience as a slave. In the first version of the "Potiphar's wife" tale, he was dismissive of the torture he would face for rejecting Manto. In the second version of the tale, the possibility of torture weighs heavily on him, and he considers, if only briefly, murdering his master. Through repetition of these traditional tales, Xenophon emphasizes how both Habrocomes and Anthia adapt to the conditions of slavery by acting and thinking like real slaves, that is, slaves who would lie to their masters or slaves who might even commit violent acts against them to defend their *sōphrosynē*.

Habrocomes and the "Potiphar's wife" tale

At Tyre, the pirates who had captured and enslaved Habrocomes and Anthia turn them over to Apsyrtus, their commander. Accompanying them are their slaves Leucon and Rhode (1.14.1), who are now the protagonists' fellow slaves. Xenophon describes them as Habrocomes' and Anthia's *syntrophoi* (2.3.3), a term that suggests the possibility that back in Ephesus Leucon and Rhode had each been brought up with their masters, a social motive for the close relationship with their (now-former) masters in Tyre.[16] As individuals accustomed to slavery, Leucon and Rhode play an important role in the first iteration of the Potiphar's wife tale. Xenophon uses their pragmatism toward their new pirate masters as a foil for the elite idealism of the newly enslaved protagonists.

After Manto falls in love with Habrocomes, she confides in Rhode and tasks her with acting as a go-between. Manto reminds Rhode that she is a slave; she promises her great rewards if her efforts prove successful and dire punishment if they do not. Rhode does not know what to do. She is still devoted to Anthia, her former master, but fears the wrath of Manto, the new master. Rather than approach Habrocomes, she confides in Leucon. Leucon takes the matter in hand and brings the four slaves, himself and Rhode, Habrocomes and Anthia, together in conference (2.3.7–9).

Accustomed to slavery, Rhode is concerned that Manto's desire for Habrocomes will split the *syntrophoi* apart and present a danger to them all.[17] "Leucon," she says, "we are totally done for. We are going to lose our dear friends" (2.3.7, νῦν οὐκέτι τοὺς συντρόφους ἕξομεν). Leucon reflects the same concerns in the meeting. He first reminds everyone not only that they are *syntrophoi* – but also that they are fellow slaves now as well (2.4.1): "What are we going to do, dear friends (σύντροφοι)? Slaves (οἰκέται), how do we take counsel?"[18] While ostensibly deferring to Habrocomes, Leucon reminds the protagonist that his choice will have consequences for them all. His implicit advice is to give in to Manto

Ephesiaca 31

(2.4.2): "So, take counsel as to what seems right to you, save us all and don't overlook those subject to the anger of masters (μὴ περιίδῃς ὀργῇ δεσποτῶν ὑποπεσόντας)." Although Leucon sees that everyone's safety is at risk, he continues to defer to the authority of his former master.

Habrocomes seems unaware of the predicament because, perhaps, he does not understand what it means to be a slave. His only work, as it were, was "to love Anthia and be loved by her" (2.4.1, οὐδὲν ἔργον ἦν ἢ φιλεῖν Ἀνθίαν καὶ ὑπ' ἐκείνης φιλεῖσθαι). This was before he learns of Manto's designs on him. After Leucon informs him of the situation and implies that he should give in, Habrocomes responds in outrage (2.4.4):

> I am a slave, but I know how to honor my agreements. They have power over my body, but I have a free soul (τὴν ψυχὴν δὲ ἐλευθέραν ἔχω). Let Manto threaten me now, if she wants, with the sword and the noose and hot plates and everything that the body of a slave can endure (πάντα ὅσα δύναται σῶμα ἀναγκάσαι οἰκέτου). I will never willingly do injustice to Anthia.

Habrocomes continues to uphold the elite honor code in which he was raised. He will keep his promise to Anthia. To do this, he is prepared to endure all sorts of physical punishment.[19] There is something Stoic in his defiance and the distinction he draws between the slavery of his body and the freedom of his soul and his disdain for physical punishment.[20] At this point, Habrocomes does not think like a real slave, that is, like Leucon.

Having received no assistance from Rhode, Manto writes directly to Habrocomes, promising that she will convince her father to betroth her to him, promising that Habrocomes will be wealthy and happy as her husband. Together they would "pack off" Anthia (2.5.2, τὴν νῦν σοι γυναῖκα ἀποσκευασόμεθα). But if Habrocomes should reject her, she threatens, both he and his fellow slaves will be punished. Habrocomes writes back to Manto what he had said to his fellow slaves in private, an unfiltered insertion of his defiant resistance into the open – a direct expression of his personal hidden transcript (2.5.4):

> Mistress, do what you want and use my body as the body of a slave (χρῶ σώματι ὡς οἰκέτου). If you want to kill me, I am ready. If you want to torture me, torture me as you see fit. But I will never come to your bed nor obey you if you command it (οὔτε ἂν τοιαῦτα πεισθείην κελευούσῃ).

In response, Manto tells her father, Apsyrtus, that Habrocomes tried to rape her. Xenophon uses the motif of false accusation in the folktale to illustrate the injustice and cruelty of the slave-owner. The author increases the seriousness of Manto's accusation by making the villainess emphasize that Habrocomes was a slave, both treacherous and violent (2.5.6–7):

> "Father," she said, "pity your daughter done outrage by a slave (ὑβρισμένην ὑπ' οἰκέτου). For chaste Habrocomes tried to destroy my virginity. He even

32 Ephesiaca

plotted against you (ἐπεβούλευσε δὲ καὶ σοί), claiming that he loved me. Exact proper punishment for this shamelessness. But if you are giving your daughter as a bride to slaves (εἰ δίδως ἔκδοτον θυγατέρα τὴν σὴν τοῖς οἰκέταις), I'll kill myself first."

Apsyrtus, too, is indignant because Habrocomes is a slave; as such, he must be made an example to the others (2.6.1):

> Apsyrtus heard her out and thought she was telling the truth. He did not investigate what had been done, but sent for Habrocomes and said, "You shameless and cursed creature. You dared to outrage your masters and wanted to destroy a maiden's virginity, slave that you are (οἰκέτης ὤν)? But you won't get away with it. I will punish you and make your suffering an example for the other slaves (τοῖς ἄλλοις οἰκέταις τὴν σὴν αἰκίαν ποιήσομαι παράδειγμα)."

Apsyrtus then orders other slaves to rip off Habrocomes' clothes, to fetch fire and whips, and to start the torture (2.6.3):

> It was a pitiful sight. The beatings covered his whole body (αἱ τε γὰρ πληγαὶ τὸ σῶμα πᾶν ἠφάνιζον), which was not used to the tortures endured by slaves (βασάνων ἄηθες ὂν οἰκετικῶν). Blood flowed down over his body and his manly beauty was extinguished (τὸ κάλλος ἐμαραίνετο).

Habrocomes' defiance implies that he was not, in Stoic terms, a moral slave. At the same time, Xenophon stresses the consequences of his real enslavement. The experienced slaves Leucon and Rhode knew that Habrocomes could not defend himself against an angry master; indeed, they feared the impact of his defiance on themselves as well. James Scott's observation that subjugated peoples tend to adopt an outward pose of deference when addressing their masters, an attitude that marked their public declarations with reservation, formulae, and flattery, may be relevant to the contrast between Habrocomes' blunt defiance and the cautious attitude recommended of the real slaves Leucon and Rhode.[21] Newly enslaved Habrocomes had not learned to speak like a slave. This direct defiance led to his torture.

The effects of that torture (αἱ τε γὰρ πληγαὶ τὸ σῶμα πᾶν ἠφάνιζον; τὸ κάλλος ἐμαραίνετο) recall the physical suffering of the protagonists as metaphorical love slaves back in Ephesus. Habrocomes had lost his manly vigor (1.5.5, τὸ σῶμα πᾶν ἠφάνιστο); Anthia's beauty had begun to fade (1.5.6, τὸ μὲν κάλλος μαραινόμενον). The linguistic parallels invite comparison between the torture Habrocomes endures as a nonmetaphorical slave and his anguish earlier as a slave of love. The vivid description of the impact of physical torture suggests that it is worse to be tortured as a slave than to be tormented as a slave of love. Xenophon may be read as criticizing how slave-owners used slavery as a metaphor to think with, exposing as hyperbole the conceit

Ephesiaca 33

that love was a kind of "slavery."[22] Those who have not experienced the real thing might indulge in such a conceit but not persons who have actually been enslaved. In addition to criticizing the metaphor, Xenophon may criticize the readiness of slave-owners to assume servile wickedness. Because Habrocomes was a slave, Apsyrtus accepted Manto's accusation against him (2.6.1, ἐρεύνεσε μὲν τὸ πραχθὲν οὐκέτι); he gave Habrocomes no chance to speak in his own defense (2.6.2, εἰπὼν οὐκέτι ἀνασχόμενος οὐδὲ λόγου ἀκοῦσαι). Apsyrtus' prejudices, the prejudices of most slave-owners, led him to commit an injustice.

Potiphar's wife: second iteration

In a reprisal of the Potiphar's wife motif at the end of Book 3, Xenophon illustrates how torture left a mark on Habrocomes' mind as well as his body. Habrocomes had left Tyre and gone in search of Anthia. At Tarsus, he heard, mistakenly, that Anthia had died and that grave robbers had taken her corpse to Egypt. He sailed after them. But his ship ran aground near the headwaters of the Nile where he was taken prisoner and sold back into slavery. His new master is an old soldier named Araxus, who lives in Pelusium. Xenophon emphasizes that Araxus is a good master who treats the protagonist like a son (3.12.4). However, Araxus is married to the dreadful Cyno, a woman whose name means "Bitch" (3.12.3). Cyno falls in love with Habrocomes and propositions him, drawing the protagonist into a conspiracy to kill her husband. Habrocomes first resists but then relents as Cyno insists, only to be appalled after Cyno carries out the murder on her own (3.12.5): "Unable to bear the unrestrained brutality of the woman, he went out of the house and left her behind, declaring that he would never get in bed with a murderess." Cyno retaliates, denouncing Habrocomes to the authorities for the murder (3.12.2–6).

Instead of offering Cyno defiant resistance, as he had Manto, Habrocomes initially relented. The lapse was momentary but still surprising. Manto was beautiful, while Cyno was repulsive. Manto's offer did not involve any plotting against her father (although such plotting was part of her false accusation). In contrast, Cyno made the murder of her husband, a man who had treated Habrocomes with kindness, a key part of the deal (3.12.4): "Cyno propositioned him for sex, pressed him to give in, and promised to take him as a husband and kill Araxus (καὶ ἄνδρα ἔχειν ὑπισχνεῖτο καὶ Ἄραξον ἀποκτενεῖν)."[23] Why would Habrocomes go along with this even for a moment? The author offers a reason for the lapse, revealing Habrocomes' thought process telegraphically but in detail (3.12.4). Habrocomes is indeed, at first, appalled. He considers many factors, two of which had inclined him earlier to reject Manto: Anthia and the promises he made her. But there was now another factor for him to consider: "the chaste self-control that had already caused him so often to suffer injustice" (τὴν πολλάκις αὐτὸν σωφροσύνην ἀδικήσασαν ἤδη). This would appear to refer to the hero's reflection on how his virtuous rejection of Manto had led earlier to his undeserved condemnation and torture. As Cyno continued to insist, he gave in (τέλος δὲ ἐγκειμένης τῆς Κυνοῦς συγκατατίθεται).[24]

34 Ephesiaca

Cyno did not threaten Habrocomes as Manto had. Nonetheless, finding himself in the same circumstances that had earlier resulted in his torture, Habrocomes feared he would be tortured again. This possibility accounts for his change of mind. In the earlier episode, Xenophon remarked that such torture had caused Habrocomes' aristocratic beauty to die away (2.6.2). In this replay, the author implies that torture has had an effect on the protagonist's nature as well. Habrocomes has experienced what it means to be tortured as a slave and, as a result, begins to think and act like one. In the course of a brief episode, he resists, yields, and finally backs out. Xenophon may have found a precedent for the vacillation in a variant.[25] But Habrocomes' indecision may also suggest an author who is triangulating to let his protagonist have it both ways. A reader, whether ex-slave or even normative elite, might understand, even sympathize with, Habrocomes' desire to avoid being tortured a second time. But his agreement to kill Araxus, not only his master but also a master who had been kind to him, would have provoked a deep-seated fear held by many slave-owners.[26] Xenophon's text may engage with an ideological conflict among his readers.

Habrocomes' lapse is only momentary but, nonetheless, implies that torture was so terrible that even an enslaved elite of good character would do anything to avoid it. At the same time, the author tries to exculpate Habrocomes through his quick reversal. Roman law, however, would not have considered the brevity of involvement in a plot against the master as exculpatory. The *senatus consultum Silanianum* did not allow slaves who were, like Habrocomes, living "under the same roof" (*Dig.* 29.5.1.26–27, *sub eodem tecto*) as their masters to remain silent when the master's life was threatened. A slave's silence would be punished as complicity.[27] Habrocomes' momentary association with servile violence would have been disturbing to many of Xenophon's readers.[28]

Cyno denounced Habrocomes to the residents of Pelusium for the murder she herself committed. She denounces him before the assembly as a newly bought slave (3.12.6, ὁ νεώνητος δοῦλος) who killed his master. As was the case in the Manto episode, Xenophon emphasizes that there is particular indignation against Habrocomes because he is a slave. The Pelusians turn him over to the Prefect of Egypt (τὸν ἄρχοντα τῆς Αἰγύπτου) in Alexandria, who reads their account of what happened (4.2.1).[29] The Pelusians, too, are indignant that Habrocomes is a slave (ὅτι οἰκέτης ὢν τοιαῦτα ἐτόλμησε). Like Apsyrtus in the Manto episode, who condemned Habrocomes without hearing from him a word in self-defense (cf. 2.6.2, οὐκέτι ἀνασχόμενος οὐδὲ λόγου ἀκοῦσαι), the prefect sentences the protagonist to crucifixion before inquiring into what had happened (4.2.1, οὐκέτι οὐδὲ πυθόμενος τὰ γενόμενα).

Set up on a cross, Habrocomes protests his innocence to the Sun (4.2.5, ἄνθρωπον οὐδὲν ἀδικήσαντα). The god pities him and raises a wind that blows the cross into the Nile. The river carries him safely to its mouth (4.2.6–7). Guards fish him out of the river and bring him back to the authorities as a slave escaping from punishment (ὡς δραπέτην τῆς τιμωρίας).[30] The prefect is even angrier than before. Habrocomes is clearly someone completely wicked, presumably because he did not die on the cross like he was supposed to (4.2.8, ὁ δὲ

Ephesiaca   35

ἔτι μᾶλλον ὀργισθεὶς καὶ πονηρὸν εἶναι νομίσας). He sentences Habrocomes to be burned on a pyre erected by the river. As the flames near him, Habrocomes prays again, and the river overflows its banks extinguishing the fire. This second miracle gives the prefect reason to pause and keep Habrocomes in jail until he can learn more about a man who seems to be such a cause of divine concern (4.2.10). He finally listens to Habrocomes' story, pities him, gives him money, and promises to send him back to Ephesus (4.4.1).

So long as the Pelusians and the prefect believed Habrocomes was a slave, he was an object of indignation and was not even permitted to give his version of events. Even if he had, Habrocomes might still have been condemned. If the person of a Roman-era official indicates the relevance of Roman law to this case, Habrocomes was required to try to prevent the crime against his master without consideration of his own safety. But in Xenophon's fictional world, divine judgment transcends the laws and social attitudes that would have condemned the protagonist. Tim Whitmarsh notes that the resort to divine intervention goes against the genre's tendency to naturalism.[31] The departure from the norm in this case may underline the earnest critique of a system that would mistreat and condemn a blameless slave.

Anthia and the Undesired Suitors

Xenophon narrates Anthia's experiences as a slave through a traditional tale type described by Thompson as the "Escape from an Undesired Suitor" (T 320). I outline the characteristic tale structure from the six iterations of the tale in *Ephesiaca*, adopting Propp's use of what he calls a function in his analysis of Russian folktales, that is, a narrative component combining a role and an action:[32] (Function 1) An antagonist holds the heroine in his power and wants to have sex with her. (Function 2) He tries to seduce her through bribes and/or threats. (Function 3) The heroine resists, typically through a strategy of deflection or deception. (Function 4) The antagonist continues his pursuit with greater vehemence, sometimes attempting to rape the heroine. (Function 5) She again resists, through renewed deception or more extreme measures; the protagonist either desists or is thwarted.[33] As is the case with Propp's analysis of Russian folktales, a given iteration of a tale may omit particular functions; however, functions will always appear in their proper order.[34]

The men who have power over Anthia vary in status – imperial and governmental officials, an Egyptian prince, bandits, a pimp – but all try to have sex with her. The sexual threat is associated with her status as a slave as well as her role as the heroine of a Greek novel: Anthia is a slave, either by sale or capture, in the last five of six tale iterations. She is under the control of one man or another in all. Her vulnerability to rape reflects the powerlessness of a slave. Sexual chasteness, or *sōphrosynē*, was a defining quality of the citizen, especially the female citizen. But sexual impurity was assumed in the case of a slave. The sexual penetrability of the slave body defined a social and legal boundary between free and slave.[35] Repetition of the tale, then, reflects Anthia's continuing corporeal

36 Ephesiaca

vulnerability as a slave. Outside the fiction of the novel, in the world of real slavery, it would have been against all odds that Xenophon's heroine manages to elude her would-be rapists again and again.

Xenophon's elite readers may have seen in Anthia's repeated defense of her virtue an affirmation of the endurance of her original elite status. However, the text allows an alternative reading. Anthia is able to remain chaste because she acts like a slave. Paradoxically, by acting like a slave she is able to remain chaste, that is, not like a slave. With two exceptions, her resistance, indicated in Functions 3 and 5 of the tale, takes on a variety of indirect forms associated with slaves, such as deferral, deception, concealment, and flattery. Such strategies did not belong uniquely to slaves. Deceptiveness and rhetorical cunning had been associated with Odysseus since Homer. But for slaves and other dominated people, as James Scott notes, indirect strategies might be the only means of resistance available. Alongside aristocratic verbal tricksters such as Odysseus, there were slave tricksters such as Aesop in the *Life of Aesop* and Anansi and Brer Rabbit in the folk tradition of African American slaves. Anthia belongs in the same tradition.

Anthia's first antagonist is Perilaus, an imperial official in Cilicia who saved Anthia's life when she was about to be sacrificed to Ares by Hippothous and his criminal gang (2.13.3).[36] After rescuing her, Perilaus is moved to pity and falls in love with the heroine (Function 1: 2.13.5–6). Perilaus does not attempt to take Anthia by force but offers her honorable marriage instead (Function 2). Anthia is not Perilaus' slave, but she is in his power.[37] As Perilaus becomes increasingly insistent, Anthia, in fear that he might become violent (δείσασα μὴ τι τολμήσῃ) attempts to deflect him, agreeing to the marriage but inventing some excuse (καὶ σκήπτεται <μὲν τι>) to put it off for a month (Functions 2 and 3 repeated: 2.13.8). As the month draws to a close and preparations for the wedding were underway, Anthia despairs of escape and determines to adopt a violent means of resistance. However, she directs the violence against herself. She procures a drug that she thinks will be fatal but that only induces sleep (Function 4: 3.5.1–11). The night of her wedding, Anthia takes the drug and falls into a death-like sleep. Stricken with grief, Perilaus entombs her in a rich monument. Anthia has definitively resisted him and preserved her *sōphrosynē* (Function 5) but at the apparent cost of her own life.

The sequence is repeated. Grave robbers raid the tomb, find the heroine alive, and take her to slave dealers in Alexandria. Psammis, an Indian king, sees her, falls in love, and buys her (Function 1: 3.11.2). He tries to rape Anthia straight away (Function 4: 3.3). She defends herself by inventing a story (σκήπτεται), that her father had dedicated her to Isis until she was old enough to marry – and that would not be for another year. The goddess would punish him harshly if he harmed her protégée (5.3.4–5). This resistance proves definitive (Function 5), because, as Xenophon notes, Psammis, an Indian, was a barbarian, and barbarians are naturally superstitious (3.11.4, δεισιδαίμονες δὲ φύσει βάρβαροι).[38]

The third iteration of the tale initially involves Hippothous, the bandit who had been preparing to sacrifice Anthia to Ares when Perilaus came to the rescue.

Hippothous himself escaped and fell in with Habrocomes, who had come to Cilicia in search of Anthia. He then left for Egypt to pursue his banditry there. There, Hippothous attacks Psammis, kills him, and captures Anthia along with other booty. Although he and Anthia had seen each other before, they fail to recognize each other on this occasion. Anthia conceals her true identity from her new master (4.3.6, τὸ μὲν ἀληθὲς οὐκ ἔλεγεν). In response to Hippothous' persistent question, "she claimed repeatedly (ἔφασκε) that she was a native Egyptian and that her name was Memphitis." It is necessary to the plot that Hippothous not realize that his captive was Anthia, the wife of his companion back in Cilicia. However, the heroine's repeated lies also align with the behavior of a slave who was wary of yielding information up to her master.

Hippothous, however, proves not to be Anthia's principal antagonist in this iteration of the tale. That role is assumed by his lieutenant Anchialus, to whom Hippothous gave Anthia and other plunder for safekeeping. Anchialus conceives a passion for Anthia and tries to seduce her, intending to ask Hippothous to give her to him as a gift (Function 1: 4.5.2). Anthia remains steadfast despite the cave, the chains, and Anchialus' threats. She is prepared, again, to die if only she can remain true to Habrocomes (Functions 2 and 3: 4.5.3). However, in this iteration, Anthia is forced again into violent resistance. Anchialus is no longer able to restrain himself and tries to rape her (Function 4). But as he got on top, she grabbed a sword lying nearby and struck him a fatal blow (Function 5: 4.5.5). As was the case in the episode involving Perilaus, in a dire moment, Anthia finds a definitive means of resistance in violence, but in this case, the violence is turned against her antagonist rather than herself.[39]

Anthia's violence here merits more discussion. An aristocratic heroine's murder of a brigand in defense of her *sōphrosynē* would seem beyond the need of justification. Xenophon, nonetheless, provides this seemingly unnecessary justification. He emphasizes that Anthia had no other means of resistance (4.5.5, ἡ δὲ ἐν ἀμηχάνῳ κακῷ γενομένη). Her action was unpremeditated. As Anchialus got on top of her, she grabbed a sword that happened to be lying nearby (τὸ παρακείμενον ξίφος) and struck only when she was on the very point of being raped (4.5.5, ὁ μὲν γὰρ περιληψόμενος καὶ φιλήσων ὅλος ἐνενεύκει πρὸς αὐτήν). If those details were not enough, the author intervenes to comment that Anthia's action was entirely justified: "He paid a fitting penalty for his wicked passion (4.5.6, δίκην ἱκανὴν ἐδεδώκει τῆς πονηρᾶς ἐπιθυμίας)."[40] This special pleading would not seem necessary in the case of an elite woman defending her honor. However, because Anthia was at that moment a slave, her act of violence was potentially concerning and in need of justification. Xenophon intervenes as author to pronounce the deed just; divinity had intervened earlier to declare that Habrocomes was an innocent man.[41]

Hippothous responds to the murder of his slain comrade as an angry master might respond to a violent slave. He sentences Anthia to be thrown in a pit and devoured by ravenous dogs, a fate which she is spared by the pity of another bandit (4.6.3). The detail reinforces the barbarity of the bandits, but, in this instance, Hippothous, who was himself an elite citizen of a Greek *polis*, may

38   Ephesiaca

have been acting like a vindictive slave-owner rather than a brutal outlaw. Behind the Grand-Guignol of this episode, there may be here an allusion to the grotesque and notorious, if rare, reality of exceptional cruelty on the part of some slave-owners.[42]

The sequence repeats a fourth time. Before Anthia's punishment can be executed, the Prefect of Egypt (the official who had earlier pardoned Habrocomes) appoints his relative Polyidus to restore public order (5.3.1). Polyidus breaks up Hippothous' gang and takes possession of Anthia (5.4.4). When he questions her about her identity, Anthia tells him not a word of truth (ἡ δὲ τῶν μὲν ἀληθῶν οὐδὲν λέγει) but that she was an Egyptian woman captured by robbers (5.4.4). Then Polyidus begins to lust for his captive as the heroine's fourth antagonist (Function 1: 5.4.5). He tries to seduce her and then to rape her (Functions 2 and 4 combined). Anthia manages to escape to a temple of Isis, becomes the goddess' suppliant (ἱκέτις γενομένη), and seeks her protection (Function 5: 5.4.5–6). This resistance proves effective. Polyidus swears an oath to respect Anthia's chastity and remains contented with merely looking at her and talking with her (5.4.7). Through his heroine's status as a suppliant, Xenophon alludes to another means of self-protection available to slaves, in this case a lawful means. Under Roman law, slaves had the right to seek protection from an abusive master by taking refuge in a religious sanctuary.[43] Polyidus, a public official, respects the law here as well as Anthia's chastity.

In the fifth and penultimate iteration of the tale, the most elaborated, Xenophon introduces an allusion to comedy that emphasizes the servile quality of Anthia's cleverness. After her arrival in Alexandria, Polyidus' jealous wife, Rhenaia, unjustly attacks Anthia and arranges for her to be sent to Tarentum and sold to a brothel (5.5).[44] As a brothel slave, Anthia faced the most serious threat of all to her *sōphrosynē*. Xenophon's account of her resistance is correspondingly more detailed than in the other iterations. The episode begins after the pimp had dressed Anthia up and led her out in front of the brothel.[45] Anthia laments her fate in the manner of a noble heroine in tragedy (5.7.2):

> Woe is me, she said. The first disasters weren't enough – the chains and bandits. But I am forced even to be a whore. O my beauty, you rightly violated. Why do you remain with me when you should not (ἀκαίρως)?[46]

The heroine interrupts her lamentation, realizing that it will not be of any help (5.7.2). She asks herself why she does not invent some scheme (οὐχ εὑρίσκω τινὰ μηχανὴν) if she will continue to preserve her purity. A crowd of customers gathers (Functions 1 and 2: 5.7.2). In her desperation, Anthia finds the necessary contrivance (5.7.4, εὑρίσκει τέχνην). She falls on the ground and pretends to be seized by an epileptic fit. The would-be customers are seized by pity and fear (ἦν δὲ τῶν παρόντων ἔλεος ἅμα καὶ φόβος); some are deterred from their desire to sleep with her, and others try to come to her aid (5.7.4). Anthia's act of resistance has proved decisive (Function 5). She continues the deception after the pimp takes her home and inquires after the nature of her disease. She invents a wild story of how she had contracted the disease from an attack by a fresh corpse when she was a young girl (5.7.6–7), capping the deception by persuading the pimp that he can recoup his money if he sells her to another owner (a sale that would deliver her from the perils of the brothel, that is, a repetition of Function 5: 5.7.8).

Anthia inspired her would-be customers with pity and fear (5.7.4). The allusion to Aristotle's *Poetics* directs us to read her resistance here in the context of tragedy and comedy. The (now-comic) heroine first adopts a pose of tragic aristocratic lament. She then realizes that her nobility will be of no use to her (τί ταῦτα θρηνῶ;). Rather, she needs to play the slave, assuming the role of a *servus callidus*, the clever slave who deceives the heartless pimp, or in Anthia's case, an *ancilla callida*.[47] Xenophon describes Anthia's deception both as a scheme (5.7.2, μηχανή) and as a contrivance (5.7.4, τέχνη). Derivatives from these Greek terms often indicated the ruse of a clever slave in Roman Comedy.[48] The allusions to tragedy and comedy serve to depict Anthia's deception as the self-conscious adoption of a servile persona. Through allusion to tragedy and comedy, Xenophon seems to suggest that the virtues of the elite citizen were of no help in slavery. Anthia needed the virtues of a slave, a heroic trickster slave.

The sixth and final iteration of the tale again involves Hippothous. After Perilaus put an end to his banditry in Egypt, Hippothous relocated to Sicily. There he married a wealthy old woman. She died and left Hippothous a wealthy widower. On a trip to Tarentum to buy slaves and other commodities (5.9.1–3), he sees the heroine at the slave market and recognizes her as the young woman who had slain his companion Anchialus. However, he does not realize that she was Anthia, the beloved of his former companion Habrocomes. He buys the heroine, takes her home, and reveals himself as the head of the Egyptian bandits. He forgives her for killing his old comrade (5.9.4–10). Then Hippothous, too, begins to desire the heroine despite his basic homoerotic orientation. He attempts to seduce her with promises (Functions 1 and 2: 5.9.11). Anthia resists, flattering her master with stilted irony: She was unworthy of intercourse with the master (ἀναξία εἶναι λέγουσα εὐνῆς δεσποτικῆς) (Function 3: 5.9.12). But Hippothous persists (Function 4), Anthia can think of nothing better to do than to tell him the complete truth about Ephesus and her marriage to Habrocomes (5.9.12). This revelation turns out to be a decisive act of resistance (Function 5). Hippothous reveals his own friendship with Habrocomes and promises Anthia that he will help her try to find him (5.9.13).

Xenophon makes his heroine accommodate the quality of her resistance in Functions 3 and 5 to the social rank of her antagonist. She resisted Perilaus by getting him to defer the wedding. When that day arrived, she resisted definitively through violence, but violence turned against herself. In Egypt, when Polyidus tried to rape her, Anthia resisted through legally sanctioned sanctuary. In the case of the two social outsiders, the heroine resorts to greater extremes of servile resistance. Anthia deterred the Indian Psammis with a quickly invented scary story involving retribution from Isis that her owner, as a superstitious

40   Ephesiaca

barbarian, believed (3.11.4).[49] She murdered the outlaw Anchialus – and even that murder needed justification. The despised pimp became the target of the most elaborate of Anthia's deceptions, when the heroine took on the role of a clever slave from comedy. Finally, Hippothous: Although he had turned to a life of banditry, Hippothous was descended from the elite of his native city (τῶν τὰ πρῶτα ἐκεῖ δυναμένων, 3.2.1) and was now a respectable widower. In this case, Anthia lays on the flattery. It is possible to recognize in the heroine's deference a common form of resistance adopted by the powerless.[50]

These modulations of Anthia's resistance seem directed to the sensibilities of readers who might be thinking of Anthia as a slave, rather than an elite who happens to be a slave but is not really. The heroine thus represents an anomalous case: a female slave who possesses *sōphrosynē*. Paradoxically, she must act like a slave to preserve her virtue. Her success, her repeated defense of her *sōphrosynē*, may be read as a pushback against the denigration faced by slaves (and many freedwomen) and asserted, if only on the level of fantasy, the chasteness of the female slave. In contrast, the author may imply a generic attack on slave-owners. Socially respectable types such as Perilaus and Polyidus share the role of Anthia's "Unwanted Suitor" with brutish barbarians such as Psammis and thugs such as Anchialus. Role sharing across the iterations of this tale type implies that the use of slaves for sex was in itself a form of brutishness, regardless of the social standing of the owner. In contrast, as I argue later in "The enslaved protagonists and ordinary slaves," Lampon, the lowly slave goatherder whom Manto ordered to rape Anthia, will take pity on the heroine and not lay a hand on her.

Habrocomes' tutor: a good slave

Xenophon's protagonists adopted the behaviors of bad slaves, including violence, in order to survive. The author also makes the converse of this point in an episode involving Habrocomes' old tutor, an idealized good slave who perishes. In the Introduction, I noted that the good-slave stereotype existed in counterpoint to that of the bad slave but was no less degrading. The good slave, like Odysseus' Eumaios, was so devoted to his owner that he did not possess his own personal subjectivity. Habrocomes' old tutor, his *tropheus*, represents such a character. Appropriately, Xenophon has not given him a name. The old tutor was among the slaves who accompanied Habrocomes on the voyage to Egypt, like Leucon and Rhode. The pirates took the protagonists, a selection of other slaves, and valuables on board their ship but left everyone else on the flaming wreck of the other vessel. A scene of pity follows, with those on board the pirate ship, including the protagonists, being carried off, while their doomed companions are wailing and calling out to them from the burning vessel. Among them is the old tutor. The episode takes place at the end of Book 1 (1.14.4–6):

> At this moment, Habrocomes' tutor, already an old man who looked like he was worthy of respect and, because of his years, worthy of pity, was not able

Ephesiaca   41

to endure Habrocomes' abduction. He threw himself into the sea and began to swim as if to seize the pirate's trireme, saying, "Why are you leaving me, child, an old man, your pedagogue? Where are you going? Kill me and bury me with your own hands, wretch that I am. For what life do I have without you?" He spoke and despairing at last ever to see Habrocomes again, he surrendered himself to the waves and died.

The scene is macabre: The old man swims after his young master's ship as it draws away; reaches out, pleading for death, pleading that Habrocomes kill him with his own hands; and then, at last, sinks beneath the waves. This over-the-top melodrama led Gareth Schmeling to condemn the episode: "Instead of a scene which elicits pity, the combination of events and speeches strikes the sensitive reader as grotesque."[51] However, what Schmeling has condemned here may have been intended by Xenophon as a satirical comment on the good-slave stereotype and the expectation that the good slave, that any human being, could so lose all sense of self.[52] The critique would anticipate a contrast with the protagonists' own behavior when they are enslaved. As we have seen, Habrocomes and Anthia adopted the behavior of bad slaves in order to survive. Habrocomes' nameless tutor, a good slave, perishes. One must act like a slave to survive as a slave.[53]

The enslaved protagonists and ordinary slaves

Habrocomes' and Anthia's bad-slave behavior blurred the distinction between the enslaved elite protagonists and real slaves. Xenophon further undermines the distinction through another traditional story. The episode involves the experiences of the enslaved heroine Anthia with a fellow slave, a goatherd named Lampon (2.9–11). After Apsyrtus punished Habrocomes for attempting to rape his daughter, he married Manto to a man from Antioch, Moeris, and gave her Anthia as a wedding gift. Manto then turned the heroine over to Lampon, the lowliest of her slaves (2.9.2, τῶν ἀτιμοτάτων), and instructed him to have Anthia as his woman and to rape her if she resisted (κελεύει γυναῖκα ἔχειν καὶ ἐὰν ἀπειθῇ προσέταττε βιάζεσθαι).

In narrative terms, Lampon is a minor character, a slave extra who figures in a single episode. In social terms and in contrast to the enslaved protagonists, he is a real slave, a lowly herdsman. Nonetheless, Lampon establishes a close and sympathetic relationship with the heroine, his fellow slave. Brought back to the farm with the goatherd, Anthia begs Lampon to pity her and respect her chastity, revealing her identity, her former nobility, her marriage, and the story of her captivity (2.9.4). The lowly goatherd pities her and promises to protect her, urging her to take heart. Manto sought to stage an iteration of the "Unwanted Suitor" tale, but Lampon does not play his part, nor does Anthia use servile trickery or violence to fend him off. The episode thus serves as a foil to the iterations of the tale where a succession of antagonists tries to force Anthia into bed, making her use trickery or violence to defend herself. Instead, the two slaves establish a relationship of trust and solidarity.

42   Ephesiaca

Manto's husband Moeris makes frequent visits to the farm and falls in love with Anthia. He offers to reward Lampon for helping him in the affair. The goatherd outwardly complies, agreeing to help Moeris, but tells Manto what her husband was up to. Xenophon notes that Lampon was motivated by his fear of Manto (2.11.2, δεδοικὼς δὲ τὴν Μαντώ); one may also read into the goatherd's actions here a slave's indirect approach to resistance. Lampon does not resist Moeris directly. Indeed, he fears Manto and what would happen to him if she learned he had assisted her husband in an affair. He also informs Manto not only because he fears her but also so that he could thwart Moeris through her.

Anthia, however, turns out to be the main victim of Manto's jealous anger. When Moeris is away, she summons Lampon and orders him to take Anthia to the middle of the woods and to kill her. In return, she promises the goatherd a reward (2.11.3). Lampon returns to the farm and, notwithstanding his fear of Manto, informs Anthia what had been decided about her fate (2.11.4, δεδοικὼς δὲ τὴν Μαντὼ ἔρχεται παρὰ τὴν Ἀνθίαν καὶ λέγει τὰ κατ'αὐτῆς δεδογμένα). Anthia asks only that he bury her and invoke Habrocomes' name (2.11.4–5). The goatherd is moved to pity. It would be unholy to kill a girl who had done no wrong and who was so beautiful. He proposes to Anthia that he sell her far away so that Manto does not learn of it and be angry with him (μὴ μαθοῦσα ἡ Μαντὼ ὅτι οὐ τέθνηκας ἐμὲ κακῶς διαθήσει). Anthia agrees, calling the gods and Artemis to reward the goatherd for his goodness (2.11.8). Lampon sells Anthia to merchants traveling on to Cilicia and collects a double price for deceiving his mistress, the money he received from the merchants and Manto's reward for killing her.

One may see a precedent for Lampon in Euripides' portrayal of the humble Mycenaean farmer who was married to Electra but did not sleep with her in deference to her nobility.[54] The episode also shares elements with the folktale of Snow White.[55] A powerful queen, stepmother, or witch is jealous of a girl who rivals her in beauty. She orders a rustic dependent to kill her rival in the forest. The dependent, however, is moved by his victim's beauty and goodness and spares the girl. He returns to his mistress with a false report or false evidence that her command had been followed. Xenophon has adapted the traditional tale to a situation involving slavery. The antagonist is a jealous slave-owner; the girl and the rustic dependent are her slaves.[56]

Lampon resisted Manto but indirectly and within the limits of his slavery. He feared his mistress and was always aware of her power to punish him. He would not defy Manto openly, but he could deceive her and get Anthia out of her way. The deception earned him a double reward. Lampon was heroic in the manner slaves might imagine heroism. He resisted his owner within the limitations of his agency and, at the same time, kept an eye to his own safety and profit. The slave gained a double reward for his moral cunning, collecting Anthia's price from the merchants and, later, the reward from his mistress. Selling the heroine to slave merchants, even with her assent, was not a heroic act by traditional measures of heroism. But the heroism of the slave differs from the heroism of an individual who possesses freedom of action. The slave has limited agency and lives in

Ephesiaca 43

a world subject to the arbitrary and often unpredictable will of the master.[57] Lampon was gathering resources for whatever would come next. Besides illustrating how a slave might be heroic, the episode illustrates the creation of a trusting bond between two slaves. After Manto ordered him to kill Anthia, Lampon informed the heroine despite his fears. He told Anthia the truth, as she first had told the truth to him. The solidarity between the two slaves is based on trust, humane feeling, and shared resistance, all of which transcend the difference between Lampon, the real slave, and Anthia, the enslaved noble protagonist.[58]

The author reaffirms this point in a later episode parallel to the Lampon episode, when Polyidus brought Anthia home with him to Alexandria (5.5). His wife, Rhenaea, was at once jealous of the slave girl. Like Manto, Rhenaea aims to punish her rival. When Polyidus is away, she attacks the heroine. She rips Anthia's clothes off. She accuses Anthia of plotting against her marriage (5.5.3, τῶν γάμων τῶν ἐμῶν ἐπίβουλε) and drunken promiscuity (ἴσως μὲν γὰρ πείθειν λῃστὰς ἐδύνασο καὶ συγκαθεύδειν νεανίσκοις μεθύουσι πολλοῖς). The accusation reflects the assumption that female slaves are morally depraved and sexually promiscuous. Rhenaea arranges for the heroine's punishment, instructing a certain trusted slave (5.5.4, οἰκέτῃ τινὶ πιστῷ) named Clytus to take the heroine to Italy and sell her to a brothel. Like Lampon, this Clytus is a supernumerary slave, another real slave character. Anthia begs him to kill her rather than to sell her into a brothel, for she had always been chaste (5.5.6). Clytus will not do that. He pities the heroine (ἠλέει δὲ αὐτὴν ὁ Κλειτός) but, fearing his mistress Rhenaea (δεδοικὼς τὰς τῆς Ῥηναίας ἐντολάς), takes Anthia to Tarentum and sells her there to a pimp.

Like Lampon, Clytus feared his mistress and felt pity for the heroine. Unlike Lampon, he did not deceive his mistress. The difference here only partly involves a distinction between a slave who was heroic and a slave who was not. Xenophon may be accommodating this repetition of the episode to the conditions of slavery in an urban household. As a trusted domestic slave, Clytus was under closer observation than Lampon, a rural slave beyond his owner's range of view. He obeyed Rhenaea out of fear, but his sympathies lay with his fellow slave. In his fearful obedience, Clytus may reveal the constraints under which he acted as well as an unheroic temperament.

Masters and slaves: hidden and public transcripts

James Scott's concept of public and hidden transcripts of master–slave relationships provides a useful framing for the episode involving Clytus. The public transcript indicates the official interaction between the master and the slave, in this case, a performance of Rhenaea's power and Clytus' obedience. Clytus acts the role of good slave. In contrast, the hidden transcript, expressed in Clytus' inner thoughts and when he was alone with Anthia, revealed his subjectivity and feelings, in particular his pity for Anthia and the censure of Rhenaea implied in this pity, all of it hidden from her. In Clytus' hidden transcript, his mistress was cruel and unjust.

44 Ephesiaca

The conceptual framework of public and hidden transcript may also be applied to an episode that took place earlier in Tyre. After Habrocomes had been punished, after Anthia had been given over to Lampon, and after the protagonists' fellow slaves Rhode and Leucon had been sold away, Apsyrtus finds the tablet containing the love letter that his daughter had written to Habrocomes (2.10.1; Manto's letter, 2.5.1–2). He summons Habrocomes from his prison cell and acknowledges his own error (2.10.2):

> Take heart, young man. I judged you wrongly because I believed my daughter. But now I'm making you a free man instead of slave (ἀλλὰ νῦν μέν σε ἐλεύθερον ἀντὶ δούλου ποιήσω). I'm giving you the job of supervising my household (δίδωμι δὲ σοί τῆς οἰκίας ἄρχειν τῆς ἐμῆς) and I'll arrange your marriage to the daughter of one of the citizens (τῶν πολιτῶν τινος θυγατέρα). Don't be angry with me (σὺ δὲ μὴ μνησικακήσῃς) over what has happened. I judged you wrongly unintentionally.

In response, Habrocomes is outwardly grateful (2.10.3, ἀλλὰ χάρις, ἔφη σοι, δέσποτα) and thanks Apsyrtus for having learned the truth and rewarding his chaste self-control (σωφροσύνης). All the other slaves in Apsyrtus' household (πάντες οἱ κατὰ τὴν οἰκίαν) rejoiced and expressed gratitude to their master on Habrocomes' behalf (χάριν ᾔδεσαν ὑπὲρ αὐτοῦ τῷ δεσπότῃ). But Habrocomes remained in great distress over Anthia. Left alone to himself, he reflects over and over again (ἐνενόει δὲ πρὸς ἑαυτὸν πολλάκις), "What do I care about freedom? Or wealth and being Apsyrtus' steward (ἐπιμελείας τῶν Ἀψύρτου χρημάτων)? That's not what I should be about. I want to find her either alive or dead." Habrocomes carries on as Apsyrtus' manager in this spirit until a letter arrived from Manto complaining to her father about her husband's interest in Anthia; as a result, Manto wrote, she had the girl sold off again (2.12.1). Habrocomes reads this letter and goes off to look for her, deserting Apsyrtus and the rest of the household (2.12.2, λαθὼν οὖν τὸν Ἄψυρτον καὶ πάντας τοὺς κατὰ τὸν οἶκον).

The first part of the episode, the scene in which Apsyrtus pardoned Habrocomes, offers a public transcript of master–slave relations that highlights the master's generosity and discourages the expression of resentment. While Apsyrtus acknowledges he had made a mistake, he insists that he was not to blame. Habrocomes and the slaves in the household express their gratitude, or *charis*, to the master for his kindness.[59] It is also interesting to note that the compensation that Apsyrtus offered to Habrocomes asserts his dominance in a new relationship, between former master and ex-slave or patron and freedman. Apsyrtus continues to define Habrocomes' identity, making him his freedman. He continues to define Habrocomes' work, making the hero his head of household. He continues to define Habrocomes' personal life, through a marriage that he will arrange. He even instructs Habrocomes how he should think about his unjust punishment.

In contrast, the second part of the episode represents a hidden transcript, expressed through Habrocomes' private thoughts, which reveals the persistence

Ephesiaca   45

of the hero's personal subjectivity, his identity, despite Apsyrtus' efforts to redefine it. Habrocomes cares nothing for his work as the head of a wealthy man's household; he thinks nothing of the comfort that this brought him personally. None of this was his real identity, the man he really should be. Even freedom, so long as it was on Apsyrtus' terms, without Anthia, meant little to Habrocomes. In the hidden transcript of his protagonist's thoughts, the author reveals that Habrocomes' survival as Habrocomes depended on *erōs*, his feelings for Anthia. Apsyrtus knew nothing of his former slave's inner life. Would he have cared if he did?

As soon as Habrocomes learns something about where Anthia was, he leaves his post in secret to find her. The detail that he leaves without Apsyrtus' knowledge (λαθὼν οὖν τὸν Ἄψυρτον) provokes a question: Why did he sneak off? Both Greek and Roman manumission practices provided for restrictions on freedom, including the frequent requirement that the freed slave continue to provide services for the former master. In Greece, this form of conditional freedom was known as *paramonē*. The freed slave's work obligations under *paramonē* would be specified in the manumission arrangements.[60] In the Roman practice of slavery, the *libertus* owed his former owner continuing obedience, or *obsequium*, and particular services, or *operae*.[61] The ex-slave's *obsequium* was a social expectation; *operae*, on the other hand, would be specified at manumission. In this episode, it seems that Xenophon was more likely to be thinking of Roman practice. Apsyrtus' proposal to marry Habrocomes to the daughter of a citizen suggests that his freedman too, like a Roman *libertus*, had become a citizen. Freed slaves in Greek city-states did not become citizens but received a status close to that of metics.[62] In fourth-century Athens, at any rate, noncitizens who married citizens were subject to penalties that included enslavement and the confiscation of property.[63] In addition, the Tyrian pirate chief Apsyrtus resembles a Roman *paterfamilias* at the head of a household with a significant urban slave family. A freedman, wealthy now himself, Habrocomes manages his former master's household and possessions. Understood in a Roman context, the protagonist's decision to go look for Anthia constituted a desertion of his obligations to Apsyrtus, his *patronus*, in particular, his social and legal obligations of *obsequium* and *operae*. Habrocomes would be, in the Roman view, a *libertus ingratus*, an ungrateful freedman, a category formally identified in law.[64] Thus, he sneaks away. Xenophon directs our sympathies to him nonetheless. His obligation to himself and Anthia are more important.

The restoration of status

At the end of *Ephesiaca*, Habrocomes and Anthia are reunited and restored to their original status as elite citizens of Ephesus. The protagonists' reunion takes place back on Rhodes, where all the main characters eventually stop off on the return to Ephesus. Leucon and Rhode had arrived earlier. At first, the protagonists' slaves in Ephesus and, then, their fellow slaves in Tyre, they are now wealthy freedmen of a Lycian who had made them his heirs (5.6.3). The two

46   Ephesiaca

stopped off at Rhodes in the hope of hearing news of their first masters (5.6.4, μέχρις οὗ τι περὶ τῶν δεσποτῶν πύθωνται). Habrocomes arrived next, on the way home from Nucerium (5.10.1–5). Anthia will arrive last when her owner, Hippothous, puts in at Rhodes on the way to taking Anthia back to Ephesus. Hippothous also brought along his lover, a young man named Cleisthenes (5.11).

Xenophon creates suspense by delaying Habrocomes's and Anthia's reunion. With some difficulty, Leucon and Rhode recognize Habrocomes in the temple of Helios, where they find him grieving for Anthia (5.10.11, κατὰ μικρὸν ἐγνώριζον). The two take Habrocomes home, care for him, try to bolster his spirits, and give him their possessions (5.10.12, καὶ τὰ κτήματα αὐτῶν παραδιδόασι), a detail that, in Roman terms, implies that Leucon and Rhode still consider themselves Habrocomes' slaves.[65] After Anthia arrives, she receives permission from Hippothous, still technically her owner, to dedicate her hair to Helios "on behalf of her husband Habrocomes" (5.11.6). When Leucon and Rhode see this dedication, they realize that Anthia is on Rhodes. They return the next day and find a woman in mourning. With difficulty, they recognize their other master (5.12.4, κατὰ βραχὺ ἐγνώριζον αὐτήν) and fall at her feet (5.12.5): "O, mistress Anthia" (ὦ δέσποινα ... Ἀνθία), they said. "We are your slaves (ἡμεῖς οἰκέται σοι), Leucon and Rhode."

The stage has been set for the reunion of Habrocomes and Anthia, which will take place in the temple of Isis before a crowd of cheering Rhodians (5.13.3). The author emphasized that Leucon and Rhode had difficulty recognizing the protagonists. It seems possible that time and hard usage had their effect on the protagonists. Both had experienced physical and emotional duress in slavery. Torture, as Xenophon noted, had earlier destroyed Habrocomes' beauty (2.6.3, καὶ τὸ κάλλος ἐμαραίνετο); he also had been put up on a cross and nearly burned at the stake. He had just arrived from Nucerium, where he worked like a slave in the quarries.[66] Nonetheless, Habrocomes and Anthia recognize one another immediately, "for this is what they desired in their souls" (5.13.3, ὡς δὲ εἶδον ἀλλήλους εὐθὺς ἀνεγνώρισαν· τοῦτο γὰρ αὐτοῖς ἐβούλοντο αἱ ψυχαί). The protagonists recognize one another at once despite the effects of time and hard usage.[67] Aldo Tagliabue may be right in his suggestion that they are able to do so because feeling for one another has evolved from physical desire to spiritual love.[68]

The protagonists have been restored to each other and their original status as elite citizens of Ephesus, even finding themselves, once again, the masters of Leucon and Rhode. They have been restored to their original status, but they have been altered by their experience. It seems possible that slavery and their other trials have taken a physical toll on the protagonists. In addition, neither is able to be completely candid about what happened during the time they were separated. The first night they are together again, Anthia gives Habrocomes an account of her ordeal that assures him of her fidelity throughout (5.14.1–2):

> Anthia embraced Habrocomes and began to cry. "Husband," she said, "and master (δέσποτα), I take you back after much wandering over land and sea. I

Ephesiaca 47

escaped the threats of bandits and the plots of pirates and the outrages of the pimps, and chains and ditches and clubbings and poison and funeral chambers. I come to you, Habrocomes, master of my soul (τῆς ἐμῆς ψυχῆς Ἁβροκόμη δέσποτα), such a one as when I first left Tyre for Syria. No one has persuaded me to sin: not Moeris in Syria; not Perilaus in Cilicia; not Psammis and Polyidus in Egypt not Anchialus in Ethiopia; not my master in Tarentum.[69] But I remain chaste for you having contrived every stratagem of chaste self-restraint (πᾶσαν σωφροσύνης μηχανήν)."

As he nears the end of his story, Xenophon returns to the concept of metaphorical slavery to love. Anthia addresses her husband as the "master of her soul" to distinguish him from a succession of men who had tried to assert control over her body. Her summary of that period includes elements that characterize the slave experience in general: geographical dislocation, sale and resale to a succession of owners, exposure to violence, vulnerability to sexual exploitation, the resort to cunning as a means of self-defense. Perhaps the only atypical aspect of Anthia's slave experience was that she was able in every instance to avoid rape or sexual exploitation. The heroine's successful defense of her *sōphrosynē* may be idealized, but it is the truth so far as concerns Xenophon's fictional narrative. Note, however, that Anthia omits Hippothous from the list of masters who tried to force her into bed. She was probably right that her husband did not need to know that his friend had tried to sleep with his wife, even if Hippothous had not known who Anthia was at the time. Anthia's confession is followed by a brief assertion from Habrocomes that he had been attracted to no woman (οὔτε παρθένος ἐμοί τις ἔδοξεν εἶναι καλή, οὔτ' ἄλλη τις ὀφθεῖσα ἤρεσε γυνή) and remained as pure as when she last had seen him in the prison in Tyre (5.14.4). Habrocomes, too, was discreet in his account, omitting the occasion on which he wavered and agreed to become the husband of the repulsive Cyno. Despite these omissions, each protagonist accepted what the other said because that was what they wanted (5.15.1, καὶ ῥᾳδίως ἔπειθον ἀλλήλους ἐπεὶ τοῦτο ἤθελον).[70]

Habrocomes and Anthia return at last to Ephesus. On their arrival they go to the temple of Artemis where they offer prayers, sacrifices, and dedications to the goddess, including the account of all they had suffered and done (5.15.2, πάντων ὅσα τε ἔπαθον καὶ ὅσα ἔδρασαν). After that, they build tombs for their parents, who had died from old age and loss of heart before their return (5.15.3, ἔτυχον γὰρ ὑπὸ γήρως καὶ ἀθυμίας προτεθνηκότες). Then, in an echo of the happy days that first followed their marriage, Habrocomes and Anthia live together like persons celebrating a festival (ἑορτὴν ἄγοντες); they are joined by Leucon and Rhode, companions who share with them in everything (5.15.4, κοινωνοὶ πάντων σύντροφοι). Finally, Hippothous and his lover, Cleisthenes, whom he had adopted as a son, join the four *syntrophoi* after Hippothous dedicated a monument to his drowned first lover, Hyperanthes.

The allusion to the first days of their marriage (1.10.2, ἑορτὴ δὲ ἦν ἅπας ὁ βίος) seems to return the protagonists to the *status quo* in place before their

48 Ephesiaca

misadventures began. However, this first period of happiness had been based on ignoring the trials prophesied for them (1.10.2, τῶν μεμαντευμένων λήθη). The happiness they celebrate on their return is salted with the memory of what they have suffered and lost. This is not a *status quo ante*. What has changed? Whitmarsh suggested that the protagonists have not only been reintegrated into their community but, through the ritual actions they perform on their return, have also been assimilated to a divine pair.[71] Tagliabue describes a change in the nature of the protagonists' love. Habrocomes and Anthia, together with their friends, appear to live apart from their fellow Ephesians, in "an exclusive society based on love." This love would be the lasting and undying love of the soul that emerged from the protagonists' trials and sufferings.[72] Tagliabue argues that the emphasis on memorialization and a prefiguration of the protagonists' own death through reference to the parents who "predeceased" them (5.15.3, προτεθνηκότες) sets this spiritual love on a mythical plane through allusion to the loving reunion of Isis with Osiris after his death. The love of Habrocomes and Anthia transcends death itself.[73]

Viewing the conclusion of *Ephesiaca* through the prism of slavery, it might also be possible to consider the society comprised of the protagonists and their friends as an ersatz family created by individuals who had lost their families. Xenophon promotes the idea that the friends who join Habrocomes and Anthia constitute a new "family" by narrating that their friends join them right after he notes the deaths of their parents. Slavery was the reason that four of the six friends had lost their original families. Habrocomes' and Anthia's original families no longer existed. Their parents had died from age and despair over the disappearance of their children (5.15.3). Leucon and Rhode had either been enslaved as children or born as slaves into the protagonists' households. The only family they had had been provided by their owners, who raised them as foster children, *syntrophoi*, a term that indicates a form of fictive kinship.[74] For these four *syntrophoi*, all ex-slaves, the emotional identity of the new family had been created in slavery and incorporated the memory of a common and painful past.[75] The protagonists' response to their painful past was not to rejoin the citizen community of Ephesus but to spend the rest of their lives in celebration within an exclusive community, that is, a replacement family with Leucon and Rhode.[76]

The final sentences of the novel, however, refer not to the protagonists and their *syntrophoi* but to Hippothous, the former brigand, and his lover, Cleisthenes. After building a great memorial for Hyperanthes on Lesbos, Hippothous adopted Cleisthenes, a young man from an elite family in Sicily (5.9.3), as a son and then went to live with the protagonists at Ephesus. The model of transient pederastic love acceptable to the *polis* did not leave room for the lasting bond the two envisioned and Tagliabue argues that the adoption functions as an alternative to marriage. In Tagliabue's reading, they, too, have a place in the "exclusive society of love" at Ephesus.[77] Fictive kinship accommodates the creation of a substitute but lasting family relationship for the pederastic couple as well as the former slaves.

Ephesiaca   49

A summary of observations

Xenophon expresses sympathy for his enslaved elite protagonists. But this sympathy is also present when Habrocomes and Anthia adopt behaviors associated, in the elite stereotype, with bad slaves. Even violence against the master may be rationalized, albeit through extraordinary means. Divine intervention absolves Habrocomes of his failure to prevent the murder of his master Araxes; the author himself intervenes to pronounce Anthia's murder of Anchialus, her owner's surrogate, a just act. The motivation for rationalizing the protagonists' bad-slave behavior is that it was necessary for their survival in slavery. This point is demonstrated through the melodramatic death of Habrocomes' old tutor, a model of a good slave who lives only for his master. Good slaves perish; bad slaves manage to survive.

In a normative elite reading, it would be expected that Xenophon sympathizes with his protagonists, both because they are his protagonists and because they are elite. However, it is possible to see in *Ephesiaca* sympathy that has been extended to real slaves, perhaps to slaves in real life. This sympathy has been suggested in the configuration of Habrocomes' and Anthia's antagonists and allies. Their antagonists are those who have power over them, most often their owners. They see Habrocomes and Anthia as they see all slaves and are quick to judge and condemn. With a few exceptions, these characters are portrayed as brutal and cruel. In contrast, the elite enslaved protagonists find allies among the other enslaved characters, the real slaves. Leucon and Rhode, their former and fellow slaves, try to teach them how to survive in slavery. At the end of *Ephesiaca*, they have become their former masters' friends and fellow freedmen. The goatherd Lampon does a heroic turn, heroic at least for a slave, and saves Anthia's life by deceiving his owner. The domestic slave Clytus has less freedom of action, but he expresses sympathy to the heroine when the two are alone.

Xenophon reveals an understanding of the constraints under which slaves could express their agency in the Lampon and Clytus episodes. His narrative of the protagonists' slavery reflects conditions and experiences endured by slaves in general: separation from friends and family, transfer from owner to owner, vulnerability to sexual exploitation, harsh treatment, torture, and personal and social denigration. In brief, the fictional slave experience of Habrocomes and Anthia reflected what many slaves endured off the page in life. Xenophon's realism in this regard can invite the reader to sympathize with slaves in general, not just the enslaved elite protagonists. In consideration of such sympathy, we might be justified in saying that Xenophon's novel has staked out an ideological position about slavery, critical of the institution and its practices.

Finally, I call attention to the role of *erōs* in the context of slavery. The protagonists' love for one another serves as a continuing link to their identities before they became slaves. Because of their enduring love for one another, Habrocomes and Anthia retain their personal subjectivity. Because of their love for one another, they could not become good slaves. *Erōs* provided them a motive to resist their masters.

50   Ephesiaca

Notes

1 This is the view of Whitmarsh 2011, 263–264, followed by Tagliabue 2017, 213. Bowie 2002, 43 suggests a *terminus post quem* as early as 65 CE on the basis of a possible allusion to Nero's embalming of Poppaea (cf. Tacitus, *Ann.* 16.6) in Aigialeus' mummification of his wife at the beginning of Book 5.

2 Cf. the comments of Ruiz-Montero 2003, 43. Xenophon's poor reputation is reflected in one edition after another of the *Oxford Classical Dictionary*. Thus, Rattenbury (1949, *OCD*[1]) described the author as "almost illiterate." Giangrande (1970, *OCD*[2]) noted a plot that is "disjointed and unclear," characterization that is "extremely poor," and language that is "full of vulgarisms." Bowie (1996, *OCD*[3], 2012, *OCD*[4]) remarked on the "occasional incoherence in a generally typical plot," which was due either to epitomization or the author's own clumsiness, and characterization that is "indeed unimpressive." Cf. Tagliabue 2017, 2–3, for another survey of disparaging assessment.

3 Rohde 1960 (1876), 429, n. 1.

4 See Tagliabue 2017, 193–201 for a review of the debate. Rohde's suggestion was argued in full by Bürger 1892. Hägg 1966 offered a refutation of Bürger currently accepted by most scholars.

5 Tagliabue 2017, 6.

6 Tagliabue 2017, 163–192. Cf. the comments of Henderson 2009, 201 in the introduction to the Loeb edition: "What X. gives us is not literature but action and adventure, in a form not unlike a screenplay for a television serial or action movie, or a graphic novel."

7 Cf. Jones 2012, 139 on slavery to love as a loss of autonomy and, thus, one's manliness (in reference to Chaereas).

8 Cf. Lyne 1979, who argues that the Roman elegists, in particular Propertius, developed the idea that love was a form of slavery into an important literary *topos* during a period when the elite were also feeling the loss of their political freedom; also, Alston 1998, 213–214.

9 In *Callirhoe*, Chaereas' friend Polycharmus is able to endure the rigors of agricultural slavery because he, in contrast to Chaereas, was not enslaved to Love, a cruel master (4.2.3, μὴ δουλεύων Ἔρωτι, χαλεπῷ τυράννῳ). In *Leucippe and Clitophon*, Clitophon teases his cousin Clinias for being in love with a boy calling him "a slave of erotic pleasure" (1.7.2, δοῦλός ἐστιν ἐρωτικῆς ἡδονῆς). Clinias responds in kind, warning Clitophon that he, too, will soon endure such slavery (Ἔσῃ ποτὲ καὶ σύ μοι δοῦλος ταχύ). In *Daphnis and Chloe*, when spring finally arrives, the protagonists drive out their flocks to pasture ahead of the other herdsmen because they are eager to see each other again, "as slaves to a greater herdsman" (3.12.1, οἷα μείζονι δουλεύοντες ποιμένι). In the *Aethiopica*, Calasiris describes the vulgar, or sexual, element of the protagonists' love (as opposed to its heavenly aspect) in terms of metaphorical slavery. He also aligns Heliodorus' heroine with Anthia; the ravages of slavery to love mar Chariclea's beauty too (3.19.1, Δεδούλωτο μὲν γὰρ ὁλοσχερῶς τῷ πάθει καὶ τήν τε παρειὰν ἤδη τὸ ἄνθος ἔφευγε καὶ τὸ φλέγον τοῦ βλέμματος καθάπερ ὕδασιν ἐῴκει τοῖς δάκρυσιν ἀποσβεννύμενον). Heliodorus later (6.3.2) contrasts the metaphorical slavery of the lover of Isias of Chemmis with the idealistic form of love that Chariclea and Theagenes share: cf. Morgan 1989b, 107.

10 Papanikolaou 1973 (Teubner), Dalmeyda 1926 (Budé), and Henderson 2009 (Loeb) have accepted A. Cocchi's 1726 suggestion of δεσμὰ δὲ μοχθήσουσι in place of the ms. reading δεινὰ δὲ μοχθήσουσι on the basis of 1.7.1, where the protagonists' parents could not understand what the oracle intended in a number of details, including "chains and the tomb" (οὔτε τίνα τὰ δεσμὰ οὔτε ὁ τάφος).

11 After referring to Habrocomes' and Anthia's enslavement, the oracle makes a puzzling reference to a tomb and obliterating fire that "would be the protagonists' wedding chamber" (καὶ τάφος ἀμφοτέροις θάλαμος καὶ πῦρ ἀΐδηλον). The reference

Ephesiaca 51

to the tomb may supplement the prediction of enslavement, glossing it as a *Scheintod*, that is, an episode in which a character is believed (mistakenly) to die. As I shall argue, even in antiquity there was an appreciation of slavery as a kind of metaphorical death. The wedding chamber and fire, that is, the wedding torches, now rendered destructive (ἀΐδηλον), would be the prelude to this disaster. A suggested translation: "The bridal chamber and gloomy wedding torches will be a tomb for them both."

For readings of the oracle in terms of its relationship to the plot, suspense, and engagement of the reader, Hägg 1971, 229–231; Morgan 2007a, 460–461; Whitmarsh 2011, 198–201. The extensive discussion in Tagliabue 2017, 53–71 focuses on the last two lines of the oracle ("And by the waters of the holy river, to revered Isis, / their savior, later will they dedicate rich offerings"), which he argues are an external prolepsis, that is, a reference to a journey that Habrocomes and Anthia will make to Egypt in order to sacrifice to Isis after the novel is over.

12 Catalogued in Thompson's 1966 index of folk-literature motifs as K2111.

13 Cueva 2004, 37–39 argues that the Phaedra–Hippolytus version plays a role in structuring the Manto story.

14 Thompson 1966, motif index T320.

15 Thompson 1966, identifies variations on the motif that can be aligned with the different means that Anthia adopts to escape her "unwanted suitors": T320.2, "Girl kills man who threatens her virtue" and T320.1, "Woman escaping from slavery kills man who would ravish her"; T322.4, "Girl pleads vow of chastity to repel lover"; K523.0.1, "Illness (madness, dumbness, etc.) feigned to escape unwelcome marriage"; T326, "Suicide to save virginity."

16 Cf. Cameron 1939: in inscriptions, the foster child or *threptos*, who could be a slave, was designated as the *syntrophos* of other children in the family, including the young master, that is, the owner's child. The *syntrophos* relationship was reciprocal; the young master would also be the *syntrophos* of the slave. The Latin equivalent of *threptos* was *alumnus*.

17 Schmeling 1980, 43 observes that the situation in which slaves seem better equipped to deal practically with a difficult situation is a literary motif present in both New Comedy and folklore and cites references in Thompson 1966: J1111.6; J1114; P361.

18 Compare the exchange in Euripides' *Andromache* between the enslaved heroine and the woman who was her attendant in Troy but is now her fellow slave. The slave still addresses Andromache as her mistress (56–58, δέσποιν'), "since it was the name I thought it right to use in your house when we lived in the land of Troy" (trans., Kovacs 1995). Andromache, however, addresses her former slave as a fellow slave (64, ὦ φιλτάτη σύνδουλε).

19 Anthia too possesses elite physical courage. She would rather die than have Habrocomes submit to torture on her behalf (2.4.5–6).

20 Cf. Seneca, *Ben.* 3.20: "It is a mistake to think that slavery penetrates the whole person. The better part is excepted. Bodies are obedient and belong to masters. The mind is in control of itself (*corpora obnoxia sunt et adscripta dominis: mens quidem sui iuris*)." On Stoic coloring in Xenophon: Doulamis 2007.

21 Scott 1990, 17–44.

22 Richlin 2017, 320 notes the expression of a related idea in Plautus' *Asinaria*, when Leonida remarks to his fellow slave Libanus that the lover is an unhappy man, to which Libanus replies that the man who is getting strung up for a whipping is much unhappier (616–617, *immo hercle vero / qui pendet multo est miserior*).

23 Xenophon may reflect in this detail a variant on the tale. Faverty 1931, 111 notes that Zulaikha, as Potiphar's wife and known in the Jewish folklore tradition, offered to kill her husband as an inducement, believing that Joseph refused her out of fear of him.

24 Konstan 2007, 38 accepts that Habrocomes' assent is genuine. De Temmerman 2014, 140 argues that he is merely trying to defer Cyno as at 2.13.8, where Anthia buys time by agreeing to marry Perilaus (συγκατατίθεται μὲν τὸν γάμον) while securing his

52   Ephesiaca

agreement to defer the marriage for thirty days. Tagliabue 2017, 91, n. 39, follows De Temmerman and cites 2.4.5 and 2.14.4, as additional instances where Xenophon uses συγκατατίθεμαι to indicate a strategy of deferring a stronger opponent by agreeing with him in the short term. However, at 2.4.5 Anthia really does seem to urge Habrocomes to save himself by sleeping with Manto (συγκατάθου δὲ τῇ τῆς δεσποίνης ἐπιθυμίᾳ); at 2.14.4 Habrocomes, albeit under compulsion, agrees to join Hippothous and his bandits (συγκατατίθεται δὲ ἀναγκάζοντι τῷ Ἱπποθόῳ), still hoping that he might find Anthia in their wanderings. The argument that Xenophon uses συγκατατίθεμαι to indicate strategic deferral may be additionally compromised by the use of the cognate noun συνθῆκαι in reference to the pledges that Habrocomes and Anthia swore to each other (2.4.4; 3.5.6 and 7; 5.1.11; 5.9.12).

25 Faverty 1931, 114–117 notes that the Jewish tradition contained a version of the tale in which Joseph hesitated briefly before he was dissuaded by a vision of Rachel, Leah, and Jacob.

26 See Gamauf 2007 on the *senatus consultum Silanianum*, a 10 CE measure providing for the collective punishment of the slaves whose master had been murdered. While it is difficult to quantify how often slaves attacked their owners, this measure suggests that the fear of such attacks was significant.

27 Thus, Ulpian, citing a Hadrianic rescript, condemns an *ancilla* who did not intervene in the murder of her mistress (*Dig.* 29.5.1.28): "Whenever slaves can give assistance to their masters, they ought not to prefer their own safety to his; but it is manifest that a slave-girl who was in the same room as her mistress could have given assistance in the matter, if not by physical act, then certainly by wailing so that those who had been in the house or nearby might hear, and this by the very fact that she has said that the murderer had threatened her with death if she cried out. She ought, therefore, to suffer the supreme penalty if only so that all other slaves may not think that when their masters are in danger each should look after himself" (trans., Watson 1985). See also the discussion of the legal tradition involving collective punishment for servile violence in Bradley 1994, 112–115.

28 The episode has also troubled Xenophon's modern readers: Konstan 2007, followed by Henderson 2009, 305, n. 45, tries to put Habrocomes completely in the clear by removing the words at 3.12.4 that refer to the intended murder: ἡ δὲ Κυνὼ προσφέρει λόγον περὶ συνουσίας καὶ δεῖται πείθεσθαι καὶ ἄνδρα ἔχειν ὑπισχνεῖτο [καὶ ῎Αραξον ἀποκτενεῖν].

29 On the identification of this magistrate with the Roman imperial prefect, see Rife 2002, 104–106.

30 Cf. *LSJ*: δραπέτης and related compounds were particularly associated with runaway slaves.

31 Whitmarsh 2011, 47–48.

32 Propp 1958, 20–21.

33 Burrus 1987, 31–67 identifies the functions of a related tale type in the chastity stories of the apocryphal *Acts*, in which an apostle inspires a woman to commit herself to chastity and reject the attentions of even her own husband. The woman endures persecution but is finally freed and allowed to remain chaste.

34 Propp 1968, 21–23.

35 See Stewart 2012, 82–95 on the codification in law and religious ritual of corporeal vulnerability as a social and legal marker that distinguished slaves from citizens during the republic.

36 Perilaus is the official responsible for peace in Cilicia (2.13.3, ὁ τῆς εἰρήνης τῆς ἐν Κιλικίᾳ προεστώς). Later, Hippothous tells Habrocomes that Perilaus had been elected to keep public order in Cilicia (3.9.5, ἄρχειν μὲν ἐχειροτονήθη τῆς εἰρήνης ἐν Κιλικίᾳ). Rife 2002 argues that Perilaus held the Roman imperial position of *eirenarch*, or "officer of the peace" (εἰρηνάρχης).

Ephesiaca   53

37 Her situation is similar to that of Callirhoe after Dionysius realized that his purchase of her was not legally valid. See Chapter 3, pp. 59 and 66.

38 Tagliabue 2017, 129–130 notes that this lie anticipates Anthia's devotion to the goddess, which becomes apparent when she takes refuge in an Isis shrine to avoid being raped by her fifth antagonist (5.4.6). On this passage, see the later discussion, p. 38.

39 Cf. Jones 2007, 117, 2012, 111–112, for a reading of the episode from the perspective of gender: Anthia is forced to assume a man's courage.

40 Hägg 1971, 100 notes that the authorial intrusion is unique for Xenophon.

41 It may be possible to see in Anchialus an acceptable substitute for the slave-owner and read this episode as a revenge fantasy from the hidden transcript, here made public in camouflaged form. Cf. the discussion in Richlin 2017, 216–224 on Plautus' dramatization of physical violence directed against masters by their slaves.

42 For example, the monstrous Vedius Pollio, who threw errant slaves into a fish pond full of ravenous eels (Seneca, *De ira* 3.40).

43 Bradley 1987, 124–125, notes that in the early imperial period the right of asylum for slaves came to be associated with temples and statues of the emperor both in Rome and in the provinces. Ulpian cites a rescript of Antoninus Pius instructing the governor of Baetica to interrogate slaves who had taken asylum and provide "relief against brutality or starvation or intolerable wrongdoing" (*contra saevitiam vel famem vel intolerabilem iniuriam*, Watson 1985). If the magistrate ruled in favor of the slave, the law provided for sale to another owner (*veniri iube ita, ut in potestate domini non revertantur*). However, the rescript also notes that "the power of masters over their slaves certainly ought not to be infringed and there must be no derogation from any man's legal rights" (*dominorum quidem potestatem in suos servos illibatam esse oportet nec cuiquam hominum ius suum detrahi*). The law would likely have ruled that if Anthia were Polyidus' slave, it would have been his right to rape her.

44 Ulpian might also have had something to say about Rhenaea's abuse of the heroine. At the conclusion of the excerpt from the *Digest* (1.6.2) noted earlier, he remarks on the case of Umbricia, a Roman matron, who was exiled for four years because of the savage treatment she meted out to her female slaves for the most trivial of reasons (*quod ex levissimis causis ancillas atrocissime tractasset*).

45 As the slave of the pimp (πορνοβοσκός), Anthia herself would be a πόρνη (cf. 5.7.1, ἀλλ' ἔτι καὶ πορνεύειν ἀναγκάζομαι). However, in describing how the pimp makes her stand in front of his brothel (5.7.1, ἠνάγκασεν αὐτὴν οἰκήματος προεστάναι and 5.7.3, ὡς δὲ ἦλθε καὶ προέστη), the author may allude to the Latin term for the occupation into which the heroine has been forced, *prostituta* from *prostare*.

46 Anthia seems to be saying that her beauty is untimely (or "out of season," ἀκαίρως) because it is a disadvantage for a female slave to be beautiful.

47 The motif in which a girl avoids prostitution by feigning madness also appears in Plautus' *Casina*.

48 Μηχανή words: In Greek the plural μηχαναί tends to carry the meaning of ruse. Plautus appears to follow this example: *machinae* at *Miles* 138, 813; *Persa* 785; *Pseud.* 550. He also uses the singular: *machina* at Bacch. 232. Also, *machinari*: Bacch. 232; *Capt.* 530–531; *Cas.* 277, 301. Τέχνη words: In Plautus, *contechnor* at Pseud. 1096; *techina* at Bacch. 392; *Most.* 550; *Poen.* 817; *Capt.* 642. Terence: *techina* at *Eun.* 718 and *HT* 471.

49 The parallels between Anthia's prayer to Isis (4.3.3–4) and the myth of Isis and Osiris imply the heroine's sincere piety: cf. Tagliabue 2017, 141–143. Her piety here contrasts with the story Anthia contrived earlier to deceive Psammis.

50 Cf. Scott 1990, 90–96.

51 Schmeling 1980, 36. Dalmeyda 1962, xxx, sees an inept imitation of the episode in Chariton in which Chaereas' parents plead with him so as he sets out to search for Callirhoe that he himself jumps overboard (3.5.4–6).

54 Ephesiaca

52 Relevant *comparanda* are the "good slave" speeches in Plautus, which, Richlin 2017, 342–349 argues, are invariably undercut by the action that follows and should not be taken at face value. Thus, Sosia, the impertinent and bibulous slave in *Amphitruo*, solemnly declares to Amphitruo and Alcumena (959–61): "This seems the right attitude for a good slave: as his masters are, let him be the same. He should take his expression from theirs: let him be sad if the masters are sad; let him be cheerful if they rejoice." On Plautus' satiric intent here, see Christenson 2000, 246, 287. Similar sentiments may be found at *Aul.* 587–607; *Men.* 966–976; *Most.* 858–884; *Pers.* 7–12; *Pseud.* 1103–1120. See Hunter 1985, 145–147, on the humor of these passages in general.

53 A similar idea is indicated in Plautus' envoi to *Epidicus*, noting his title character's manumission, a bad slave who was freed because he was bad (732): *hic is homo est qui libertatem malitia invenit sua.*

54 Cf. Henderson 2009, 265, n. 23.

55 ATU 709 in Uther 2011, a catalogue of folktale types begun by Aarne and Thompson. Anderson 2000, 47 notes versions that make a Greek Snow White, that is, Chione, one of the daughters of Niobe. Manto the prophetess commands Chione to acknowledge the superiority of Apollo and Artemis; the latter detail appears in Ovid's version of the Niobe story (*Met.* 6.157).

56 Anderson 2000, 50–57 also discusses Xenophon's use of the Snow White story.

57 Cf. Levine 2007, 81–135 on the didactic function of African American folklore for slaves who live in an arbitrary world, discussed earlier, p. 15.

58 Cf. the comments in Richlin 2017, 246–247 on the significance of on-stage friendships between slaves in Plautus.

59 Scott 1990, 17–44 discusses how dominated peoples emphasize the virtues and paternalism of the master to promote better conditions for themselves.

60 On *paramonē*: Garlan 1982, 78–82; Zelnick-Abramovitz 2005, 222–248.

61 On *obsequium* and the ungrateful freedman: Mouritsen 2011, 51–65.

62 Zelnick-Abramovitz 2005, 308–319; Youni 2008.

63 Zelnick-Abramovitz 2005, 312.

64 For example, the *lex Aelia Sentia* provided for an accusation against an ungrateful freedman: cf. *Dig.* 40.9.30.

65 Under Roman law, the *peculium* was *de facto* at the disposal of the slave but *de iure* the property of the master. Habrocomes would own what "belonged" to his slaves Leucon and Rhode if they were his slaves. On the legal status of the slave's *peculium*, cf. Crook 1967, 188–189.

66 Montiglio 2013, 47–54 sees lack of verisimilitude in the characters' difficulty in recognizing one another and notes Xenophon's use of the traditional patterns (e.g., Anthia's dedication of a lock of hair) in the protagonists' unusually protracted recognition.

67 Cf. Hägg 1971, 200, who observes, "The large sum of separate episodes, the wide geographical frame, and the many iterative-durative passages (with occasional explicit stressing of "a long time") are all factors which make for the impression of an action extending over a number of years."

68 Tagliabue 2017, 104–105.

69 That is, the pimp, who is never named.

70 Tagliabue 2017, 37–39 identifies the reunion of Odysseus and Penelope as an intertext for this episode in which Anthia aligns both with Odysseus' wanderings and Penelope's *sōphrosynē*.

71 Whitmarsh 2011, 50; cf. the observations of Fusillo 1997, 217–218, that the conclusion of the novel was impersonal, "without direct speech and without focalizing the characters' emotions."

72 Montiglio 2013, 54 remarks on the absence of Ephesian participation in the protagonists' return.

Ephesiaca   55

73 Tagliabue 2017, 152–161.
74 Cameron 1939, 47 notes the familial connotations of *syntrophos*, a term "applicable to children brought up together without regard to their legal status."
75 Cf. Gutman 1976, 213–224, who discusses the creation of fictive kinship associations among African American slaves as an adaptive reaction to slavery's disruption of natural family ties.
76 The ex-slave status of the protagonists and their companions, their emphasis on memorialization and the prefiguring of their own deaths (cf. 5.15.3, προτεθνηκότες), and the decision to lead their lives "like a festival" apart from the rest of the community suggest a parallel to Petronius' portrait of another ex-slave, Trimalchio, whose celebration and extravagance may be considered in the context of his marginalization as both slave and ex-slave. Cf. Bodel 1994, 253: "Hence the mood of melancholy many have felt pervades the determined merriment at Trimalchio's table; hence also Trimalchio's preoccupation with death, the final emancipation. Once property, now propertied, he and his fellow freedmen live neither redeemed nor effaced."
77 Tagliabue 2017, 156–157.

2 *Callirhoe*

Narratives of slavery explicit and implied, told and retold

Introduction

Stefan Tilg's thorough discussion proposes a date for *Callirhoe* in the middle decades of the first century CE.[1] There exist significant narrative parallels between Chariton's novel and Xenophon's. The pairs of protagonists marry early; their marital happiness is short-lived. Both heroines are buried alive and discovered by tomb robbers. Both heroines are wooed by noble suitors from whom they have concealed the existence of a husband. Both heroes are crucified.[2]

Chariton's novel also features the enslavement of both protagonists, Chaereas and Callirhoe; their trial of slavery; and their redemption from slavery. His plot, however, is more complicated than Xenophon's. Events have been located in the late fifth century BCE through reference to the historical Hermocrates, who led Syracusan resistance to the Athenian expedition of 415–413, and whom Chariton makes the heroine's father. Chaereas' family is noble too, second in prestige only to Callirhoe's. After the protagonists marry, Chaereas is tricked into suspecting Callirhoe of infidelity. He kicks her in the stomach, and Callirhoe, who is already pregnant, falls into a coma. Taken for dead, she is buried in a lavish tomb. Robbers wake her up and sell her across the sea, to Dionysius, the leading citizen of Miletus. Dionysius falls in love with his beautiful new-bought slave. She agrees to marry him after she discovers that she is pregnant with Chaereas' child, deciding to pass the child off as Dionysius' rather than bear him into slavery.

Back in Syracuse, Callirhoe's tomb is found empty, and soon after the Syracusans learn that she was still alive. Chaereas sets off to find her. He arrives near Dionysius' estate outside Miletus where Persian troops attack him and his crew. The Persians take Chaereas and others prisoner and sell them to an agricultural estate belonging to Mithridates, the Persian governor of Caria. Mithridates, too, falls in love with Callirhoe, whose beauty he has glimpsed. When he learns that one of his slaves claims to be Callirhoe's first husband, he seeks to undermine Dionysius' position under the pretext of helping Chaereas. Everyone goes to Babylon, Dionysius and Callirhoe, Mithridates and Chaereas, for a trial that will determine Callirhoe's rightful husband, a trial presided over by Artaxerxes, the Great King himself. However, such is the heroine's beauty that Artaxerxes, too,

Callirhoe   57

falls in love with her. As a result, although Chaereas and Callirhoe see each other in the courtroom, they are not able yet to be reunited.

Their reunion becomes possible after the Persian province of Egypt revolts. Chaereas deserts to the rebels, leads them to victory, and takes possession of Callirhoe along with the Great King's harem. Hero and heroine return to Syracuse in triumph, although circumstances force them to leave their son behind in Miletus, where Dionysius will raise him, still believing that he himself is the boy's father.

Chariton's historical placement of his narrative, in Syracuse at the end of the fifth century BCE after the victory over Athens, has led scholars to consider this love story in a political dimension that involves questions of freedom, tyranny, and empire from the perspective of the Greek elite in the eastern half of the Roman empire.[3] These previous readings regard the protagonists' slavery as a means of thinking about political freedom and tyranny.[4] However, Chariton also shows significant concern for the protagonists as enslaved persons. He depicts their mental and physical suffering. He narrates with sympathy the difficult choices they are forced to make. He exposes the selfishness and hardness of their masters. In brief, Chariton treats the slavery of his protagonists as an important human story in its own right.

Xenophon and Chariton are similar in their ideological perspective on slavery but differ in their narrative approach. Like Xenophon, Chariton criticizes aspects of the normative thinking of slave-owners and of the regular practices of slavery. Like Habrocomes and Anthia, Chaereas and Callirhoe adopt bad-slave behavior in order to survive. However, where Xenophon told the story of his protagonists' enslavement through the use of repeated traditional tales and occasional glimpses into the inner thoughts of his enslaved characters, Chariton employs more sophisticated narrative approaches. For Callirhoe, he creates two narratives, explicit and implicit, that give the reader contrasting perspectives on the heroine's slave experience.[5] The theme of the explicit narrative is the power of *erōs*, how Dionysius falls in love with his beautiful slave and ends up marrying her. This narrative is transacted in the open, through public statements of the characters and Chariton's direct and authoritative intrusion.[6] The implicit narrative, in contrast, has been embedded in allusions, silences, and inconsistencies in the explicit narrative. Its theme is power, specifically, the power of the slave-owner and how circumstances compel Callirhoe to marry her master. Both explicit and implicit narratives are marked in ideological terms. The explicit narrative reflects normative elite ideas regarding slaves and slave–master relations. The implicit narrative presents an alternative and critical view of master–slave relationships. The author's explicit narrative, reflecting the perspective of the dominant elite, shares characteristics with Scott's concept of the public transcript; Chariton's implicit narrative, with its critique of slave-owners and slavery, shares characteristics with the hidden transcripts of subjugated groups. Tim Whitmarsh has noted that the Greek novels offer a nuanced representation of the elite view of class relationships, a representation that admits the expression of alternative points of view.[7] In Chariton, the implicit narrative, the narrative that reflects the perspective of

58 Callirhoe

the enslaved protagonists, acts as a critique, or even a corrective, for the explicit narrative of the master.

Chariton adopts an approach that might be called "retelling" in the narration of the central event in Chaereas' enslavement. The protagonist and his companion Polycharmus were implicated in the murder of a guard and an escape attempt from Mithridates' estate. The episode is narrated three times: The first version is told by Chariton as the external third-person narrator; the second and third versions, by Polycharmus and Chaereas as embedded narrators. Polycharmus, who addresses his version to his master, Mithridates, is trying to save Chaereas' life and his own. Chaereas' version, addressed to the Syracusan assembly at the end of the novel, is a feature of his summary of the protagonists' slave experiences that he has edited and spun in other respects.[8] In these retellings, Polycharmus and Chaereas obscure their adoption of bad-slave behavior, in this case, murder and running away. However, for the reader who keeps in mind the author's original version of the event, the discrepancies and illogic of the retellings serve instead as a reminder that Chaereas and his friend were implicated in a slave rebellion and afterward covered it up, from others and possibly themselves.[9] Like Xenophon, Chariton depicts enslaved nobles who adopt slave-like behavior to survive; however, he also represents how such characters choose to remember (or not remember) this behavior.

Chariton also gives his protagonists an opportunity to absolve the corrupting effects of slavery by giving them an opportunity to "re-act"; that is, he gives them each a second chance. When the action moves to Persia, Chaereas and Callirhoe confront situations analogous to what they had experienced earlier as slaves. Callirhoe had felt forced to accept Dionysius as a second husband, but when the Great King falls in love with Callirhoe, she rejects him, in a sense reclaiming her *sophrosyne*. Chaereas had been implicated in a slave rebellion, but when he joins the Egyptian rebels in revolt against Persia, he converts his association with servile violence into the sanctioned violence of elite male *arete*. These re-actions, or second chances, purge the protagonists of the moral taint they acquired in slavery.

The explicit narrative of Callirhoe's slavery

The explicit narrative of Callirhoe's slavery features the noble characters Callirhoe and Dionysius. Callirhoe had become Dionysius' slave through the series of melodramatic events that began with her false death and burial alive and concluded when tomb robbers took her across the sea to Miletus and sold her to Leonas, Dionysius' financial steward, or *dioiketes*, a slave but a high-ranking one. Leonas purchased the beautiful slave to cheer up his recently widowed master (1.4–14).

After he found Callirhoe alive in the tomb, Theron, the chief of the tomb robbers, realized that she could bring him even more profit than the gold and silver grave offerings he had come to steal (1.9.6): "Let her be part of the funeral offerings (τῶν ἐνταφίων μέρος). There is much silver here, much gold.

Callirhoe 59

But the beauty of the woman is worth more than it all." The characterization of Callirhoe as a commodity recurs when the tomb robbers try to decide whether they should kill her or sell her as a slave. A robber who sees danger in selling Callirhoe warns that, while gold and silver cannot declare they were stolen, their captive was merchandise with eyes, ears, and a tongue (φορτίον δὲ ἔχον ὀφθαλμούς τε καὶ ὦτα καὶ γλῶσσαν) that might denounce them (1.10.6–7). He concludes that no one would believe Callirhoe was a slave because of her exceptional beauty; selling her would bring only danger, not profit.

In the explicit narrative, even a bandit reflects the elite prejudice that associated physical beauty and nobility. No one would believe that this noble-looking girl was a real slave. But greed decides the matter. Theron decides that the robbers should look for a buyer for merchandise (κτῆμα) that was "not for the mass of people or just anyone but for some wealthy prince" (1.12.1). He finds such a buyer far from Syracuse in Miletus. Claiming that he had bought the heroine in Sybaris in Italy from a mistress jealous of her beauty, Theron sells Callirhoe to Leonas, who buys Callirhoe because the heroine's beauty makes her a possession worthy of his master (1.12.10, δεσποτικὸν ... κτῆμα). Although he is a slave, Leonas is able to enter into contracts on his master's behalf.[10] The transaction is completed on Dionysius' country estate, away from the eyes of the Milesian tax officials (1.12.4). Leonas pays a significant amount, one talent, before he can obtain a proper bill of sale, or *katagraphē* (1.14.3–5).[11] On completion of the exchange, Theron promises to meet Leonas in the city the following day to register the sale and confirm its legality. But Theron takes the money and sails off. The next day, Leonas searches all over the city, questioning the merchants and harbor men and even taking a boat back down to Dionysius' estate but does not find him (2.1.6–7).

Chariton reminds the reader of the illegality of the sale through Leonas' anxiety over his inability to secure a *katagraphē*.[12] Laws regulating the sale of slaves belonged to the public transcript of master–slave relations or, here in *Callirhoe*, the explicit narrative of the heroine's slavery. In the explicit narrative, Callirhoe has not been legally sold; she was not a real slave. Chariton also uses the legal dimensions of Callirhoe's sale to frame an ethical difference between Leonas and his master. Leonas is anxious about the proper bill of sale because he fears punishment. He is barely able to bring his master the bad news (2.1.7, μόλις οὖν καὶ βραδέως ἀπῆλθε πρὸς τὸν δεσπότην). Leonas' ethical outlook is shaped not by the law, but by his master. However, the money is not a concern to Dionysius, who warns Leonas only to be more cautious in the future (2.1.8). He wants to obey the law even though it will cost him a talent. Hearing that Theron had disappeared, he surmises that the seller had kidnapped someone else's slave. He instructs Leonas to inquire if there were any people from Sybaris in town, presumably so that the slave can be returned to her proper owners (2.1.9).

Chariton also makes Dionysius a mouthpiece for the aristocratic prejudice that masters and slaves are essentially different from one another. When Leonas first tells him of the new slave girl's beauty, Dionysius objects that a slave could not be so beautiful. Leonas is exaggerating: physical beauty is a concomitant of

60   Callirhoe

nobility and cannot belong to someone born a slave. He draws on aristocratic *paideia* to make the point (2.1.5):

> "O, Leonas," he said. "It is impossible for someone to be physically beautiful unless she has been born free (μὴ πεφυκὸς ἐλεύθερον). Have you not heard the poets when they say that beautiful people are children of the gods, but well before that, they are children of nobles?"

Chariton depicts Dionysius as a model aristocrat, endowed with physical, mental, and moral gifts that make him a *kaloskagathos*. He is handsome, tall, and dignified in appearance (2.5.2, ἦν δὲ καὶ φύσει καλός τε καὶ μέγας καὶ μάλιστα πάντων σεμνὸς ὀφθῆναι). In the explicit narrative, Dionysius' own slaves esteem him as a master. He is conscious of the example he sets and at several points proclaims his adherence to a code of correct behavior. However, after falling in love, he fails to live up to these expectations. He fails because *Callirhoe* is an erotic novel, not a narrative of Stoic heroism. Nonetheless, in the explicit narrative, although he yields to the power of love, Dionysius' moral sense is not completely destroyed. He never uses physical force against Callirhoe. In the context of the explicit narrative, he remains a sympathetic character.

When Callirhoe is first brought to Dionysius' rural estate outside Miletus, Plangon, the head female slave and domestic partner of Phocas, Dionysius' estate manager, or *oikonomos* (ἡ τοῦ οἰκονόμου γυνή), assures the heroine that her new master is a decent and a kind man (2.2.1, χρηστός ἐστι καὶ φιλάνθρωπος).[13] Soon after that, Callirhoe is introduced to her master in the shrine of Aphrodite.[14] He falls in love with her at once (2.3.5–8). Chariton asserts that as "an educated man who made a particular claim on virtue" (2.4.1, οἷα δὴ πεπαιδευμένος ἀνὴρ καὶ ἐξαιρέτως ἀρετῆς ἀντιποιούμενος), Dionysius first tries to conceal his passion. In the struggle between reason and passion that ensues, the author affirms Dionysius' nobility of character (2.4.4): "although drowning in desire, as a noble man (γενναῖος) he tried to resist." Dionysius reproaches himself in a soliloquy (2.4.4–5), ashamed that, as a man famed in Ionia for his reputation and virtue (ἀνὴρ ὁ πρῶτος τῆς Ἰωνίας ἕνεκα ἀρετῆς τε καὶ δόξης), he was thinking of marriage with a slave girl (καὶ γάμους δούλης), one for whom he even lacked a proper bill of sale, and this at a time when he had not even finished mourning for his recently deceased wife.[15]

The explicit narrative contrasts Dionysius' character with that of his slave Leonas. Although he is overcome with desire, he demurs from Leonas' suggestion that he just have his way with her (2.4.9). Dionysius will not do that before learning who the woman is and where she comes from (2.4.10, "οὐκ ἂν ποιήσαιμι," φησὶν ὁ Διονύσιος, "πρὶν μαθεῖν τίς ἡ γυνὴ καὶ πόθεν."). Dionysius arranges the interview not in his private residence but in the shrine of Aphrodite, in order, he tells Leonas, to avoid any suspicion that he was intimidating the woman (2.4.10, μὴ καί τινος βιαιοτέρου λάβωμεν ὑποψίαν). For the same reason, on the day of the interview, he takes with him friends, freedmen, and his most trusted slaves as witnesses (2.5.1, φίλους τε καὶ ἀπελευθέρους καὶ τῶν οἰκετῶν τοὺς πιστοτάτους, ἵνα ἔχῃ καὶ μάρτυρας). Leonas also affirms his master's nobility of character to Callirhoe. Dionysius is exceptionally just and law-abiding (2.5.3, δικαιότατός ἐστι καὶ νομιμώτατος). She can count on receiving from him the assistance that is her due (οὐ γὰρ ἀτυχήσεις οὐδεμίας δικαίας βοηθείας). However, Leonas continues, she must hide nothing of the truth; in fact, the complete truth would incline the master to greater kindness (τοῦτο γὰρ αὐτὸν ἐπικαλέσεται μᾶλλον <πρὸς> τὴν εἰς σὲ φιλανθρωπίαν). Finally, in front of the audience assembled in the shrine, Dionysius himself proclaims to Callirhoe that he is famed for his piety and kindness (2.5.4, ἐπ᾽εὐσεβείᾳ καὶ φιλανθρωπίᾳ διαβόητος).

The explicit narrative of the interview represents both Callirhoe's nobility and that of Dionysius. The heroine's quality had already been acknowledged by the slaves who escorted her to the shrine of Aphrodite on the occasion of her first encounter with Dionysius, when the other slaves followed her as if she had been elected their mistress on account of her beauty (2.3.10, καθάπερ ὑπὸ τοῦ κάλλους δεσποίνη κεχειροτονημένη). The author, too, affirms the elite constellation of beauty, birth, and nobility: Nobility is a matter of birth (φύσει γίνονται βασιλεῖς). The heroine's beauty and noble demeanor prepare Dionysius to believe her. After Callirhoe refutes what Theron had told Leonas, that he had acquired her in Sybaris from a jealous mistress, Dionysius comments to Leonas that he knew she was not a slave, but probably, in fact, of noble birth (2.5.6).[16] Dionysius encourages her to tell him her story because, as two nobles, they share a kinship of character (2.5.8, τρόπου συγγένεια). Callirhoe tells him some of the truth: She is the daughter of Hermocrates, the ruler of Syracuse. However, in the same breath, she lies, telling Dionysius that she had lost consciousness after a fall and was believed to have died (2.5.10).[17] Then she lies a second time. Callirhoe does not tell Dionysius that was married, an omission that Chariton notes but leaves unexplained (2.5.11). Dionysius is heartbroken. As a nobleman, he is constrained to do the right thing – return Callirhoe to her family. This he promises to do, rejecting her offer of compensation for the talent that Leonas had paid out (2.5.11–12). In addition, he assures Callirhoe that, in the meantime, she will be treated like a mistress rather than a slave (ἐν δὲ τῷ μεταξὺ θεραπείαν ἕξεις παρ᾽ ἡμῖν δεσποίνης μᾶλλον ἢ δούλης).

Dionysius does not keep his word. He is, after all, in love. Nonetheless, in the explicit narrative, he continues to behave with a degree of honor despite his love-sickness. After the interview, as he laments to Leonas that he must send Callirhoe home, the slave encourages his master a second time just to have his way with her (2.6.2):

> Master, don't call curses down on yourself. You are her lord and have authority over her (κύριος γὰρ εἶ καὶ τὴν ἐξουσίαν ἔχεις αὐτῆς), so that, willing or not, she will do what you decide. I did buy her for a talent.

When Leonas made the same suggestion earlier (2.4.10), Dionysius merely demurred. This time, he erupts in indignation. He will not play the tyrant with

62 Callirhoe

the body of a free person.[18] He will not prove worse than Theron the pirate! Famed as he is for his virtue, he will not take Callirhoe against her will (2.6.2–3, ἐγὼ τυραννήσω σώματος ἐλευθέρου, καὶ Διονύσιος ὁ περιβόητος ἐπὶ σωφροσύνῃ ἄκουσαν ὑβρίω, ἥν οὐχ ὕβρισεν οὐδὲ Θέρων ὁ λῃστής;). Dionysius reflects an attitude typical of his class. When there was a possibility that Callirhoe was rightfully his slave, he left the door open to the possibility of having his way with her. Only when he knew her true status, would rape, in his view, constitute an act of *hybris*.

Still, Dionysius does not give up hope (2.6.4). He sets out to persuade Callirhoe to love him, enlisting the assistance of Plangon. He trusts Plangon; she has already shown him sufficient proof of her diligence (2.6.4, πεῖραν ἱκανὴν τῆς ἐπιμελείας). Through Plangon's agency as a go-between, the explicit narrative of this phase of Dionysius' courtship of Callirhoe draws on the stereotype of the cunning and deceitful slave of the *palliata*, the *ancilla callida*.[19] Plangon will manipulate and deceive her master as well as the heroine. She begins by gaining Callirhoe's trust (2.6.5). In an initial deception, she employs some dramatic playacting to convince her that Dionysius is murderously angry with Phocas and herself. By his nature, she explains, Dionysius is severe just as he is kind (2.7.2, φύσει δέ ἐστι βαρύθυμος, ὥσπερ καὶ φιλάνθρωπος). Their only hope of salvation lies in Callirhoe (2.7.3). In fact, Chariton notes, Dionysius had corrected Phocas on some aspect of his estate management but did not go beyond verbal correction (2.7.2). Callirhoe agrees to help, although she, too, considers herself to be a slave with no right to speak out (2.7.3, κἀγὼ μὲν, φησὶν, εἰμὶ δούλη καὶ οὐδεμίαν ἔχω παρρησίαν). When Callirhoe goes to appeal on behalf of her fellow slaves, Dionysius sees through the charade (2.7.6, Συνεὶς οὖν ὁ Διονύσιος τὸ στρατήγημα τῆς Πλαγγόνος) but joins in, pretending to spare Phocas' and Plangon's lives because of Callirhoe's entreaty (2.7.5–6). As Callirhoe turns to him to thank him, Plangon gives her a shove, Callirhoe stumbles, and Dionysius catches her and steals a kiss (2.7.6–7).

The kiss worsened Dionysius' lovesickness to the point of endangering his life (2.8.1). He summons Plangon and urges her to intensify her efforts promising both her freedom and something worth even more to her than freedom, her master's life (2.8.2, γίνωσκε δὲ ἐλευθερίαν σοι προκειμένην τὸ ἆθλον καὶ ὃ πέπεισμαί σοι πολὺ ἥδιον εἶναι τῆς ἐλευθερίας, τὸ ζῆν Διονύσιον). Dionysius idealizes the relationship with Plangon from his perspective as her master; Plangon values his life, her master's life, even more than her own freedom. Plangon redoubles her efforts, but Callirhoe remains true to Chaereas (2.8.2). Then, seeing Callirhoe's swelling stomach, Plangon realizes that she is pregnant.[20]

In what follows, Chariton contrasts the two women. In the explicit narrative, the cunning real slave uses the pregnancy as a means to manipulate the noble heroine. Plangon calculates that a mother's love will overcome the heroine's sense of female honor, her *sōphrosynē* (2.9.1, νικήσει σωφροσύνην γυναικὸς μητρὸς φιλοστοργία). Noble Callirhoe, on the other hand, sees the matter as a question of honor (2.9.2): Would a descendant of Hermocrates be born a slave, whose father no one knew? And her reputation – what would her child

Callirhoe   63

say about her?[21] But then, the same sense of nobility pushes her in the opposite direction as she remembers the sons of gods and kings who were born into slavery but grew up to claim the rank of their father (2.9.5). Perhaps her child would one day go to Syracuse and tell Chaereas what had happened to her! As she debates the question, a vision of her husband appears and entrusts the child to her. The issue is settled. Callirhoe will have the baby (2.9.6).

Cunning Plangon anticipated that a mother's love would prevail. She now has the leverage she needs.[22] She tells Callirhoe that their master (2.10.1, ὁ γὰρ δεσπότης ἡμῶν) would be jealous and not allow the child to be raised. Her affection for the heroine (ἐγὼ δέ σε φιλοῦσα) moves her to urge Callirhoe to abort the child and avoid the pain of labor (2.10.1–2). In despair, Callirhoe asks the slave to devise some stratagem (2.10.2, τινὰ τέχνην) that would allow her to raise her baby. Plangon returns a few days later and declares to the heroine that she will betray her master because of her affection for Callirhoe (2.10.3). Since Callirhoe is only two months' pregnant, Plangon advises her to sleep with the master and pretend that Dionysius is the father. Callirhoe is appalled at this gross deception (2.10.6): "I would rather have it die!" In response, Plangon turns the heroine's nature against her (2.10.6–7):

In response to her, Plangon dissimulated (κατειρωνεύσατο αὐτῆς). "O, woman, your preference for an abortion shows your good sense. It is less risky than deceiving Master (ἀκινδυνότερον γὰρ ἢ ἐξαπατᾶν δεσπότην). Forget everything that reminds you of your nobility (πανταχόθεν ἀπόκοψόν σου τὰ τῆς εὐγενείας ὑπομνήματα) and give up the hope of seeing your homeland. Accommodate yourself to your present fortune and truly become a slave" (ἀκριβῶς γενοῦ δούλῃ).

At this point, Chariton intervenes to comment that Callirhoe had no idea that Plangon was manipulating her because she was "a well-bred young lady with no experience of servile wickedness" (2.10.7, μεῖραξ εὐγενὴς καὶ πανουργίας ἄπειρος δουλικῆς).[23] The authorial intervention affirms the explicit narrative's contrast between nobility and servile wickedness.

In a melodramatic soliloquy that evening, Callirhoe turns the decision into a trial in which she, her unborn child, and her husband all have a say (2.11.1–3). The heroine herself decides to remain faithful to Chaereas; the unborn child, however, votes to live. Chaereas had already indicated his wishes in a dream vision that Callirhoe now interprets as a vote to raise the child. The following morning, Callirhoe declares that she would surrender her honor, not for her own sake but that of the child (2.11.1–4). She tells Plangon to take charge (2.11.5, σὺ πρᾶττε τὸ συμφέρον). Still, Callirhoe is worried that she will have surrendered her *sōphrosyne* in vain if Dionysius treats her as a mere concubine rather than as a wife (ὡς παλλακὴν μᾶλλον ἢ γυναῖκα) and not raise her child (τὸ ἐξ ἐμοῦ γεννώμενον).[24] Dionysius, in fact, had been wanting to marry Callirhoe ever since he learned that she was noble. Nonetheless, Plangon took the credit for this too, claiming to have anticipated Callirhoe in her concern (2.11.6, κἀγὼ

64 Callirhoe

περὶ τούτων προτέρα σοῦ βεβούλευμαι). She describes a plan to compel Dionysius (as much as slaves could compel a master) to marry the heroine:

> I respect Dionysios' character. He is a good man (χρηστὸς γὰρ ἐστιν).
> Nonetheless, I will have him swear an oath, even though he is our master
> (κἂν δεσπότης ᾖ). We have to guard against all risks. And you, child,
> trust him when he swears.

The explicit narrative worked through the characters' own declarations and the
author's assertions. Dionysius' slaves repeatedly affirmed that their master was
a good man. Before interviewing Callirhoe, he assembled an audience of witnesses, as he asserted to Leonas, to avoid any suspicion of intimidation. He reas-
sured Callirhoe of his piety and kindness in front of this audience. Chariton
himself endorsed Dionysius' nobility, noting that he prided himself on his aristocratic refinement and virtue and his struggle to behave well though in the
throes of passion. As for the heroine, Chariton intervened to certify that Callirhoe was "a well-bred young lady with no experience of servile wickedness" as
Plangon manipulated her into joining in on a deception of the master.[25]

Transacted through this combination of public declaration and authorial assertion, Chariton's explicit narrative resembles a public transcript of the relations
between Dionysius and his slaves. Dionysius' slaves are loyal and admiring.
They repeatedly affirm the fairness and kindness of their master. Dionysius is
confident that Plangon values his life over her own freedom. The explicit narrative affirms the essential difference between masters and slaves. Dionysius at
once recognized Callirhoe as a fellow noble. He ordered his slaves to treat her
as their mistress. He angrily rejected the suggestion of Leonas to have his way
with her. The power of *erōs* strained but did not rupture his code of conduct.
In fact, he has earned the sympathy of not a few modern readers as a cultivated
man who would eventually be disappointed in love.[26] As for Callirhoe, she would
have remained faithful to her husband Chaereas but for her cynical manipulation
by Plangon. The heroine herself was, thus, absolved of responsibility for the
deception and would never stop loving Chaereas.

The implicit narrative of Callirhoe's slavery

An implicit narrative of Callirhoe's enslavement to Dionysius has been embedded in the allusions, silences, and incongruities of the explicit account. One
aspect of this version is a critique of the discourse that dehumanized slaves
as animate tools or objects. The critique is anticipated in the character of the
grave robber who described Callirhoe as "property which has eyes, ears, and a
tongue" (1.10.7). The idea is connected to Aristotle's definition in the *Politics*
of the slave as a "living piece of property," a possession necessary for leading
the good life (1253b32, ὁ δοῦλος κτῆμά τι ἔμψυχον). Similarly, the first-
century CE Roman agricultural writer Varro described the slave as a tool with
a voice, an *instrumentum vocale*, one of the things necessary for the cultivation

Callirhoe   65

of fields, along with oxen and ploughs (1. 17, *De agri cultura*). The concept of the *instrumentum vocale* aligns Varro with the robber who characterized Callirhoe as "merchandise having a tongue" (φορτίον ἔχον γλῶσσαν) who needed to be put to death because she could inform against them. The robbers' brutality and inhumanity are givens, evidence that these men operated outside the law and human decency.[27] However, through the association of the robbers' ideas with the sort of respectable and educated thinking about slavery found in Aristotle and Varro, Chariton connects the inhumanity of his grave robbers with the normative thinking of slave-owners in general.

The implied association of bloodthirsty pirates with the educated elite anticipates aspects of the implicit narrative's unflattering portrait of Dionysius. When he replied to Leonas' praise for the beauty of the new-bought slave by remarking that only freeborn individuals can be beautiful (2.1.5), Chariton does not note how Leonas reacted to the implied insult. The slave's silence figures in a later incident. Welcoming her into Dionysius' household, Plangon had assured Callirhoe of the master's kindness and decency (2.2.1). When Callirhoe first meets Dionysius, Leonas directs her to greet her master. Callirhoe begins to cry as she hears the word *master* (2.3.6, κυρίῳ) for the first time, understanding at last what it means to lose one's freedom (2.3.6, ὀψὲ μεταμανθάνουσα τὴν ἐλευθερίαν). Dionysius' reaction to all this is startling. He strikes Leonas (πλήξας τὸν Λεωνᾶν) and rebukes him for calling Callirhoe a slave (2.3.6): "Blasphemer (ἀσεβέστατε)! You address the gods as if they were mortal beings?" Again, Chariton says nothing about how Leonas reacted.[28] Would Dionysius have even cared? He shows no regard for the feelings of his steward (the most responsible and trusted of his slaves!), or perhaps, he had no consciousness that Leonas even had feelings: a tool with a voice. In any event, Dionysius follows up his violence with a courtly citation from Homer (*Od.*, 17, 485, 487), suggesting that Callirhoe was a goddess who had come to observe both the insolence, or *hybris*, and righteousness of men (2.3.7, ἀνθρώπων ὕβριν τε καὶ εὐνομίην). Dionysius, who strikes a slave who had done nothing wrong, seems unconscious of his own potential for *hybris*.[29]

Chariton does not describe how Leonas reacted to this rebuke, much less the blow. As for Callirhoe, at the moment she realizes she has lost her freedom, she observes that her master, a man reputed to be just, is given to sudden fits of violence and changes of affect. What is her reaction to what she has just seen? Was she reminded, for example, of when she herself had been struck by her husband? Chariton does not say directly. But he may have implied his heroine's response in her wary and self-denigrating deflection of Dionysius' compliment (2.3.7): "Stop making fun of me," she said, "and calling me a goddess, who am not even a fortunate mortal" (τὴν οὐδὲ ἄνθρωπον εὐτυχῆ).[30] A bit later, before her interview with Dionysius (2.5.3), Leonas urges Callirhoe to tell the truth about herself because the master was exceedingly just (δικαιότατος) and law-abiding (νομιμώτατος). Chariton does not describe how Callirhoe reacts to the incongruity of Leonas' praise of his master so soon after Dionysius had struck him. Did he really think his master was just or was he just afraid of him?

66 Callirhoe

In preparation for his interview of the heroine, Dionysius had assembled an audience of friends, freedmen, and trusted slaves (2.5.1) in the shrine of Aphrodite ostensibly to avoid suspicion that he was intimidating Callirhoe (2.4.10). The actual effect (perhaps the true intent) could have been the opposite. The assembly of retainers and dependents signals Dionysius' power. Callirhoe had plenty of reason to believe he had fallen in love with her: He had paid her a courtly compliment in their first meeting and then sent her special food, instructing his slaves to tell her that it was "from Dionysius" rather than "from her master" (2.3.2). In preparation for the interview, he had dressed himself like a man going to talk with his beloved (2.5.1). The astute heroine, alone as she was, would have been wary of disappointing this powerful and impulsive man whose power to compel was more apparent than his commitment to fairness, despite the assertions of his slaves. Callirhoe uses her rhetorical skill to secure Dionysius' sympathy and his promise to send her home (2.5.12).[31] Part of this skill involves remaining silent about certain things. Callirhoe does not tell Dionysius that she is married, an omission that Chariton notes but does not explain (2.5.11, πάντα εἰποῦσα μόνον Χαιρέαν ἐσίγησεν).[32] The implicit narrative may embed the reason for this omission in the heroine's wariness of this powerful man and her dependence on his goodwill.

Realizing that Callirhoe had been unlawfully enslaved, Dionysius has promised to send her home. Nonetheless, he continues to think of her as his slave. To Leonas, he referred to her as a new-bought slave who was running away (2.6.1, φεύγει δὲ ἡ νεώνητος). When he enlisted Plangon as a go-between, he described Callirhoe as the most valuable of his possessions (2.6.4, τὸ μέγιστον καὶ τιμιώτατόν μου τῶν κτημάτων). In his description of Callirhoe as a valuable possession Dionysius uses the same language as Theron the grave robber, who described the heroine as a slave fit to be the possession of some rich prince (cf. 1.12.1, κτῆμα ... πλουσίου τινὸς καὶ βασιλέως); he uses the same language as his own slave Leonas, who bought Callirhoe as a possession fitting for his master (cf. 1.12.10, δεσποτικὸν ... κτῆμα).

Callirhoe's concealment of her marriage, a deception by omission, later blew back on her when she realized she was pregnant. The crisis leads to her collusion with Plangon, a real slave.[33] The explicit narrative depicts this collusion as a manipulation of the noble and naïve heroine by the unscrupulous and cunning slave, an *ancilla callida* drawn from comedy. In contrast, the implicit narrative blurs the distinction between noble heroine and unscrupulous slave. Plangon is more pragmatic than unprincipled, and Callirhoe, perhaps, not so naïve. Indeed, a later event lends credence to Plangon's assertion that Dionysius, as a jealous lover, would never consent to raise another man's child (2.10.1, θρέψαι δὲ παιδίον οὐκ ἐπιτρέψει διὰ ζηλοτυπίαν). In the explicit narrative, this appeared to be another instance of Plangon's cynical maneuvering of the heroine into marriage. As it turns out, however, after Dionysius and Callirhoe are married, his wife's beauty causes Dionysius to be in a state of perpetual suspicion and fear (3.9.4). When questioning his estate manager about a possible threat to his marriage, Dionysius comes to a point where he is ready to torture Phocas and all the

Callirhoe 67

slaves who worked on his farm (3.9.5–7). The jealousy of the erotically obsessed is, of course, a literary *topos*. However, in the implicit narrative, Dionysius is a slave-owner as well as an erotically obsessed lover. His jealousy has consequences for his slaves – and Plangon knew it.[34] She was right to have been concerned regarding what Dionysius could do on learning that the object of his erotic obsession had concealed her pregnancy from him. The implicit narrative transforms Plangon from a cunning and immoral slave into a discerning and pragmatic slave, a slave who knows her master's character and how best to cope with it.

It is Callirhoe herself who initiates the collusion when she asks Plangon to devise some scheme (τινὰ τέχνην) to get her out of her predicament (2.10.2). In this context, *technē* indicates not just a scheme but some sort of servile deception, a connotation that was emphasized in the *palliata* through Latin words derived from *technē*. Callirhoe's deception of Dionysius is thus a slave's scheme, a *technē*, comparable to the *technē* Anthia employed to deceive the pimp in the *Ephesiaca* (5.7.4).[35] However, where Anthia adopted servile deception to preserve her *sōphrosynē*, Callirhoe deceives in order to negotiate the loss of her *sōphrosynē* on the best terms possible. In the explicit narrative, Callirhoe professed to turn herself over to Plangon's direction. The implicit narrative suggests a more active role for the heroine. While outwardly turning things over to Plangon, Callirhoe makes her own negotiating points clear, expressing the fear that if he took her as a mistress rather than a wife, he would not raise the child and she would have lost her *sōphrosynē* for nothing (2.11.5, ὡς παλλακὴν μᾶλλον ἢ γυναῖκα νομίσας οὐ θρέψῃ τὸ ἐξ ἐμοῦ γεννώμενον κἀγὼ μάτην ἀπολέσω τὴν σωφροσύνην).[36]

The heroine's collusion with Plangon continues after her marriage. Chaereas had set out as part of a Syracusan mission to recover Callirhoe after learning from Theron that he had sold her at Miletus (3.4–5). But the rescue mission ended in disaster. Soon after Chaereas drew his boat up near Miletus, on Dionysius' estate, Phocas, having learned the identity and intent of the strangers, instigated an attack by the local Persian forces (3.7.1–3). Chaereas was captured and sold together with his friend Polycharmus to Mithridates' estate in Caria. Soon after, Callirhoe has a dream of Chaereas in chains and calls out his name in her sleep. Her grief impels her at last to tell Dionysius about Chaereas, who, she infers, had died because of the chains he was wearing in her dream (3.7.5). Since Dionysius now knows of her first marriage, Callirhoe realizes that her other secret was also in danger. She asks Dionysius to free Plangon, who alone shares in this secret, that she came to Dionysius already pregnant (3.8.1, τὴν μόνην αὐτῇ συνειδυῖαν ὅτι πρὸς Διονύσιον ἦλθεν ἐγκύμων).

The request uncovers a detail obscured in the explicit narrative: Dionysius has not honored his promise to free Plangon as a reward for getting Callirhoe to marry him (2.6.4). The recollection of this broken promise might recall another. Dionysius had promised to send the heroine home (2.5.12).[37] In the explicit narrative, Chariton glozed over Dionysius' breach of promise to Callirhoe with the near-death melodrama of his lovesickness. In contrast, the implicit narrative reveals that nothing prevents a master from breaking a promise to a

68   Callirhoe

slave. Dionysius kept Callirhoe because he could, by virtue of the same power he held over Plangon and all his other slaves.[38] It did not matter that Callirhoe is not a real slave, that she was noble, beautiful, and freeborn; it did not matter that Dionysius' power over her lacked both moral and legal sanction. In the implicit narrative, power alone was sufficient to make one person the master of another.

The episode in which Phocas incited the attack on Chaereas and his crew contains explicit and implicit versions of the slave's actions (3.7.1–3). Chariton notes that Phocas acted as a slave who loved his master (3.7.2, οἷα δὲ φιλοδέσποτος) and who wanted to avert disaster for his master's household. However, a report about the arrival of strangers reached Callirhoe, who heard that one of them, a young man, fainted on seeing a golden statue of the heroine that Dionysius had dedicated in the shrine to Aphrodite (3.9.1). Callirhoe had to find out who he was. She enlists the aid of Plangon, whose freedom she has recently arranged. The two ex-slaves maintain the solidarity that they had forged earlier in slavery. They remain united by mutual danger and a shared secret. Callirhoe takes the lead in the new intrigue (3.9.3): "Let us look for him, but do keep quiet about it (ἀλλὰ σιγῶσαι)."

She manipulates her husband into conducting the investigation, telling him what she had heard, knowing that jealousy would motivate him to busy himself in finding out what had happened (3.9.4, κἀκεῖνος δι᾿ἑαυτὸν πολυπραγμονήσει περὶ τῶν γεγονότων). However, Dionysius was not only provoked into conducting an investigation; he was also convinced there was a plot to seduce his wife. He summoned Phocas. The estate manager had not told Dionysius anything about the attack on the ship, not out of fear of Dionysius but, as Chariton says, "because he knew that Callirhoe would destroy him and his family" (3.9.6, γινώσκων δὲ ὅτι Καλλιρόη καὶ αὐτὸν ἀπολεῖ καὶ τὸ γένος αὐτοῦ).[39] The slave's silence made Dionysius even more suspicious that there was a plot against his marriage. He ordered preparations be made to torture Phocas and the other slaves, calling for whips and the torture wheel to be brought out (3.9.7, μάστιγας ᾔτει καὶ τροχὸν). That even kind Dionysius possessed these implements of torture is a reminder of the harsh reality of slavery. The threat of torture got Phocas to talk – but in private, without Callirhoe knowing. He told Dionysius about the arrival of Chaereas and how he had arranged for the hero's destruction. This news clears away the black cloud that had descended on Dionysius. He swings from murderous rage to abject gratitude and embraces Phocas, calling him his benefactor and his true and most trusted protector in his confidential business (3.9.11, εὐεργέτης ἐμός, σὺ κηδεμὼν ἀληθὴς καὶ πιστότατος ἐν τοῖς ἀπορρήτοις). The master's mood swings must have been dizzying for Phocas.

For all his gratitude, Dionysius tries to parse a distinction between himself and his slave, declaring that he would not himself have ordered his slave to kill Chaereas, but he does not fault Phocas for having done so (3.9.12, σοῦ δὲ ποιήσαντος οὐ μέμφομαι). It was a crime committed by a slave who loved his master (τὸ γὰρ ἀδίκημα φιλοδέσποτον). It is possible to see here an explicit narrative that Dionysius tells himself: Phocas is loyal, but he goes too far and without sanction in protecting his master's interests. As for condoning Phocas'

Callirhoe 69

crime, well, one may sympathize. What is done is done. The reader of the implicit narrative, in contrast, would align slave and master closely here. Phocas contrives Chaereas' murder as a slave who loved his master (3.7.2, οἷα δὲ φιλοδέσποτος); Dionysius sees the crime in the same way (3.9.12, τὸ γὰρ ἀδίκημα φιλοδέσποτον). Master and slave agree on what it means for a slave to be *philodespotos*. In the implicit narrative, Phocas provides Dionysius with "plausible deniability" while doing his master's will nonetheless.[40] He was derelict only in failing to make sure that Chaereas was out of the way for good. He faults Phocas only for not learning whether Chaereas had been killed or sold off into slavery.

To return to Dionysius and Callirhoe: The explicit narrative was a story involving the power of *erōs* and elite honor. If Dionysius broke his promise to return Callirhoe home, he did so because he was in love, so much so that he was close to dying and was even making out his will and the plans for his funeral (3.1.1). Love tested Dionysius' commitment to his code of conduct. He did not fail completely. He did not rape the heroine. The implicit narrative, in contrast, emphasizes Dionysius' power as a master.[41] This power is evident even when he is in danger of death, a victim of disappointed love (3.1.1, ἀποτυγχάνων τοῦ Καλλιρόης ἔρωτος), that is, before the heroine's pregnancy would force her into marriage. As he lay dying, in his will, "he called on Callirhoe to attend him even if dead" (παρεκάλει δὲ Καλλιρόην ἐν τοῖς γράμμασιν ἵνα αὐτῷ προσέλθῃ κἂν νεκρῷ). George Goold's translation, "he begged Callirhoe to visit him," reflects the perspective of the explicit narrative and obscures Dionysius' continuing exercise of power.[42] However, the meaning of παρεκάλει ranges from "beg" to "command."[43] The latter signification may be present in another silence in the implied narrative, a detail absent from Dionysius' – Callirhoe's manumission. Dionysius not only failed to honor his promise to send the heroine home; he also intends to keep her in his power even after he has died, requiring her to visit his grave. Dionysius' determination to maintain control over Callirhoe eventually forces her into his bed.[44]

Chariton drew a line in the explicit narrative between the heroine's naïve and well-bred nobility and Plangon's wicked and manipulative servile cunning (πανουργίας δουλικῆς, 2.10.7). The implicit narrative blurs that line. Both Callirhoe and Plangon are slaves subject to Dionysius' power.[45] Callirhoe acts like a real slave, increasingly in concert with Plangon: first enlisting her to come up with some servile scheme, then insisting on the conditions under which she would sleep with Dionysius, and, finally, arranging for Plangon's freedom in order to safeguard the deception they had together arranged. Chariton's heroine faces a paradox similar to that of Anthia. She was compelled to act like a slave in order to retain her nobility. However, Chariton makes the paradox more pointed. Anthia deceived a succession of masters to protect her *sōphrosynē*. Callirhoe surrendered her elite honor, procuring, as might a slave, better conditions in return for sex.

I argued in the previous chapter that Xenophon accommodated the sensibilities of his elite readers by adjusting the extent of Anthia's servile resistance to

70 Callirhoe

the social rank of her antagonist: the lower the villain, the more extreme the resistance. A similar process of accommodation is present in *Callirhoe*, transacted, however, not only on behalf of the elite reader but also on behalf of the elite heroine. Thus, Callirhoe makes her decision to agree to Plangon's deception a choice on which her child and her husband out vote her (2.11.1–3). In a sense, the heroine is creating here an explicit narrative for her own benefit, which transfers the responsibility for the loss of her *sōphrosynē* to her unborn child and her absent husband. A reader of the implicit narrative may be able to see this episode as an act of self-deception, through which the heroine assuages her feelings of guilt and rationalizes her bad-slave behavior to herself.

Retelling the tale: the mystery of the dogs who barked

After learning that Callirhoe had been sold as a slave – but not to whom – Chaereas set out to find her (3.4–5). At Miletus, however, the protagonist and his friend Polycharmus were captured and sold as slaves to work on Mithridates' estate in Caria. Chaereas and his fellow slaves endure brutal conditions and hard labor. By day, they labor in the fields; they are beaten for failing to work their quota. At night they are quartered together in a slave barracks, 16 slaves chained together and confined to a gloomy cell (4.2.1–5).

Chaereas endured harsher conditions on the farm than what Callirhoe faced in domestic slavery, but Chariton draws a parallel between the emotional impact of slavery on the two.[46] Under these harsh conditions, Polycharmus and Chaereas finally realize what it means to lose one's freedom (4.2.4, ὀψὲ μεταμανθάνοντες τὴν ἐλευθερίαν). Callirhoe had learned the same lesson earlier when she was first directed to bow before her master Dionysius (cf. 2.3.6: ὀψὲ μεταμανθάνουσα τὴν ἐλευθερίαν). The formula indicates that enslavement causes both protagonists to suffer a psychic shock. However, the shock is worse for Chaereas. He is completely demoralized. Unable to work his quota, he is beaten every day (4.2.2, ἐργάζεσθαι μὴ δυνάμενον, ἀλλὰ πληγὰς λαμβάνοντα καὶ προπηλακιζόμενον αἰσχρῶς). He wants to die but clings to life in the slight hope of seeing Callirhoe again. Chaereas' friend Polycharmus comes to the rescue and contrives to complete Chaereas' quota of work as well as his own. Chariton notes that unlike the hero, Polycharmus is not doubly enslaved to Eros, a hard master, as well as Mithridates (4.2.3, καὶ μὴ δουλεύων Ἔρωτι, χαλεπῷ τυράννῳ).[47] Chariton may be playing with the contrast between the conditions of Chaereas' real slavery, which he describes in realistic detail, and his metaphoric slavery to Eros, which he notes here in a literary cliché.[48]

Then, the barracks-mates of Chaereas and Polycharmus attempt to escape. Chariton provides three accounts of the event. The first account is the author's (4.2.5–6):

> At night, some of the workers who were chained together with Chaereas (τῶν ἐργατῶν τινες τῶν ἅμα Χαιρέᾳ δεδεμένων) – 16 of them were confined in a gloomy cell – broke their chains and killed the overseer. Then they

Callirhoe 71

made a run for it. But they did not get away. Barking dogs betrayed them (οἱ γὰρ κύνες ὑλάσσοντες ἐμήνυσαν αὐτούς). So, they were caught that night and bound more carefully in the stocks, all of them. After daybreak, the estate manager told Mithridates what had happened. He immediately ordered that the 16 cellmates be crucified, without seeing them or listening to their defense. So, they were brought out chained together at the feet and around their necks. Each one was carrying a cross. Those administering the punishment added this gloomy spectacle to the necessary punishment as fearful deterrent to similarly minded slaves.

Chaereas' companion Polycharmus provides the next account. As the crucifixions are underway, he speaks Callirhoe's name out loud. This act leads to an interrogation in which Polycharmus gets a chance to tell his story to Mithridates. He describes how he and his friend had come to be slaves on Mithridates' estate. He states that he and Chaereas had been bearing their misfortune virtuously (σωφρόνως) but that certain others, who had been chained together with them but whom they did not know (ἕτεροι δέ τινες τῶν ἡμῖν συνδεδεμένων, οὓς ἀγνοοῦμεν), broke their chains and committed the murder (4.3).[49] Near the end of the novel, Chaereas provides a second retelling of the episode in the course of the summary account of his adventures to the Syracusan assembly (8.7.9 – 8.8.11). He describes how he and Polycharmus had come to be enslaved and how they were chained and put to working on the estate (8.8.2, σκάπτειν ὄντας πεπεδημένους). Then he describes the revolt (8.8.2–3): "After some of the bound slaves (τῶν δεσμωτῶν ... τινες) killed the prison guard, Mithridates ordered us all to be crucified. I, too, was being led off. But Polycharmus said my name as he was about to be tortured and Mithridates recognized it."[50] Chaereas concludes by describing how this all then led to his rescue.

Polycharmus' and Chaereas' retellings of the episode separate out the protagonist and his friend from their fellow slaves. Each retelling attributed the violence to "certain slaves" distinct from Chaereas and Polycharmus. Polycharmus underlined this distinction through his assertions that he and Chaereas had been bearing the misfortune of the slavery virtuously and that they did not know the slaves who had been responsible for the violence.[51] Chariton's and Polycharmus' versions both noted that the "certain individuals" responsible for the outbreak had been chained together with the protagonist and his friend. In contrast, while Chaereas described how he and Polycharmus worked as chained laborers, he omitted the detail that he and Polycharmus had been chained together with the other slaves. Chaereas' account at the end of the novel completes a process of disassociation in the explicit versions that dissolves the bonds, both figurative and literal, that connected the protagonist to his fellow "real" slaves.

On the face of it, Polycharmus' assertion that he and Chaereas did not know their cellmates is implausible. For some time now Chaereas and Polycharmus had worked with these 14 other men; they suffered the same harsh discipline and beatings; they took their meals together; they were confined at night

72   Callirhoe

chained together in the same barracks. The author's account of the episode is marked by a curious silence. Chariton does not say what Chaereas and Polycharmus were doing during the breakout. That night in the cell, when those "certain slaves" broke their chains, they broke chains that bound them together with Chaereas and Polycharmus. Where were the protagonist and his friend captured? Sitting on the floor of the gloomy barracks with the broken chains around their ankles? Or making their way through the fields with the others?

We only know that Chaereas and Polycharmus did not betray their cellmates because the author in his version tells us that the escape attempt failed when barking dogs betrayed the runaways. We might then (with apologies to Conan Doyle) call the collective tellings of this episode the "Mystery of the Dogs Who Barked" or perhaps the "Mystery of Two Slaves Who Remained Silent." The implausibility of the re-tellings, in particular, raises the possibility of collusion between Chaereas and Polycharmus and the real slaves. Thus, like Callirhoe, Chaereas acted like a slave or was forced to act like a slave. He rebels to escape the hard work, chains, frequent beatings, physical neglect, and emotional deprivation of slavery. He rebels in order to survive.

Finally, it is worth noting that Chariton's version of the episode contains a critique of slave-owners similar to what we have seen in *Ephesiaca*. Like Apsyrtus, who accepted his daughter's accusation against Habrocomes without allowing him to speak, and like the Prefect of Egypt, who accepted the Pelusians' indictment of Habrocomes without further inquiry, Mithridates was ready to condemn Chaereas and his fellow slaves without inquiring into the outbreak or its causes. Chariton, however, may go further in his sympathies and antipathies than Xenophon. Sympathy for Chaereas may be read as extending to the protagonist's fellow slaves, who endured the same harsh conditions of agricultural slavery and who were no more guilty than he was. As for Mithridates, his cruelty is indicated by Chariton's authorial comment that the torture and punishment of his slaves provided him some consolation for his erotic illness (4.2.5, τινος ἔτυχε παραμυθίας) at a time that he was sick with desire for Callirhoe.

Re-action in Babylon

Chariton implies ambivalence about his protagonists' servile behavior even as he indicates that such behavior was necessary. Callirhoe and Chaereas acted like slaves because they had to; that excused them to a degree but not entirely. The characters themselves seem aware that they had not acted well, at least from an elite perspective. Thus, Callirhoe deceived herself that the decision to deceive Dionysius about the paternity of her child was not hers but that of the unborn child and her husband. Chaereas obscures the likelihood of his involvement in the slave revolt on Mithridates' estate, affecting, in his account to the Syracusans, not to have known his fellow slaves and omitting mention of the fact that they had been chained together.

The protagonists' ambivalence suggests they felt they had been morally compromised in slavery, tainted, one might say, by the *macula servitutis*. However,

Chariton gives them each a second chance, a chance to re-act, as it were, when subjected to similar circumstances. This re-action is transacted in Persia, where Callirhoe and Chaereas face, as ex-slaves, the same choices they had faced earlier as slaves. In Miletus, Callirhoe had relinquished her sexual modesty by marrying Dionysius. In Persia, she rejects the attentions of Artaxerxes, the Great King himself and reclaims her *sōphrosynē*. In Caria, Chaereas had been tainted by the possibility of his involvement in a slave rebellion. In Persia, he helps lead a rebellion against the tyranny of the Great King, transforming servile violence into the elite male violence of *aretē*. Through these second chances, the protagonists expunge the taint they had acquired in slavery. It is significant that Chariton has set the process of rehabilitative renarration in Persia, or rather "Persia," that is, a Greek cultural construction going back at least to Herodotus and built on an antithesis between free Greeks and servile barbarians. Chariton's "Persia" is a complete slave society, a *doulotopia*, as it were, where, in the words of the Great King's fawning eunuch Artaxates, everything worth having is a slave to the Great King (6.3.4, ᾧ τὰ καλὰ πάντα δουλεύει, χρυσός, ἄργυρος, ἐσθής, ἵπποι, πόλεις, ἔθνη).[52] This complete slave society serves as a foil for the protagonists. In the Persian *doulotopia* Chaereas and Callirhoe stand out as the only characters who are free.

The events that take the story to Babylon are complicated. After learning about the attack on Chaereas' ship, Dionysius directed Phocas to tell Callirhoe that her husband was dead (3.10.1–2). To console her in her grief, he advised his wife to build a cenotaph in honor of her first husband (4.1.3–4). Mithridates, satrap, or governor, of Caria (and Chaereas' owner), present as a guest at the sumptuous dedication of the cenotaph, saw Callirhoe and fell in love (4.1.9). Shortly after, he learned that Chaereas was alive, one of the runaway slaves he was about to crucify. Mithridates saw here an opportunity to get Callirhoe for himself under the pretext of restoring her to her first husband. However, Dionysius caught on to the satrap's scheming and his complaint reached Artaxerxes, the Great King. Artaxerxes summoned all the parties to Babylon, Dionysius and his wife, and Mithridates, to answer a charge of adultery (4.4–6). Mithridates took Chaereas and Polycharmus as witnesses (4.7.4).

By producing Chaereas at the trial Mithridates convinces everyone that he had not been aiming to seduce Callirhoe but to return her to Chaereas. The Great King now faced another dilemma: To which husband should he award Callirhoe, Dionysius or Chaereas? Or, perhaps, to himself? For Artaxerxes had fallen in love with the heroine and he, too, set about trying to seduce her (5.8.1). Thus, Callirhoe was confronted with the same situation she had faced in Miletus while Dionysius' slave. Both Dionysius and Artaxerxes were powerful men with a reputation for justice. Both fell hopelessly in love with Callirhoe. Both found themselves in the position of deciding Callirhoe's fate. Neither was able to do the right thing because of *erōs*.[53] Each rejected the idea of taking the heroine by force (Dionysius 2.6.2; Artaxerxes, 6.3.7 and 6.7.2); however, each entrusted the wooing of Callirhoe to a trusted slave. Dionysius had assigned that task to Plangon (2.5.4–5). Artaxerxes relies on his eunuch Artaxates (6.4.8).

74 Callirhoe

Callirhoe had yielded to Dionysius, but in Babylon, with Chaereas nearby, she resists the Great King. Chariton emphasizes that his heroine resists because of her noble character. The confrontations between Callirhoe and the eunuch Artaxates at 6.5 and 6.7 contrast the heroine's free Greek nobility with the uncomprehending servility of the slave. Artaxates thought that the task of seducing Callirhoe for the king would be easy because, "as a eunuch, as a slave, as a barbarian, he did not understand the noble spirit of a Greek, especially that of Callirhoe, who was chastely modest and faithful to her husband" (σώφρονος καὶ φιλάνδρου). Even before Artaxerxes' seduction attempt began and Callirhoe rejected him, Chariton has begun to correct his heroine's story. Callirhoe's second chance in "Persia" enables her to reclaim the honor she had lost in Miletus.

When Artaxates first propositions her, Callirhoe's impulse was to pluck his eyes out (6.5.8). But remembering her situation and the eunuch's influence, she sets anger aside and deflects Artaxates with irony (κατειρωνεύσατο λοιπὸν τοῦ βαρβάρου): She, a slave of Dionysius, was unworthy of the Great King (6.5.9, Διονυσίου δούλη); Artaxates had mistaken his master's pity for love.[54] The heroine's ironic indirection here takes the reader back to Miletus, when Plangon earlier deployed similar irony to get Callirhoe to yield to Dionysius (2.10.6, κατειρωνεύσατο αὐτῆς). On that occasion, Chariton remarked on the cunning slave's wickedness (2.10. 6–7, δουλικὴ πανουργία). Now in Babylon, Callirhoe resorts to similar cunning, but to reclaim her elite *sōphrosynē*.[55]

On a second attempt at persuasion, Artaxates presents Callirhoe with a stark choice: either become the king's mistress or suffer horrible torture (6.7.7). Callirhoe laughs at the threat and recounted all she had already gone through, the worst of which was being near Chaereas but not able to see him. When Artaxates expresses his astonishment that Callirhoe would prefer a slave of Mithridates to the King, the heroine proudly responds that Chaereas was of noble blood, the first man of a city which not even the Athenians could defeat, the Athenians who conquered the Great King at Marathon and Salamis (6.7.10).

Realizing that Callirhoe loves Chaereas, Artaxates sees at last how to persuade her. As he leaves, he pronounces a threat against Chaereas, who runs the risk of a horrible death if he should best the king as a rival in love (6.7.13). This threat alone (a figurative Parthian shot from a real Parthian) seems to affect Callirhoe. In Miletus the heroine had yielded to Dionysius for the sake of her unborn child. Would Callirhoe yield now to Artaxerxes, to spare her beloved a horrible death? Chariton does not put her to the test. Egypt rises in rebellion and the Great King must direct his attention from love to war (6.8). Chance enables Callirhoe to be virtuous, just as Chance led her earlier to act like a slave.[56] Or perhaps we could read the sudden plot twist as emphasizing the arbitrary and fictive quality of Callirhoe's rehabilitation. The author saves his heroine from another difficult choice.

Chaereas and Polycharmus join the rebels and Chaereas becomes the chief commander of the rebelling Egyptian king. The protagonist's heroic actions as a rebel commander displace the darkly hinted association with servile violence

Callirhoe   75

back in Caria with military *aretē*. Chariton aligns the two episodes in which Chaereas participates in violence, as different as they were. At the beginning of Book 7, as the King is directing all his minions and underlings to war, Chaereas had nothing to do. He was neither the king's slave nor part of the general muster. He had been left, the author remarks, the only free man in Babylon (7.1.1, βασιλέως γὰρ δοῦλος οὐκ ἦν, ἀλλὰ τότε μόνος ἐν Βαβυλῶνι ἐλεύθερος).[57] Chaereas has not been Mithridates' slave for some time now; this explicit mention that Chaereas is a free man functions programmatically for the coming action, in which the protagonist will reassert his agency as a free person.

Amidst this general mobilization, Chaereas hears that the Great King had decided to give Callirhoe to Dionysius. The report was false, put out by Dionysius in the hope of convincing Chaereas to give up hope. Polycharmus redirects his friend's despairing impulse to commit suicide into anger against Artaxerxes. The two run away to the Egyptian side (7.2.2, ηὐτομόλησαν πρὸς τὸν Αἰγύπτιον). The verb, ηὐτομόλησαν, associates their desertion with servile *automolia*, a regular term for the desertion of slaves, especially in wartime.[58] Any rebellion against the Great King might be considered a slave rebellion because all his subjects were notionally slaves. However, when the rebellion broke out, Chaereas and Polycharmus were once again free Syracusans. The characterization of their going over to the rebels as *automolia* may connect their current actions with their attempt to run away while slaves in Caria.[59]

In Caria, slavery had demoralized Chaereas. Now in the rebel army, he displays intelligence and boldness in his zeal to punish Artaxerxes. Chariton's protagonist at last becomes a hero.[60] Although Chaereas' transformation may seem abrupt and unrealistic, its function is clear. He becomes a hero worthy of Callirhoe. In addition, Chaereas' military valor functions as a redo of his earlier involvement with the violent slave breakout on Mithridates' estate. The rebel king makes Chaereas his advisor, recognizing his noble character and learning (7.2.5, οἷα δὴ καὶ φύσεως καὶ παιδείας οὐκ ἀπρονόητος), and this impels the protagonist even more to show that he is worthy of honor (7.2.6, ἄξιος τιμῆς). When the rebel king despairs of taking the impregnable citadel of Tyre and proposes a retreat back to Egypt, Chaereas volunteers to lead an assault with Polycharmus, paraphrasing a line from the *Iliad* that recalls the valor of the hero Diomedes (9.48, νῶι δ᾽, ἐγὼ Πολύχαρμός τε μαχησόμεθα). He assembles a force of 300 Dorian Greek volunteers.[61] In a speech before the battle, Chaereas recalls the heroism of Leonidas and the Spartan 300 at Thermopylae (7.3.4–5). He also employs a ruse. He presents himself and his small force before the gates of Tyre as a group of Greek mercenaries who were deserting the Egyptian king because they had not been paid. The Tyrian commandant himself arrives and opens the gates; Chaereas kills him on the spot and then rushes headlong at the other defenders (7.4.6). Koen De Temmerman notes that Chariton heralds the slaughter that follows with a citation from the *Odyssey* (22.308) that describes Odysseus' slaughter of the suitors in his palace.[62] Duplicity is potentially a servile trait, but reference to Odysseus associates Chaereas' ruse with the sanctioned martial craftiness of the Homeric warrior.

76 Callirhoe

A second engagement follows. The rebel king faces Artaxerxes and his army on land but gives Chaereas command of his navy. The spirits of the fleet rise because they have in Chaereas the bravest and noblest leader (7.5.11, ὅτι τὸν ἀνδρειότατον καὶ κάλλιστον εἶχον ἡγούμενον). Artaxerxes and his Persians prevail in the fighting on land. Dionysius distinguishes himself by hunting the Egyptian rebel king down and bringing his head back to the Great King. He receives Callirhoe as his reward (7.5.12–14). But in the fighting at sea, Chaereas prevails and takes control of Aradus, the island where Artaxerxes had left his entourage, the wealth of his court, Queen Statira and, as Chaereas will learn to his joy, Callirhoe.

Chaereas' victory at sea gains him possession of all these prizes and recalls a theme that was signaled in Dionysius' detention of Callirhoe in Miletus: Slavery depends on power rather than on law or morality. The Persian queen is now his slave by right of conquest. Statira and the members of the Persian court antici-pate a future of physical punishment, outrage, and death, with slavery as the most humane of what they would endure (7.6.5, τὸ φιλανθρωπότατον δέ, δουλείαν). The sanctioned violence of military valor also allows Chaereas himself to take Callirhoe back as his own rather than wait for the Great King's judgment. The protagonist himself makes this clear in a letter he sent to Artaxerxes after the battle: "You were hesitating to judge my case, but I have won already according to the most just of judges. For war is the best judge of the stronger and the weaker" (8.4.2, πόλεμος γὰρ ἄριστος κριτὴς τοῦ κρείττονός τε καὶ χείρονος).[63] In his letter, Chaereas also asserts a moral advantage over the Great King. He notes that, at Callirhoe's urging, he is returning Queen Statira and not following the king's own bad example in delaying judgment in the matter of a man's wife.[64] He even lectures Artaxerxes on statecraft, advising him to come to terms with the rebels, since it behooves a king not to hold a grudge (8.4.3).

In the meantime, without Chaereas' knowledge (8.4.4, τοῦτο μόνον ἐποίησε δίχα Χαιρέου), Callirhoe writes a letter to Dionysius. She addresses him as her benefactor (8.4.5, εὐεργέτης) because he had freed her from pirates and enslavement (σὺ γὰρ εἶ ὁ καὶ λῃστείας καὶ δουλείας με ἀπαλλάξας).[65] In Roman terms, she would be defining him as her *patronus* and herself as his *liberta*.[66] In brief, she reminds Dionysius that their relationship had been grounded in asymmetrical power, not love. Then she turns the tables on her ex-owner. She and her child had first been separated when they arrived in Babylon for the trial; now the fortunes of war force the heroine to leave her son behind with Dionysius.[67] She instructs him to raise and educate the child (8.4.5, ὃν παρακατατίθημί σοι ἐκτρέφειν τε καὶ παιδεύειν). Dionysius still does not know the truth about the child's paternity. These are the duties of a father; however, the verbs *ektrephein* and *paideuein* may also evoke in this case the servile offices of *tropheus* and *paidagogos*, in which case Callirhoe would be commanding Dionysius now as if he were her slave. She also places restrictions on his sex life, enjoining him from remarriage, a form of symmetrical retribution for the man who had forced her into an unwanted marriage. Finally, she enjoins Dionysius to marry the boy to his half-sister (Dionysius' daughter

Callirhoe 77

from his first wife) and send him to Syracuse to see his famous grandfather. Callirhoe's letter recalls the "world-turned-upside-down" fantasy of dominated peoples.[68] The (ex-)slave orders about the (ex-)master. Her letter concludes with a salutation to Plangon (ἀσπάζομαί σε, Πλαγγών), a sign from Callirhoe to maintain their deception. The two ex-slaves of Dionysius remain in solidarity. Thus, Callirhoe and Chaereas not only redeem themselves from the moral blemish they contacted in slavery; they also assert their superiority over those who once held them in their power.[69]

In "Persia" both protagonists receive a second chance in which they encounter a situation similar to that in which they earlier had resorted to bad-slave behavior. This second chance, that is, the corrective reenactments of the earlier situations, ends up functioning as a homeopathic cure of sorts for the protagonists. Both Callirhoe and Chaereas get things right the second time around. That is what matters.

Telling the story of slavery

The process of reenactment in Babylon points to the author's interest in slavery itself as a theme for narration. When the action moves to Babylon, and when Chariton puts his protagonists into situations similar to what they had faced earlier, he retells, in a sense, the stories of their enslavement in new versions that restore their lost honor. Narration is arbitrary and much depends on it. Even in Babylon, Callirhoe might have been forced to surrender her honor a second time in order to save Chaereas had not the Egyptian rebellion intervened.

Chariton engages with the question of narration again in the final book, when the protagonists return to Syracuse. This engagement is introduced in an address to the readers at the beginning of Book 8. The author assures his audience that the story he is telling them will end well. Specifically, the conclusion of *Callirhoe* will provide a purgation, or *katharsion*, of the grim events narrated earlier (8.1.4):

> I think that this last book will be one that gives the readers the most pleasure (ἥδιστον). For it will be a purgation of the grim events in the first books (καθάρσιον γάρ ἐστι τῶν ἐν τοῖς πρώτοις σκυθρωπῶν). No more piracy and slavery (λῃστεία καὶ δουλεία) here; no law trials, battles, and suicide; no war and being taken captive (πόλεμος καὶ ἅλωσις); only honest love and lawful marriage (ἔρωτες δίκαιοι <καὶ> νόμιμοι γάμοι).

As many have noted, the reference to pleasure and purgation alludes to Aristotle's thesis in the *Poetics* (1449ᵇ), that through the representation of pitiable and fearful actions or events, tragedy produced a pleasurable purgation, or catharsis, of these same emotions in the audience (δι' ἐλέου καὶ φόβου περαίνουσα τὴν τῶν τοιούτων παθημάτων κάθαρσιν). Chariton seems to say something different, that the happy events of the final book will purge the grim ones that happened earlier and that this would be a source of pleasure to the reader – the

78 Callirhoe

displacement of bad things by good things in the plot rather than a homeopathic release of unpleasant emotions within the audience.[70] Some maintain that Chariton has misunderstood or sentimentalized Aristotle.[71] Stefan Tilg has argued that Chariton is consciously engaging with the philosopher to articulate a new poetics for the erotic novel, centering on the innovation of a happy ending, a convention that, in the case of tragedy, Aristotle had deplored.[72]

Chariton glosses the grim events, *ta skythrōpa*, of the earlier books as piracy, slavery, trials, fighting, suicides, war, and being taken prisoner. Slavery, *douleia*, itself is noted as only one of the protagonists' many misfortunes; nonetheless, their enslavement seems to be the calamity foremost in the author's mind.[73] The first two items on the list, piracy and slavery, *leisteia* and *douleia*, may be taken as hendiadys for Callirhoe's enslavement; the last two items, war and captivity, *polemos* and *halōsis*, may be similarly understood for the enslavement of Chaereas.[74] Conversely, the good things that happen at the end of the story are associated with freedom. Only free individuals had a right to *erōtes dikaioi* and *nomimoi gamoi*. Slaves could not be legally husband and wife. Thus, Chariton's *katharsion tōn skythrōpōn*, that purgation of grim events, is associated specifically with a transition from slavery to freedom.

Chaereas summarizes what has happened to himself and to Callirhoe in a lengthy recapitulation that concludes the novel (8.7.3–8.11). Tomas Hägg connects this summary with the address to the readers, arguing that the summary offers the readers a repetition and concentration of the experience of catharsis.[75] However, Chariton seems also to be interested in the effect of this summary on the summarizer himself; put another way, in Chaereas' summary, the author narrates a former slave remembering and narrating his own experience of slavery. For when he returns to Syracuse, Chaereas is an ex-slave. The protagonist is a reluctant teller of his own tale; he speaks only at the insistence of the crowd and with the encouragement of his father-in-law, Hermocrates, who steps up to encourage him (8.7.4):

> Do not be ashamed, my son, if you should talk about something that is painful or unpleasant for us (λυπηρότερον ἢ πικρότερον ἡμῖν). For the end of your story, in its brilliance, overshadows everything that came before (τὸ γὰρ τέλος λαμπρὸν γενόμενον ἐπισκοτεῖ τοῖς προτέροις ἅπασι).

This encouragement aligns with Chariton's address to his readers, where the happy ending provides the readers "a purgation of the grim events in the first books." According to Hermocrates, the brilliant conclusion of Chaereas' story, its *lampron telos*, will overshadow "everything that came before," that is, the things that would be painful and unpleasant to his listeners. However, the process that Chariton has in mind may also reflect the influence of an Aristotelian homeopathic purgation, in this case for Chaereas himself. By telling his story, Chaereas relives the things that happened to him and feels again the pain associated with those events. This is the reason why it is more difficult for the protagonist to tell his story than it is for his eager audience to hear it.

Callirhoe   79

To help his son-in-law, Hermocrates takes over the first part of the story himself, summarizing what had happened up to Chaereas' departure from Syracuse (8.7.5–8). Chaereas resumes the account with his arrival near Dionysius' estate in Miletus. Even after the head start that Hermocrates provided, he has difficulty with the parts of his story that deal with slavery. For example, he interrupts himself after noting that Dionysius had bought Callirhoe for a talent, saying to his listeners (8.7.10):

> Don't be frightened. She did not serve as a slave (οὐκ ἐδούλευσεν). For he immediately made his bought slave the mistress of himself (τὴν ἀργυρώνητον αὐτοῦ δέσποιναν ἀπέδειξε). Although he was in love with her, he did not dare to force himself on a woman of noble birth; however, he could not bear to send the woman he loved back to Syracuse.

Steven Smith attributes Chaereas' unease here to a concern for the expectations and sensibilities of his listeners, but the reluctance may also be motivated by the protagonist's own discomfort with what his wife had endured.[76] Chaereas then tells about Callirhoe's realization of her pregnancy and her decision to deceive Dionysius, which he depicts to the Syracusans as a heroic act that has saved the life of a fellow citizen (8.7.11, σῶσαι τὸν πολίτην ὑμῖν θέλουσα). He reassures his listeners that his son, their own fellow citizen, is being raised by the wealthy and distinguished Dionysius. He encourages the assembly to acquiesce in this arrangement and not begrudge his son his birthright (8.7.12).

When Chaereas comes to the attack on his ship and how he himself became a slave, the Syracusans burst forth in a groan. It is painful to hear about slavery. But it is painful, too, for Chaereas, the ex-slave, to talk about it. In language that connects his summary with the address to the reader, Chaereas asks his listeners permission to skip over that part because it was grimmer than the start of his account (8.8.1, σκυθρωπότερα γὰρ ἐστι τῶν πρώτων). But the crowd will have none of it: "Tell us the whole story!" Chaereas continues and relates his work as a slave on Mithridates' estate, the murder of the guard by some of the prisoners, and the crucifixion from which he and Polycharmus were saved when his friend uttered his, Chaereas' name, which Mithridates recognized. Then the concluding events: a failed attempt to communicate with Callirhoe through letters, the summons to Babylon and the trial, the Great King's futile infatuation with Callirhoe, his own despair and the loyalty of Polycharmus, and, finally, the Egyptian revolt, his military triumph, and the protagonists' reunion and triumphant return home (8.8.4–11).

Chaereas' audience loved his account if one is to judge from the acclamation they accord it and their adoption of his proposals, that Polycharmus marry his sister and that the 300 Dorian Greeks who fought with him at Tyre receive Syracusan citizenship (8.8.13).[77] The author, however, does not indicate the effect of narrating his story on Chaereas himself, whether the act of narration provided him with homeopathic relief of what he had endured or whether the glorious

80 Callirhoe

conclusion of his adventures, the *lampron telos*, that is, freedom, reconciled him to the suffering that he and Callirhoe had endured as slaves.

Chariton does imply, however, that recollecting slavery was difficult and painful for this former slave. Chaereas' summary is thus marked by omission, emendation, and spin.[78] As Chaereas told it, Callirhoe was never a slave; her loss of *sōphrosynē* and her deception of Dionysius were patriotic acts. He slides past the likelihood of his involvement in a slave revolt, "certain" that his fellow prisoners murdered their guard (cf. 8.8.2, τὸν δεσμοφύλακα τῶν δεσμωτῶν ἀπέκτεινάν τινες). His recollection that Polycharmus called out his own name, not Callirhoe's, possibly results from a lapse on Chariton's part. But he could also be trying to distance Callirhoe from responsibility for his enslavement and crucifixion.[79] Finally, Chaereas glosses over the painful fact that circumstances have forced him and Callirhoe to leave their child in Asia with Dionysius. The protagonists' abandonment of their son recalls the circumstances of slavery, which often separated biological parents from their children. Chaereas' anticipation of his son's future glory may then serve as a form of consolation, a means of dealing with that pain.[80]

Through Chaereas' summary of his story (and the novel), Chariton offers a commentary on what it means to remember and narrate the experience of slavery. For an ex-slave, as was Chaereas at this point, the *lampron telos* of freedom might overshadow the grim events of a servile past. However, sometimes a happy ending alone might not be enough. The ex-slave may feel the need to remember selectively, even to lie, to put a good face on things and produce an account that is pleasurable to his listeners (or readers) and, despite the pain of recollection, even pleasurable to himself.

Notes

1 Tilg 2010, 36–82.
2 These parallels have been adduced in support of the first-century CE date for Xenophon. For additional parallels, see Gärtner 1967, 2082–2084. Other discussions in Dalmeyda 1962 (1926), xxix–xxxi; Henderson 2009, 208–210; Trzaskoma 2010b, xxiii–xxvii. Cf. Whitmarsh 2011, 67, who cites thematic parallels in favor of a first-century CE date for both.

   Regarding the relative chronology, most scholars are of the view that Chariton came before Xenophon. Tilg 2010 has laid out the most extensive case. For the anteriority of Xenophon, see O'Sullivan 1995. Xenophon's repetitive prose and simple characterizations led some to see him as a clumsy imitator of the more rhetorically refined and psychologically insightful Chariton. However, it is also possible, as Henderson 2009, 209–210 noted, that Chariton sought to refine and improve what he found in Xenophon.
3 Refraction of Roman power through Persia: Alvares 2001–2002; Schwartz 2003; significance of the relationship between Aphrodisias and Rome: Edwards 1991, 1994; allusions to Roman imperial power: Connors 2002; general reflection on freedom and tyranny: Smith 2007.
4 Hunter 1994, 1077–1078 sees Callirhoe as the embodiment of Syracuse and her enslavement as a metaphor for the loss of political freedom; Chaereas' violence against his pregnant wife, Hunter argues (p. 1080), assimilates him to tyrants such

as Periander. Alvares 2001–2002, 123–124 emphasizes the corrupting influence of slaves on their masters; Schwartz 2003, 381, 385, notes Persia as a place where all but the Great King are slaves; Smith 2007, 244–245 sees the protagonists' enslavement and Dionysius' coercion of enslaved Callirhoe as a modulation on the general theme of political freedom and tyranny.

5 Hägg 1971 discusses the characteristics of the explicit narrative in terms of its narratological elements: the treatment of time, point of view, the handling of parallel action, and the anticipation and recapitulation of action.

6 Cf. Morgan 2004a, 481, who notes that Chariton "takes us into the minds and hearts of his characters and tells us, as objective fact, what they thought or felt."

7 Whitmarsh 2008, 72–87.

8 On Chaereas' summary, see the later discussion, pp. 78–80.

9 Callirhoe, too, denies responsibility for her own bad-slave behavior, perhaps even to herself, when she rationalizes her decision to marry Dionysius (and sacrifice her *sōphrosynē*) as a decision that Chaereas and her unborn child made for her (2.11.1–4).

10 Leonas' purchase of the heroine reflects commercial practices that evolved in the Roman villa system, in which a *servus actor*, a slave who acted as the legal extension of his master, had the authority to enter into contracts and agreements: cf. Aubert 1994, 415–417, with reference to this episode. Another indication of Leonas' importance is implied in the description of his lodgings on the estate, which were very much like a free person's home (1.13.2, τὴν οἴκησιν τὴν ἑαυτοῦ σφόδρα ἐλευθέριον οὖσαν).

11 The episode appears to reflect laws regarding the sale of merchandise that applied in Greek cities during the imperial period, as opposed to the historical time of the story: cf. Karabélias 1990, 282.

12 Zimmermann 1957 argues that Chariton had acquired knowledge of the law in his capacity as secretary, or *hypographeus*, to the public speaker Athenagoras.

13 Domestic partner: as slaves, Plangon and Phocas are not legal spouses. In Roman terms, they would correspond to the *vilicus* and *vilica*, the enslaved male and female managers on a slave-run estate. Plangon and Phocas are both subordinate to Leonas, who oversees all of Dionysius' wealth. The management hierarchy aligns with our understanding of practices in the evolved villa economy: cf. Aubert 1994.

14 When Leonas received Theron at his master's villa, the robber marveled at the size and magnificence of the home (1.13.1, τὸ μέγεθος καὶ τὴν πολυτέλειαν), which had been built to receive the Great King. According to Rossiter 1989, 104–105, the estate reflects some of the features characteristic of Roman villas in the Greek East: the estate is close to town; as noted, the main house is beautifully built (also, 1.13.5, ἔπαυλις κατεσκεύασται πολυτελῶς); the shrine to Aphrodite on the property has its analogue in a chapel that Gregory of Nyssa (*Ep.* 20) describes on an estate belonging to a certain Adelphius.

15 Cf. the discussion in Balot 1998, 146–154, on the subversion of Dionysius' elite male identity through *erōs*.

16 Fakas 2005, saw in the reference to Sybaris and its reputation for loose morals a prefiguring of Callirhoe's decision to marry Dionysius. Tilg 2010, 146–155 argues that Chariton refers to Sybaris and the salacious content of the *Sybaritica* as a foil for the chaste Callirhoe.

17 Kaimio 1995, 124–125 suggests that Callirhoe would have cast suspicion on herself by telling the truth, that her husband had assaulted her because he suspected her of adultery.

18 Smith 2007, 244–245 discusses the passage in the context of political tyranny and Plato's discussion in the *Republic* of the role played by *erōs* in the transition from democracy to tyranny.

19 Plangon as New Comic clever slave: Schmeling 1974, 144; Smith 2007, 106.

82   Callirhoe

20 Plangon's knowledge about such matters (2.9.5, ὡς δὴ πεῖραν ἔχουσα τῶν γυναικείων), suggests a character who had dealt with slave pregnancies as the estate's head female slave. Columella (12.3.7–9) notes that monitoring the health of the slaves and maintaining standards in the *villa* infirmary were among the duties of the *vilica*.

21 Callirhoe first tried to abort herself, striking her stomach, but was stopped by Plangon, who promised to provide her with an easier means of terminating the pregnancy (2.8.7). Kapparis 2002, 120–124 argues that the episode gives insight into real-life circumstances, such as slavery and social dislocation, that could lead a woman to consider an abortion. Doody 1996, 37–38 sees in this episode "a source of female conflict, as well as an anguish that only a slave can know," and argues that Callirhoe faces the same dilemma as Sethe in Toni Morrison's *Beloved*, who killed her daughter to prevent her from being taken back into slavery.

It is useful to remember that fiction here is tied to the real world. Morrison's Sethe was based on Margaret Garner, a slave who escaped with her family to Cincinnati. Garner killed her two-year-old daughter before they could be seized by federal marshals and taken back to Kentucky under the terms of the 1850 Fugitive Slave Act. The unsympathetic citizen interlocuter in Dio Chrysostom's discourse on slavery may also reflect actual conditions in the first and second centuries in his assertion that enslaved women aborted pregnancies in order to avoid the burden of raising a child in addition to the burden of slavery (15.8, ὅπως μὴ πράγματα ἔχωσι παιδοτροφεῖν ἀναγκαζόμεναι πρὸς τῇ δουλείᾳ).

22 Schmeling 1974, 96 absolves Dionysius from involvement with Plangon's trickery, arguing that, like many slaves in comedy, Plangon aided her master "in all the wrong ways, namely by believing that her master had all the baser instincts that she had." Smith 2007, 157–158 follows Schmeling on the parallels between Plangon and comic clever slaves but also notes that Plangon was operating in her own interests, that is, to gain her freedom.

23 Cf. the comment of the tyrant of Rhegium to the son of the tyrant of Acragas, who advises that Callirhoe be taken from Chaereas by wicked cunning rather than by force, because that is the way that tyrants take power (1.2.5): καὶ γὰρ τὰς τυραννίδας πανουργίᾳ μᾶλλον ἢ βίᾳ κτώμεθα. Plangon's servile *panourgia*, that is, the amoral willingness to do whatever it takes to achieve an end, associates slavery with tyranny in that both tyrants and slaves attain their ends through this attribute.

24 The emendation suggested by Trzaskoma 2010a, "ἐξ ἐμοῦ," makes sense of the manuscript reading, "τὸ ἐξ ἄλλου." Whatever decision Callirhoe made, Dionysius was not to know that her child was "from another man," ἐξ ἄλλου.

25 The insightful interpretation of De Temmerman 2014, 61–70, who regards the heroine as an inexperienced victim of a cunning slave, should be qualified as a reading of the explicit narrative.

26 In his study of characterization in Chariton, Helms 1966, 66–80 acknowledges Dionysius' imperfect self-control, his jealousy, and his readiness to deceive in order to keep Callirhoe. However, his summative judgment is positive (p. 70): "Being her master he has complete control over her, yet he reveals self-control over his emotions and treats her with great respect and tact. Although finally overcome by his desires he nevertheless is guided by a sense of decency and self-respect, exhibiting a kind of humaneness so totally lacking in the *dramatis personae* of the other romances." Schmeling 1974, 95 notes Dionysius' "high moral character and discipline." Reardon 1982, 23 argues that Dionysius is given charge of Callirhoe's son as a consolation because Chariton has "represented him throughout as a noble soul and as *sympathique*, and cannot bear to leave him out in the cold altogether." Liviabella Furiani 1989, 51 compares him favorably to Chaereas. In the view of Egger 1990, 193–194, Chariton's depiction is too sympathetic to justify his loss of the heroine. "He is 'a good guy,' humane, mature,

Callirhoe   83

sophisticated, a man of the world, tactful, charming – in one word, πεπαιδευμένος ἀνήρ (2.4.1; 3.2.6; 5.5.1), and genuinely dedicated to the heroine and her wellbeing." Hunter 1994, 1062, sees Dionysius as "an educated and sensitive Greek in the service of the Persians," who is "a worthy foster-father" for Callirhoe's child. Fusillo 2003, 297 remarks that Dionysius "receives a quite positive characterization as a noble, well-educated and self-controlled man according to a Menandrean pattern; he has to fight not only his moral code but also the memory of his dead wife (2.4); his destructive passion finally finds the only canonical and acceptable expression for the ideology of the Greek novel, marriage." For Schwartz 1999, 25, n. 5, Dionysius stands out among Chariton's male characters for his *sōphrosynē* because he did not force himself on the heroine. Whitmarsh 2011, 52 suggests that "in an other life, in an other romance, he might have been quite a catch."

27 When Theron and his crew reached the area around Athens, they told Callirhoe to wash and rest (1.11.5) because, Chariton comments, they wanted to preserve her beauty (διασώζειν θέλοντες αὐτῆς τὸ κάλλος) after the long voyage. Shortly after, in the territory of Miletus, Theron ordered his men to do everything for her comfort. The author again intervenes to comment that Theron did this not out of human concern for Callirhoe but as a merchant hoping for a good price for his merchandise rather than a pirate (1.12.1, ταῦτα δὲ οὐκ ἐκ φιλανθρωπίας ἔπραττεν ἀλλ᾽ ἐκ φιλοκερδίας, ὡς ἔμπορος μᾶλλον ἢ λῃστής). In Xenophon's novel, the pirates who take Anthia from Cilicia to sell her in Egypt also take good care of their merchandise so that they can get a good price for her (3.11.1, οἱ δὲ ἔτρεφόν τε αὐτὴν πολυτελῶς καὶ τὸ σῶμα ἐθεράπευον, ζητοῦντες ἀεὶ τὸν ὠνησόμενον κατ᾽ ἀξίαν).

   These villains reflect the practices of real slave dealers, who tried to show off their merchandise in the best light and who were commonly suspected of fraud. Bodel 2005, 192–193 notes that the stereotype of the slave dealer, or *mango*, as a retail-level deceiver is reflected the term's connection with μαγγανεύειν, a word that indicated the use of charms in magic and which referred metaphorically to deception; that is, it was assumed that a *mango* would try to cover up defects in his human merchandise, a practice that Roman law attempted to curb: cf. Bradley 1994, 51–54.

28 See the remarks in Barton 2001, 11–14. Actual slaves felt the dishonor of insulting treatment: perhaps, too, Leonas. Barton cites the *de Constantia*, where Seneca notes (5.1) that some slaves would rather suffer physical injury than personal insult: "Thus, you will find the slave who would rather be whipped than punched, who thinks that death and whip-lashing is more easily endured than tongue-lashing (*qui mortem ac verbera tolerabiliora credat quam contumeliosa verba*)."

29 *Hybris* was commonly defined as the act of treating a fellow citizen as if he were a slave (cf. MacDowell 1976, 23–24), an idea that suggests one could not commit *hybris* against someone who was, in fact, a slave. However, the issue is complicated; in Athens, at any rate, slaves were included among the classes of persons protected by a law against *hybris* (see the discussion in Dmitriev 2016). Dover 1974, 285–286 argues that the concern of this law may have been to discourage *hybris* against citizens (an *a fortiori* approach to discouraging civil violence). In that context, Dionysius' violence against Leonas anticipates the misuse of his power against Callirhoe, an incontrovertible instance of *hybris*. It may also be the case that Chariton's implicit narrative is insinuating a protest against the normative idea that one could not commit *hybris* against a slave.

30 *LSJ* II: ἡ ἄνθρωπος may indicate a female slave with a tone of contempt or pity.

31 De Temmerman 2014, 51–52 remarks on Callirhoe's rhetorical astuteness in this episode, an attribute that undermines the explicit narrative's presentation of the heroine as a naïve, young girl manipulated by Plangon.

32 Schmeling 1974, 95 notes that Callirhoe's failure to tell Dionysius about her husband may have been a Freudian slip indicating her unconscious desire for him, or that it

84 Callirhoe

could have been based on her fear of him. Liviabella Furiani 1989, 50–52 argues that the heroine was attracted to Dionysius and that her second marriage was better grounded than her first. Egger 1990, 57, n. 2 argues that Callirhoe was manipulating Dionysius – but unconsciously; Egger 1994a, 39–42 makes a stronger case for the heroine's attraction to him.

33 Egger 1990, 98–100, 103–104 on the genre's use of a female slave as the heroine's confidante; p. 104 on Plangon; Egger 1999 (1988), 123, n. 49 sees the motif as derived from tragedy and comedy.

34 Chariton may suggest that this quality is generic to slave-owners rather than specific to Dionysius. At the beginning of the story, when he suspected Callirhoe of infidelity, Chaereas, too, spent a whole night torturing her slave attendants, including her particular favorite, whom he tortured twice over (1.5.2, Χαιρέας δὲ ἔτι τῷ θυμῷ ζέων δι' ὅλης νυκτὸς ἀποκλείσας ἑαυτὸν ἐβασάνιζε τὰς θεραπαινίδας, πρώτην δὲ καὶ τελευταίαν τὴν ἅβραν).

35 On this episode, see Chapter 1, pp. 38–39.

36 Cf. Trzaskoma 2010a, 207, who notes Callirhoe's full understanding of her circumstances and her collaboration with Plangon "to bind freedom, marriage, and the production of children together as inseparable."

37 A failure similarly noted by Alvares 2001–2002, 128.

38 Thus, Plangon reassures Callirhoe that even though Dionysius was an honorable man, she would nonetheless have him swear an oath to marry the heroine (2.11.6, ἐξορκιῶ δὲ ὅμως αὐτόν). In the implied narrative, the astute Plangon knows that slaves have little protection from the master's power. Because they are slaves, she and Callirhoe must do everything carefully: δεῖ πάντα ἡμᾶς ἀσφαλῶς πράττειν.

39 Note that Phocas fears Callirhoe because she, too, now has power over him as his master's wife.

40 Bradley 1990, 145–146 notes evidence in Roman law for slaves who were coerced into criminal activity by their masters.

41 Cf. the comment of Doody 1996, 42, that, in contrast to Aristotle's idea of the natural slave, "[a]uthors like Chariton know that it is the imposition of power that makes slavery." Also, Smith 2007, 130, who comments on Dionysius' tyrannical power as a metaphor for political tyranny.

42 Goold 1995, 133; similarly, Reardon 1989, 49; Trzaskoma 2010b, 37 "begged Callirhoe," and Omitowoju 2011, 39: "he addressed Callirhoe in the hope that she would visit him."

43 *LSJ* IV, "demand, require"; V. "beseech, entreat."

44 Curran 1978, 220–221, in his discussion of rape in Ovid's *Metamorphoses*, notes episodes that take the form of a seduction but a seduction in which the rapist has "disproportionally unfair advantage over the woman." Curran cites contemporary parallels involving professor and student or employer and secretary; the advantage of master over slave is greater.

An analogue to Dionysius' coercion of Callirhoe may be present in *Ephesiaca*, in Perilaos' determined efforts to get Anthia to marry him (2.13.5–8 and 3.5 – 3.6). Like Dionysius, Perilaos was a powerful man, the official in charge of public peace in Cilicia (2.13.3). He did not rape the heroine, but he was strongly insistent (2.13.8, βιαζομένῳ καὶ πολλὰ ἐγκειμένῳ). Anthia feared worse violence (2.13.8, δείσασα μὴ καί τι τολμήσῃ βιαιότερον) and used a variety of oblique strategies to put Perilaos off. In the end, however, the only way she could escape from an unwanted marriage was by trying to kill herself.

45 The view of Karabélias 1990, 382–386, that Callirhoe was not really ever a slave because Theron had sold her illegally, reflects the perspective of the explicit narrative. Cf. Zimmermann 1957, who argues that the sale was completed *de facto* but not *de iure*. From the perspective of the implicit narrative, Callirhoe was Dionysius' slave because she was subject to his power, right or wrong.

Callirhoe   85

46 Both Dionysius' and Mithridates' estates possess characteristics associated with Roman agricultural *villae*. In the case of Dionysius' *villa*, the narrative focuses on the luxury of the main house. The description of Mithridates' estate, with its supervisors, chained slaves, assigned work quotas, and slave barracks, recalls the slave-run *villa* of the Roman agricultural writers: cf. Baslez 1992, 202. The contrast in focus, house or fields, reflects a contrast in the slave experience, domestic or agricultural, of the two protagonists.

47 Polycharmus was an invaluable friend to the protagonist throughout: Hock 1997, 147–157.

48 Romantic cliché may lead the author into inconsistency: on one hand, the slim hope of seeing Callirhoe again keeps him alive; on the other hand, love renders him incapable of doing enough work to avoid daily beatings.

49 Hägg 1971, 256–257 considers Polycharmus' account in terms of the formal aspects of narrative repetition.

50 Another inconsistency: Chariton said that Polycharmus called out Callirhoe's name. On this, see the later discussion, p. 80, n. 79.

51 Saïd 1999, 96–97 appears to take Polycharmus at his word: The indignation of the author and his readers comes from the fact that Chaereas and his friend, "two innocent people, moreover young people of noble birth," were going to be condemned with the guilty.

52 For an overview of the sources, literary, artistic, and historical that informed Chariton's composite construction of Persia, see Baslez 1992. On Herodotus' representation of all Persian subjects, including nobles, as the king's slaves, see Hunt 1998, 46–51. Hunter 1994, 1058–1059 notes the influence of Herodotus and Xenophon's *Cyropaideia*. Schwartz 2003 observes that Chariton's Persia reflects the Greek literary tradition but, at the same time, stands as a complex symbol of Roman imperial power.

53 Smith 2007, 195–197 on *erōs* and the association between loss of personal self-control and political tyranny.

54 Cf. Anthia's attempt to deflect Hippothous in *Ephesiaca*, by demurring that she was "unworthy of the master's bed" (5.9.12).

55 In his comparison of the two episodes, De Temmerman 2014, 71–73 argues that while Callirhoe was the defenseless and emotionally vulnerable victim of Plangon in Miletus, in Babylon she fended off Artaxates by means of emotional self-control and rhetorical astuteness. Kaimio 1995, 128–129 notes examples prior to the Plangon episode of the heroine's astuteness and ability to size up a situation.

56 According to Liviabella Furiani 1989, 47, Chariton opens the possibility that Callirhoe may have been disposed to have sex with Artaxerxes if that is what it would have taken to save Chaereas.

57 Smith 2007, 87–89 suggests that the author's remark is programmatic of the hero's reclamation of his identity as a Syracusan noble.

58 On the desertion of slaves in wartime, see Hunt 1998, 102–120, who characterizes the phenomenon as "an ubiquitous background to classical warfare" (p. 106). On the word *automolia* as a cue for servile desertion in wartime, cf. Aristophanes, *Eq.*, 21–26, produced in 424 BCE, during the Peloponnesian War. Two slaves of the character Demos conjure up the idea of desertion by combining disjointed syllables into the word αὐτομολῶμεν: "Let's run away!"

59 Chaereas himself later refers to his participation in the revolt as *automolia* (8.1.17, to Callirhoe, and 8.5.8, to the Syracusans). Artaxerxes also characterizes Chaereas' participation in the revolt as *automolia* while acknowledging that he himself had given the hero good reason to desert (8.5.8).

60 Rohde 1960 (1876), 527 comments on the sudden transformation: "man verwundert sich, am Schluss des Ganzen den bis dahin so wenig energischen Chaereas urplötzlich zum siegreich handelnden und herrschenden Kriegshelden sich umwandeln zu sehen."

86 Callirhoe

Also, Helms 1966, 129. Schmeling 1974, 135 argues that Chaereas proves himself worthy of Callirhoe through his martial heroism; for Balot 1998, 156, Chaereas finally displays the virtue of his class; Haynes 2003, 85, 97–100 considers psychological and sociological contexts for Chaereas' transformation. Scourfield 2003 argues that Chaereas realizes himself as a man when he learns to control and focus his anger in the context of battle; De Temmerman 2014, 82–95, argues that the hero learns to control himself and others, in particular, through rhetoric.

61 Syracuse was a Dorian colony. De Temmerman 2014, 96 observes that Chaereas appeals to his Dorian ethnicity as a means of aligning himself with his men.

62 De Temmerman 2014, 92: τύπτε δ᾽ ἐπιστροφάδην· τῶν δὲ στόνος ὤρνυτ᾽ ἀεικής. Cf. *Odyssey* 24.184 (in Hades the suitors describe their own slaughter) and *Iliad* 10.483 (Diomedes attacks the Thracians).

63 Chaereas' letter echoes Aristotle's description of the thinking that justifies victory or defeat as the arbiter of slavery or freedom (*Pol.*, 1255ᵃ 13–16): "in a certain manner (τρόπον τινά), virtue (ἀρετή), when it obtains resources has in fact very great power to use force (βιάζεσθαι), and the stronger party (τὸ κρατοῦν) always possesses superiority in something that is good (ἀγαθοῦ τινος), so that it is thought that force (τὴν βίαν) cannot be devoid of goodness" (μὴ ἄνευ ἀρετῆς εἶναι; Rackham 1932).

64 Chaereas had at first thought of keeping Statira as a slave attendant for Callirhoe. The heroine, however, refused this gift; she would not be so mad as to have the Queen of Asia as her slave (8.3.2, ὥστε τὴν τῆς Ἀσίας βασιλίδα δούλην ἔχειν). She steered Chaereas to a nobler course of action.

65 Callirhoe's rhetoric posits Dionysius in opposition to the pirates but at the same time may align him with them. Dionysius had "rescued" Callirhoe, the pirates' kidnapping victim, but by buying her as his slave; by freeing her from slavery, he "rescued" her from a second dire condition but one into which he himself had forced her.

66 Cf. Eilers 2002, 110; Bowersock 1965, 12–13 notes that εὐεργέτης functioned as the equivalent of *patronus* in the epigraphy of the Greek cities of the empire.

67 A point recognized by Schwartz 1999, 30.

68 Cf. Forsdyke 2012, 49–53; also, Richlin 2017, 204–224 on Plautine slaves who get even with their masters.

69 I suggest an ironic take on the letter's closure, "Farewell, good Dionysius, and remember your Callirhoe" (ἔρρωσο, ἀγαθὲ Διονύσιε, καὶ Καλλιρόης μνημόνευε τῆς σῆς). Callirhoe did not think of Dionysius as particularly "good," and she knew that his memory of her would be for him a source of pain.

70 Thus, Reardon 1982, 21–22: "Chariton seems to mean that the good will replace the bad, will make you forget it."

71 Misunderstood or trivialized: Mueller 1976, 134–135; sentimentalized: Reardon 1982, 21–22.

72 Tilg 2010, 130–137.

73 Slavery figures in two earlier occurrences of *skythrōpos*. At 2.5.7 the statue of Aphrodite itself seemed to take on a grimmer (σκυθρωποτέραν) aspect as Callirhoe acknowledges she is now just a slave; the crucifixion of Chaereas and his cellmates is described as a grim spectacle (φαντασίαν σκυθρωπήν) to dishearten other slaves inclined to escape.

74 Cf. Callirhoe's reference to piracy and slavery (8.4.5, λῃστείας καὶ δουλείας) in her farewell letter to Dionysius.

75 Hägg 1971, 258–260; followed by Tilg 2010, 130–137.

76 Smith 2007, 223.

77 De Temmerman 2014, 103–104 sees the success of this speech as evidence of Chaereas' acquisition of rhetorical skill, an "essential quality of male adulthood."

78 Cf. De Temmerman 2009, who argues that Chaereas plays up his own heroism and lies about other actions that may have caused him embarrassment. For example,

the hero asserts how he was encouraged on seeing Callirhoe's statue in the shrine to Aphrodite after his arrival near Dionysius' estate (8.8.1, τότε δὲ καταχθεὶς ἐν τῷ χωρίῳ, μόνην εἰκόνα Καλλιρόης θεασάμενος ἐν ἱερῷ ἐγὼ μὲν εἶχον ἀγαθὰς ἐλπίδας). In fact, Chaereas had fainted and needed to be revived (3.6.3, κατέπεσεν οὖν σκοτοδινιάσας).

79 Cf. De Temmerman 2009, 259. Hägg 1971, 258 implies that Chaereas' (deliberate?) lapse of memory reflects his belief that Mithridates was a noble helper and his ignorance of the satrap's true motivations.

80 Cf. Richlin 2017, 243–245, 387–388 on characters in Plautus whose families have been broken apart by slavery. In Chariton, the abandonment of the protagonists' child has been a source of perplexity; thus, Whitmarsh 2011, 67, "a significant loose end." Some commentators have judged Callirhoe as a hard-hearted mother: cf. Perry 1930, 101, n. 11, 104; Reardon 1982, 22–23; Johne 2003, 180. On the other hand, Kanavou 2015, 948 argues that in relinquishing custody of her child to Dionysius, Callirhoe "practises self-restraint by controlling her motherly instinct in order to take a morally optimal decision for all parties involved (considering also, in a sensible manner, the benefits for her child)." Schwartz 1999 is more persuasive in her view that both the law and social convention would have regarded Dionysius as the father and given him custody of the child, a view noted in Egger 1994b, 263.

3 Two novels about slavery

Introduction

In this chapter, I discuss the possibility that Xenophon and Chariton had themselves been slaves and directed their novels in part to readers who were also former slaves. I consider how these ex-slave readers may have responded to particular motifs relevant to slavery. Enslavement and the experience of slavery play a central role in *Ephesiaca* and *Callirhoe*. Anthia is a slave for almost the entire plot of *Ephesiaca* (1.13–5.13). Habrocomes is twice enslaved (1.13–2.10 and 3.13–4.4). When he is not a slave, he is looking for his wife, who is. The first half of *Callirhoe* focuses on the illegal enslavement of the heroine (1.14–3.2). Chaereas' slavery is related more concisely (3.7–4.3). However, Chariton is still processing the moral consequences of both his protagonists' enslavement in the second half of the novel, when the action moves to Persia and then back to Syracuse. In the next section, I draw attention to three aspects of the representation of slavery in *Ephesiaca* and *Callirhoe*: Both novels depict slavery with a significant degree of realism, with reference to Roman practices of slavery in particular; both novels express sympathy for their enslaved protagonists even when they adopt bad-slave behavior; both novels, in contrast, depict slave-owners unsympathetically, as unchecked in their power, as cruel and quick to punish. This configuration of sympathies and antipathies, I argue, may have had a particular appeal to readers who knew about slavery from the perspective of the slave.

It is possible that an author imbued with elite *paideia* and exposed since childhood to the normative opinions of his class regarding slaves could, nonetheless, have sympathized with slaves in an imaginative and empathetic act. However, in the section titled "The status of the authors," I consider evidence that Xenophon and Chariton imply authorial personas suggestive of individuals who had been slaves. In a similar fashion, it is also possible that readers imbued with elite *paideia* and exposed since childhood to the normative opinions of their class could, nonetheless, have aligned themselves with the sympathies of these novels in an act of imaginative and empathetic reading. There is no reason to doubt that such readers existed. However, in two sections that follow, "Ex-slaves as readers: a hypothesis," and "Ex-slave readers: means, opportunity, and motive," I note evidence suggesting that ex-slave readers existed as well. The response of these readers depended less on their capacity for imagination and empathy than on their memory and experience. Thus, in "Reading Xenophon and Chariton as an ex-slave," I consider how such readers may have responded to selected motifs in these two novels. In the final section, I argue that an important achievement of Xenophon and Chariton was to take narrative ideas about slavery that reflected a slave's point of view, some of them possibly originating from the hidden transcripts of slaves, and incorporate them into works of extended prose fiction and thus to mark the new genre, the erotic novel, as a form that was, in some way, about slavery.

Realism, sympathy, antipathy

Ancient slave-owners often used slavery as a metaphor to reflect on their own concerns, a means to think with, as it were.[1] However, *Ephesiaca* and *Callirhoe* thematize slavery itself as an object of concern. Both novels narrate how their protagonists respond to slavery; how they are affected by it, both physically and psychically; how they resist and survive it; and how they remember it. Broadly speaking, the protagonists of these novels experience many of the things that real slaves experienced: geographical dislocation, separation from family, sexual coercion, and harsh punishment. The response of the protagonists to these conditions is realistic. Like actual slaves, they resist slavery, and they desire to escape from it.

Such realism supports the contention that slavery itself is an object of interest in these novels. The realism is present in details that align with evidence for Roman conditions but that could also apply to Greek slavery. For example, both heroines receive good treatment from their captives prior to being put up for sale, a detail reflecting the practices of slave dealers, who wished their human merchandise to look its best.[2] A number of other details in *Ephesiaca* align with aspects of Roman slaveholding. The close relationship between the protagonists and Leucon and Rhode, their *syntrophoi*, reflects the affective ties that sometimes existed between Roman slave-owners and slaves who had been raised with them since childhood, their fellow *alumni*.[3] Habrocomes' services and continued subordination to his ex-master as a freedman correspond to the *operae* and *obsequium* that the Roman *libertus* might owe his *patronus*.[4] When he goes to look for Anthia, Xenophon may have had his protagonist sneak off from Apsyrtos (2.12.2, λαθὼν οὖν τὸν Ἄψυρτον) because he was behaving like a *libertus ingratus* by deserting his post.[5] Lampon, a rural slave living on his own, had more scope to subvert the will of his owner and assist the heroine than did Clytus, an urban slave. The contrast aligns with a concern of Roman estate owners regarding the trustworthiness of inadequately supervised rural slaves.[6]

Callirhoe also reflects aspects of the Roman villa system. The slave Leonas, Dionysius' steward (*dioikētēs*), corresponds to the *dispensator*, a slave empowered to buy and sell on his master's behalf.[7] The slave couple who administer

90 *Two novels about slavery*

Dionysius' estate, Phocas and Plangon, align with the *vilicus* and *vilica* in charge of the *familia rustica*.[8] Mithridates' estate in Caria exhibits additional aspects of the slave-run *villa* in Roman agricultural writers: chained work teams, the assignment of specific work quotas, and the slave barracks or *ergastulum*.[9] While Chariton's fictional depiction of the slave-run estates of Dionysius and Mithridates does not offer dispositive evidence regarding the existence of the villa system in the eastern part of the empire, these episodes can indicate that educated Greeks at least knew about it. In addition, Greeks would have had direct experience of the Roman practice of employing educated slaves and freedmen as their agents in matters of importance both private and official.[10] As Neville Morley notes, "Rome did not export the villa mode of production to any great degree, but it did export its beliefs, habits, practices and anxieties; the provinces were confronted with, and clearly influenced by, a culture that was permeated by slavery."[11]

The violence that attended the slavery of both pairs of protagonists also reflected reality. Brigandage and war were important sources of slaves in the real world.[12] After their enslavement, slaves were subject to systematic coercion and frequent violence. The purpose of this systematic coercion and violence of slavery was to instill fear.[13] In *Ephesiaca*, Apsyrtos has Habrocomes tortured in order to frighten his other slaves (2.6.1, τοῖς ἄλλοις οἰκέταις τὴν σὴν αἰκίαν ποιήσομαι παράδειγμα). In *Callirhoe*, Mithridates stages the mass crucifixion of the 16 rebel slaves, a grim spectacle with the same end in mind (4.2.7, εἰς φόβου παράδειγμα). This "Persian" cruelty was, in fact, typically Roman in both its means and its aims. The Romans used crucifixion to punish slaves who had rebelled and to deter future rebellion.[14]

The realism of these novels does not count for a documentary description of slavery, nor should we expect that in a work of fiction. However, this realism does suggest that the enslavement of the protagonists and how they respond to it is a theme of interest in itself and that slavery in these novels was not only a metaphor indicating, for example, the fragility of one's identity or alienation from a secure and predictable world. The Roman context of much of this realism indicates that *Ephesiaca* and *Callirhoe* are engaged with ideas and attitudes about slaves and ex-slaves that were characteristic of early imperial culture.

The sympathy expressed for slaves noted in the previous chapters is sometimes expressed through narration from the perspective of the enslaved protagonist.[15] It is also useful to note that this sympathy is sometimes associated with servile emotions that may also be realistic. Xenophon, for example, takes the reader into Habrocomes' thoughts as he considers the worthlessness of freedom without Anthia (2.10.3, ἐνενόει δὲ πρὸς ἑαυτὸν πολλάκις) and later outlines the thinking that led his protagonist to plot against the life of his master Araxus (3.12). These passages not only encourage sympathy for the protagonist; they also encourage sympathy for the protagonist as he faces the sorts of dilemma that real slaves faced: separation from family and fear of torture. Chariton focalizes Callirhoe through one anguished soliloquy in which she tries to decide whether to abort her pregnancy or to bear a child in slavery (2.11.1–3) and another in which she expresses the despair she felt on crossing the Euphrates and the immense distance that now separated her from home (5.1.3–7). Here, again, the text suggests sympathy for a protagonist suffering as a real slave might: hesitating whether to bear a child into slavery and despairing at the loss of the world she knew.[16] Xenophon and Chariton also sympathize with and even justify their protagonists' adoption of bad-slave behaviors as a form of resistance that was necessary for their survival. Sympathy for bad-slave behavior is not restricted to the elite protagonists but is extended to slaves as a class. A cast of real slaves aid and enable the enslaved protagonists: In *Ephesiaca*, the protagonists' *syntrophoi* Leucon and Rhode, Lampon, the goatherd who pities Anthia and spares her life, and even Clytus, who also feels pity for the heroine but is afraid to help her; in *Callirhoe*, Plangon starts out manipulating the heroine, soon becomes her co-conspirator, and remains her confidante at the end of the novel.

Xenophon and Chariton complement the sympathetic representation of enslaved characters with an unsympathetic depiction of slave-owners. This may have touched on a reality in which at least some masters were quick to anger and to punish. William V. Harris, in his study of anger in antiquity, *Restraining Rage*, notes that master–slave relations were "a great locus of classical anger."[17] Excessive anger on the part of masters was a target of critique, not out of concern for the well-being of the slave but out of concern for the functioning of the system or out of moral or medical concern for a slave-owner who had lost control of himself.[18] The prescription was not that masters should not punish their slaves but that they should not punish them in anger and that they should have others do the job. Harris notes that we cannot establish "that the Greeks and Romans expressed, or felt, much more anger than we do, though we cannot exclude the possibility either."[19] It may be the case that the power of the slave-owner gave rein to unchecked expressions of anger and made such anger a characteristic of the system rather than the individual owner. Xenophon and Chariton signal this aspect of master–slave relations in the frequent episodes in which masters either strike their slaves in anger or arrange for their summary punishment. In Xenophon, both Apsyrtos and the prefect of Egypt condemn Habrocomes without allowing him a word of explanation (2.6.2; 4.2.1). Rhenaea assaults Anthia with her bare hands (5.5.2). In Chariton, Mithridates sentenced his slaves to death at once, before seeing or hearing them (4.2.6). Chariton plays up the cruelty of the Persian governor. At the time, he was pining with love for Callirhoe, whom he had glimpsed in Miletus. He would have died had he not found some consolation in the execution of the rebel slaves (4.2.5, εἰ μὴ τοιᾶσδέ τινος ἔτυχε παραμυθίας).

It may be possible to discount the depiction of cruel masters such as Apsyrtos, who was a barbarian, and Mithridates, who was both a barbarian and a Persian.[20] In the normative view, barbarians were subject to savage emotion. But Xenophon and Chariton seem to blur the line between the barbarian and respectable Greek or Roman slave-owner. Apsyrtos' reaction to what he thought was an attempt to rape his daughter aligns with the response of a protective Roman *paterfamilias*

92 *Two novels about slavery*

concerned about his daughter's marriageability. He tortures Habrocomes not only as a cruel example to the other slaves (2.6.1) but also to prove Manto's virginity to a prospective bridegroom (2.6.4). In *Callirhoe*, the hard-hearted villains who find the heroine in the tomb and commoditize her as a share of the grave goods (1.9.6) and merchandise, albeit with eyes, ears, and a tongue (1.10.7), reflect a way of thinking about slaves that aligns with Aristotle's "living sort of property" (κτῆμά τι ἔμψυχον) and Varro's "tool with the ability to speak" (*instrumentum vocale*). Even Dionysius, a paragon of Greek *paideia*, nonetheless refers to Callirhoe as the most prized of his possessions (2.6.4) – and this after he acknowledged the heroine's noble identity.[21] A kind and humane master in the words of his own slaves, in impulsive irritation, Dionysius nonetheless strikes Leonas, the highest ranking and most trusted of his slaves (2.3.6). He is also ready to torture all the slaves on his rural estate when he suspects a plot against his marriage (3.9.7). In brief, this most humane of masters, a character imbued with humanizing *paideia*, is not far removed from the barbarian or the heartless criminal.[22]

* * *

Xenophon and Chariton sympathized with their protagonists as slaves who were subject to cruel domination. Both authors entered into their protagonists' minds as they tried to cope with slavery. They sympathized with the protagonists even when they acted like stereotypical bad slaves. They rationalized or justified the protagonists when they deceived their masters or engaged in violent resistance: Such acts were necessary for survival in slavery. The authors' sympathy was also extended to ordinary slave characters, who pitied the protagonists, shared their dangers, and assisted them. In contrast, their unrestricted power enabled the masters, even when imbued with humanizing Greek *paideia*, to be quick to anger, quick to condemn, and quick to punish.

The status of the authors

The authors of these two novels – novels that represent their protagonists' enslavement from a perspective both sympathetic to slaves and critical of masters – may have themselves been slaves; at any rate, each at least associated himself with the experience of slavery. Thus, Chariton in the first sentence of his novel (1.1.1):

> I, Chariton of Aphrodisia, under-clerk of the lawyer Athenagoras (Ἀθηναγόρου τοῦ ῥήτορος ὑπογραφεύς), am going to narrate a love story that happened in Syracuse.

Tim Whitmarsh notes that Chariton the Aphrodisian, or "Mr Favours from the city of Aphrodite," is perhaps too good to be believed for the author of an erotic novel;[23] however, many accept the nonfictional character of the information.[24] Aphrodisias was the site of an important cult of Aphrodite, the goddess from whom the city took its name, and enjoyed close connections with Rome, having chosen sides well during the conflicts that ended in Augustan rule. The goddess plays a role in motivating the action of *Callirhoe*, and the famous cult may have provided Chariton with some of his inspiration.[25] Epigraphical evidence indicates that individuals named Chariton and Athenagoras lived in Aphrodisias.[26] An Ulpius Claudius Chariton, a physician, was commemorated in a late second- to early third-century funerary inscription (*IAph2007* 12.1112), too late to refer to the author. The importance of the Athenagoras family at Aphrodisias has been attested over the first century and into the second. Tilg suggests an identification with the Athenagoras of a first- to second-century dedication, who was honored as "a fine and good man and a lover of his city who had been a gymnasiarch, a *stephanēphorus* and president at contests, and an ambassador" (*Iaph*2007 13.302; translation Tilg).[27]

However, the nature of Chariton's self-presentation may be no less important than its historical accuracy.[28] It was conventional for authors to identify themselves, or to be identified by others, with reference to their city. "Chariton of Aphrodisias" follows in the tradition of Thucydides of Athens, Herodotus of Halicarnassus, and other authors whose identities are so constructed at the start of their books.[29] In social terms, Chariton's reference to his employment and his employer distinguishes him from the two historians and indicates a subservient status.[30] In Roman epigraphy, for example, slaves and freedmen identified themselves by occupation and through reference to their masters and former masters. The connection with the patron and the work itself may have formed a part of the freedman's personal identity.[31] In addition, Chariton's occupation, that of *hypographeus*, secretary or clerk, is a type of position associated with educated slaves and freedmen. If his boss Athenagoras functioned in some official capacity, Chariton's employment might align with that of the *scribae*, or public scribes, who assisted Roman magistrates, and whose ranks included many ex-slaves.[32] The author of *Callirhoe* thus constructed an authorial persona appropriate to the story that follows, a tale of *erōs* that is also a narrative about slavery that reflects the perspective of enslaved characters. These servile associations are also implied in an alignment between Chariton as narrator and his protagonist. In Book 8, when Chaereas summarizes the story that Chariton has just told, the protagonist becomes a narrator. As a narrator, Chaereas may serve as a projection of the author. He may have something else in common with Chariton. Chaereas was not merely a narrator; he was also a former slave who told a story about slavery.

The possibility that Xenophon had been a slave does not attach to the author's persona (indeed, Xenophon of Ephesus is little more than a name)[33] but may have been implied through his significant use of folktales.[34] In the Introduction, I noted that the folktale, like the fable, while by no means the exclusive property of slaves, was available to slaves for the expression of their hidden transcripts. Xenophon's extensive use of folktales such as "Potiphar's Wife," "Escape from an Undesired Suitor," and "Snow White" may not only indicate a choice of narrative mode but also suggest an origin for some of his narrative ideas. The sixfold repetition of

94 *Two novels about slavery*

the "Escape from an Undesired Suitor" tale reveals its formulaic structure and, in that, suggests the possibility of the tale's oral character; Xenophon may thus allude to oral transmission of the tale among slaves as well its origins.[35]

Xenophon's versions of these folktales represent matters that were of concern to real slaves: false accusation and punishment, the need for slaves to form bonds with one another, the unpredictability of the slave's life, how a slave may resist the master, and the slave's necessary use of circumspection and cunning.[36] Repetition of the unwanted-suitor tale may also support the thematic agenda, reflecting the enslaved heroine's sense of entrapment and uncertainty as she passes from owner to owner.[37] The same repetition can also emphasize Anthia's servile circumspection – as when she conceals her true name from Hippothoos and Polyidus – and her cleverness – as when she claims to Psammis, the Indian king, that her chastity was under the protection of Isis or persuades the pimp that she suffered from epilepsy. Collectively, the ensemble of iterations emphasizes that Xenophon's heroine managed against all odds to preserve her *sōphrosynē*.

By incorporating these folktales into his novel, Xenophon indicates, if indirectly, an author who relates the kind of stories slaves told to one another.

Ex-slaves as readers: a hypothesis

Ephesiaca and *Callirhoe* express sympathy for slaves and antipathy toward slave-owners. Xenophon and Chariton suggest authorial personas of individuals who had been slaves: Xenophon indirectly through his use of the fable and Chariton through reference to his employment and employer. In this section, I consider their readers and argue that Xenophon and Chariton wrote for a complex audience that included literate ex-slaves. It is necessary to describe the relationship between these ex-slave authors and their ex-slave readers now before moving on to the later novelists; the argument for a special ex-slave readership is particular to Xenophon and Chariton and does not apply to them. Longus, Achilles, and Heliodorus each reflects an ideological perspective on slavery closer to the elite norm; each of them constructs a traditional elite authorial or narratorial persona.

As one may expect in the matter of a new genre that drew scant explicit notice in antiquity, the identity of actual readers of the novels has been a long-standing question.[38] In the general lack of external evidence, scholars have read and interpreted the novels in their contemporary historical and social contexts and from this hypothesized different audiences of ancient readers. In other words, novel scholars became reader-response critics, if only to the extent that they were trying to identify the genre's original readers. The effort to infer the reader from the text has hazards. The familiar hermeneutical pitfall of privileging one among several potential readings may be amplified in the case of the novel, a genre noted for its polyphony, a genre which represents multiple points of view, male and female, slave and slave-owner, Greek and non-Greek and which contains rhetoric and ideas drawn from genres high and low, including epic, tragedy, comedy, elegiac poetry, folktale, and fable. This polyphony widens the range of plausible interpretation (although not infinitely) and problematizes the attempt to infer particular readers from any one reading.[39] There is also the risk of simplifying the role that social and historical factors play in the creation of a literary text. As Tim Whitmarsh notes, "literary works are shaped by multiple influences, which may include, alongside social, political and cultural shifts, the conservatising effects of canons and traditions as well as the idiosyncratic creative aspirations of individual authors."[40] The same multiple influences are at play in how a text draws its readers.

Despite these challenges, the demographics of ancient literacy and other evidence for ancient readers allow us to narrow the genre's potential readers to an elite literate enough to read complex texts. Literacy was on the rise during the time the novel emerged; nonetheless, the degree of literacy required to read and enjoy literature was always limited in the ancient world. William Harris concluded that few in the ancient world were literate, perhaps 10% to 20% of the population. Fewer still would have had access to the education that conferred the literacy sufficient for reading literary texts, perhaps 5% of the population.[41] These limitations would apply to readers of the Greek novel. The rhetoric and literary allusiveness of Longus, Achilles Tatius, and Heliodorus presume a reader who was sophisticated and well educated. Chariton, too, is replete with allusions to Homer.[42] Susan Stephens's study of the papyrus fragments of the novels from the Fayum and Oxyrhynchus provides material support for the same point. Papyri preserving novel texts are similar to papyri of the traditional classics in general appearance, letter size, and rate of error. Stephens suggests that the readers of the novel did not constitute a separate audience apart from the elite, a conclusion she suggests we may generalize outside Egypt.[43] Such a generalization need not be limited to Greek-speaking parts of the empire. Romans acknowledged the status of Greek as an international language of high culture, and many in the Roman elite were literate in Greek as well as Latin.[44]

Finally, the limited evidence that makes explicit note of novel readers points to individuals of high social status. In the latter half of the fourth century, Julian censured pagan priests in Asia Minor who appear to have been reading the novels.[45] Other evidence points to wealthy male slave-owners. The physician Theodore Priscianus recommended reading Iamblichus, author of *Babyloniaca* (*The Babylonian Tale*) as a cure for male sexual dysfunction.[46] Immediately before his Iamblichus prescription, Priscianus advises the same patients to procure attractive slave girls or boys (*puellarum speciosarum vel puerorum similiter servitium procurandum est*).

These factors inform a consensus that the ancient readership was limited, well-off, and well educated.[47] From this, Harris suggested that the novels, with their erotic themes and tales of adventure and travel, constituted the leisure reading of the empire's urban elite, the "light reading of a limited public possessing a real degree of education."[48] Even the highly educated read to relax, and this would likely be an apt description for some readers of Xenophon and Chariton – but not necessarily all of them.

96 *Two novels about slavery*

One important and influential reader hypothesis suggested that the genre addressed the concerns of individuals who felt lost in a wider world, in Ben Edwin Perry's phrase, "the poor in spirit."[49] Perry associated the spiritual crisis of the individual with a cultural shift in the late Hellenistic and Roman imperial world, a time when the search for identity and a meaningful life was transacted on the level of the individual rather than that of the community:

> In the vastly expanded world of Hellenistic and Roman times, the individual lost nearly all his quondam importance and representative significance, having become too tiny to be tragic, or heroic, or poetic, or symbolical of anything more than himself or a particular segment of contemporary society.... The bigger the world the smaller the man. Faced with the immensity of things and his own helplessness before them, the spirit of Hellenistic man became passive in a way that it had never been before, and he regarded himself instinctively as the plaything of Fortune. All this is conspicuous from first to last in the Greek romance.[50]

Taking *Callirhoe* as his model of an ideal novel, Perry projected a primary readership of average individuals, well meaning but perhaps not up to the challenge of a complex world, readers lacking in a degree of sophistication, "a law abiding, well-established, optimistic, tender and conventionally-minded, middle-class, pagan gentry."[51] It is difficult to know what Perry intends by "middle-class," an anachronism apparently intended to disparage the intellectual level of these readers.[52] In addition, the evidence that we do have for novel readers indicates an economic and educational elite, not an ancient middle class. As John Morgan put it, the genre was by no means "down-market of 'normal' literature."[53]

Many now dispute Perry's premise, that the *polis* was giving way to the individual as the locus for identity during the time the genre emerged. Simon Swain, for example, argues that the Greek urban elite were experiencing a cultural revival under imperial rule. The novels celebrate "being Greek and living and continuing to live in the traditional Greek city."[54] The centrality of the protagonists' conjugal bond, the ideal of conjugality, expresses the value that this revival placed on the family as an agent of Greek cultural inheritance and transmission.[55] The readers of the novel were the elite of the urban upper classes in the eastern half of the empire who were proud of their Greek identity and who wished to reflect on their cultural traditions and the sources of their privilege, the traditional *polis*.[56] A shortcoming of Swain's construction of the reader may derive from his reading of the genre, which glosses over the ways in which the surviving novels may end ambiguously, satirize the values of the *polis*, or problematize identity itself.[57]

Several scholars have suggested that women readers had a reflexive affinity for the novel heroines, who overshadow their male counterparts in their eloquence, resolution, and courage.[58] Others, reflecting an anachronistic and sexist tradition that disparaged both the female gender and the novel genre, argued that the sentimental and erotic focus of the novel appealed to the "weaker sex," for whom love was all.[59] Brigitte Egger advanced this discussion with her proposal of a more complex model for the engagement of male and female readers, grounded theoretically in reader-response criticism and contextualized in the social conditions under which ancient women readers would have lived.[60] According to Egger, the novel heroine conquers men with her irresistible erotic power but remains, nonetheless, socially powerless, circumscribed by social norms that render her incapable of direct action. However, the heroine's constricted social agency, Egger notes, would not have aligned with the lives of potential women readers.[61] The notion of a woman who possessed irresistible erotic power but who was, at the same time, socially restricted, was, first of all, the stuff of male fantasy and had been since the time of Homer and heroines such as Helen and Penelope.[62] At the same time, Egger argues, this notion also appealed to elite women readers. On one hand, these readers could indulge in the fantasy of the heroine's irresistible power over men. On the other hand, the archaizing representation of gender roles that were, in Egger's words, "secure, traditional, circumscribed" offered women readers a form of escapist, possibly infantilizing, comfort in an imagined simpler world that presented fewer difficult choices.[63] Thus, for different but complementary reasons, the novel was a form of pleasure reading for both well-educated men and well-educated women.[64]

The hypothesis here, that Xenophon's and Chariton's readers included literate ex-slaves is offered in the context of a model that also assumes a normative elite reader, that is, a reader whose engagement with slavery was limited to owning slaves. By the time the novel emerged in the first century CE, educated freedmen had already made important contributions to imperial culture, in particular in the field of literature. I shall discuss the significance of their contribution in the following section. The existence of these literary freedmen, ex-slave authors and scholars, suggests the existence of a still larger population of ex-slaves who were literate enough to read for pleasure. The hypothesis for ex-slave readers in no way posits a down-market readership.

Adapting for my purposes Iser's notion of a hypothetical reader implied in the text, I argue that Xenophon's and Chariton's novels configure a reader who was knowledgeable about slavery.[65] Much of this reader's knowledge was indicated in the realistic aspects of Xenophon's and Chariton's depiction: the representation of domestic and agricultural slaves; the master's reliance on particular slaves, such as a steward; and the phenomenon of *syntrophoi*, the possibility of an affective bond between master and slave. The implied reader would also have been familiar with the normative elite opinions about slaves, the role that coercion played in the institution, and servile strategies of acquiescence and resistance. Actual readers, however, could have construed or, in Iser's term, concretized, the significance of this representation differently, depending on whether they were normative readers or ex-slave readers. Both authors indicate sympathy for their enslaved protagonists and express disapproval of slaveowners. Granted, most literary works evoke sympathy for a struggling protagonist and antipathy for his or her adversary. But Xenophon and Chariton indicate

98 *Two novels about slavery*

sympathy for their protagonists even when they adopt bad-slave behaviors; in addition, they imply sympathy for ordinary slaves who become their allies.

At the same time, these authors salted their sympathy with unease, ambivalence, or reservation. For example, in Xenophon, the gods twice save Habrocomes from execution because he was a man who had "done no wrong" (4.2.5, ἄνθρωπον οὐδὲν ἀδικήσαντα). The divine intervention suggests discomfort with Habrocomes' even brief complicity in the plot against his master and his failure to report the plot at all. Chariton excused Callirhoe's decision to deceive her master and pass off Chaereas' unborn child as his, at least on the level of the explicit narration, by characterizing his heroine as the victim of the manipulative slave Plangon. Callirhoe herself was "a well-bred young lady with no experience of servile wickedness" (2.10.7). Both Chaereas and Polycharmus either lied about or obscured their participation in the slave revolt on Mithridates' estate.

Xenophon's and Chariton's sympathy for bad-slave behavior ran counter to the ideology of normative elite readers. It is possible that some of these readers would have revisited their assumptions regarding slaves who deceived their masters, tried to run away, or even committed acts of violence. However, *Ephesiaca* and *Callirhoe* also contain details that would have enabled normative readers to excuse or to rationalize the protagonists' actions in accord with their ideological assumptions. Normative readers might have reasoned that the protagonists were elites and therefore not real slaves (despite the fact they were acting like real slaves). They could have rationalized the brutality of the slave-owners as the brutality of outlaws and barbarians. The ambivalence and discomfort that Xenophon and Chariton attached to their protagonists' bad-slave behavior reflected the normative reader's own discomfort with such behavior and gave them the rhetorical leverage to justify, obscure, or deny that the heroes of the story were slaves acting badly.[66]

In contrast, their experience of slavery could have equipped Xenophon's and Chariton's ex-slave readers to sympathize with the protagonists as slaves rather than elites who happened to be slaves. The normative reader, who knew slavery only as a slave-owner, had been conditioned to ignore socially marginalized slaves except when they were following (or not following) his commands. Such readers may have been inclined to overlook or discount the significance of ordinary slaves, characters such as Leucon and Rhode, Lampon and Clytus, Leonas and Plangon, and the 14 slaves chained up with Chaereas and Polycharmus. In contrast, ex-slave readers would have been sensitive to the sympathy that was implied for these real slaves in addition to the enslaved protagonists. Finally, ex-slave readers, because of their ambiguous social status, could have been in particular sympathy with Xenophon's and Chariton's ambivalence to bad-slave behavior. In this case, the author's ambivalence may have resonated with readers who were no longer slaves, but freedmen who had themselves become slave-owners and who were assimilating the attitudes of their new status. The defensiveness and ambivalence that these authors attached to their sympathy for enslaved protagonists may reflect the complicated perspective of these readers.[67]

In their representation of slavery, *Ephesiaca* and *Callirhoe* accommodated the reading of both the normative elite reader and the ex-slave reader. However, it is useful to recall that Xenophon and Chariton each suggested, directly or indirectly, the authorial persona of a person who had been a slave. It is also possible that Chariton had ex-slaves in mind at the beginning of Book 8, when he promises his readers a happy ending that seems to be grounded in a transition from slavery and events associated with slavery (e.g., piracy, war, captivity) to freedom and what freedom affords (e.g., lawful marriage).[68] The reading concretized by the ex-slave reader may be more complete and, possibly, the reading indicated by these authors. For example, the normative elite reader would have read the explicit narrative of Callirhoe's enslavement to Dionysius as a love affair between two noble individuals; the ex-slave reader would have read both this narrative and another, implicit one that dealt with the power and coercion of the master and the desperation and resistance of the slave. The normative reader was likely to pass over the episode in which Dionysius struck his slave Leonas as a minor incident in the main love story; an ex-slave reader (someone who had once been struck herself?) was more likely to pause and wonder what Callirhoe was thinking in her silence at that moment.

Ex-slave readers: means, opportunity, and motive

During the first century CE, that is, around the time when Xenophon was writing *Ephesiaca* and Chariton was writing *Callirhoe*, literate slaves and freedman were contributing significantly to the cultural and intellectual life of the empire. The epigraphical record indicates that elite households employed educated slaves in a wide range of occupations. Slaves and freedmen worked as accountants, business agents, stewards, architects, doctors, secretaries, librarians, and clerks. However, literate slaves and ex-slaves distinguished themselves, especially as teachers and scholars. Fifteen of the 21 *grammatici* in Suetonius' biographical survey of teachers and scholars of literature and rhetoric from this period, the *De grammaticis et rhetoribus* (*DGR*), were ex-slaves.[69] As teachers these ex-slaves introduced the children of the elite to the study of literature and philology. They authored original works in a range of genres: grammatical and philological studies and textual commentaries in addition to historical and geographical studies, philosophy, satire, and mime. These teachers and literary men belonged to a wider group of educated slaves on whose expertise and judgment the nobility relied in the full range of their personal, political, and economic endeavors. During the republic, a noble household would have been invested in the education of such slaves.[70] Noble patrons freed such slaves not only to secure their continued loyalty and service but also in recognition of their expertise and attainments. During the principate, the practice of relying on the expertise of educated slaves led to the evolution of the *familia Caesaris*, the slaves of the imperial family, who assisted their master, that is, the emperor, in the administration of the empire.[71] This ex-slave elite would have been literate in both Greek and Latin; many would have been native speakers of Greek.[72]

100 *Two novels about slavery*

Educated ex-slaves held the trust of their patrons. They were charged, for example, with the education of their patron's children. Cornelius Epicadus (*DGR*, 12), a freedman of Cornelius Sulla, taught Sulla's son Faustus. Q. Caecilius Epirota, the *verna*, or home-born slave, of Cicero's friend Atticus tutored Attica, his patron's daughter. Connections of a personal nature may be indicated in the example of the first-century BCE freedman Lutatius Daphnis (*DGR*, 3) who assisted his patrons, M. Aemilius Scaurus (cos. 115) and Q. Lutatius Catulus (cos. 102), in the composition of their memoirs; Epicadus completed the memoirs of his patron, Sulla. There is some evidence of esteem of a more general character between ex-slave *grammatici* and the nobility. Staberius Eros (*DGR*, 13) won praise for teaching gratis the sons of the proscribed during the Sullan proscriptions. M. Verrius Flaccus (*DGR*, 17), who tutored Augustus' grandsons, wrote books on Latin philology, Etruscan history, and Roman religion, and edited the *Fasti Praenestini*, was honored at Praeneste with a statue erected in his honor displayed together with a marble copy of the *Fasti*.[73] Ex-slave *grammatici* publicly proclaimed their relationship with their noble patrons. Epicadus liked to think of himself as Faustus' freedman as well as Sulla's. Melissus, a freedman of Maecenas, rejected an opportunity to assert freeborn status so that he could remain Maecenas' freedman (*DGR*, 21). The evidence in Suetonius suggests that these slaves and ex-slaves identified with their owners and patrons, that is, with the slave-owning elite, more than they identified with other slaves or ex-slaves.

The example of *grammatici* indicates that in the first centuries BCE and CE, there were educated ex-slaves who had the necessary education, leisure, and resources not only to read novels such as *Ephesiaca* and *Callirhoe* but even to write them. That is, they had means and opportunity. But would they have had motive? If their experience of slavery had been, as it seems from the evidence of the *DGR*, relatively benign, would educated ex-slave authors have felt a need to make slavery a focus of their literary efforts, much less to write critically about slavery? Then, would educated ex-slave readers have constituted a receptive audience for such narratives?[74]

I believe an argument for motive can be found in imperial society's continuing degradation of even elite freedmen. The evidence that follows is Roman. However, the representation of slavery in *Ephesiaca* and *Callirhoe* reflects details particular to the Roman practice of slavery.[75] First of all, we should be wary of taking Suetonius' account of the amicable relations between ex-masters and their educated ex-slaves at face value or as typical. Elite writers cannot be relied on as objective recorders of the attitudes of slaves and ex-slaves. Slave-owners had motive to emphasize the positive affectual ties between patrons and ex-slaves; such ties helped prove that slavery was a just institution that could recognize worthy individuals even if they were slaves. Conversely, elite sources might ignore or misrepresent educated ex-slaves who were resentful and embittered because of slavery. Second, even in the more benign form experienced by educated slaves, slavery entailed degradation. Despite their education and intellectual attainment, these slaves were still owned as property. They could be bought, sold, and even punished like other slaves in the *familia urbana*, the cooks, chambermaids, and

Two novels about slavery 101

doormen. Like other slaves, educated slaves had no recognized legal identity and no right to their own family.[76] They may have felt apart from the majority of slaves in the household; however, at the same, because of their intelligence and education, and, in some cases, their familiarity with the law, educated slaves may have recognized that they were subject to the constraints faced by all slaves. The educated slave could have felt injustice no less keenly than an ordinary slave.[77]

Nor did manumission erase the past. As I noted in the Introduction, despite their wealth, accomplishments, and connections, ex-slaves still had to cope with legal and social subordination to their former masters, civil disabilities, and social degradation. Freeborn elite were often uncomfortable with the literary attainment of the *grammatici*.[78] From the elite perspective, the freedman bore this stigma of slavery, the *macula servitutis*, regardless of his accomplishments.[79] This prejudice is well attested in a range of texts, literary, legal, rhetorical, and historical. I have chosen three passages that illustrate the meanness of this prejudice, its broad acceptance among the elite, and the significant degree to which it might inform elite behavior.[80] Martial's mean-spirited portrait of a wealthy freedman in the Theater of Marcellus (2.29) treats the *macula servitutis* as an actual scar. A freedman sits in the *subsellia*, prestigious seats reserved for magistrates and other VIPs. He is beautifully and expensively dressed, bejeweled, coifed, and scented. But what are those bandages stuck to his forehead? Well, Martial says, peel them off and read! The man's bandages cover brand marks. He had been a slave and not merely a slave but a bad slave, one whose forehead had been branded in punishment, perhaps for trying to run away.[81]

The Elder Seneca relates a cautionary tale for public speakers involving Quintus Haterius (*Controversiae* 4. pr. 10): While defending a freedman client alleged to be his patron's concubine, Haterius tried to deflect the charge by arguing, "Sexual impurity (*impudicitia*) is a crime in the case of a freeborn citizen (*in ingenuo crimen*); in the case of a slave, it is a necessity (*in servo necessitas*); in the case of a freedman, an obligation (*in liberto officium*)." The jurors must have found this funny, but not only the jury. Seneca notes that *officium* became a popular joke, a double entendre for shameful sexual submission among an elite who were ready to see a freedman's pretensions to *dignitas* as a motive for laughter: "You're not doing your 'duty' to me and he really spends a lot of time doing his 'duty' to him" ("*non facis mihi officium" et "multum ille huic in officiis versatur*").[82]

This assumption of servile and, therefore, libertine sexual unchasteness provides the context of the humor in a letter Pliny wrote to his friend and fellow senator, Pontius Allifanus (*Ep.* 7.4). While reading a book by Asinius Gallus, Pliny writes, he came across an erotic epigram that Cicero was supposed to have written about his secretary Tiro (*epigramma Ciceronis in Tironem suum*). It is unclear whether Tiro is to be imagined as a slave or freedman at the time, and it may not matter. For classicists, the existence of such an epigram itself may trigger a sensation of cognitive dissonance: the *maximus orator* and his diligent amanuensis canoodling? Tiro a boy toy? A consensus emerged

102 *Two novels about slavery*

that Cicero could not have written such a poem; rather, Asinius Gallus was himself the author and sought to traduce Cicero, his father's political rival.[83] However, even if Cicero had not written the epigram, it is significant that Pliny believed he had and then taken the orator as a model for his own playful imitation.

The historical question of author and addressee is less relevant than the fact that a slave-owner (or *patronus*) cast himself in the active role of *erōtēs* and his slave (or freedman) in the passive role of *erōmenos* in a game of homoerotic poetry (*lascivum … lusum*). Part of the game entails that Pliny make fun of himself. But the rules of the game also reflected how Pliny and his class thought about freedmen. Even a highly educated and erudite ex-slave such as Cicero's Tiro could be reduced to an object vulnerable to shameful sexual penetration. Taking Cicero (or "Cicero") as his model, Pliny shifts into hexameters and complains that his own favored slave or freedman, that is, his own "Tiro," has cheated him of some kisses he was owed after dinner. He concludes (*Ep.* 7.4.6):

> When I read this I said, "Why do I hide my love and make nothing public? Do we admit that we have known Tiro's sly tricks (*Tironisque dolos*), Tiro's fleeing charms (*Tironis nosse fugaces blanditias*) and his thefts, which add fuel to my fire (*furta nouas addentia flammas*)?"

Pliny makes fun of himself but at the expense of the slave (or ex-slave). His play reflects a broadly held attitude that entailed the freedman's continuing subordination and the patron's entitlement to his freedman's compliance. This play also reflects the key aspects of the freedman stereotype. Pliny casts doubts on the freedman's sexual purity by casting him as the object of his erotic attention. He evokes Tiro's servile character (or the persistent servile character of the *libertus*) through reference to "Tiro's" coyness as sly tricks (*dolos*), runaway charms (*fugaces blanditias*), and thefts (*furta*).[84] He is, of course, only joking, playing a game. Pliny and Allifanus may have enjoyed a good laugh. Ex-slaves maybe not so much. In the elite imagination, "*Tiro erōmenos*" displaced and degraded the ex-slave who would have been like a real Tiro, someone who earned his freedom because he was his master's (or patron's) educated, accomplished, and trusted confidant, not as a return for sex.[85]

It seems plausible that disdain of this sort would work against an educated ex-slave's inclination with his ex-master and motivate instead pushback and counter-assertion, that is, a continuation of the resistance practiced in slavery, but now under new conditions.[86] In this context, we might consider the evidence of the *Suda* (II. 414/3045), which notes a Phoenician ex-slave of the Hadrianic period, Hermippus of Berytos, the title of whose book, *On Slaves Who Distinguished Themselves in Education*, may indicate that slaves and ex-slaves were proud of their intellectual achievement and thought of themselves as a distinct group.[87] Other educated ex-slaves might have been motivated to tell the story of what it meant to be a slave from a slave's point of view. They could have found a form for such a story in the emerging genre of prose fiction, a genre

Two novels about slavery 103

not burdened by the elite or citizen ideological agenda of epic, or lyric, or tragedy and a genre that was able to accommodate new voices. I suggest that we have surviving examples of such stories in Xenophon's *Ephesiaca* and Chariton's *Callirhoe*.[88]

Reading Xenophon and Chariton as an ex-slave

Consider first the plots of these two novels in terms of the protagonists' enslavement, their experience as slaves, and their escape from slavery. It seems possible that a plot of this design would have signified differently for an ex-slave reader, who, in some sense, had lived it, than for readers who had never been slaves. However, in addition to the main arc of their narratives, Xenophon and Chariton made use of particular motifs and themes that could also have elicited responses from ex-slave readers peculiar to their experience as slaves. Some of these motifs and themes, such as the nobility of the protagonists and the chasteness of the heroine, would seem, as literary phenomena, universal in their application and appeal.[89] This section argues that even these seeming universals had a peculiar appeal for the ex-slave reader.[90]

The Scheintod *motif*

Novel scholars use the German term *Scheintod*, or "false death," in reference to the motif in which a character is believed to have died but is actually alive.[91] The motif was well established long before the novel emerged.[92] As a narrative strategy the false-death motif was useful in creating dramatic suspense and melodramatic reversal in a variety of situations; for example, Orestes' shocking discovery of his sister Iphigeneia at Tauris, rescued by Artemis from sacrifice long ago. An important point of a false death was that it was false and, in that, signaled that there was hope even in a time of great despair, that even death, perhaps, might be conquered. This powerful message is implicit in a version of the motif in which a hero journeys to the Underworld and returns: Heracles, Theseus, Odysseus, and Aeneas.[93] From the perspective of Christian doxology, Christ really did die and his resurrection would not represent, properly speaking, an instance of *Scheintod*; nonetheless, a related idea may be implied in the motif of the empty tomb.[94]

Scheintod could have had a particular appeal for enslaved persons. In *Slavery and Social Death*, Orlando Patterson described enslavement as a ritual process that began with the symbolic death of a free person. The slave lived but as a marginalized individual in the master's household, someone of no importance, someone who was "dead" in social terms. The comments of jurisprudents in the *Digest* reveal the presence of this idea in Roman thinking. Florentinus observed, for example, that slaves are called *servi* because the commanders *spare* the lives of those whom they take prisoner instead of killing them (*Dig.* 1.5.4, *servare nec occidere solent*). In a discussion regarding the inheritability of legacies, Ulpian made the association between slavery and death explicit. A

104 *Two novels about slavery*

legacy would terminate in the event of the legatee's death; a legacy would also terminate if the legatee should be sentenced to slavery, "because slavery is likened to death" (*Dig.* 35.1.59 *quia servitus morti adsimulatur*).

In *Callirhoe*, the heroine's false death and burial in Syracuse led directly to her enslavement in Miletus. Callirhoe expressed the idea that her enslavement was a form of death, calling her slavery "another tomb, lonelier than the first" (1.14.6, ἰδοὺ," φησὶν "ἄλλος τάφος ... ἐρημότερος ἐκείνου μᾶλλον). Chaereas' enslavement was also associated with his symbolic death. Dionysius allowed Callirhoe, now his wife, to construct a cenotaph for her first husband, after he convinced her that Chaereas had died (4.1.2). The author connected Chaereas' symbolic entombment explicitly with his enslavement. As Callirhoe consecrates the memorial to her first husband in Miletus, Chariton switches the scene to Caria, where Chaereas is working as a slave on Mithridates' estate (4.2.1, Καλλιρόη μὲν οὖν ἐν Μιλήτῳ Χαιρέαν ἔθαπτε, Χαιρέας δὲ ἐν Καρίᾳ δεδεμένος εἰργάζετο).[95]

The association of *Scheintod* with enslavement is also present in Xenophon. The same oracle (1.6.2) that instructed protagonists' parents to marry them also prompted them to send Habrocomes and Anthia on the sea voyage during which they were captured by pirates and enslaved. After predicting their enslavement, the oracle suggested a puzzling association between the protagonists' common tomb, their wedding chamber, and obliterating fire (καὶ τάφος ἀμφοτέροις θάλαμος καὶ πῦρ ἀΐδηλον). This may depict the protagonists' wedding as the ill-fated prelude to their metaphorical death as slaves.[96] Later, in the course of the pirate attack itself, Xenophon implies the idea that slavery was a substitute for death when his protagonists surrender themselves as slaves in return for their lives (1.13.6, ἡμᾶς οἰκέτας ἔχε, φεῖσαι δὲ τῆς ψυχῆς). The connection between *Scheintod* and slavery is more certain in Anthia's second enslavement, which Xenophon may have modeled on the events leading up to the enslavement of Callirhoe.[97] Anthia is on the point of being sacrificed to Ares by a gang of Cilician bandits when she is saved by the imperial official Perilaos, who then falls in love with her. As he grows more insistent in pressing her to marry him, Anthia tries to kill herself. The potion she swallows, however, merely induces sleep. Robbers find her alive in the rich tomb where she had been buried. They then sell her to slave dealers in Egypt (3.7–9). After that, she passes, by sale or capture from one owner to another until she is freed by Hippothoos. Habrocomes, in the meantime, having learned of Anthia's death, has set out to retrieve her body (3.9–10).

This search takes him to Sicily, where, in another episode, Xenophon seems to play with the *Scheintod* motif. Habrocomes is staying with Aigialeus, a poor fisherman who had mummified the corpse of his beloved wife, Thelxinoe (5.1.2). Aigialeus tells his guest how he continued to speak to Thelxinoe, to lie with her, and to dine with her as if she were alive. When he returns home weary from fishing, he finds in her a source of consolation. He still looks on her as the young girl with whom he had fallen in love, not the mummified corpse of an old woman (5.1.10–11). Habrocomes and Aigialeus act under complementary misperceptions of how things were. Habrocomes acts within the narrative conventions of the *Scheintod* in his search for Anthia's corpse, believing that she was dead when, in fact, she was still alive. Aigialeus reverses the scenario. He has preserved Thelxinoe's corpse and continues to live with it as if she were alive. Was Xenophon playing with the motif and creating a *"Scheinleben"* as the counterpoint to the *Scheintod*?[98] If the *Scheintod* is a precursor to slavery, that is, a state of being (socially) dead while living, the *"Scheinleben"* might then show how love may keep "socially alive" (i.e., alive in spirit) someone who has died.[99]

The traditional narrative motif of false death contained a universal human message of the possibility of hope even during a time of deep despair. In spiritual or religious terms, the motif expressed the hope that even death might be overcome. The same motif could have had particular significance for enslaved persons. Even in slavery, a kind of living death, there was the hope of freedom. As the protagonist was revealed as alive, so would she be released from slavery. Such an idea could have been present in the hidden transcripts that slaves told one another. Similarly, the *Scheintod* motif could have reminded Xenophon's and Chariton's ex-slave readers of the despair they felt in slavery and the hope that had been confirmed in their manumission, a metaphorical return from death to life.[100]

The themes of symmetrical erōs *and* sōphrosynē

In *Sexual Symmetry*, David Konstan argued that the construction of love distinguished the Greek novel from other literary genres, which tended to represent *erōs* as a transitory, nonreciprocated passion, involving individuals, homosexual as well as heterosexual, of different status.[101] Instead, the protagonists' love was reciprocal. They themselves were of equivalent age and status. Their bond was lasting, realized fully in marriage, and conceived as lasting even after one of the lovers had died. In the case of the protagonists of *Ephesiaca* and *Callirhoe*, this commitment persisted even through slavery. While Konstan may, in some instances, overstate the symmetry between novel protagonists,[102] his observation seems on target in broad outline.[103]

Reciprocal *erōs*, Konstan argued, evolved in the context of the decline of the *polis* as the focus of political life:

> [C]orrespondingly, social relations among individuals were apprehended as private affairs, motivated not by traditional civic concerns but by personal desire. Where obligations to family, patrimony, and the city had formerly constituted the ideological matrix for marriage, the motive for marriage was now constructed as spontaneous love or passion.[104]

It can be argued that the novels' emphasis on reciprocal love between equal partners would also have had a particular appeal for enslaved individuals. Love and the need for love, an affirming confirmation of one's human worth, are human universals. For slaves, however, love took on additional significance in the

106   *Two novels about slavery*

context of their systematic degradation. The symmetry between the male and female lovers in the novel might also have had a particular significance. Male and female slaves, who had no family, no property, and no rights as citizens, were made more equal than male and female citizens, who possessed different and unequal rights and privileges. Asymmetric and transgressive love is present in the novels; however, it is represented by the individuals who have power over the protagonists, who wish to exploit them sexually: in Xenophon, the pirates, the wicked mistresses Manto and Cyno, and the succession of Anthia's would-be rapists and in Chariton, Dionysius and Artaxerxes. Finally, the emphasis of *erōs* in the context of marriage corresponded to a particular concern of slaves and ex-slaves. Slaves had no right to legal marriage; they might be separated from their partners, sold apart, even given to other partners according to the dictate of the owner. The natural relationships of parent, child, and sibling had no legal standing under slavery. Freedom, however, gave the ex-slave the right to legitimate marriage and to establish a secure family, one that could not be broken up according to the master's will.

Enslavement separates the married protagonists of *Ephesiaca* and *Callirhoe*, who then strive to remain faithful and be reunited. The two novels also indicate a concern for a reunion that included the broader family. In Xenophon, Habrocomes' and Anthia's parents die from despair at their separation from their children (5.15.3). On their return to Ephesus, Habrocomes and Anthia create an ersatz family that included Leucon and Rhode, who were their former slaves, their former fellow slaves, and who were now their fellow freedmen. In Chariton, circumstances forced Chaereas and Callirhoe to return to Syracuse without their son, whom they left behind with Callirhoe's former master. They consoled themselves by thinking of him as a fellow citizen of Syracuse (8.7.12), with whom one day they would be reunited (2.9.6).[105]

The right to create a secure family was thus a major benefit of freedom for the ex-slave. Henrik Mouritsen notes the valorization of this benefit in freedman inscriptions that emphasized family relationships through naming patterns that commemorated family beyond the nucleus of parents and children.[106] Rose MacLean notes patterns of freedman commemoration that emphasized the relationships freedmen had formed in slavery with their fellow slaves over the connection with the former master and patron; freedman husbands and wives, for example, referred to one another as *contubernales*, a reference to their relationship before they had been able to marry as *iusti coniuges*.[107]

These inscriptions implied the fidelity of the spouses, in possible rejection of elite stereotyping. Michele George sees a similar valorization of family in family relief portraits of freedmen that begin to appear in Rome and Italy in the late republic. George notes that husband and wife commemorations were most common; children were often included; sometimes individuals outside the nuclear family group were present too. The inclusion of nonfamily members in some group portraits may have reflected a continuing relationship among former *conservi*. Slaves and freedmen valued loyalty and permanence in their nonerotic relationships as well.[108]

George also observed how these group portraits represented the freedwoman as possessing the virtues of a Roman *matrona*: through her costume, with the *stola* and *vitta* of the *matrona*, and through her gesture, both the traditional *pudicitia* gesture and the *coniunctio dextrarum*, or clasping of right hands with her husband.[109] George argued that freedwomen, in representing themselves in the style and manner of the *matrona*, "could reform the moral universe they had inhabited as slaves and declare their willingness to be judged by the same standards of decency as freeborn women."[110] The freedwoman's assertion of *pudicitia* was thus a form of counter-assertion against the degradation that it was assumed she had experienced in slavery and that was still attached to her after manumission.[111]

For the ex-slave reader, Xenophon's and Chariton's representation of the enduring *erōs* that motivated their protagonists to be rejoined could also have functioned as an affirmation of moral worth. The female protagonists of *Ephesiaca* and *Callirhoe*, who strove against all odds to be reunited, expressed in narrative form the sculptural motif of the *coniunctio dextrarum*. Anthia's repeated defense of her *sōphrosynē* and Callirhoe's reassertion of this virtue, despite having had to surrender it, align as narrative with the representation of the freedwoman in funerary commemoration as a Roman *matrona*.[112] In the context of the slave experience, Xenophon's and Chariton's ex-slave readers may have also seen the heroines' devotion to *sōphrosynē* as an affirming pushback against the sexual denigration of female slaves and freedwomen.

The motif of the unheroic hero

Scholars of the novel have perceived a relative passivity in the protagonists but remarked on this quality with particular reference to the hero.[113] In *Ephesiaca*, for example, when pirates attack their ship, Habrocomes is not among those who resist. He and Anthia surrender themselves at once into slavery. In *Callirhoe*, Chaereas gives in to despair and was twice ready to kill himself (3.5.6 and 7.1.5). Callirhoe was, in comparison, a resolute, if anguished, heroine.

Various explanations, cultural and literary, have been offered for the unheroic-hero motif.[114] However, it may be productive to consider the idea specifically in the context of a male protagonist who has been enslaved. In certain respects, the novel hero lost more in becoming a slave than the heroine did. Enslavement denied recourse to elite self-assertion through direct speech or direct action, in particular violent action. The female protagonist did not possess these freedoms to begin with.[115] A similar dynamic was at play in American slavery. Historians have noted that the system worked to emasculate the male slave, depriving him of any right to self-defense against his owner and allowing him no legal standing as a husband or father and, thus, depriving him of his role as provider and protector of his wife and children.[116] Many enslaved African American men tried to resist the emasculating effect of slavery as they resisted other aims of the institution, but not all succeeded to the same degree.[117] This is the context in which Frederick Douglass prefaced the episode in which he finally attacked his abusive

108 *Two novels about slavery*

overseer: "You have seen how a man was made a slave; you shall see how a slave was made a man."[118] Violence made the man.

It may be possible to read the representation of this motif in *Ephesiaca* and *Callirhoe* in the context of the emasculating effect of slavery on the enslaved male. Ex-slave readers of Xenophon might have understood, although not necessarily have approved, Habrocomes' unheroic failure to stand up to Cyno. But they might have foreseen how his earlier heroic resistance to Manto was foolish for a slave. The sympathies of ex-slave readers in this case may have aligned with Habrocomes' fellow slave Leucon, who warned Habrocomes not to bring disaster on himself and his fellow slaves. Indeed, disaster was the immediate outcome of Habrocomes' heroic but ill-advised rejection of Manto. Similarly, Chaereas is unheroic for much of *Callirhoe*, worthy, perhaps, of pity but not admiration. However, he is able to redeem himself at the end of the novel through a display of military valor. Chaereas' *lampron telos* is all that matters. For ex-slave male readers in particular, the hero's definitive self-assertion could have served as a form of vicarious redemption for indignities they had to endure passively when slaves.

The motif of the protagonists' nobility[119]

Ex-slave readers may also have found a form of pushback against degradation in the representation of Xenophon's and Chariton's protagonists as elite citizens.[120] In narration, it seems a given that a protagonist is noble. In addition, the temporary enslavement of a noble, or even divine, protagonist was a familiar move in traditional storytelling. Heracles, for example, was made a slave to Queen Omphale as punishment for the murder of Iphitus. Apollo and Poseidon were enslaved to King Laomedon of Troy after joining in a revolt against Zeus.[121] In the context of this tradition, normative elite readers were likely to discount the slavery of the novel protagonists. Chaereas and Callirhoe, Habrocomes and Anthia would have been no more real slaves and no more affected by slavery than Heracles, Apollo, or Poseidon. But an ex-slave might have read this motif differently. Rather than seeing it as an illustration of the idea that a noble might become a slave, ex-slave readers might see it as an affirmation that a slave could actually be noble. For such readers, the motif could have served as a form of wish fulfillment or a negation of social degradation.

It is possible to observe the desire to assert one's nobility in historical slaves. Eunus, the leader of a slave rebellion in Sicily in the 130s BCE, assumed the royal name of Antiochus, a name traditional for the Seleucid kings who ruled the region where he had been born. In like manner, Salvius, the leader of the second Sicilian slave rebellion at the end of the second century BCE, called himself Tryphon, associating himself with another Seleucid ruler, Diodotus Tryphon. Tacitus noted that Claudius' freedman Pallas claimed that he was a descendent of Arcadian kings through Pallas, the son of Evander (*Ann.* 12.53.3). The historian and other elite writers regarded these claims of nobility with derision.[122] But for persons who had been systematically degraded as slaves

Two novels about slavery 109

and who faced continued scorn as freedmen, such claims expressed an assertion of worth and dignity and a negation of degradation.[123]

The theme of ambivalence

Xenophon and Chariton salt their sympathy for slaves with ambivalence and reservation. Xenophon, for example, implies this ambivalence in the accommodation of Anthia's many deceptions to the social rank of her antagonist: The lower the assailant, the grosser the deception. Chariton's heroine herself expresses reservations about her role in the deception of Dionysius. Callirhoe passes responsibility for the deception on to others: first, to her unborn child and absent husband who overrule her desire to die and, later, to the clever real slave Plangon to whom she entrusts the execution of the deception. However, in the implicit narrative, Chariton represents Callirhoe as a full participant in this necessary deception of her owner.

The apologetics for the protagonists' behavior intensify when the protagonists are forced to turn to violent resistance. Xenophon justifies Anthia's violence by making her victim a brigand on the very point of raping her. Habrocomes earns a degree of exoneration when he backs out of the conspiracy to murder his master before the crime was committed. When he was nonetheless punished for the crime, Xenophon asserts his protagonist's guiltlessness through two divine interventions. In *Callirhoe*, Chaereas' implied involvement in a slave outbreak is only darkly hinted in the silences and incongruities of the author's third-person version. In their own accounts of the event, Polycharmus and Chaereas disassociated themselves from their fellow slaves against the logic of events.

These expressions of ambivalence could suggest texts that were unresolved ideologically, in conflict with themselves. The protagonists' bad-slave behavior was necessary for their survival. Why, then, the reservations, the need for apologetics? In part, these reservations would accommodate the sensibilities of normative elite readers who instinctively disapproved of bad-slave behavior. But we may also see here the operation of a rhetorical reflex from slavery, the disinclination to express the thoughts of the hidden transcript in direct and unmuted form. The apologetics and ambivalence provide camouflage for the bad behavior. Finally, the ambivalent affirmation and reservation of the protagonists' servile behavior may have reflected contradictions in the consciousness of ex-slave readers themselves. As ex-slaves, they would remember what they once had to do to survive. The memory of their previous life prepared them to understand and condone the protagonists' bad-slave behavior. However, these ex-slaves had now become slave-owners themselves and were acquiring the normative attitudes of their new status. They found themselves in the uncomfortable situation of learning to despise what they had once been. Such readers had reason to mute and veil memories of slavery from themselves. The contradictions in the representation of bad-slave behavior in *Ephesiaca* and *Callirhoe* may have reflected contradictions of their own conflicted social identities.[124]

110   *Two novels about slavery*

In brief, while the motifs and themes discussed above can be treated as literary phenomena, perhaps universal in their narrative interest, they nonetheless could have had particular significance for ex-slave readers, to whom they offered a reflection of lived experience, the possibility of consolation for past suffering, the rationalization and redemption for morally dubious acts, and the affirmation of personal worth and counter-assertion against past and continuing degradation.

Two novels about slavery

As Sara Forsdyke reminds us through the title of her 2012 book, slaves told tales. Slaves had access to fables, myths, folktales, anecdotes, rumors, gossip, jokes, mimes, and songs – all of which they could select and adapt to fashion their own hidden transcript of master–slave relations.[125] The tradition of servile literary production and intellectual resistance has been lost as such to us. However, it was available to Xenophon and Chariton. These and other authors did not have to invent the negative representation of slavery that appears in their novels. Rather, they could draw on a tradition of criticism that had originated during slavery itself, the tales that slaves told. They could adapt themes and ideas they found in the hidden transcripts of slavery and insinuate them in a new form, the novel, and for a new audience mixed of traditional elite and literate ex-slaves.

During the late first century BCE and first century CE, literate freedmen were contributing significantly to imperial cultural and intellectual life. Their social position was complex and contradictory. They were ex-slaves who now owned slaves. They possessed wealth and influence but endured continuing social disdain. The stories they had told as slaves did not speak to their new condition as wealthy and influential freedmen. Nor did the literary canon of elite *paideia* address their life experience as degraded ex-slaves. Authors such as Xenophon and Chariton, who themselves may have been among these elite ex-slaves, turned to the medium of extended prose fiction to tell their story – a new kind of story for a newly important population of reader, the literate ex-slave.[126] These authors fashioned a narrative that focused on the enslavement and slave experience of the protagonists. They pushed back against normative elite thinking about slaves. They sympathized with their protagonists when they were forced to act like stereotypically bad slaves. They held up slave-owners to critical inspection.

The novel allowed Xenophon and Chariton to represent master–slave relations in more complexity and detail than, for example, the fable. In place of the fable's animal allegories, the novel represented human slavery directly, as human slavery. The genre's human point of view focused on the personal interactions between masters and slaves and the complex emotions that affected both. The genre's ability to contain multiple voices allowed Xenophon and Chariton to combine their adaptation of hidden transcripts with the elements drawn from established genres such as epic, tragedy, comedy, history, rhetoric, and philosophy.[127] The learnedness of their novels spoke to the sophistication of their readers, both traditional elite and ex-slave.

Two novels about slavery 111

We cannot be sure, but Xenophon and Chariton may have played a role in associating the new genre with the narration of slavery, perhaps making the enslavement of the protagonist a marker of the genre. The surviving novels that were published after *Ephesiaca* and *Callirhoe*, Longus' *Daphnis and Chloe*, Achilles Tatius' *Leucippe and Clitophon*, and the *Aethiopica* of Heliodorus all narrate the enslavement of one or both of the protagonists. But each of these novels in their own way rejects or ignores the ideological position on slavery staked out by Xenophon and Chariton. Longus' novel represents slavery as a culturally articulated expression of the inequality that exists in nature, something both natural and inevitable. Achilles Tatius exploits the slavery for generic experimentation and play. Heliodorus uses slavery as a metaphor to distinguish the chaste, almost Platonic, love of his protagonists from earthly physical love, a form of *erōs* that he likens to a kind of slavery.

Notes

1 Cf. Edwards 2009, 156–157, who, in her study of Seneca's complex use of the master-slave metaphor, observed (while channeling Lévi-Strauss) that ancient elites found slaves "irresistibly good to think with." Edwards also suggests that Seneca's use of slavery as a metaphor could have drawn some of his readers into sympathy with actual slaves and their predicament.
2 Cf. Bradley 1994, 51–54; Bodel 2005.
3 On *alumni*, cf. Rawson 2003, 250–263, who notes that such children could be of free or slave status but tended to be subordinate (pp. 250–251): "poor orphans, poor relations, foundlings, sometimes apprentices." The *alumnus*, Rawson also notes, was known as a *collacteus* in relation to other children in the family. *Collacteus*, like *syntrophos*, was a reciprocal term. The Lex Aelia Sentia included *collactei* among the individuals who could be freed when the master was below the age of 20, suggesting a real-world parallel to the close relationship among the *syntrophoi* in *Ephesiaca*.
4 On obligatory *operae*, cf. Crook 1967, 52–54. Mouritsen 2011, 224–226, however, argues that the prominence of *operae* in the legal sources misrepresents the day-to-day reality. Habrocomes' obligation to stay with Apsyrtos may also be understood in terms of a Greek *paramonē* agreement between ex-master and freed slave: see the earlier discussion, p. 45.
5 On *obsequium* and the *libertus ingratus*, Mouritsen 2011, 51–65. Cicero wished to rescind the manumission of two freedmen who deserted their post while escorting his son in Cilicia (*Att.* 7.2.8); cf. Mouritsen 2011, 54–55 on the incident.
6 Cf. Columella 1.7.6.
7 See Aubert 1994, 183–199 on the managerial staff of agricultural estates. Kirschenbaum 1987, 148–160 surveys the range of activities in which slaves and freedmen would operate on their master's or patron's behalf; Broekaert 2016 surveys a range of views regarding the relationship between owners or patrons and their slave or freedmen agents; from epigraphical evidence, he proposes different models for interaction between the principals and their agents.
8 Columella 1.8 on the character and responsibilities of the *vilicus*; 12.1–3 for the character and duties of the *vilica*, on which Carlsen 1993. The relationship between Phocas and Plangon may have been exceptional. Roth 2004 argues that the evidence was tenuous for the consensus view that *vilicus* and *vilica* tended to be *contubernales*.
9 Baslez 1992, 202.

112 *Two novels about slavery*

10 For example, Marc Antony installed Theophilus, a Greek freedman, as his chief agent in Corinth (cf. Plutarch, *Antony*, 67, τὸν ἐν Κορίνθῳ διοικητὴν). The practice continued under the principate. Slaves and freedmen are found at all levels of administration, from clerks to administrators: cf. Bowersock 1965; Weaver 1972; Morley 2011.

11 Morley 2011, 284–285.

12 Bradley 1994, 32–46 discusses five principle sources for new slaves: warfare, breeding, infant exposure, trade, and piracy and kidnapping. While the relative importance of these sources varied according to time and circumstance, warfare and piracy played a role throughout; cf. Harris 1980, 117–125; Schumacher 2001, 34–43, with discussion of literary and archaeological evidence of piracy during the Bronze Age and archaic period.

13 On fear as a tool for controlling slaves, cf. Bradley 1987, 113–137; Rodríquez Gervás 2007.

14 Cf. the catalogue of crucifixions assembled from Latin texts by Cook 2014, 51–214, who notes that legal reasons for the penalty included (p. 216) "brigandage or political disturbance such as rebellion, slave revolts, disobedience of slaves, various crimes of soldiers including acts of disobedience, and piracy." The most famous instance of a mass crucifixion was Crassus' execution of 6,000 slaves captured after the defeat of Spartacus in 71 BCE.

15 Cf. Booth 1961, 129–133; Stanzel 1984, 127–130 notes how focus on the consciousness of a protagonist can produce intimacy and sympathy. Doody 1996, 33, on the desired impact of the erotic theme, may also be applied to how Xenophon's and Chariton's representation of slavery worked on the reader: "'The sufferings of love' is a generalizing phrase, but novels are never abstract, they deal always with particulars, and must aim to get the reader engrossed in specific characters, incidents, descriptions and observations."

16 On Callirhoe's consideration of abortion as a reflection of the reality for some slaves, see the earlier discussion, pp. 62–63, n. 21; on this passage as a reflection of the geographical and linguistic isolation of real slaves, see Bradley 1994, 47–48.

17 Harris 2001, 12.

18 Harris 2001, 317–336.

19 Harris 2001, 15.

20 The *topos* of Persian cruelty goes back at least to Herodotus.

21 Chariton repeatedly stresses that Dionysius is an *anēr pepaideumenos*, an individual imbued with the humanizing values of Greek *paideia*: 2.4.1; 3.2.6; 4.7.6; 5.5.1.

22 Chaereas, too, was capable of such excess. Seething with anger (τῷ θυμῷ ζέων), he had all Callirhoe's slaves tortured with whips and hot brands, including her favorite, whom he tortured twice over (1.5.1–2, ἐβασάνιζε τὰς θεραπαινίδας, πρώτην δὲ καὶ τελευταίαν τὴν ἄβραν. ἔτι δὲ καιομένων καὶ τεμνομένων αὐτῶν ἔμαθε τὴν ἀλήθειαν). Only then was he convinced that his wife was innocent of adultery.

23 Whitmarsh 2011, 26.

24 Tilg 2010, 50.

25 Tilg 2010, 24–36; also, Ruiz-Montero 1994, 1032–1033; Bowersock 1994, 40; Bowie 2002, 62; Reardon 2003, 328. Edwards 1994, 707–708 argues that Chariton's novel helped promote Aphrodisias' relationship to Rome through common investment in Aphrodite as both the city's tutelary deity and ancestor of the Julian *gens*.

26 Cf. Jones 1992; Tilg 2010, 49–50.

27 See Tilg 2010, 52–54, for discussion of the dedication. Athenagoras' designation as *stephanēphorus*, or crown-wearer, indicated that he had been (at some point) chief magistrate of Aphrodisias; Chariton's Athenagoras was a rhetor, a capacity that Tilg sees implied in this Athenagoras' activity as an ambassador.

Two novels about slavery   113

28 Cf. the comments of Whitmarsh 1998, 97 on Heliodorus' self-representation, biographical or not, as a Hellenized non-Greek. Such self-representation, Whitmarsh suggests, is intended to tell the reader something of the novel's perspective.

29 The parallel to Herodotus and Thucydides would align with the historical frame in which Chariton has set his love story, with its allusions to the Peloponnesian War and a war between Greeks and Persians. Herodotus is also identified as a citizen of Thurii.

30 Hunter 1994, 1069 sees Chariton's self-characterization as *hypographeus* in literary terms, as a narratorial move "away from authorial control of the material to the accurate recording of 'historical fact.'"

31 Cf. Joshel 1992. In the view of Edwards 1994, 701, "[a]s secretary for a rhetor Chariton would have intimate knowledge of the administrative operation of a city in the Greek East." Schwartz 2003, 379 notes that Chariton was "an insider with regard to the law."

32 Cf. Purcell 1983 on the various public assistants of magistrates, or *apparitores*, including, in addition to *scribae*, the *praecones*, *lictores*, and *viatores*. For those who had been excluded from society, such appointments, Purcell notes, provided (p. 171) "a licensed mechanism for social mobility." As Athenagoras' secretary Chariton would be distinct from the *hypographeis* of Hellenistic and Roman Egypt, who served as signatories and witnesses for illiterate individuals in their legal dealings: cf. Youtie 1975. However, Treu 1989b, 181–182 appears to have in mind these *hypographeis* and their monotonous work of drafting wills, contracts, and other legal documents in the suggestion that Chariton found a more varied use for his abilities in writing *Callirhoe*.

33 The name itself may have been a pseudonym. The *Suda* lists Xenophon of Ephesus between two other novel writers, a Xenophon of Antioch and a Xenophon of Cyprus. O'Sullivan 2014, 47 notes that authors of love novels may have assumed the name Xenophon to acknowledge Xenophon of Athens, whose *Cyropaedia* related the tragic love story of Pantheia and Abradatas.

34 Ruiz-Montero 1981 argues that the common underlying structure of the five surviving novels derives from the functions described by Propp in *Morphology of the Folktale*; Ruiz-Montero 2003, 45–47, argues that *Ephesiaca* has been structured as a whole in alignment with two folktale paradigms, the heroic quest, reflected in Habrocomes' search for Anthia, and the victimized hero, reflected in Anthia's travails. Anderson 2000, 50–57, 89–91, 145–157 argues that folktale paradigms underlay the structure of each of the five surviving novels. A weak form of this thesis seems correct: ancient writers of fiction had traditional narrative materials at their disposal and adapted them to suit their requirements; however, it is harder to demonstrate closer and interpretively significant dependence applied to the structure of an entire novel.

35 O'Sullivan 1995, 2014 argues on the basis of repeated scenes, scene elements, and formulaic language that the novel as a whole (2014, 50), "is a work deriving from a background of oral storytelling." In the view of Ruiz-Montero 2003, Xenophon adapted an oral style to the reworking of oral material of local origin. On the basis of stylistic elements such as repetition and recapitulation, Hägg 1994, 59–64 hypothesizes that Xenophon's (and Chariton's) readers included less experienced readers as well as listeners. König 2007 sees evidence for Xenophon's self-conscious use of an oral style in a narrative that moves "from voice to written text, from unpredictable to authoritative words"; a text that is "increasingly monumental, increasingly fixed and circumscribed"; and a text that mirrors the protagonists' life upon their return to Ephesus. Kim 2013, 309–311 discusses oral elements in Xenophon in a wider context of interaction between oral and literary texts.

114 *Two novels about slavery*

36 While Xenophon may have drawn inspiration for his heroine's cleverness from the trickster of folktale, he also aligns Anthia with the clever slave of Plautine comedy in her deception of the pimp.

37 Cf. König 2007, 3, who comments on the narrative impact of such repetition: "[T]hat very repetitiveness sometimes gives a sense of the difficulty of escaping from endlessly recycled patterns of action."

38 Cf. Hunter 2008, 261: "Who read this? is a question which scholars of the ancient novel, perhaps more than those engaged with any other Greek or Roman literary form, have persistently and anxiously posed." The fundamental nature of the question is reflected in other interrogative titles: "To whom did the ancient novelists address themselves?" (Levin 1977); "Who read ancient novels?" (Stephens 1994); "Κερκίδος παραμύθια? For whom did Chariton write?" (West 2003).

39 Not infinitely: in an essay on Bakhtin, Whitmarsh 2005b offers a sensible caveat on the extent of novel polyphony and openness.

40 Whitmarsh 2011, 10.

41 Harris 1989, 259–299. Cf. Wesseling 1988; Stephens 1994; Bowie 2003a. Possibility of increasing literacy: Holzberg 1995, 33–34.

42 The simple language and repetitive plot of *Ephesiaca* seem to demand less of the reader. However, as Tagliabue 2017 advises, we should consider Xenophon as an author with his own artistic agenda rather than condemn him as an unskilled hack.

43 Stephens 1994. Morgan 1995, 136 notes another possible index for the affluence of novel readers in mosaics found in a wealthy private home at Daphne, near Antioch, that may illustrate scenes from two novels, the *Ninos Romance* and *Parthenope and Metiochos*. See Quet 1992, 129–131, 135–137 for a description of the mosaics and the controversy regarding the identification of the Parthenope and Metiochos mosaic with the novel.

44 Thus, Cicero, in the *Pro Archia*, 23 (albeit in a forensic context): "Greek literature is read in nearly every nation, but Latin is confined within its own rather limited boundaries." Adams 2003, 9–14 surveys the anecdotal evidence for the Roman elite's knowledge of Greek; the anecdotal evidence, however, does not help us determine the extent and quality of this bilingualism.

45 Julian *Epistle* 89b, ἐρωτικὰς ὑποθέσεις καὶ πάντα ἁπλῶς τὰ τοιαῦτα.

46 Priscianus, *Rerum Medicarum Libri Quattuor*, 2.11.34.

47 Cf. Wesseling 1988; Treu 1989b; Bowie 2003a; Morgan 1995. In the view of Hägg 1983, 90–100, 107–108, the sophistication of the later novelists (and their readers) is not in doubt, but Xenophon and Chariton may have reached a wider audience through oral readings.

48 Harris 1989, 227–228; cf. Bowie 1989, 128 "lighter reading for the intelligensia" and Reardon 1991, 41, "the relaxation of the literate" – but not just that, because even escapism and entertainment are not simple ideas since "they imply a cultural context."

49 Perry 1967, 90.

50 Perry 1967, 48; cf. Holzberg 1995, 29–32.

51 Perry 1967, 98–101. Reardon 1991, 29 on Chariton, who wrote for the inhabitants of the late Hellenistic and imperial Greek world of the Eastern Mediterranean, offering a myth "of the private individual isolated and insecure in a world too big for him, and finding his security, his very identity in love." A similar view of Chariton's readers is found in Schmeling 1974, 30–33: "a literary creation built for the middle class by a middle-class writer" and 1980, 133 on Xenophon, whose readership was "one which suspends its intellectual judgments and appreciation for reality and adopts a view that events in life are simple." Hägg 1983, 97–90, posited that the new genre came into being as the epic of an atomized and multicultural Hellenistic world, "an open form for an open society," in which the certainties of the past no longer sufficed.

Two novels about slavery   115

52 Earlier Perry 1930, 130, n. 43, 134 suggested that, in the ideal novel's idealized view of romance, we have evidence for ancient juvenile literature, a genre meant for a primary audience of young readers and speculates whether Chariton himself was "a youngster."

53 Morgan 1995, 135. Hägg 1994 argues that the novels were accessible to both sophisticated readers and less sophisticated auditors. Cf. Doody 1996, 23, who argues that the genre's core audience were highly educated readers; however, such readers may well have read the novels aloud to the illiterate. In addition, the sophistication and erudition of the novels did not "preclude lower classes of readers, of course, for any novel can be enjoyed by people who do not 'get' all the literary play or by-play."

54 Swain 1996, 109; cf. Whitmarsh 2011, 7–9.

55 Swain 1996, 118–129.

56 Swain 1996. Cf. Haynes 2003, 161–162; Lalanne 2006, 60–65; Hunter 2008, 266–267.

57 On the novels and the construction of Greek identity, Whitmarsh 2011.

58 On women as novel readers (or listeners): Hägg 1994, 59–62; Konstan 1994, 78 (Chariton); Sandy 1994, 133–135, who sees "a *prima facie* case for supposing that the ancient novel was intended for, and catered to, female readers"; also, Holzberg 1995, 33–35; Johne 2003, 156–164, who moots an additional hypothesis (without evidence) that women were novel authors; Bremmer 1998, with a parallel argument for women readers of the *Apocryphal Acts*; West 2003, following Hägg's hypothesis of aural reception, proposes that Chariton composed his novel for women to listen to as they did their wool work. West herself expects the suggestion to be taken *cum grano salis* (p. 68); nonetheless, she may well have identified one of the ways Chariton was enjoyed.

59 On the sexist rationale for women as readers, see Egger 1999 (1988), 108–109, 1990, 1–20, noting in particular, Lesky 1966, 861 (cited by Egger 1990, 7, 1999 (1988), 109), who could not see the chatty Alexandrian housewives Gorgo and Praxinoa in Theocritus, *Idyll 15* as readers of Sophocles but who could imagine them as readers of the novel.

60 Egger 1990, 21–26 on the reader-response criticism in identifying novel readers; cf. Wesseling 1988 for a similar approach.

61 Egger 1990, 392–396 notes, for example, the evidence of papyri indicating that Greek women in Hellenistic Egypt had extensive rights in marriage law in comparison to classical Athenian law. Also, Egger 1999 (1988), 129–133.

62 Elsom 1992 and Montague 1992 investigate the possibility of a modern feminist reading of the genre: Elsom, in comparing Chariton's depiction of Callirhoe as an object of the male gaze to the objectification of women in pornography and Montague, in identifying elements of male fantasy implied in the virtue and vulnerability of the heroines Chloe and Leucippe.

63 Egger 1990, 397–398, suggests a parallel to the escapist appeal for women readers of contemporary romance fiction. Also, Egger 1999 (1988), 135.

64 For a counterview, cf. Haynes 2003, who finds support for Swain's hypothesis for an elite male readership in the genre's management of gender. Haynes argues that the genre revises traditional gender expectations for men as well as women and sees here a reflection of elite male preoccupations rather than evidence for women readers.

65 Iser 1978, 27–38.

66 Another path of access to Xenophon and Chariton for freeborn elite readers is suggested in Rose MacLean's hypothesis (2018, 97–101) that the servile perspective in Phaedrus' *Fables* offered first-century elite readers a model of how to cope with the autocratic power of the emperor; similarly, freeborn elite readers of Xenophon and

116 *Two novels about slavery*

Chariton could have read in their elite protagonists' enslavement a metaphor for their own loss of *libertas*.

67 Cf. additional remarks on this theme in the later discussion, pp. 102–110.

68 On this passage, see the earlier discussion, pp. 77–78.

69 On the *DGR*, see Kaster 1995. For a general overview of the contribution of slaves and freedmen to literature and scholarship, see Christes 1979b.

70 In the view of Mohler 1940, slave schools or *paedagogia*, in both noble households and the *familia Caesaris*, offered elements of a liberal education beyond mere training. See also Forbes 1955; Booth 1979.

71 Weaver 1972 describes the complex and extensive bureaucracy of the *familia Caesaris* and its contribution to imperial administration.

72 See Adams 2003, 761–762 on slave bilingualism.

73 Kaster 1995, 190–192.

74 Cf. Fitzgerald 2000, 2–3: "formally manumitted slaves became Roman citizens, and they spoke with the voice of the masters." Cf. Treggiari 1969, 241–243, in whose view freedmen authors such as Terence, Publilius Syrus, and Phaedrus "seem to have accepted without question the inevitability of the institution of slavery. They cared, however, about the behavior of individual masters and slaves and as philosophers they tended to hold that a man could triumph over slavery." Cf. Christes 1979a for a similar reading of Publilius Syrus and Phaedrus; however, in the latter, Christes sees signs of a partial protest, not against slavery but against the enslavement of gifted and capable people (*die Versklavung auch begabter und tüchtiger Menschen*). On the other hand, Schtajerman 1964, 112–136 sees evidence in both Phaedrus and Publilius Syrus of protest against the ideology of the slave-owning class, a germ of nascent class consciousness uniting slaves, freedmen, and free poor. Bloomer 1997, 73–109 offers a complex reading of Phaedrus as a freedman trying to secure social acceptance and reputation through literary merit.

75 Slaves manumitted under Greek practice could have experienced similar marginalization and subordination: They did not become citizens; they remained subject to the former master, who acted as a guarantor (ἐπίτροπος or προστάτης); *paramonē* agreements requiring them to continue to serve the former master were common. Youni 2010, 325–326 discusses clauses in Greek manumission agreements that aimed to protect the freed slave from *hybris*, a possible indication of continuing public degradation after freedom.

76 Weaver 1972, 210 suggests that even for an elite slave of the *familia Caesaris*, it was preferable to establish a family with his own female slave (*vicaria*), if he could afford one, rather than take on a fellow slave assigned by the master, who had the power to separate the couple if it suited his interests.

77 Note Keith Hopkins's suggestion, 1993, 6, that the presence of highly educated and responsible slaves and former slaves in Rome helped to intensify the "implicit struggle between masters and slaves and the oppressive cruelty of the Roman slave system."

78 Cf. Bloomer 1997, 67–71.

79 Bloomer 1997, 105 suggests that the imperial freedman Phaedrus was alluding to such snobbery in the prologue to his third book when he complained that he was allowed only grudging entrée into literary society (23): *fastidiose tamen in coetum recipior.*

80 There is no need here to review the (in)famous case of Trimalchio: Petersen 2006, 1–13, argues that Trimalchio has led some scholars to confuse the stereotype with real freedman, a phenomenon she calls "Trimalchio Vision."

81 Cf. Gaius, *Inst.* 1.1.13 on branded slaves. The man might have been branded with the letters TMQF, that is, *tene me quia fugi*: "Arrest me, for I have run away." For literary examples, Apuleius 9.12; Petronius 103.

Two novels about slavery 117

82 Perry 2011 analyzes Haterius' gaffe in terms of a conflict between the normative expectations of male citizens and the legal and social latitude allowed to a patron in dealing with an ex-slave.

83 See Romano 1980, 441–447, who argues that Cicero, in fact, wrote the poem as a form of neoteric poetic play when a young man. His addressee was not Tiro but some imaginary *puer*. Asinius Gallus' mistaken assertion that the poem was an *epigramma in Tironem* misled Pliny.

84 For a discussion of the sexualized stereotype of the freedwoman in literature, see Perry 2014, 138–148.

85 The tradition, reported in Suetonius' *Vita Terenti*, that Terence, the ex-slave comic playwright, had had sexual relations with his patrons Scipio Africanus and Laelius, provides what may have been a real-life example of the degradation of an accomplished ex-slave. In this case, the degradation would have gone even further. The same tradition reported that Terence's noble friends were the real authors of his plays.

86 Note the perceptive comment of MacLean 2018, 17, that "basic inequalities and stigmas persisted from one status to another, and these forces prompted reactions from *liberti* that are in some respects comparable to those undertaken by slaves."

87 Christes 1979b, 137–140. Hermippus studied with Philon of Byblos. The lack of a Roman *gentilicium* suggests Hermippus likely had been a slave in his native Phoenicia and came to Rome already a freedman. Philon may have sponsored Hermippus and recommended him to his own patron Herennius Severus.

88 Thus, I conclude *contra* Morley 2011, 283–284, who argues in reference to the *familia Caesaris* that "educated freedmen who were in a position to give an account of the life of a slave, admittedly an exceptionally privileged slave, chose not to do so; not only was there no ready audience for such a memoir, but they thought of themselves less as former slaves than as members of the imperial household – even if rivals and jealous aristocrats preferred to emphasise their servile origins."

89 Cf. Létoublon 1993.

90 Cf. Sara Forsdyke's readings of selected fables from the point of view of slaves and other dominated groups noted earlier in the Introduction, p. 17.

91 According to Billault 1991, 202–205, the proper *Scheintod* only involved the heroine, because one must see the *corpus* of the presumed *delictae*. Billault connects the motif to a broader tradition of legend, fantastic narration, miracle stories, and philosophical speculation on the human condition. The innovation of the novel was to make the *Scheintod* one of the protagonists' adventures, one that always ends for the best.

92 Thompson K426. A familiar example from myth: Artemis' rescue of Iphigenia at Aulis.

93 And in popular culture, the Marvel Comics hero T'Challa, the Black Panther.

94 Bowersock 1994, 99–119 on the empty tomb as a Christian motif.

95 Létoublon 1993, 188 also notes the association between the dedication of Chaereas' cenotaph and his enslavement.

96 See Chapter 2, p. 29, nn. 10 and 11.

97 If the chronological relationship between the authors is reversed, as some think it should be, Chariton could have adopted Callirhoe's enslavement from the example of Anthia.

98 Létoublon 1993, 188 describes the Aegialeus scene as a reversal of the usual motif.

99 Cf. Tagliabue 2017, 49–52 on the relevance of the Aigialeus episode to the novel's central love theme.

100 The narrative sequence of a storm at sea, a shipwreck, and survival may also preserve servile thinking associated with enslavement and redemption. The lexicographer Nonius Marcellus (848) notes that newly freed slaves shaved their heads, like

118 *Two novels about slavery*

survivors of a shipwreck, because they had escaped from "the storm of slavery": *Qui liberi fiebant ea causa calvi erant, quod tempestatem servitutis videbantur effugere, ut naufragio liberati solent.* Cf. Bodel 1994, 251, commenting on one of Trimalchio's freedmen guests who "swam out" of troubles thanks to his master's goodwill (57.10). One might "swim out" of troubles that had nothing to do with slavery, but Nonius' testimony suggests that popular perception saw manumission as a figurative deliverance from a hostile sea. Xenophon and Chariton reflect the idea, perhaps as "disaster associated with a sea voyage": In *Ephesiaca*, the pirate attack on the protagonists' ship; in *Callirhoe*, the enslavement of each protagonist at the conclusion of a journey by sea. A shipwreck resulted in Habrocomes' second enslavement, in Egypt to Araxus and Cyno. Shipwreck and slavery are also associated in Longus, when pirates kidnap Daphnis to sell him as a slave; as they set out from shore, their boat is upset by the cattle they had also put on board. The pirates drown, but Daphnis swims safely to shore. Achilles Tatius and Heliodorus include actual storms and shipwrecks, which are followed by the capture of the protagonists by brigands, a prelude to enslavement, but one that is not realized. Achilles' heroine Leucippe, however, is sold into slavery after she is kidnapped by pirates at Alexandria and taken to Miletus.

101 Konstan 1994.

102 Cf. Winkler 1990, 101–126 on growing differentiation between Daphnis and Chloe.

103 Fusillo 1989, 186–196 earlier noted the outlines of such reciprocity between the protagonists of *Ephesiaca*, *Callirhoe*, and *Aethiopica*, less so for Leucippe and Clitophon.

104 Konstan 1994, 226–227.

105 Bradley 2011, 370–371 on the importance to Roman slaves of a secure family. Family is a recurring theme in the African American slave narrative. Charles Ball illustrates the intensity of the feeling that could have been involved. As a child in Maryland, Ball was separated from his parents when they were sold to a plantation in Georgia. As an adult, he was separated from his family when he was sold to a South Carolina plantation: "I had at times serious thoughts of suicide so great was my anguish." Ball escaped to the North and went into Maryland in search of his family only to learn that his wife and children had been sold away: "They had now passed into hopeless bondage and were gone forever beyond my reach.... . I rushed out of my own house in despair and returned to Pennsylvania with a broken heart."

106 On the centrality of family to the freedman's identity, Mouritsen 2011, 284–289.

107 MacLean 2018, 136–143; cf. the discussion in Perry 2014, 118–127 on inscriptions that note *patronus*/husband and *liberta*/wife.

108 George 2005. Flory 1978 discusses epigraphic evidence for a range of professional, social, and affective relationships among the slaves of a *familia*.

109 Perry 2014, 148–153 argues that marriage served to redeem the freedwoman of the shame she had incurred earlier in life as a sexually available slave.

110 George 2005, 50.

111 On the sexual exploitation of slave women: Kolendo 1981; Bradley 1994, 49–51; Harper 2011, 281–325; Perry 2014.

112 Callirhoe reclaimed the *sōphrosynē* she had surrendered while Dionysius' slave by rejecting the Great King and reasserting her devotion to her first husband, Chaereas. It may be possible to see in the second chance that Chariton offered his heroine in Babylon a fictionalization of the social process argued for by Perry 2014, 148–153, in which lawful marriage had the power to redeem a freedwoman of the sexual shame she incurred in her previous life as a slave, remaking her, at least in the ideal, as a *materfamilias*.

113 Haynes 2003, 82–100 is a good starting point for consideration of this topic. She argues that the genre revises the classical conception of the hero as a warrior and

Two novels about slavery 119

replaces it with the idea of the hero as a steadfast lover, a husband, whose tendency to lamentation and despair is a manifestation of the intensity of his feelings. Others who have commented on the genre's unheroic male protagonists: Sandy 1982a, 60–61 (on Theagenes); Hägg 1983, 210; Anderson 1984, 63–64; Konstan 1994, 15–26, 30, 34; Reardon 1991, 82; Morgan 1995, 145 suggests that it would have been easier for (male) readers to identify with colorless heroes, "blank screens," as it were, than with strongly drawn protagonists; Lalanne 2006, 154–180; Whitmarsh 2011, 223–225. Perry 2014, 19–22 discusses evidence for slavery's attenuation of gender in the case of female slaves.

114 Konstan 1994, 26 suggests that the submissive hero of the novel was a function of the equivalence between the male and female protagonists as lovers. Haynes 2003, 81–83 argues that motif reflected a societal crisis in masculinity itself. Whitmarsh 2011, 224–225 sees the hero's despondency as a crisis in narration, "a form of hermeneutic and actorial incapacitation, an inability to see how the plot might be progressed."

115 Jones 2012, 138–144, identifies personal autonomy in connection with the ability to defend one's self and exact revenge as an essential element in the manliness of novel heroes. Autonomy and power over others were central to the conception of manliness in elite Greek and Roman thought; cf. Fisher 1998 on the connection between violent self-assertion and personal honor in classical Athens, and Alston 1998 on the evolving relationship between *libertas* and masculinity in Rome in the transition from republic to empire.

116 That, at any rate, was the intent of the system. The degree to which it succeeded is a theme of debate: cf. the discussion in Lussana 2016, 1–5.

117 On the resistance of African American men to the emasculating aims of the slaveowner: Lussana 2016. But resistance was not always feasible: Genovese 1974, 484–486.

118 Douglass 1845, 65–66.

119 Richlin 2017, 439–451 discusses the Plautine slaves who imagine themselves as *reges* and sees in the motif a servile fantasy of omnipotent wealth and power.

120 Baslez 1990 notes the association of the nobility motif with the protagonists' beauty and *sōphrosynē*. She distinguishes between Xenophon and Chariton, who stress the importance of legitimate, endogamous marriage for nobility within the *polis*, an attitude that looks back to the time of the classical city, and Achilles Tatius and Heliodorus, who open nobility to non-Greeks and depict marriages involving spouses from different cities.

121 Cf. Trenkner 1958, 39–41 on enslaved protagonists in Euripides.

122 Suetonius (*Nero*, 28.1) reports that Nero forced men of consular rank to swear falsely that his freedwoman concubine Acte was of royal origin (*regio genere ortam*). It may be possible, however, to attribute some of the motivation to be acknowledged as royal here to Acte herself. Petronius may be making fun of servile assertions of royalty when one of Trimalchio's freedman guests pushes back against Ascyltos' mockery (57): "You're a Roman knight? Well, I'm the son of a king. – 'So, how did you come to be a slave,' you may say. – Because I voluntarily became a slave (*me dedi in servitutem*) and I preferred being a Roman citizen to paying taxes as a provincial (tributarius)."

123 Cf. the authors of slave narratives, such as Olaudah Equiano or Charles Ball, who claimed noble or royal status for their original families in Africa.

124 Cf. the discussion of conflicting values in elite freedmen in Patterson 1991, 243–244.

125 Scott 1990, 160–166 on oral aspects of the hidden transcript.

126 Tilg 2010 goes too far in concluding that Chariton invented the genre itself of the ideal love romance. Nonetheless, some of the arguments he adduces in support of

120 *Two novels about slavery*

this conclusion are worth considering. These include Chariton's apparent concern with literary innovation (pp. 164–188). Tilg also argues that Rumor (Φήμη) serves a metaliterary function in the novel, standing for "an allegory of the author's voice" (p. 241); thus, when Dionysius imagines Rumor hurrying to Sicily with a new sort of story about Callirhoe's fate, that she is still alive, that tomb robbers kidnapped her and sold her into slavery at Miletus (3.2.7, φέρουσα τὸ καινὸν εἰς Σικελίαν διήγημα, "ζῆ Καλλιρόη, καὶ τυμβωρύχοι διορύξαντες τὸν τάφον ἔκλεψαν αὐτήν, καὶ ἐν Μιλήτῳ πέπραται."), one might infer an authorial claim of originality in *kainon diēgēma*, that is, a new sort of narrative. I see evidence for a narrower claim to originality here, in the narration involving Callirhoe's false death and subsequent enslavement. Chariton's best claim to originality may be as a novelist of the experience of slavery.

Tilg is on firmer ground in arguing that Chariton knew the *Aeneid* and may have drawn the inspiration for his Rumor from Virgil's *Fama* (pp. 261–283). If Chariton, Athenagoras' *hypographeus*, had been an ex-slave, he would, in his knowledge of the *Aeneid*, join literate ex-slaves such as Q. Caecilius Epirota (ca. 70 – 15 BCE), a *verna* and *libertus* of Atticus, who helped introduce Virgil into the standard curriculum, and Polybius, Claudius' secretary for petitions (*a libellis*), who wrote prose paraphrases of Homer and Virgil.

127 Fusillo 1989, 17–109 surveys the genres subsumed by the novel.

4 *Daphnis and Chloe*
Slavery as nature and art

Introduction

Daphnis and Chloe is rich in allusion to earlier Greek literature – to Homer, Sappho, Thucydides, and New Comedy but especially Theocritus and pastoral poetry. However, the novel lacks references indicating its chronology relative to the other Greek novels. In addition, there are no reliable internal details, explicit or implied reference to historical events, that would point to a date.[1] Thus, the consensus that Longus wrote *Daphnis and Chloe* sometime in the second century or early in the third has been based on analysis of the novel's language and style and their affinity with the prose of the Second Sophistic.[2]

Daphnis and Chloe begins with a proem in which an anonymous first-person narrator, while hunting on Lesbos, sees, in a beautiful grove dedicated to the Nymphs, a painting that was even more beautiful (Pr. 2):

> In the picture were women giving birth. Other women were wrapping them in swaddling clothes. Babies were exposed and herd animals were suckling them. Shepherds adopted them. Youngsters pledged their love to one another. There was a pirate attack and an enemy invasion. And many other details, all having to do with love.

The hunter marvels at the painting and, desiring to create a rival version in words (Pr. 3, ἀντιγράψαι τῇ γραφῇ), seeks an expert (ἐξηγητής) to explain it. The story follows. The action takes place on the island of Lesbos, in a rural district 200 stades (or about 22 miles) from the city of Mitylene. Two infants are exposed, a boy, and two years later, a girl. The children will survive, however, because, in Longus' idealized pastoral narrative, the god Eros is watching after them. It may have been the god, then, who led a goatherd to find one of his stray nannies in a thicket nursing a baby boy. He had been exposed along with funerary offerings (1.2.3; cf. 4.24.1, ἐντάφια), markers of his high status: a purple mantel with a golden clasp and a little sword with an ivory hilt. The herdsman, named Lamon, is tempted to take the offerings and leave the boy, but he feels shame not to imitate the humanity of the goat (1.3.1, αἰδεσθεὶς εἰ μηδὲ αἰγὸς φιλανθρωπίαν μιμήσεται). Lamon takes

122 Daphnis and Chloe

the baby home, where he lives with Myrtale, and together, they raise him as their son, naming him Daphnis.

Two years later, another herdsman, while pasturing his sheep in a neighboring field, finds a baby girl in a cave of the Nymphs nursing under one of his errant ewes. This baby, too, had been set out with expensive offerings: a headband threaded with gold, gilt sandals, and golden anklets. The shepherd, whose name is Dryas, takes the foundling home where he and his wife, Nape, raise her as their daughter. They call her Chloe (1.4–6). As the two foster children grow it became clear that their beauty was greater than what was usual for peasants (1.7.1, καὶ κάλλος αὐτοῖς ἐξεφαίνετο κρεῖττον ἀγροικίας). Conscious of their foundling's high birth, each pair of foster parents hoped for a destiny greater than that of herding goats or sheep (1.8.1). But then, in response to the same dream, both fathers send the children to tend the flocks, 15-year-old Daphnis to herd Lamon's goats and 13-year-old Chloe to tend Dryas' flock of sheep.

Together, the two savor the beauty around them and delight in imitating the sights and sounds of nature. They worship at rustic sanctuaries of the Nymphs and Pan. They amuse themselves in rustic games. They fall in love. They will encounter obstacles before they can be together as husband and wife. Dorcon the cowherd will fall in love with Chloe. But the heroine naturally prefers Daphnis. Pirates seize Daphnis and try to carry him off. A party of wealthy young men from the neighboring city of Methymna on a hunting vacation in the district also try to seize the hero, holding him responsible for the loss of their boat. However, Daphnis is rescued in both instances. An army from Methymna invades and carries off Chloe as war booty. She, too, is rescued when the god Pan intervenes.

Daphnis' and Chloe's ignorance of the facts of life may be an even greater obstacle to the consummation of their love than romantic rivals or pirates or war parties. Neither, at first, understands what is making them feel so strange and to suffer so. They learn the name of their ailment from an old shepherd named Philetas.[3] The disease is called *erōs* and, Philetas tells them, there is no cure "except for kissing, embracing, and lying down together with naked bodies" (2.7.7, ὅτι μὴ φίλημα καὶ περιβολὴ καὶ συγκατακλιθῆναι γυμνοῖς σώμασι). They do all that but cannot figure out what follows. Daphnis, but not Chloe, will learn that only when Lycaenium, a city woman living in the district with an old farmer, teaches him what Philetas did not and what nature, apparently, could not. He rushes off to share with Chloe what he has just learned, but Lycaenium stops him: Chloe will scream and cry and bleed profusely, like one slain. Because of Daphnis' reluctance to cause her harm, Chloe's virginity is spared for the time being. In the meantime, the heroine's beauty has begun to attract suitors from the surrounding area, each promising her foster parents a tempting bridal present (3.25.1). Daphnis, of course, wants to put himself forward. However, he and his family are poor; he cannot compete with the rival suitors. The Nymphs remove this obstacle. They appear to Daphnis in a dream and reveal where a considerable sum of money, 3,000 drachmas, has washed ashore, treasure from the lost boat of the young gentlemen vacationers from Methymna

(3.26–28). Daphnis takes the money and goes to Dryas, who is happy now to accept him as Chloe's future husband. But then another obstacle arises. Lamon reminds Daphnis that he and his family are slaves. They must obtain the consent of the master before Daphnis can marry Chloe (3.31.3).

The opportunity to ask permission arrives when the master, Dionysophanes, comes from Mitylene, with his wife, Cleariste, and their son, Astylus, to inspect his rural estate. The master's visit presents an additional complication. Astylus agrees to give handsome Daphnis as a companion to his friend Gnathon, a heavy drinker, a gourmand, and a lover of boys (4.11.2, φύσει παιδεραστὴς ὤν). Lamon is indignant that Daphnis be made to be the love toy of such a one as Gnathon, especially given his knowledge of Daphnis' high birth. He shows his master the birth tokens. Thus, Dionysophanes and Cleariste learn that their goatherd slave Daphnis was the son they had exposed to die 16 years before, a fourth child who, Dionysophanes worried, would have forced an unacceptable division of his estate (4.24.1–2). The recognition of Daphnis' true status leads swiftly to the revelation of Chloe's status. Dryas shows Dionysophanes her birth tokens. The couple are betrothed. All return to Mitylene, where Dionysophanes contrives to discover Chloe's true parents by means of her birth tokens. They, too, are wealthy citizens, Megacles and Rhoda. Megacles explains how, at the time of Chloe's birth, having exhausted his estate on liturgies, he was too poor to raise a daughter (4.35.3). Since then he has become rich but remained childless. The protagonists at last are able to wed and to consummate their relationship.

Daphnis and Chloe stands apart, as John Morgan notes, both in its pastoral setting and in its deviation from the narrative norms that characterize the other four novels.[4] The protagonists, although of elite birth, are raised as peasants. They seldom venture from their homes and the hills, fields, and woods that surround them. Longus also spares his protagonists the misadventures experienced by other novel protagonists, such as kidnapping by pirates or being taken captive by armed raiders. The two, in fact, are seldom apart. Longus' countryside is not only a world apart; it is also an artificial world, a bucolic bubble. Lia Raffaella Cresci demonstrates persuasively that Longus drew the inspiration for his countryside from Theocritus and the later bucolic tradition rather than from nature itself.[5] The idyllic countryside provides a setting in which Longus considers nature, art, and imitation and the role they play in the birth and growth of *erōs* and the perception of beauty. The artificial and literary character of the setting and the author's apparent philosophical and aesthetic concerns seem at first to suggest a narrative with little interest in social realia such as slavery.[6] However, despite the artificiality of the bucolic setting, Longus is realistic in the broad outline of his representation of the economic relationship between city and countryside, the power relations between masters and slaves, and even certain agricultural practices.[7] The protagonists' status figures in the resolution of the novel in a manner that reflects social reality: When he was thought to be a slave, Daphnis needed to obtain his master's permission to marry Chloe.[8] With the revelation of Daphnis' true status, the apparent fact that Chloe was a

124 Daphnis and Chloe

mere peasant became an obstacle to their marriage. Only when she, too, was revealed as an elite did the marriage become possible.

H. H. O. Chalk provides a point of departure for the present reading, arguing that Longus makes Eros the prime mover of events in the novel.[9] This god not only controls what happens to the protagonists; he is also the supreme controller of the cosmos, the cause of both its beauty and the destruction that is necessary for rebirth and continued life. Chalk sees in Longus' Eros a religious vision that was aligned with Orphic–Dionysiac mystery religion. Daphnis and Chloe are initiates into the human dimension of the god, the rites of sexual love.[10] In this chapter, I take these insights and consider them in terms of human social relations. An important aspect of the cycle of birth–destruction–rebirth involves a struggle for domination and survival in nature. This struggle produces a natural hierarchy: wolf over lamb, human over beast, man over woman. However, Longus represents society as an elaboration of nature, including the natural struggle for domination. This struggle is present in human society (which is also part of nature): the pirate raid, for example, and the invasion of the Methymnaean army. In such cases, a natural hierarchy of domination has been further expressed according to social conventions and relations: Pirates are defined as predators not so much by their nature but in the context of their relationship to the conventions of the law and the *polis*; the Methymnaean army practices violence with the sanction of the state according to the arts of war.

However, while domination exists both in the countryside and in the *polis*, Longus clarifies relationships of domination in social terms only in the latter. Social differences do exist in the countryside, but the author has obscured them, for example, the fact that Daphnis and his family are slaves and Chloe and her family are not.[11] Longus is not, however, implying that social status does count or should count for nothing. In Book 4, when the outside world, the world of the city, definitively invades Daphnis' and Chloe's bucolic bubble, status counts for a great deal and the author becomes an acute observer of social relations and rank, especially in relation to slavery: Daphnis' friendship with his fellow slave Eudromus, his fear of his master, his master's absolute control over his life. Finally, only when the protagonists' true status is revealed will they be able to marry.[12]

Longus' representation of slavery is embedded in his concern for the relationship between nature, or *physis*, and art, or *technē*. In Chalk's reading, human arts and skills, the *technai*, enable human beings to live in an informed harmony with Eros and nature.[13] In a second line of interpretation, Froma Zeitlin emphasizes the aesthetic dimension of the relationship between nature and art and the role that both play in the protagonists' erotic education.[14] I suggest a third approach that considers the relationship between nature and art in the context of social relations, with particular reference to relations involving slavery. An important text here will be the myth that Plato attributes to Protagoras in the sophist's account of the evolution of the *politikai technai*, the political arts that make it possible for human beings to live together in communities. Longus, I argue, represents slavery as an expression of the domination that exists in nature but that

Daphnis and Chloe   125

has been articulated and enhanced (even mitigated and aestheticized) through the application of the *politikai technai*; thus, slavery is the legally defined ownership and exploitation of human beings. As something that is in essence natural, slavery, at least in Longus' idealizing narrative, is both right and inevitable.

Love, beauty, and violence in the countryside

The action takes place in an idealized countryside, the *agroikia* (cf. 2.11; 2.23; 2.27; 4.13; 4.38). This *agroikia* is eroticized in several senses. It is, first of all, a place of natural beauty and a source of pleasure. Longus has arranged his descriptions of the countryside according to the progression of the seasons and notes the beauty and pleasures (as well as the work) associated with each (spring 1.9–10 and 3.12–13; summer 1.23–27 and 3.24; fall, 2.1–2 and 3.33; winter, 3.3 and 3.5). Even the description of frozen winter is a source of pleasure to the reader, although for the protagonists, winter was itself even more bitter than the war with Methymna (3.3, τοῦ πολέμου πικρότερος) because it kept them apart. In addition, Daphnis and Chloe fall in love in the *agroikia*, in sympathetic accord with the seasons and the beauty around them, inspired, for example, by the goats in springtime rut (cf. 3.13.3) or made all hot by the summer sun (cf. 1.23.2). Or was it that the landscape was in sympathetic accord with the young lovers? For Longus describes Daphnis' and Chloe's first summer in the fields as if nature, too, were a lover (1.23.1): pleasant (ἡδεῖα) like the sound of the cicadas, sweet (γλυκεῖα) with smell of the fruit, and as delightful (τερπνή) as the bleating of the sheep. The rivers sang, the wind sounded like the panpipes, and the apples "fell to the ground because they were in love" (1.23.2, τὰ μῆλα ἐρῶντα πίπτειν χαμαί). The sun, like a lover of beauty (φιλόκαλον), made everyone take off their clothes. Finally, Longus' landscape has been eroticized in the sense that the god Eros himself is present, immanent in Nature, and the cause of both the beauty of the *agroikia* and of the protagonists' love that comes to be in it.

The garden of the old herdsman Philetas, who first teaches the protagonists about love, serves as a microcosm of the *agroikia* in its seasons and makes clear the part that Eros plays in making the countryside beautiful. The old herdsman describes his garden to Daphnis and Chloe while they are helping with the vintage. In it grows, he says, (2.3.3–4):

> everything, season by season, that the seasons produce: in spring, roses, lilies, hyacinths, and both kinds of violet; in summer, poppies, pears, and all varieties of apple; now there are grapes, figs, pomegranates, and green myrtle.

That day, Philetas says, a beautiful young boy had invaded his garden. The old herdsman could not catch him and ended up offering him a gift of apples and pomegranates and permission to pick the fruit and flowers of his garden in exchange for a kiss. The boy laughed and told Philetas that despite his appearance, he was not really a boy but older even than Cronus and time itself (2.5.2). The young-looking but ancient god tells Philetas that long ago he had joined

126   Daphnis and Chloe

him with Amaryllis, who became the mother of his sons; now he is "herding together" (2.5.4, ποιμαίνω) Daphnis and Chloe. Besides this, the god continues, he makes the flowers and trees in Philetas' garden beautiful by bathing in the springs that water them.

Philetas recognizes the god of love, Eros. He tells Daphnis and Chloe that they are thus consecrated to Eros, that Eros is looking after them (2.6.2, Ἔρωτι, ὦ παῖδες, κατέσπεισθε καὶ Ἔρωτι ὑμῶν μέλει). This Eros, Philetas continues, is a god who is (2.7.1–5)

> young and beautiful and winged. Thus, he delights in youth and chases after beauty and makes souls grow wings. He has more power than even Zeus. He rules the elements, the stars, and his fellow gods (κρατεῖ μὲν στοιχείων, κρατεῖ δὲ ἄστρων, κρατεῖ δὲ τῶν ὁμοίων θεῶν) – even more than you rule over your goats and sheep. The flowers are all his works; all the plants are creations of this god. The rivers flow and the winds blow because of him. I have known a bull in love, and he bellowed as if stung by a gadfly; a billy goat in love with a nanny goat followed her everywhere. I myself was young and in love with Amaryllis. I took no notice of food or drink. I didn't sleep. My soul was ill at ease; my heart leapt in my chest; I shivered with cold. I would cry out as if struck. I would be as silent as a corpse. I would dive into the rivers as if on fire.

Eros is immanent in nature. He is the cause of nature's beauty and is himself a lover. No wonder then that nature itself seems to fall in love, in harmony with the protagonists. The visits of Eros to Philetas' garden have done no damage to tree, fruit, flower, or stream (2.7.5). But the god, the most powerful force in all the universe, is also violent. He is the cause of the elemental and irresistible urge to procreate. Philetas emphasizes this aspect of Eros through his repetition of *kratei*, a word implying dominance as well as control, and the concluding picture of the powerful impact that Eros had on the bull and himself. The violence of Eros is present throughout Longus' *agroikia*, which was, despite its beauty, a place of material scarcity and the locus of struggle for survival and domination.[15] Longus notes this struggle on several levels. There is, first of all, a struggle among animals. A she-wolf preys on the flocks in order to feed her cubs – and becomes herself the target of countermeasures taken by the herdsmen (1.11.1–2); two billy goats in Daphnis' flock butt heads in a dominance display that results in one of them breaking a horn and running off with the other in pursuit (1.12.1); a swallow chases a cricket that takes refuge in Chloe's bosom (1.26.1).

Another level of struggle involves the domination of animals by human beings. Daphnis and Chloe care for the animals entrusted to them not for the benefit of the goats and sheep but because the animals are a source of food and clothing. Human domination of animals in the *agroikia* is also indicated in the ritualized violence of sacrifice. After he is rescued from a pit that had been dug to trap the marauding she-wolf, Daphnis sacrifices a goat (1.12.5). After Pan rescued Chloe from the Methymnaean army, Daphnis sacrificed a nanny goat to the

Nymphs (2.30.5). Chloe's family sacrificed a ram to Dionysus while Daphnis was visiting during the winter (3.10.1). Daphnis had gone bird hunting near Chloe's house as a pretext for this visit; he had already killed a good number (πόλλοι) before Dryas came out of the house, saw him, and invited him in (3.6). The birds were collateral victims in Eros' plan to bring together the protagonists: "Because of you I'm killing the poor blackbirds," Daphnis tells Chloe (3.10.3, διὰ σὲ ἀπολλύω τοὺς ἀθλίους κοψίχους).

Longus represents the struggle among human beings in the countryside as a struggle engendered by Eros, that is, the struggle to reproduce, which has been articulated in the narrative as a contest for Chloe. Daphnis first defeats the cowherd Dorcon in a ritualized poetic contest to win a kiss from her (1.16–17). Soon after, Dorcon dresses in a wolf skin and tries to seize Chloe and carry her off, but he is foiled by the dogs who mistake him for a real wolf (1.26). Near the end of the novel, Lampis, another herdsman, tries to carry Chloe off, but he is foiled at the last moment (4.28).

Chloe's vulnerability to seizure and rape serves as a reminder that male dominates female in the natural hierarchy. Longus foreshadows the coming subjugation of the heroine in three inserted myths, each of which involves male violence directed at a doomed female protagonist. Each narrates the destruction of a girl and her metamorphosis: into a wood pigeon (1.27); into panpipes (2.34); into an echo (3.23). Daphnis tells the first myth to Chloe to explain the origin of the wood pigeon's song. The story's violence is indirect. An unnamed female cowherd is disconsolate at a male cowherd's ability to sing better than she. This other cowherd had enticed eight of her cows into his own herd. In despair, she asks the gods to turn her into a bird, and thus, she becomes the wood pigeon (φάττα), a bird, like the girl, noted for its song. The violence here is indirect; however, the story references another tale in which male violence is direct: The female cowherd sings about Pitys, a nymph who was changed into a pine tree to escape Pan, a god who embodies aggressive male sexuality.

Male sexual aggression is the explicit theme of the second and third inserted myths and Pan is the aggressor in both. In the second myth, Lamon tells about Pan's pursuit of Syrinx during the celebration that followed Chloe's rescue from the Methymnaean raiders (2.34). Pan loved the musical nymph Syrinx, who rejected him because he was neither fully man nor goat. The god gave chase, intent on rape. Syrinx fled into a marsh and was changed into reeds. The god, who had followed her into the marsh, realized what had happened, cut the reeds into unequal lengths, and joined them together, creating the panpipes. Daphnis narrates the final myth to explain to Chloe why she heard the rowing song of a ship at sea repeated by the land (3.23). Like the Syrinx tale (and the tale of Pitys), the third myth concerns Pan's pursuit of a nymph who rejected him. In this myth, however, the musical nymph Echo did not just reject Pan but was committed to chastity altogether. Pan, in his anger, maddened herdsmen who tore Echo limb from limb. Earth hid the scattered remains of the nymph, preserving her voice so that they imitate everything just as Echo did.

128 Daphnis and Chloe

Previous readings of the inserted tales have noted in particular their relevance to the protagonists, either as foreshadowing or unrealized alternative.[16] The male and female cowherds, Pan, and the nymphs Syrinx and Echo, are all musical, like the protagonists. Daphnis observes that the cowherd, like Chloe, was a beautiful maiden (1.27.2, ἦν παρθένος, παρθένε, οὕτω καλή) who also sang and herded animals in the forest. The relevance of the Syrinx story is also emphasized when Daphnis and Chloe enact it in dance as Pan and Syrinx (2.37). But the inserted myths point especially to Chloe. Longus characterizes each of them as a *mythos* (1.27.1, ὁ Δάφνις μυθολογῶν; 2.33.3, ὁ δὲ Λάμων αὐτοῖς ἐπηγγείλατο τὸν περὶ τῆς σύριγγος ἀφηγήσασθαι μῦθον, 3.23.5, ταῦτα μυθολογήσαντα τὸν Δάφνιν). Chloe, too, was fated to be the protagonist of a *mythos*: Pan warns the Methymnaean commander to release the girl about whom Eros intends to create a myth (2.27.2, παρθένον ἐξ ἧς Ἔρως μῦθον ποιῆσαι θέλει).[17]

Jack Winkler was troubled by the possibility that the Pan and Syrinx myth, which Daphnis and Chloe enact in dance, foreshadowed Chloe's eventual submission in a system of socially constructed *erōs*.[18] Thalia Pandiri made a more general point, that the inserted stories show the possibility of a tragic and violent outcome for the protagonists; however, as Pandiri argues, the pain and suffering of these tales are converted into pleasure. "Music, man's artistry, transforms violence and turns even tragedy into something *terpnon* – a source of pleasure."[19] The point holds even in reference to the most violent of the myths. So pleased was Chloe with Daphnis' telling of the story that climaxes in the ghastly dismemberment of Echo, that she rewards him with many more than the ten kisses she had promised in return (3.23.5). Pandiri applies her observation regarding the transformative power of art and the skillful artist to the novel as a whole. Thus, the "Myth of Chloe" will end not in rape but in loving and lawful marriage.

However, I shall argue later in this chapter that it is not so much the *technai* of the fine arts that mitigate and aestheticize the subjugation of the heroine as the *politikai technai* that define marriage, which possess a similar transformative power, no less than do the *technai* of the fine arts.

Intrusions: violence and social relations

So far I have discussed instances of violent struggle that emerge from within the bucolic bubble of the *agroikia*. Longus also narrates five episodes in which violence from without punctures the bubble. The author articulates this external violence in terms of social domination and economic compulsion. The first intrusion involves the Tyrian pirates who try to kidnap Daphnis. When the pirates see the handsome hero, they realize that his value on the slave market would be worth more than the plunder from the fields (1.28.2, κρεῖττον τῆς ἐξ ἀγρῶν ἁρπαγῆς). A second episode involves wealthy young men from Methymna taking a holiday in the countryside around Mytilene. The young gentlemen arrive in a boat that, Longus notes, was oared by their domestic slaves (2.12.2, οἰκέτας προσκώπους καθίσαντες).[20] This intrusion of the city into the countryside raises a socially configured danger for Daphnis. Wrongly blaming him for the loss of their

Daphnis and Chloe   129

boat and the valuables on it, the Methymnaeans seize him, strip him, tie him up, and beat him (2.13–14). They intend to take him back to Methymna to be their slave in compensation for their losses (ἀνθ᾽ ὧν ἀξιοῦμεν ἄγειν τοῦτον πονηρὸν ὄντα αἰπόλον). But in the end, the city boys get the worst of it. Daphnis' fellow *agroikoi* come to his defense, and Philetas judges that Daphnis was not to blame (2.16–17). The Methymnaeans return home to give a distorted report of the incident to their assembly (2.19).

These events lead to a third intrusion, whose violence is enacted through the political agency of the state. The Methymnaean assembly votes to avenge the young men by sending an army to raid the district where they had been insulted, including the farms where Daphnis and Chloe live (2.19–20). The raiding party seized crops; livestock, including Chloe's and Daphnis' flocks; and many others who worked in the fields (2.20.1, καὶ ἀνθρώπους δὲ οὐκ ὀλίγους ὅσοι τούτων ἐργάται). Chloe is among those seized. When Daphnis learned what has happened, he goes to the shrine of the Nymphs, to remonstrate with them for failing to protect Chloe and their flocks. The animals would be slaughtered, and Chloe would, from now on, "live in a city" (2.22.2, Χλόη δὲ λοιπὸν πόλιν οἰκήσει). In the middle of his protest, Daphnis falls asleep and sees a vision of the Nymphs. They reassure him that they will take care of Chloe and that she would not "serve as a slave" in Methymna (2.23.3, ὡς μήτε εἰς τὴν Μήθυμναν κομισθεῖσα δουλεύοι μήτε μέρος γένοιτο λείας πολεμικῆς). The Nymphs keep their word. Pan himself rescues Chloe and the protagonists' flocks (2.25–29).

The fourth intrusion involves Lycaenium and the tutorial she gave Daphnis in sexual intercourse (3.15–19). Like the pirates and the Methymnaeans, Lycaenium is an outsider: an attractive city woman (3.15.1, τούτῳ γύναιον ἦν ἐπακτὸν ἐξ ἄστεος), refined in comparison to rural standards, brought into the protagonists' neighborhood by Chromis, a man who farmed his own land and who was already past his prime. An old farmer, a sexy young woman who lives with him, a handsome neighbor lad – all elements suggesting the outline of a comic plot. Readers have seen in Lycaenium a variety of stock characters. Some see a reflection of the "kind-hearted courtesan." Others see a predatory *femme fatale* (albeit predatory in a manner different from that of the pirates or the Methymnaeans), as her name, "Little She-Wolf," suggests.[21] However, Longus also indicates a social and economic identity for Lycaenium in addition to her literary persona. While it is possible that she was Chromis' wife,[22] her name associates her with prostitution. In Latin, at any rate, *lupa* was a regular term for prostitute; a *lupanar*, a wolf's den, designated a brothel.[23] An additional hint regarding Lycaenium's economic role may be contained in the detail that she had been "imported" from the city (ἐπακτὸν ἐξ ἄστεος), suggesting that she had been brought to the countryside not as a legally wedded wife but, rather was "imported," as in a commercial transaction. Lycaenium is, of course, well qualified to be Daphnis' tutor in terms of her sexual experience. If she were a hired prostitute, she would be an acceptable tutor in a social context as well.[24]

In a fifth intrusion, Daphnis and Chloe catch sight of a fishing boat as it comes into view headed back to the city. The fishermen are pulling hard at the oars.

130 Daphnis and Chloe

When the boat rounded a headland, the protagonists were able to hear the echo of their rowing song. Chloe is puzzled by the phenomenon, which, as noted earlier, Daphnis explains through the myth of Pan and Echo (3.21–23). As the boat speeds on to the city, the author himself intrudes to set the episode in the context of social and economic relations. The fishermen, he notes, were striving at the oars so that they could deliver their catch while it was still fresh to a wealthy man in the city (3.21, ἠπείγοντο γὰρ νεαλεῖς ἰχθῦς εἰς τὴν πόλιν διασώσασθαι τῶν τινι πλουσίων).

Each of these external intrusions reflects a situation that involves social or economic domination and compulsion. The pirates who kidnapped Daphnis to sell him as a slave were outlaws who live through predation on legal communities. The young Methymnaeans possess wealth that allows them to go on a hunting and fishing vacation and are accompanied by a slave retinue. The Methymnaean raiding party provides a state-based example of violence. The raiding party seized Chloe and would have sold her as a slave in Methymna. Even Daphnis' *praeceptrix amoris* Lycaenium has been articulated in terms that suggest her adaptation to economic compulsion. The fishermen, of course, lived off the fish they caught. But their strenuous rowing to bring their catch in fresh for a wealthy city dweller also suggests a response to economic need.

Longus has represented the struggle within the *agroikia* as a natural struggle for survival and domination driven by Eros. In contrast, he articulates instances of the same struggle occurring outside the countryside in terms of social and economic relationships. I argue later that Longus describes social and economic relations as products of art, or *technē*, in particular, *politikē technē*. *Politikē technē* configures the social and economic structures that would have enabled the pirates to sell Daphnis as a slave, that afforded Methymnaean youth leisure, that determine how Methymna goes to war, that defines Lycaenium's status, and that create a market for fishermen to sell their catch. Within their bucolic bubble, Daphnis and Chloe are ignorant of these relations. As Daphnis understood it, Chloe's seizure meant that she would have to live in the city (πόλιν οἰκήσει). With characteristic irony, Longus makes nature goddesses, the Nymphs, clarify the consequences of Chloe's seizure, telling Daphnis in a dream that, were it not for their protection, she would become a slave. Longus intervenes to reveal the economic compulsion under which the fishermen lived to the reader but not to the protagonists, who remain beguiled by the echo of their singing and the myth it prompts Daphnis to tell. While the author depicts a struggle for domination as a part of nature, his representation of the *agroikia* obscures the social configuration of this struggle. If status is playing a role in the countryside, the protagonists seem not to notice.

The suppression and revelation of status

Longus' readers may well have been familiar with a rural population composed of slaves, free tenants or sharecroppers, or free peasants.[25] Even Daphnis and Chloe are of different social statuses, despite the remarkable parallelism of

Daphnis and Chloe 131

their lives. Exposed as an infant, Daphnis was rescued and raised by slaves belonging to Dionysophanes. As the son of these slaves, Daphnis, too, is Dionysophanes' slave. Chloe, on the other hand, was rescued and raised by two peasants who were not slaves, although Longus does not clarify whether they were free or freed. In any event, like Daphnis, Chloe inherited the free or freed status of her foster parents.

The nonslave status of the heroine and her family is implied *ex silentio* at the same time that Daphnis' slave status is revealed. When Dryas comes to arrange with Lamon for Daphnis to marry Chloe, Daphnis' foster father declares that as a slave he has no authority over his family but must defer to his master (3.31.3, δοῦλος δὲ ὢν οὐδενός εἰμι τῶν ἐμῶν κύριος, ἀλλὰ δεῖ τὸν δεσπότην μανθάνοντα ταῦτα συγχωρεῖν). There is no suggestion that Dryas is obliged to seek similar permission for Chloe. Another detail makes the free or freed status of Dryas and Nape explicit. They were hoping that a hefty bride price in return for Chloe would provide for their natural and legitimate infant son (3.25.2, γνησίῳ παιδίῳ). Their status is implied on another occasion, after the true identities and natal social status of the protagonists have been discovered. Daphnis' former owner and newly revealed father Dionysophanes rewards his slaves Lamon and Myrtale with their freedom; in contrast, he rewards Chloe's foster parents with money (4.33). Lamon and Myrtale are not the slaves of Dionysophanes, nor are they slaves of the man who will be revealed as Chloe's real father, Megacles. Megacles, too, rewards them with a generous cash gift (4.37).[26]

As I have noted, up to the time of these late revelations, Longus obscures the status difference between Daphnis and Chloe.[27] Daphnis himself is never labeled as a slave; rather, Longus describes him as a naïve and innocent rustic, an *agroikos* who does not realize he has fallen in love (1.32.4) and who is full of innocent eagerness to share with Chloe what he has just learned from Lycaenium (3.18.1). The same obscurity applies to the other inhabitants of the countryside. They are Daphnis' fellow *agroikoi*, his country neighbors (cf. 2.13.1; 2.14.4; 2.17.1; 2.25.2). These *agroikoi*, whatever their status, come out to defend Daphnis when he is seized and beaten by the wealthy tourists from Methymna (2.17). Communal work effort also obscures any status differences among them. Everyone comes to help out with the vintage (2.1.1, πᾶς ἦν κατὰ τοὺς ἀγροὺς ἐν ἔργῳ). When raiders from the neighboring city of Methymna pillaged Mitylene's territory and carried off Chloe and other peasants, Longus refers to them generically as farmworkers, *ergatai*, without indication of status (2.20.1).

The inhabitants of the *agroikia* seem themselves not to care about status. In a contest for Chloe's kiss, Daphnis' rival Dorcon, whose courtship gifts suggest his relative prosperity, cites a number of advantages he possesses over the protagonist, but none have any connection with legal status. Dorcon is a cowherd, and Daphnis, a mere goatherd; Dorcon is fair, rosy-cheeked, a grown man, and Daphnis, small, dark, and beardless; Dorcon was nursed by his mother, and Daphnis, by a nanny goat. Finally, Daphnis smells like a goat and is so poor he cannot even afford a dog (1.16). Dorcon's relative prosperity suggests that he himself was not a slave. The cowherd also knows a great deal

132   Daphnis and Chloe

about Daphnis; however, he does not mention the protagonist's slave status among his many other disadvantages.

Chloe, too, knew Daphnis' status; she awards him the kiss nonetheless. A kiss is one thing, but Daphnis' status does not seem to matter to Chloe even when the two seek to marry: or better, "marry," because the union could not be a legal marriage given Daphnis' status. Daphnis himself seems untroubled or unaware that his status would be an impediment to his suit for Chloe's hand. He competes against rivals who are both many and wealthy, at least in the rustic scheme of accounting (3.25, πολλοὶ καὶ πλούσιοι), who offer Chloe's foster parents gifts that poor Daphnis cannot match. Nonetheless, he takes heart and enters the competition, concerned only by his family's poverty (3.26, ἕν αὐτὸν ἐτάραττεν· οὐκ ἦν Λάμων πλούσιος· τοῦτο αὐτοῦ τὴν ἐλπίδα μόνον λεπτὴν εἰργάζετο). The emphasis that Daphnis was troubled only by his poverty suggests an authorial ellipsis of that other thing, something a reader might think should trouble the protagonist but does not – his slavery. Daphnis' parents are of a similar mind. They expect that Daphnis' poverty will result in the rejection of their foster son's suit; in this case, expectation is allied with calculation. Although Myrtale is sympathetic to her foster son's feelings for Chloe, she and Lamon expect Daphnis will find a bride far wealthier than Chloe if his true parents are ever found (3.26–27). However, the fact that both they and Daphnis are slaves does not enter into their calculation of how the courtship of Chloe could progress. Myrtale also anticipates that Dryas would veto the match, not because Daphnis was a slave but because he had richer suitors for Chloe (3.27.1). Indeed, after the Nymphs tell Daphnis the location of a hidden treasure, which he recovers and presents to Dryas and Nape as a bride price, Chloe's parents readily accept him as a "son-in-law" (3.27–30).

Longus represents his idealized *agroikia* as a place where social status is an obscured distinction without a meaningful difference. Apart from the intrusions, this holds until the visit of Daphnis' master Dionysophanes, a final and definitive intrusion of the city into the countryside. Earlier, Daphnis seemed even not to know what being a slave entailed, that he needed his master's permission to live with Chloe. His master, in fact, had been little more than a name to him (4.6.2, πρότερον μόνον ἤκουε τὸ ὄνομα). With the visit, however, slavery and status become very important. The author makes slavery and the consequences of master–slave relations explicit. Events will depend first on Daphnis' apparent status as a slave and then the eventual revelation of his aristocratic birth; Chloe's birth status as an aristocrat and her virginity will prove to be of no less importance.[28]

Dionysophanes' visit, an inspection tour to assess whether his property had been damaged by the Methymnaeans (4.1.1), gives Daphnis an opportunity to ask permission to marry Chloe. In late summer, a messenger arrives to announce that the master will arrive during the vintage. Longus notes not only that the messenger is a slave but also a fellow slave of Lamon, both the property of the same master (4.1, ὁμόδουλος τοῦ Λάμωνος). The announcement stirs Lamon into action in order to make everything right for the master and his family. He cleans the wells

Daphnis and Chloe   133

and mucks the yards, work through which Longus reveals the filth and manure that were part of the reality of the life of agricultural slaves.[29] Longus also reveals the mentality of the protagonist and his family as slaves, who strive to secure the favor of the master. Lamon urges Daphnis to work harder and take special care of his goats because the master would see the results of his work (4.4.2, λέγων ὄψεσθαι τὸν δεσπότην).

The maneuvering for advantage also draws in other slaves belonging to Dionysophanes. A second messenger, Eudromus, arrives from the city to urge the vintage workers to finish their work as quickly as possible. The master determines the parameters of Eudromus' life no less than that of Lamon or Daphnis. His name means "Good Runner," and Longus notes that Eudromus is so named because his slave job is to deliver messages (4.5, οὕτω γὰρ ἐκαλεῖτο, ὅτι ἦν αὐτῷ ἔργον τρέχειν); the slave's identity has been defined by the work he does for his master. Before Eudromus' departure, Daphnis gives him gifts of cheeses, a kid, and a goatskin. Eudromus promises to assist Daphnis in his request to marry Chloe by putting in a good word for him with the master (4.6.2, ἀγαθόν τι ἐρεῖν περὶ αὐτοῦ πρὸς τὸν δεσπότην ἐπηγγέλλετο). Longus represents the master as now the center of gravity in his slaves' lives; their actions and emotions bend in reference to him. Lamon and Daphnis spring into anxious action at the news of the impending visit. Longus represents here an experience peculiar to agricultural slaves, for whom a visit from the master to his rural estate was an occasion for anxious preparation and inspection.[30] Daphnis, of course, has an additional and even greater reason to feel anxious. He needs his master's permission for him and Chloe to live together; thus, he makes a friend of his fellow slave Eudromus to better his odds.

Lamon and Daphnis are responsible in particular for a beautiful pleasure garden on the estate, which Longus describes as a *paradeisos*, after the famous pleasure park, or paradise, of the Persian kings. This *paradeisos* is the subject of an elaborate and extended ecphrasis at the beginning of Book 4 of the novel (4.2–3). In the midst of all Lamon's and Daphnis' anxious care, another herdsman, Lampis, who had been a rival of Daphnis for Chloe, vandalizes the pleasure park in order to make Dionysophanes angry at his slaves (4.7, τέχνην ἐζήτει δι᾽ ἧς τὸν δεσπότην αὐτοῖς ποιήσειε πικρόν). When Lamon and his family see the destruction, they are all distraught, less for the garden's ruined beauty than fear of their master.[31] Longus' representation of the emotions of his slave characters in this episode may have been observed from life. Keith Bradley notes Galen's account in the *de Praecognitione* (6.11–13) of a slave accountant who had fallen into a state of debilitating anxiety after discovering a missing sum of money before his master's audit and concludes that "there is every reason to think that the steward's experience was common among the Roman slave population at large, especially among those whose occupations brought them into direct personal contact with their owners."[32]

There is potential for sympathy here for slaves who will be unjustly punished; however, Longus undercuts this potential sympathy through art. When Lamon and his family see the ruined *paradeisos*, they weep in anticipation of punishment.

134 Daphnis and Chloe

Even a stranger who came upon the scene, the author notes, would have wept not, however, at the fate of the slaves but at the devastation of the garden. The author deflects the reader's sympathy (i.e., the sympathy of the stranger who comes upon the scene) from the slaves to the ruined garden by means of the explanatory *gar*-clause (4.8.1, ἀποκεκόσμητο γὰρ ὁ τόπος). Indeed, in a rhetorically elaborate lament, Lamon himself dwells as much on the ruination of the garden as on his coming punishment (4.8.3–4):[33]

> Alas for the rosebush, how it has been crushed. Alas for the violets, how they have been trampled. Alas for the hyacinths and the narcissi; some wicked man has dug them up. Spring will come, but these flowers will not be in flower. In summer, they will not be in full bloom. There will be another autumn, but they will garland no one. Even you, Lord Dionysus, did not pity these wretched flowers, whom you looked on – your neighbors, flowers with which I crowned you many times. How will I now show the pleasure garden to Master? How will he react when he sees this? He will hang an old man from one of the pine trees – like Marsyas – and probably Daphnis too, blaming his goats.

Lamon mourns the individual varieties of flower, anticipates missing them in the coming seasons, and reproaches Dionysus, to whom the garden was dedicated, for not protecting the flowers. He concludes with a consideration of his coming punishment. The enslaved character has aestheticized his punishment through rhetorical lament and mythological reference. One might read this aesthetic distancing as a form of psychological displacement. The reader's potential distress at the unjust punishment of Lamon and Daphnis is transferred to the garden. The devasted garden anticipates the ruined bodies of the slaves. If that is the case, Longus would be replacing the sympathy that Xenophon and Chariton express for an unjustly punished slave with aesthetic pleasure for the reader.

However, in contrast to Habrocomes and Chaereas, Lamon and Daphnis will not actually be punished. In the midst of all this lamentation, Eudromus returns with the news that the master will arrive in three days. Lamon and Daphnis ask him for his advice. Eudromus suggests that they open the matter first with the master's son, Astylus. He himself can help them in making the overture, boasting that the young master treats him as a fellow nursling (4.9.3, καὶ αὐτὸς συμπράξειν ἐπηγγέλλετο, τιμώμενος ὡς ὁμογάλακτος).[34] Longus appears to treat the motif involving the assistance the protagonist receives from a fellow slave differently from Xenophon and Chariton. Eudromus will turn out to be a valuable ally, not only because of servile solidarity but also because of his position in the hierarchy of slaves who belong to Dionysophanes. When Astylus arrives, Lamon and Daphnis fall before his feet and beg him to save them from the anger of his father (4.10). The young master takes pity and agrees to help. His horse would take the blame, not the slaves. In gratitude, Lamon and Myrtale bless Astylus; Daphnis presents him with rustic gifts: kids, cheeses, fruit, and wine.

Accompanying Astylus is his companion, a parasite (4.10.1, παράσιτος) of voracious appetites, appropriately named Gnathon, or "Jaws." This character represents a final danger for Daphnis so long as he remains a slave. The parasite falls in love with him and tries to exploit his relationship with Astylus to get his hands on him. Both Greek New Comedy and Roman social relations provide a conceptual framework for understanding Gnathon. In Greek New Comedy, the parasite was a stock character, a social dependent associated with characteristic behaviors: flattery of his patron, an obsequious desire to please, but, most of all, ravenous hunger. The comic parasite was a man ruled by his belly. Longus connects Gnathon with the stock type through his name.[35] Longus does not leave it to the reader to pick up on the reference. Gnathon "was nothing but a jaw and a belly and what is below the belly" (4.11.2, οὐδὲν ἄλλο ὢν ἢ γνάθος καὶ γαστὴρ καὶ τὰ ὑπὸ γαστέρα) with a natural proclivity for boys (ἀλλὰ καὶ φύσει παιδεραστὴς ὤν). In brief, the parasite was ruled by his physical appetites, a character trait in ancient comedy often associated with slave characters in contrast to free characters who are inspired by ideals.[36]

The contexts of Roman comedy and social practice point to the possibility of a servile background for this character. In Roman comedy, as Cynthia Damon observes, the parasite and the slave possessed similar characteristics.[37] In Roman social practice, the new relationship between masters and their ex-slaves was assimilated to the Roman patronage system. The former owner became the freed slave's *patronus* and the former slave became his *cliens*, albeit of a sort distinct from *clientes* of nonservile origin.[38] Whether *cliens* or ex-slave *cliens*, Gnathon the parasite represents an additional point of articulation in the hierarchy of status and power, between master and slave – but closer to the latter. However, it may be possible to read him as an ex-slave, a freedman *cliens*, like the Plautine slave Epidicus.[39] As such, Longus' Gnathon would also play the part of an ex-slave with pretensions to learning. He was a clever talker and learned in all the stories that had to do with love, an education he acquired in licentious drinking parties (4.17.3, πᾶσαν ἐρωτικὴν μυθολογίαν ἐν τοῖς τῶν ἀσώτων συμποσίοις πεπαιδευμένος). In Astylus' youthful and naïve opinion, he was a witty and learned sophist (4.18.1, ὡς μεγάλους ὁ Ἔρως ποιεῖ σοφιστάς). Understood as this sort of ex-slave, Gnathon may evoke the stereotype of the educated, urban freedman from whom neither education nor freedom could erase the marks of a servile character.

In his account of Gnathon's attempt to seduce Daphnis, Longus illustrates the absolute power the master had over a slave. After Daphnis rebuffed the parasite (4.11–12), Gnathon turns to his patron Astylus for help. He confesses his love, and Astylus, after some teasing, promises to ask his father to send Daphnis to the city, to be his personal slave, and, at the same time, Gnathon's lover (4.17.1, αὐτῷ μὲν δοῦλον, ἐκείνῳ δὲ ἐρώμενον). Fortunately, Eudromus overhears the whole conversation. He likes Daphnis, a fine young fellow, and was aggrieved that someone so handsome would end up the object of Gnathon's drunken pleasure (4.18.1). Eudromus tells Daphnis and Lamon. Daphnis is appalled and decides to run away or die, taking Chloe with him. Lamon realizes that the time has come to reveal Daphnis' birth tokens.

136 Daphnis and Chloe

Astylus in the meantime tells Dionysophanes that he wants to take Daphnis to the city because he is handsome, too good for the countryside, and one capable of being quickly tutored in city ways by Gnathon (4.19.1, καὶ ταχέως ὑπὸ Γνάθωνος τὰ ἀστικὰ διδαχθῆναι δύναμενον). Dionysophanes must know what that really means, but straightaway, he happily (4.19.2, χαίρων) grants the request, summoning Lamon and Myrtale to inform them and promising them two goatherds to recompense them for the loss of Daphnis (4.19.2). As the other slaves in Dionysophanes' urban family express their pleasure at the prospect of having so handsome a fellow as Daphnis as their fellow slave (4.19.3, ὅτι καλὸν ὁμόδουλον ἕξουσιν), Lamon steps forward. He expects to be disbelieved. His story is fantastic and he himself is a slave, so he swears by Pan and the Nymphs that he will tell no lies: Daphnis is not his son but a foundling. He does not take offense at the fact of Daphnis' status as a slave in Dionysophanes' family but at the thought that he would be used by someone like Gnathon (4.19.5):

> In my view, he is not unworthy to be Astylus' slave, a handsome slave of handsome and noble master (καλὸν οἰκέτην καλοῦ καὶ ἀγαθοῦ δεσπότου). But I cannot permit him to become a toy for Gnathon, who is all eager to take him to Mitylene and use him like a woman.

Dionysophanes is astonished. He silences Gnathon, who had begun to threaten Lamon, with a dark look. Dionysophanes exhorts his slave to tell the truth and not to make up stories to keep his son (4.20.1, παρεκελεύετο τἀληθῆ λέγειν μηδὲ ὅμοια πλάττειν μύθοις ἐπὶ τῷ κατέχειν τὸν υἱόν). Lamon's dilemma is that the truth about Daphnis is like a myth: the protagonist's high birth, his exposure, and his rescue by a nursing animal align with several myths: Romulus and Remus and the wolf, Heracles' son Telephus and the deer, and Zeus and Amalthea. In response, Lamon offers to give his account under torture (4.20.2, ἐδίδου βασανίζειν αὐτόν εἰ ψεύδεται), the normative conditions for a slave's testimony. This offer may motivate the master to reexamine what Lamon is saying. Dionysophanes considers that it would be unlikely for the slave to lie when he was going to receive two goatherds in exchange for Daphnis. It also seems unlikely that a simple rustic such as Lamon could invent such a story (4.20.2, πῶς δ᾽ ἂν καὶ ταῦτα ἔπλασεν ἄγροικος;). It seems unlikely yet again that handsome Daphnis could have come from a father like Lamon and a lowly (εὐτελοῦς) mother like Myrtale. Fortunately, Lamon has the proof to verify his account: the birth tokens. The seeming myth about Daphnis is a true *logos*.[40]

The episode reflects, first of all, the power of the master to determine the basic circumstances of a slave's life and the possibility of the master's blindness to any feelings the slave might have. Neither Astylus nor Dionysophanes takes Daphnis' wishes into account or even consider the possibility that he had wishes. When Daphnis hears what has been decided for him, he decides either to run away with Chloe or die together with her (4.18 and 22). He is a late learner of the lessons of slavery, but he learns them in short order: fear, powerlessness, and despair. Longus also illustrates through Dionysophanes key aspects

Daphnis and Chloe   137

of how elites thought about slaves. The offer of compensation to Lamon and Myrtale, two herdsmen for the herdsman they would lose, reduces Daphnis to the work he performed as a slave, much as Eudromus' name reduced him to his work. The offer also assumes that the two slaves will be motivated by material reward more than love for their son. Dionysophanes also has a low opinion of his slave's intellect. He begins to suspect that Lamon is telling the truth when he considers the unlikelihood that someone so simple could not have made up such a story (4.20.2). Ironically, Dionysophanes does not realize that Lamon had anticipated how his master would perceive him. Thus, the slave begins by swearing he was telling the truth. His compliment to Astylus as a noble master (καλοῦ καὶ ἀγαθοῦ δεσπότου) may reflect genuine respect. We may also see in the flattering compliment the rhetorical strategy of a slave who understands that Daphnis' fate depends on what the master decides.

After the birth tokens prove the truth of Lamon's account and reveal that Daphnis is Dionysophanes' own son, the reunited family rejoice. Dionysophanes appeals to his two sons not to be angry with him (4.21–24). He explains to Daphnis the rationale that led him to expose the youngest of his four children, something he did not do willingly (4.24.3, ἑκὼν γὰρ οὐκ ἐβουλευσάμην); he explains to Astylus, who will now lose half of his inheritance to Daphnis, that for a sensible person "no possession is worth more than a brother" (κρεῖττον γὰρ τοῖς εὖ φρονοῦσιν ἀδελφοῦ κτῆμα οὐδέν). By possession, *ktēma*, Dionysophanes refers to the value of his estate, part of which was the "very beautiful property" where baby Daphnis had been exposed (1.1.2, κτῆμα κάλλιστον). But the word also applies to Daphnis himself, who, minutes before, was a *ktēma*, part of that estate and one day to be inherited by Astylus. He has now been revealed as Astylus' brother.[41]

Nature and art in the garden of Dionysophanes

The revelation of Daphnis' true status and paternity occurs in Dionysophanes' magnificent *paradeisos*. The pleasure park is also the place where Chloe's true status is revealed, the second installment of the happy ending. The heroine's birth tokens – the gilded sandals, the anklets, and the headband – reveal her high birth, although not her parentage.[42] After this, Cleariste leads Chloe off to dress her in a manner appropriate to her role as the wife of an elite citizen (4.31.3). The status revelations serve as a prelude to the upper-class marriage of the denouement.[43] It is useful to consider the *paradeisos*, where the importance of status takes center stage, in comparison and contrast with Philetas' garden.[44] It was there that the old herdsman saw the god Eros, in form a playful boy-god but, in fact, the natural force that steers the universe. In contrast, the *paradeisos* anticipates the acculturated form of this natural force, that is, lawful marriage, *erōs* as it is sanctioned and regulated by the community. The contrast is present in other respects. Both garden and park are examples of cultivated nature, places where nature and art meet. However, in Philetas' garden, nature seems to dominate. The beauty of the herdsman's garden was chiefly owed to the visits of the god (2.5.4).

138 Daphnis and Chloe

If one were to remove the wall surrounding this garden, it would resemble a natural grove (2.3.5, ἄλσος); that is, it would seem to be no one's property at all, except, perhaps, some god's.[45] In contrast, Longus' ecphrasis of the pleasure park emphasizes the role of human *technē*. The *technē* of geometry has been implied in Longus' specification of the park's dimensions, a stade long and four plethra wide, or 185 by 120 meters (4.2.1). The *technē* of horticulture has been implied in the park's careful design. Each tree stands in its proper spot, separated by borders planted with flowers: in a middle ring, a variety of fruit trees; in an outer ring, cypress, laurel, plane, and pine; and around them, a stone wall (4.2.2–6). While Eros himself was present in Philetas' garden and his power manifest in all that grew there, divinity is present in the *paradeisos* through *technai* belonging to the fine arts. At the very center of the park stands a shrine to Dionysus (4.3.1, ἵνα τοῦ παραδείσου τὸ μεσαίτατον ἐπὶ μῆκος καὶ εὖρος ἦν). The change in divinity is only apparent. As Chalk argued, Eros and Dionysus represent different aspects of Longus' religious vision.[46] The temple is decorated with paintings that celebrate the power and violence of the god (4.3.2): Semele giving birth, Ariadne asleep on Naxos, Lycurgus in chains, Pentheus torn limb from limb, the Indians conquered, the Etruscan sailors transformed into animals. The shrine was decorated everywhere with satyrs treading grapes and Bacchantes dancing; a statue of Pan was there too, playing his syrinx as if he were providing music for the satyrs and the Bacchantes (4.3.2).

The myth that Plato attributes to the sophist Protagoras of how human beings acquired *technai* may have served Longus as a conceptual framework for the representation of *technai* in the *paradeisos*.[47] Protagoras divides the *technai* that human beings needed for survival into two groups, *dēmiourtikē* and *politikē*. The *demiourgikai technai* encompass not only creative skills and crafts, such as the construction of houses, the manufacture of clothing, shoes, bedding, medicine, and agriculture, but also the fine arts, such as poetry and music. In Protagoras' myth, however, human survival depended on more than the *demiourgikai technai* alone. Humankind also needed to acquire the *politikai technai*, involving the exercise of justice, modesty, and shame, if they were going to live together in cities (*Prt.*, 322). The exercise of justice, of course, is a different sort of skill than, say, bricklaying or painting; however, *technē* was an elastic term of broad application.[48] Both varieties are present in Dionysophanes' *paradeisos*. The *demiourgikai technai* are represented in Lamon's and Daphnis' horticultural skills, which enhance and maintain the beauty of the park, and in the paintings in the central shrine that depict the power of the god Dionysus. But the presence of the *politikai technai*, which determine the rules of social status, the conventions of lawful marriage, and the rights of ownership and property, has also been implied: The park provides the setting for the revelation of Daphnis' and Chloe's status, the prelude to their lawful marriage. The precise description of the dimensions of the park recalls laws and conventions that demarcate property and establish the rights of ownership. In this case, however, Dionysophanes owns not only the land on which the park is situated but also the slaves, Lamon and Daphnis, whose labor makes it beautiful. In

Daphnis and Chloe   139

Philetas' garden, Eros is conceived as a natural force of domination (cf. 2.7, κρατεῖ μὲν στοιχείων, κρατεῖ δὲ ἄστρων). In Dionysophanes' pleasure park, domination is again present but as a culturally articulated system, that is, chattel slavery, whose proper practice is part of *politikē technē*.[49]

Froma Zeitlin has discussed the relationship between *physis* and *technē* with particular reference to the garden; however, her focus is on the *demiourgikai technai*.[50] The following section, in a sense, extends Zeitlin's discussion to include *politikē technē*. Zeitlin notes that art is related to nature principally through the act of imitation, or *mimēsis*. Longus reflects an idea found in Aristotle's *Poetics*, that the impulse to imitate nature is natural (σύμφυτον) from childhood and distinguishes human beings, who are exceptionally given to imitation (μιμητικώτατον), from the other animals; in addition, human beings learn first from imitations and find pleasure in them (1448b5–8). Thus, in their first spring together in the pastures Daphnis and Chloe imitated what they heard and saw in nature (1.9.2, μιμηταὶ τῶν ἀκουομένων ἐγίνοντο καὶ τῶν βλεπομένων). Hearing the birds sing, they learned to sing; seeing the lambs prance, they learned to dance; they gathered flowers in imitation of the bees (τὰς μελίττας δὲ μιμούμενοι). Longus, Zeitlin observes, also reflects Aristotle's thinking as it has been elaborated in the *Rhetoric*, the idea that skillful *mimēsis* is a source of pleasure, even if the object of the *mimēsis* is not itself pleasurable (1371b):

> And since learning and admiring are pleasant (ἐπεὶ δὲ τὸ μανθάνειν τε ἡδὺ καὶ τὸ θαυμάζειν), all things connected with them must also be pleasant; for instance, a work of imitation, such as painting, sculpture, poetry, and all that is well imitated, even if the object of imitation is not pleasant (καὶ πᾶν, κἂν ᾖ μὴ ἡδὺ αὐτὸ τὸ μεμιμημένον); for it is not this that causes pleasure or the reverse, but the inference (συλλογισμός) that the imitation and the object imitated are identical (ὅτι τοῦτο ἐκεῖνο), so that the result is that we learn something.
>
> (Freese 2000, 125)

Aristotle appears to be talking about two varieties of pleasure, an aesthetic pleasure that one takes in admiration of something beautiful (τὸ θαυμάζειν) and an intellectual pleasure that one takes in the learning and inference (τὸ μανθάνειν, συλλογισμός) that occurs in contemplation of an imitation. A skillful imitation of something even unpleasant or painful, it seems, can produce both kinds of pleasure: aesthetic pleasure taken in the skillful *mimēsis* and intellectual pleasure associated with the learning that follows upon consideration of a *mimēsis*. In the case of *Daphnis and Chloe*, however, both the object of imitation, *erōs*, and its *mimēsis*, that is, the novel, are productive of pleasure. In addition, the reader appreciates not only Longus' *mimēsis* of the protagonists' *erōs* but also a second level of imitation, the imitation of earlier imitations, that is, a whole tradition of erotic writing to which the novel alludes and belongs.[51] As Zeitlin concludes, two kinds of pleasure, the pleasure of *erōs* and the pleasure of reading are intertwined.

140 Daphnis and Chloe

Zeitlin also notes that Longus drew on an important idea in later mimetic theory, that conceived of *mimēsis* as a creative enhancement of nature.[52] In the proem, the narrator notes that the grove was beautiful (Pr. 1, καλὸν μὲν τὸ ἄλσος), but the picture was more beautiful because of its exceptional artistry and erotic theme (ἀλλ᾽ ἡ γραφὴ τερπνοτέρα καὶ τέχνην ἔχουσα περιττὴν καὶ τύχην ἐρωτικήν). An amusing illustration of the same idea comes near the end of the novel. After the birth tokens have signaled Chloe's high-born status, Cleariste leads her off to dress her in a manner appropriate to her impending role as the wife of an elite citizen (4.31). When she returns with her future daughter-in-law, Daphnis can hardly recognize Chloe because her natural beauty has been so enhanced by adornment (4.32.1, ἦν οὖν μαθεῖν οἷόν ἐστι τὸ κάλλος, ὅταν κόσμον προσλάβῃ).[53]

The notion that *technē* can enhance or improve nature seems to be associated with the idea that nature alone is deficient. This deficiency is illustrated in the protagonists' inability to figure out how to have sexual intercourse. After Philetas informed Daphnis and Chloe that the only cure for *erōs* was in "kissing, embracing, and lying down together with naked bodies" (2.7.7), they are unable to translate this advice into action (cf. 2.9–11). Nature alone did not clarify what the final bit of instruction intended. Nature again was found wanting as an instructor the following spring, when Daphnis tried to mount Chloe in imitation of the billy goats mounting the nanny goats (3.14, μιμούμενος τοὺς τράγους). Wretched, he felt less learned than the billy goats in matters pertaining to love (κριῶν ἀμαθέστερος εἰς τὰ ἔρωτος ἔργα). To the extent that it is conceived as sexual intercourse, *erōs* requires a variety of *dēmiourtikē technē*. This is supplied to Daphnis by Lycaenium. Noting the protagonists' difficulty with sex and having conceived a passion for Daphnis, she contrives a scheme (3.15, ἐπιτεχνᾶται τι) to help both them and herself. If Daphnis becomes her pupil (3.17, παραδίδου μοι σαυτὸν μαθητήν), she will teach him (διδάξω). Getting him alone in the deep woods by a spring, she takes Daphnis through the first two stages of Philetas' advice, kissing and embracing. Then at the third stage, when the two are lying naked together and Lycaenium sees that her pupil is taut and ready, she artfully slips herself under him (3.18, αὐτὴν δὲ ὑποστορέσασα ἐντέχνως) and shows him the path he had been looking for (τὴν τέως ζητουμένην ὁδόν). Longus notes with irony that at that point nature taught Daphnis what needed to be done (αὐτὴ γὰρ ἡ φύσις λοιπὸν ἐπαίδευσε τὸ πρακτέον).

The final stage of the protagonists' erotic education is transacted in the acculturated context of marriage, which Zeitlin notes has been signaled with a shift in genres in Book 4, from pastoral to comedy.[54] *Politikē technē*, I argue, plays an implied role in articulating this final stage of the protagonists' education, which is not merely erotic but also social. For Daphnis and Chloe not only learn the final mysteries of *erōs* in the context of citizen marriage, they also enter into their roles as elite citizens and slave-owners. Before that, in the *agroikia* where social distinctions were effaced, the protagonists were as naïve about status as they were about sex. In addition, Longus appears to transfer the notion that *mimēsis* enhances the object of imitation from the realm of the *demiourgikai technai* to that of the *politikai technai*, which also enhance or improve what is

Daphnis and Chloe 141

found in nature. In this case, however, the objects imitated and enhanced are by nature unpleasant, for example, the violence of domination. But *techne* can render even that pleasant. As Aristotle noted, a skillful artistic *mimesis* can give pleasure, "even if the object of imitation is not pleasant."

Aristotle's examples of the kinds of skillful *mimesis* that could even make something pleasurable that was painful belonged to fine arts *technai*: painting, sculpture, and poetry. Longus shows how *politikai technai* work in a similar manner. The violence of male aggression that victimizes the female cowherd, Syrinx, and Echo in the inserted nature myths is mitigated in the "Myth of Chloe" through the *politike techne* that defines legal marriage and accords the heroine protection and honor as the wife of a citizen and the mother of legitimate children. The *politike techne* that defines the ownership of human beings also created a benign experience of domination for Daphnis and his family in what might be called "The Myth of Daphnis' Slavery." Before his master's visit, Dionysophanes was only a name to Daphnis (cf. 4.6.2, πρότερον μόνον ἤκουε τὸ ὄνομα). Although Daphnis and his family were exploited and lived lives of material scarcity, they had enough to live. Daphnis himself rejoiced in the beauty of nature. At work, he had long hours to play the panpipes, swim in the stream, rest in the shade, and fall in love with Chloe. As slaves, he and his foster father also had a role to play in the creation of beauty, the *paradeisos*. Longus has also represented real slaves as endorsing the values of the system. Lamon and Eudromus could accept that Daphnis be Astylus' slave, but they did not want him to be put under the control of the ignoble Gnathon.

In the *mythos* of Daphnis' slavery, Longus acknowledges the potential for injustice in slavery; however, the *politike techne* of humane slaveholding helps prevent this injustice from being realized. Daphnis and Lamon fear they will be beaten for the devastation of the *paradeisos*. But Astylus listens to their explanation, pities them for their misfortune, and arranges for his horses to be blamed for the destruction (4.10.2). Also relevant may be the contrast between Dionysophanes, who examines the testimony of his slave Lamon (4.20.2, ἐδοκίμαζε τὰ λελεγμένα), and masters such as Apsyrtus and Mithridates, who made no investigation and refused even to hear what their slaves had to say in defense of their actions.[55] Dionysophanes, in contrast, possesses the slave-owner's proper *techne*.

Longus and his readers were, no doubt, aware that individuals of noble birth and character could be enslaved, could suffer as slaves, and could die in slavery. Longus' *mythos* of slavery is thus idealizing but may be nonetheless read as an affirmation of slavery as an institution that was grounded in nature, an institution in which domination, enhanced and moderated by *politike techne*, tended toward justice and humanity.

* * *

An episode that occurs shortly before the revelation of his birth tokens sets the *politike techne* of slave-mastery in the same continuum of artistic *technai* and

142 Daphnis and Chloe

illustrates how both forms of *technē* may play a role in aestheticizing and mitigating domination. Soon before the revelation of his true status, Daphnis entertains his masters Dionysophanes and Cleariste with a demonstration of his ability to herd his goats by means of the music of his syrinx alone (4.14–15). Playing a series of tunes, he commanded his goats to stand still and attend, to graze, to lie down, to flee, and to gather together again. Longus comments that Daphnis' goats were more obedient to his command than slaves to the command of a slave owner (4.15.4, οὐδὲ ἀνθρώπους οἰκέτας εἶδεν ἄν τις οὕτω πειθομένους προστάγματι δεσπότου).[56] The author, of course, anticipates the coming revelation and the position in society that Daphnis would soon occupy as the master of enslaved human beings. But the comparison also associates the two forms of *technē*, *politikē* and *dēmiourtikē* Daphnis' musical command of his goats indicates that a master possessed of the proper *technē* may also mitigate the violence of slavery. The goats are not Daphnis' pets. He exploits them for their milk, their meat, and their hides. But he also protects them and cares for them. As a good goatherd benefits his goats, so might a slave-owner possessing the proper *technē* benefit his slaves even as he exploits them.

Antigraphē and the representation of slavery

In the proem, Longus' narrator describes the beautiful painting he found dedicated in a grove of the Nymphs while he was hunting on Lesbos. The lovely painting instilled in the narrator a desire to emulate the painting in response (Pr. 3, ἰδόντα με καὶ θαυμάσαντα πόθος ἔσχεν ἀντιγράψαι τῇ γραφῇ). The verb *antigraphō* connotes the notion of writing something as a response to something else. Longus suggests that the narrative that follows is competing with the painting.[57] Competition here involves a process of revision and correction, and *antigraphē* provides a framework for understanding the author's reversal of his chosen genre's treatment of motifs. As noted, Daphnis and Chloe do not fall in love at first sight but over time. John Morgan has noted that the aborted wars, the foiled kidnappings, and the trials are "dead-pan caricatures of conventional romantic adventures."[58] In contrast to other novel protagonists, Daphnis and Chloe never leave the island of Lesbos; in fact, they never stray very far from the fields and pastures of their district.[59]

Daphnis and Chloe may also be regarded as an *antigraphē* of how previous novels, such as *Ephesiaca* and *Callirhoe*, represented the protagonists' enslavement. For example, the exposure of the protagonists with their expensive recognition tokens would have raised a reader's expectation that the two infants would be enslaved before the discovery of their true status.[60] However, for three-quarters of the novel, Longus defers both the confirmation and defeat of that expectation (confirmation for Daphnis, defeat for Chloe) by obscuring reference to status. The exposure of the infants itself represents a Longan twist on the motif of *Scheintod*, the false death that Xenophon and Chariton associated with a protagonist's enslavement.[61] In contrast to the violent episodes in which Xenophon's and Chariton's protagonists are enslaved, Longus represents the episode in which Daphnis becomes a slave as one of peaceful quiet and humanity (1.2–3): Baby

Daphnis lay in a wood on soft grass, surrounded by wandering ivy and protected by a thicket. A nursing nanny goat stood over him, careful not to tread on him with her hooves, and fed him. Lamon the goatherd chanced on the scene and, after a moment of hesitation, rescued the baby from death. Again, in contrast to the protagonists of *Ephesiaca* and *Callirhoe*, who at once acknowledged and lamented their enslavement, for most of the novel, Daphnis seemed unaware of the significance of his servile status. In contrast again to Xenophon's and Chariton's enslaved protagonists, Daphnis and his foster family endure, or even enjoy, a benign experience of slavery.

It may also be possible to take Longus' novel as an *antigraphē* of how the ex-slave protagonists in *Ephesiaca* and *Callirhoe* remember their past. The memory of slavery casts a shadow on the present in both novels. Xenophon emphasizes his protagonists' loss. Habrocomes and Anthia returned to Ephesus but not to the *status quo* that had existed before their enslavement. Chariton's Chaereas was reluctant to talk about what he and his wife had experienced in slavery. In contrast, Longus depicts how his protagonists would commemorate their past in a brief flash-forward before the end of his novel (4.39). They would return to the place where Daphnis had been a slave. There they would live as an integral family with their own children. Through these children they would commemorate their exposure as infants: the boy they would put to suckle at a she-goat, as Daphnis had; the girl at a ewe, like Chloe. Daphnis and Chloe would own many flocks and thus, it is implied, many slaves. Slavery cast a lingering shadow over the lives of Habrocomes and Anthia, Chaereas and Callirhoe; in contrast, Daphnis and Chloe's memory of their childhood in the *agroikia*, including Daphnis' life as a slave, becomes the focus of fond commemoration and the foundation on which both protagonists build a happy present and future.

An aspect of *antigraphē* may also figure in Longus' construction of his narrator's persona. "While I was hunting on Lesbos," (the novel's first words: Pr. 1, Ἐν Λέσβῳ θηρῶν), the narrator stops to admire a beautiful painting and then hear from an interpreter what the picture represented, that is, the protagonists' love story. It is clear from this that the narrator is a member of the elite, who hunts not because of necessity but as a form of leisure.[62] This elite persona contrasts with that of Chariton, whose self-description as clerk to a legal rhetor seemed intended to connote that author's subordinate status, and possibly that of Xenophon, who structured much of his novel around folktales involving slaves. Granted, Longus inserts a series of myths. However, in contrast to Xenophon's folktales, which feature themes of slave resistance and solidarity, the inserted myths in Longus aestheticize and naturalize domination.

Thus, *Daphnis and Chloe* may be read as an ideological *antigraphē* to novels such as *Ephesiaca* and *Callirhoe*. Longus justifies slavery in the context of his religious vision of a broad cosmic order. He represents slavery not as the cruel and violent result of malign fortune in a chaotic world but as a reflection of a world in which violence and domination are natural. But for all its violence, in Longus' idealizing *mythos* the cosmos is steered by a providential god. In addition, the natural violence involved in some human beings dominating others may be transformed and mitigated through the application of humane

144 Daphnis and Chloe

techne into slavery. Slavery is thus both natural and humane.[63] Longus also justifies slavery on aesthetic grounds. In Lamon's and Daphnis' creation of the *paradeisos*, Longus indicates that slaves have a role to play in the enhancement of nature and the creation of beauty and pleasure.[64]

* * *

And yet ... Jack Winkler's reading of the novel focused on Chloe's socialization as an inevitable and necessary process of subordination culminating on the wedding night and the violence of her loss of virginity. When sex became real, the heroine learned that what she and Daphnis used to do in the woods were only games that shepherds play (4.40.3, ποιμένων παίγνια). Winkler was troubled by a text that seemed to make of Chloe a necessary victim of "socially constructed sexuality" and mooted the possibility that Longus was, in the words of Helene Foley, "taking a very conscious and polemical stance towards the question of violence and sexuality."[65] In any event, Winkler urges that we be "resisting readers" of the text, in the spirit suggested by Judith Fetterley. In contrast to an "assenting reader," Fetterley argues, a resisting reader aims to "accurately name the reality," that is, the ideology, indicated in the text and "so change [s] literary criticism from a closed conversation to an active dialogue."[66]

As far as slavery is concerned, the possibility of a resisting reading is not in doubt for a modern reader, who possesses a deep conviction of the injustice of slavery and who is prepared to see behind the wrongfulness of Daphnis' enslavement the wrongfulness that anyone should be enslaved.[67] However, the text may have made room for even an ancient reader to resist, a reader whose education and culture did not view slavery as inherently unjust. Beside the novel's naturalizing myth of slavery was an alternative account. Bernard Williams notes that it was a commonplace in antiquity to think of enslavement as an arbitrary event, the result of chance and necessity, that is, very bad luck and compulsion imposed by force.[68] This commonplace view informs Stoic thinking but may also be seen in tragedy and Homer. In Sophocles' *Ajax*, Tecmessa refers to enslavement as a fated necessity (485, ἀναγκαίας τύχης), and in the *Iliad*, Hector foresees the fated day when Andromache will be enslaved, forced in Argos to ply the loom or fetch water because powerful necessity will be upon her (6.458, κρατερὴ δ' ἐπικείσετ' ἀνάγκη).[69] The idea is also present in the novels of Xenophon and Chariton, whose protagonists come to be slaves as through a concatenation of violent misfortunes. Williams suggests that this perception of slavery's arbitrariness raises the theoretical possibility that even ancient peoples could have realized its injustice.[70]

Aspects of this alternative account, which framed slavery as arbitrary, brutal, and potentially unjust, were present in *Daphnis and Chloe*, albeit in the background. The reader gets a glimpse of the slave-owner's power to coerce and compel in Lamon's and Daphnis' fear of punishment after the *paradeisos* was vandalized and in Daphnis' despair when he expects to be placed under Gnathon's authority and taken to the city. The idea that slavery came about as the

Daphnis and Chloe   145

result of violent misfortune, in particular, war, has been implied in Longus' co-optation of Thucydides. In the proem, the narrator calls the picture that inspires him to write a "history of love", ἱστορίαν ἔρωτος (Pr. 1). The narrator notes that he intends his written version of the "history of love" in the painting to be "a pleasing possession for all humankind" (Pr. 3, κτῆμα δὲ τέρπνον πᾶσι ἀνθρώποισι). Many have remarked on the allusion to Thucydides indicated in *historia* and *ktēma*.[71] The allusion was competitive. Edmund Cueva notes that Longus has reversed the authorial judgment of Thucydides (1.22.4).[72] The historian anticipated that his account would be less pleasurable (ἀτερπέστερον) for some readers because of its lack of a mythological element (τὸ μὴ μυθῶδες). However, while less pleasurable, the history would be a possession for all time (κτῆμά τε ἐς αἰεὶ) because it would provide a reliable picture (τὸ σαφὲς σκοπεῖν) of what happened in the war. Longus, in contrast, rejects Thucydides' either–or choice, asserting that his story will be both pleasing and useful, a *ktēma terpnon*, "that will heal the person sick from love, console the person in pain because of love, remind the person who has been in love what it was like, and be a lesson for the future for the person who has yet to love." As John Morgan notes, for Longus the mythological element, which was untrue insofar as it was fiction, might nonetheless contain "higher truths than mere fact" regarding love and the human condition.[73]

However, Longus has exploited Thucydides for more than staking out a truth claim for the mythological element of his fiction. His allusion to the historian also presented the ancient reader with a representation of enslavement as a violent and arbitrary instance of bad luck. This is a harsher account than what Daphnis experienced as a slave, a *logos* rather than a *mythos*. Allusion to Thucydides resumes in the account of the mini-war between Mytilene and Methymna. Stephen Trzaskoma has discussed parallels to the historian in language and content in the Methymnaean decision to attack and the operations that followed (2.19–20) and in the actions taken by the Mytilenaeans in response (3.1–2).[74] While the Methymnaeans are plundering the district in which the protagonists live, they seize Chloe along with many others who were then working in the fields (2.20.1, καὶ ἀνθρώπους δὲ οὐκ ὀλίγους, ὅσοι τούτων ἐργάται). Divine intervention saves Chloe, because, of course, she is the girl about whom Eros intends to make a myth (2.27.2). But the heroine's unfortunate fellow captives are taken to Methymna as slaves, where they will remain until an army from Mitylene forces the Methymnaeans to return them along with rest of the plunder (3.2).[75] These unnamed characters have thus been assigned roles as supporting cast in a Thucydidean *logos* about the realities of war and enslavement rather than an idealizing *mythos*. Their brief appearance could have motivated some of Longus' ancient readers to reflect on the difference between the author's *mythos* of slavery and slavery's *logos*, a process of reflection that could have, to paraphrase Fetterley, more accurately named the reality of slavery, a system that was so arbitrary that, in one moment, a man could be someone's property and, in the next moment, become his brother.

146   Daphnis and Chloe

Notes

1 Morgan 1997, 229–231 notes the difficulty of associating the text with contemporary cultural or social conditions.
2 On Longus' style, Hunter 1983, 84–98. See Henderson 2009, 3–5; Whitmarsh 2011, 263 for the consensus on date, see Perry 1967, 350–351, n. 17; Hunter 1983, 3–15, and MacQueen 1990, 196–203.
3 It is apt that Longus names Daphnis' and Chloe's instructor in erotics after the Hellenistic love poet Philetas of Cos, who was also, antiquity believed, Theocritus' instructor in poetry. Hunter 1983, 76–83, reviews the evidence for an allusion to Philetas in the novel.
4 On Longus' originality in this regard, see Morgan 2004d, 4–5: "His is the most original and the least bound by generic convention of all the novels." Also, Morgan 1994a, 64–67.
5 Cresci 1981 notes in detail how Longus adapted or accommodated characters, motifs, and scenes from pastoral to the requirements of the novel. Effe 1999, on the other hand, emphasizes that the typical motifs of the novel have been transformed by the bucolic setting.
6 Scarcella 1970 is critical of what he reads as Longus' prettified vision of the countryside; Longo's 1978 Marxist reading sees the countryside as transformed into an object of aesthetic and economic exploitation by an elite whose dominance is masked by pastoral illusion; in the view of Di Virgilio 1991, the representation of economic domination has been obscured by the theme of bourgeois love, another form of possession. Saïd 1994 argues that Longus created a countryside that would have been plausible to the urban elite.
7 Kloft 1989 notes details that align with our understanding of ancient Lesbian agricultural economy and the management and labor practices described in Roman agricultural writers. Even Cresci 1981, who argues that Longus' countryside is a literary product, suggests (p. 120) that Longus made Daphnis, whose name denotes a cowherd in pastoral, into a goatherd so that he and Chloe could pasture their animals together.
8 If Daphnis were a slave, however, his relationship with Chloe would not have been a legitimate marriage but concubinage sanctioned by his master.
9 Chalk's 1960 reading is deservedly influential: cf. Morgan 1997, 2257–2258.
10 Cf. Merkelbach 1962, 192–224, and 1988, who interprets the novel as an allegory of Dionysiac myth and ritual.
11 The obscuring of status in the countryside has led to confusion and vagueness on this point: Winkler 1990, 102 argues that Daphnis and Chloe are both of "dependent (though not servile) status." Cf. Morgan 1994a, 64, who comments on the humble, nonelite status of the shepherd protagonists, without indicating whether it was servile or not. Both protagonists are slaves according to McCulloh 1970, 15; also Heiserman 1977, 140, 142; Longo 1978, 102; Schönberger 1989, 35; Egger 1990, 313, n. 1. Scarcella 1970, 109, 1972, 77–78 classified Chloe's foster parents, and thus Chloe herself, as slaves but later, 2003, 257, changed his judgment on Chloe and her foster parents.
12 Zeitlin 1994, 162 characterizes the revelation of status in Book 4 as a shift of genre, from pastoral to New Comedy. In the view of Pandiri 1985, 127–130, comedy cuts short the potential of an unhappy ending. On Longus' allusions to New Comedy (with particular reference to Menander): Berti 1967, 353–357.
13 Chalk 1960, 49–50.
14 Cf. Zeitlin 1990, 1994.
15 Winkler 1990, 107–108 notes that predation is one of the paramount features in an economy of scarcity. He cites the incident in which a peasant steals the rope used to secure the boat belonging to the gentleman vacationers from Methymna (2.13.1).

Daphnis and Chloe   147

At the beginning of the novel, Lamon's first impulse on finding the infant Daphnis was to take the valuable death offerings and leave the baby behind (1.3.1).

16 For example, McCulloh 1970, 65–66, who aligns the myths with the protagonists' erotic development, and Pandiri 1985, 130–133, who argues that the myths represent a tragic version of what could have happened to Chloe but did not. MacQueen 1990, 41–81 observes a structural role for the myths, each functioning as a center point in the chiastic ordering of the book in which it appears.

17 MacQueen 1990, 82–97, followed by Wouters 1994, 157–160, identifies this myth with the episode in Book 4 in which Lampis tries to carry the heroine off. Lalanne 2006, 141–143 also argues that these myths anticipate a "Myth of Chloe."

18 Winkler 1990, 119–120; Morgan 1994a, 69–70, acknowledges this violence but maintained that it was necessary for the heroine "to be acculturated into the passive role because that is the only way that she can escape the sterility of innocence" (p. 70). In response to Winkler and Morgan, Bowie 2003b, 374–376, argues that Chloe was an eager bride and was not in any sense a victim.

19 Pandiri 1985, 132. Cf. Morgan 1994a, 69–70, who observed how each inserted myth issues in musical beauty. The song of the wood pigeon, the reeds that may be made into panpipes, and the phenomenon of echo are all produced out of violent struggle. On the other hand, Winkler 1990, 119–120 appears more inclined to see censorship than aesthetic transformation, noting how Daphnis and Chloe omit the "sinister and essential elements of force" when they perform the Pan and Syrinx story in dance.

20 This is the only explicit reference to the presence of slaves in the countryside before the dramatic moment when Lamon tells Daphnis that as slaves they must ask the master's permission for Daphnis to marry (3.31). A reference to the protagonists as slaves within their bucolic bubble is metaphorical: Longus characterizes both Daphnis and Chloe as the slaves of Eros. At the start of spring they return to the pastures eagerly ahead of the other herdsmen, "because they were slaves to a greater herdsman" (3.12.1, οἷα μείζονι δουλεύοντες ποιμένι).

21 For "Little She-Wolf" cf. Pandiri 1985, 121. Kind-hearted courtesan: Hunter 1983, 68. Winkler 1990, 120 sees Lycaenium as a "benign predator," who seduces Daphnis partly out of sympathy for his sexual difficulties. *Femme fatale*: Reardon 1991, 82 and Montague 1992, 242. Suggestion of sexual predation: Chalk 1960, 47; McCulloh 1970, 58; Konstan 1994, 84, n. 56.

22 Chromis' wife: McCulloh 1970, 18; Heiserman 1977, 139; Hunter 1983, 68–69; Holzberg 1995, 96; Winkler 1990, 120; Montague 1992, 242; Konstan 1994, 84.

23 Lycaenium's name may allude to New Comedy. Julius Pollux's second-century CE *Onomasticon* included a *lykainion*-type among the stock comic masks, although he described this character as a somewhat tall and wrinkled old woman (150, τὸ μὲν λυκαίνιον ὑπόμηκες· ῥυτίδες λεπταὶ καὶ πυκναί), perhaps a procuress. Lycus was the name of the pimp in Plautus' *Poenulus*.

24 Scarcella 1972, 66–67, moots the possibility that Lycaenium was a paid courtesan or *pallakē*.

25 The agricultural writer Columella (1.7.1) implies a rural labor pool of mixed status and notes conditions in which free-tenant labor is more profitable than slave labor.

26 Longus may anticipate his protagonists' status difference when each is first exposed. The land where Lamon lives is a property, a *ktēma* (1.1.2), belonging to a wealthy Mytilenaean. The author thus raises the possibility that the goatherd who grazes his flocks there is also the property of the man who owned the land. Longus notes that Dryas works fields adjacent to those of Lamon; however, the author indicates nothing regarding the ownership of those fields. In retrospect, a reader could infer that Dryas was working fields that he owned or leased.

27 See the earlier discussion, p. 124, n. 11.

148 Daphnis and Chloe

28 Longo 1978 anticipated the argument here that social and economic relations have been obscured; however, the present reading argues that the exposure of these relationships at the end of the novel is of equal significance.

29 Cf. related details that remind the reader of the discomfort of life in the *agroikia*: During the first summer, for example, noisome flies pester and bite Chloe as she presses the milk into cheese (1.23.3); at the end of the novel, during the celebration of Daphnis' and Chloe's wedding, goats grazed nearby, "as if they too were joining in the celebration." The smell of the goats was not particularly pleasing to the guests from the city (4.38.4, τοῦτο τοῖς μὲν ἀστικοῖς οὐ πάνυ τερπνὸν ἦν).

30 Cato's advice in *de Agricultura* 1.2 on how a master should interrogate his slaves and examine their work suggests that such visits could be anxious ordeals for the slaves. Consider also Seneca's dramatization of his own querulous interrogation of a *vilicus* and the latter's anxious excuses in *Ep.* 12.

31 Pandiri 1985, 126–127 notes that Lamon fears his master's reaction.

32 Bradley 2011, 376–377.

33 See Morgan 2004d, 228 on the "incongruity of the lament's high art and the speaker's rusticity and the triviality of the loss." But a possible consequence of this loss would not have been trivial for Lamon and Daphnis: cf. McCulloh 1970, 114.

34 Eudromus' boast refers to a relationship in which two infants were nursed by the same wet nurse. Such ὁμογάλακτοι or, in Latin, *collactanei* were often of different status, one slave, one free. Bradley 1991 notes that the common employment of wet nurses (*nutrices* in Latin) led to familial-like relations between individuals who were not blood relatives, including the *nutrices* and their nurslings (pp. 26–27) and between fellow nurslings themselves, although not, according to the epigraphical evidence, between *collactanei* of vastly different social status (p. 154). Cf. Leucon and Rhode, the protagonists' *syntrophoi* in *Ephesiaca*; Melite's *syntrophos* in *Leucippe and Clitophon*, 6.1.2.

35 Gnathon was also the name given to the parasite in Menander's *Kolax*, a character whom Terence transferred, with the same name, to his *Eunuchus*.

36 Cf. Fitzgerald 2000, 26, cited earlier, p. 22, n. 24.

37 Damon 1995, 1997, 23–36. Also, Richlin 2017, 133–136.

38 Mouritsen 2011, 36–37. Damon 1997, 146–191 argues that in authors such as Juvenal and Martial the parasite became a symbol for the unhealthy aspects of patronage relationships in contemporary society.

39 Epidicus is transformed into a parasite at the end of the play. Along with his freedom, he demands and receives from his master articles of clothing characteristic of the parasite (*Epid.* 725–726, *soccos, tunicam, pallium*) and the guarantee of meals (727, *novo liberto opus est quod pappet*). See Tylawsky 2002, 107–123 on *socci* and the *pallium* as parasitic insignia.

40 On verifiability as a key distinction between *mythos* and *logos*, see Fowler 2011.

41 Longus' intention that his novel itself be "a pleasing possession for all mankind," (Pr. 3, κτῆμα δὲ τερπνὸν πᾶσιν ἀνθρώποις) will be reconsidered in the context of this episode: see the following discussion, p. 145.

42 At 4.22.1 Astylus rushes from the park (ἔθει κατὰ τοῦ παραδείσου), where Lamon had revealed his master Daphnis' birth tokens, to embrace his newfound brother. At 4.30.2 Dryas brings Chloe's birth tokens to Dionysophanes and Cleariste while they are seated in the park (καθημένοις ἐν τῷ παραδείσῳ).

43 Zeitlin 1994, 161–165.

44 Forehand 1976, noting the possibility of the influence of Platonic ideas from the *Symposium* and *Phaedrus* on Longus' conception of love, suggests that Philetas' garden and Dionysius' *paradeisos* symbolize the pure Form, the *idea*, of the pastoral world.

45 Cf. *LSJ* on ἄλσος as "sacred grove" and Henderson 2009, 63, who translates: "If the stone fence were removed it would look to be a sacred grove."

Daphnis and Chloe 149

46 Chalk 1960, 34–35, 45–48.
47 Herrmann 2007, 207 notes parallels to the *Protagoras* in the instruction that Daphnis and Chloe receive from Philetas about love.
48 On this point, cf. Adkins 1973, esp. 3–6.
49 Cf. Doody 1996, 52–53, who remarks on the *paradeisos* as a product of Dionysophanes' rights over property and human labor.
50 Zeitlin 1990, 1994, a shorter version of the earlier study.
51 The relevance of this observation is underscored by the fact that Longus frames *Daphnis and Chloe* as an imitation of another work of art, the painting described in the proem, which itself was the imitation of the life and love of the protagonists.
52 On *technē* as an enhancement of *physis*: Zeitlin 1994, 153–154. Hunter 1983, 45–46 stresses the interplay and tension between art and nature; Teske 1991 treats the relationship of *physis* and *technē* as a key theme for interpreting the novel as both an erotic and aesthetic text. For Teske, the two elements exist in a complementary relationship in which *technē* makes *physis* complete in such a way that it renders the structure inherent in nature visible, in an exaggeration of nature (p. 35, daß die τέχνη die φύσις in der Weise ergänzt, daß sie in der φύσις angelegte Strukturen sichtbar macht, die φύσις gleichsam überhöht). Longus' ideal is symbolized in both Philetas' garden and Dionysophanes' *paradeisos*: artistically formed nature (die kunstvoll gestaltete φύσις).
53 The detail may reverse a motif in which it has become difficult to recognize a novel protagonist because of the ravages of slavery; for example, the difficulty that Leucon and Rhode have recognizing Anthia and Habrocomes at the conclusion of *Ephesiaca* (5.10.11; 5.12.5).
54 Zeitlin 1994, 161–162. Cf. Winkler 1990, 103: "Longus' tentative and exploratory fiction is, we might say, more about culture than about nature, and at times it seems to lead us in the direction of the thesis that sex itself is in no recoverable sense a natural act but is through and through a social reality."
55 After hearing Manto's accusations against Habrocomes, Apysrtus made no investigation (2.6.1, ἠρεύνησε μὲν τὸ πραχθὲν οὐκέτι) and did not allow him to say a word in self-defense (2.6.2, ἀνασχόμενος οὐδὲ λόγου ἀκοῦσαι). Mithridates ordered the crucifixion of Chaereas and his fellow slaves without seeing them or listening to a defense (4.2.6, κἀκεῖνος οὐδὲ ἰδὼν αὐτοὺς οὐδὲ ἀπολογουμένων ἀκούσας).
56 As an anticipation of his role as an elite citizen and slave-owner, Daphnis, with his skillful musicianship, may allude humorously to *Prt.* 327A-B, when the sophist imagines the consequences if a city's existence depended on everyone being a good flute player instead of the citizens having a sense of justice and shame.
57 Zeitlin 1990, 151–152 notes that the narrator's "infatuation with the painting makes him an aesthetic rival." Cf. Henderson 2009, 12, who translates, "a longing seized me to rival the depiction in words."
58 Morgan 1994a, 66.
59 The name of the slave who exposed baby Daphnis, Sophrosyne, is revealed by the protagonist's mother at 4.21.3, after the hero's true identity has been discovered. The name may be read as an oblique reference to the absence of this ideal in Longus' novel in contrast to the novels where the protagonists' *sōphrosynē* figures importantly. Daphnis and Chloe are the only protagonists who do not devote themselves to *sōphronsynē*. Herrmann 2007, 225–226 sees a connection between the slave's name and the narrator's prayer at the end of the proem that he be able to maintain his own sense of chaste modesty while writing Daphnis' and Chloe's story (Pr. 4, ἡμῖν δ' ὁ θεὸς παράσχοι σωφρονοῦσι τὰ τῶν ἄλλων γράφειν).
60 Harris 1980, 123–124 argues that child-exposure was an important source of new slaves. Kudlien 1989 argues that in Longus and Heliodorus, in whose novel the heroine Charicleia was also exposed as an infant, the theme was exploited for the

150   Daphnis and Chloe

purpose of suspense and the drama of the recognition scene; at the same time, the parents' motives for infant exposure (economic circumstances for the fathers of Daphnis and Chloe; the need of Charicleia's mother to avoid an accusation of adultery) reflected parental motives in the real world.

61 Cf. Brulé 1987, 132, who reads the exposure of gods and heroes in myth as a *topos* of "fausse mort" in the context of religious initiation.

62 On hunting as elite activity: Anderson 1985, esp. 17–29. Morgan 1995, 137 notes that Longus is portraying himself "as a member of the leisured urban classes." Hunter 1983, 2 cites inscriptional evidence (*IG* XII.2.88 and 249) indicating that Longus could have belonged to an important Graeco-Roman family on Lesbos.

63 Longus' defense of slavery appears to take the form of an *argumentum a fortiori*: If the life of a slave goatherd can be happy, despite its hard work, scarcity, and peril, so may be the life of any slave. In reference to real herdsmen, Kloft 1989, 51–53 notes that critics of slave-owning practices, such as Posidonius, saw the conditions under which slave herdsmen lived as excessively harsh, unjust, and a source of rebellion.

64 As a text that works first to obscure the reality of relationships of domination in the countryside and then to gloze over and mystify them, *Daphnis and Chloe* is situated firmly in the pastoral tradition: cf. Leigh 2016 on Virgil, *Ec.* 2.

65 Winkler 1990, 125–126.

66 Fetterley 1978, xxii–xxiii.

67 Including, for example, the unnamed slave (4.25.2, τις ἄλλος) who was sent to tend the goats after the protagonist's identity was revealed.

68 Williams 1998.

69 See Williams 1998, 2–3 on these passages.

70 Williams 1998, 5–7, 18–19.

71 Cueva 1999, 429, n. 1 for reference to earlier discussion. More recently: Luginbill 2002; Cueva 2004, 54–61; Trzaskoma 2005.

72 Cueva 2004, 54–61.

73 Morgan 2004d, 182, who notes that Daphnis and Chloe seem not to understand the deeper truth of Philetas' account of the epiphany of Eros in his garden. In an ironic reflection on the transcendent truth value that he claimed for his *mythos*, Longus notes that his protagonists took so much pleasure in Philetas' story that they regarded it as a myth rather than an actual account, that is, a *logos* (2.7.1, Πάνυ ἐτέρφθησαν ὥσπερ μῦθον οὐ λόγον ἀκούοντες).

74 Trzaskoma 2005.

75 If these workers were already slaves at the time of their capture, they would have been enslaved to new masters and then returned later to their old masters; on the other hand, if they were free peasants, they would have regained their freedom on returning home.

5 Slavery and literary play in *Leucippe and Clitophon*

Introduction

A second-century papyrus fragment containing an episode from Book 6 of *Leucippe and Clitophon* suggests that Achilles' novel was already in circulation at the end of the second century.[1] In the consensus view, Achilles wrote before Longus. His novel is remarkable for its succession of melodramatic events, remarkable even in the context of a genre noted for melodrama. In an opening frame, an anonymous first-person narrator has arrived in the Phoenician city of Sidon after a stormy sea voyage. While this character is admiring a painting depicting Zeus' abduction of Europa, a young man interrupts him. He tells the narrator that he, too, has suffered the indignities of love (1.2.2, τασαύτας ὕβρεις ἐξ ἔρωτος παθών). At the narrator's invitation, the young man, Clitophon, functioning now as a secondary embedded first-person narrator, tells the story of his love affair with Leucippe. The first narrator vanishes, never to return, and Clitophon begins his tale.

He is a native of Tyre and the son of a Greek father and Phoenician mother. In his cultural attitudes and education, however, he is Greek. His father had been planning to marry him to his half-sister Calligone. But Clitophon falls in love with his cousin Leucippe when she arrives in Tyre from Byzantium. He tries to seduce her with the help of his slave Satyrus. Their scheming is thwarted, and the lovers flee to Alexandria. They are shipwrecked and captured by bandits. Then they are separated. The bandits take Leucippe away for a virgin sacrifice, and Clitophon is soon after rescued by the Egyptian army. The next day he looks on in horror as Leucippe appears to be disemboweled on an altar some distance away; in fact, Satyrus has contrived her rescue. Although reunited with Clitophon, Leucippe must still escape the snares of Gorgias and Charmides, two Egyptians who also fall in love with her, before she and Clitophon can finally arrive in Alexandria. They are not there long when Chaereas, another Egyptian, sets his sights on the heroine and arranges to kidnap her by boat. As Clitophon pursues them in another vessel, he looks on in horror (again) as the kidnappers behead a woman and throw her into the water. He gives up the chase and retrieves what he believes is Leucippe's headless torso. The episode will later turn out to have been the heroine's second *Scheintod*.

152   Leucippe and Clitophon

Clitophon is left grieving in Alexandria when Melite, a beautiful widow from Ephesus, falls in love with him. After some months, he agrees to sail with her to Ephesus and marry there. However, after arriving in Ephesus, he discovers that Leucippe is alive, a slave on Melite's rural estate, where she was being abused for resisting the advances of the slave-foreman Sosthenes. Using Satyrus as a go-between, Clitophon contrives a means for their escape. However, the situation is thrown into even greater confusion by the appearance of Melite's husband, Thersander, who had actually not died at sea. Thersander seizes Clitophon as his wife's adulterous lover. With the assistance of her slaves, Melite tries to help Clitophon escape even though she has lost him to Leucippe. This scheme is thwarted too, and Clitophon is put in jail. Then Thersander falls in love with the heroine prompted by the wicked Sosthenes, who convinces his master to take the beautiful slave as his mistress. These and other complications are resolved through a trial, the arrival in Ephesus of Leucippe's father, Sostratos, on a sacred embassy, and chastity tests for both Melite and Leucippe. The villains are put to rout; the lovers are reunited and soon will marry. However, the novel ends *in medias res*, without a return to the opening frame and an explanation of why Clitophon was in Sidon, not Tyre, seemingly unhappy and without Leucippe.

At first view, Achilles seems less interested in slavery than the other novelists. A critique of normative ideas regarding slaves and slavery was central to the novels of Xenophon and Chariton. Longus aligned slavery with his conception of *physis* and *technē* as an institution whose natural violence has been mitigated by *politikē technē*. Heliodorus, as I argue in the next chapter, makes slavery a metaphor central to his conception of love. In contrast, while *Leucippe and Clitophon* includes the generic motif of the enslaved protagonist, only Achilles' heroine is enslaved and that occurs only after the novel has passed its midpoint. Clitophon, too, finds himself cast in what can be considered "the role of a slave" in narrative situations typical of master-slave relations, but without actually having been enslaved.

Nonetheless, slavery figures as a meaningful theme for Achilles. He has made his elite first-person narrator's perception of slaves a significant element of Clitophon's characterization. He also depicts a complex and conflicted master–slave relationship in Clitophon's relationship with his slave attendant Satyrus. Finally, and most important, Achilles shows a keen interest in slavery as an object of literary representation. He draws on traditional narrative materials associated with slavery and reframes them in a context that has been detached from actual slavery. This reuse of these materials in contexts detached from slavery suggests an interest in texts associated with slavery but not in slavery itself. Texts treating slaves and slavery furnish Achilles with ideas and *topoi* to be exploited in literary experimentation and play.

Achilles' representation of slavery is focused first through the eyes of the narrator Clitophon, the scion of a wealthy Phoenician Greek slave-owning family. The novel thus represents slaves from the perspective of someone implicit in the system as a slave-owner rather than the universalizing perspective of an omniscient third-person narrator. Achilles filters every observation and judgment in the

Leucippe and Clitophon   153

novel about slaves (about everything else, for that matter) through him. However, Achilles' own perspective might be problematized as well. He, too, was a slave-owner in the real world outside the novel. However, the author distances himself from his narrator when it comes to his observations involving slavery and other matters. Achilles may even, as John Morgan observed, make his narrator the target of ironic humor by implying an alternative "authorial" version of events.[2] When, for example, the evil slave Sosthenes runs away in a panic to avoid judicial torture, Clitophon remarks, "Slaves as a class are exceedingly craven in matters involving fear" (7.10.5, μάλιστα γὰρ τὸ τῶν δούλων γένος ἐν οἷς ἂν φοβηθῇ σφόδρα δειλόν ἐστιν). However, Clitophon had already shown himself on numerous occasions to be a coward. The author implies his narrator's blithe lack of self-knowledge. Is he also criticizing the normative view that slaves are cowards? The broader context suggests not; the author seems to be exploiting the stereotype for the sake of humor.[3]

Clitophon is also a problematic narrator in terms of his personal character.[4] His Phoenician background itself suggests unreliability.[5] His declaration at the beginning of his story that what he has to say is like a work of fiction (1.2.2, τὰ γὰρ ἐμὰ μύθοις ἔοικε) hints in the same direction.[6] The reference to *mythos* recalls the Platonic distinction between fictional and true narrative (*logos*).[7] Clitophon's unreliability is further implied, as Morgan noted, in the discrepancy between the self that the young man wished to project and the person that he inadvertently revealed.[8] In other words, Clitophon's narration is both "character-defined," that is, limited to his first-person point of view, and "character-defining," that is, indicating Clitophon's limitations as a person. For all his rhetorical training and book learning, the narrator is still a young man, self-absorbed, blind to others, blind to himself, and, at the risk of anachronism, blind to his privilege as an elite male.[9] In brief, as Tim Whitmarsh has written, Clitophon is "the most unreliable of narrators."[10]

Helen Morales has demonstrated that Achilles' novel is broadly concerned with vision and watching and their relation to narration.[11] The story is told, first of all, by what the young and erotically obsessed male narrator sees.[12] Through Clitophon's eyes, as David Konstan notes, Leucippe is turned into an object of beauty and desire.[13] The narrator coopts the reader into looking at the heroine in the same way so that even when he is a spectator to Leucippe's suffering in two grisly *Scheintode*, his rhetoric and privileged perspective produce aesthetic pleasure out of the atrocity.[14] Yet, for all Clitophon's gazing at Leucippe, it is not clear that he really sees her. Koen De Temmerman has described, for example, how Leucippe's actions, as reported in Clitophon's own narration, undermine his repeated assertions that the heroine felt about him as he felt about her.[15] In his erotic obsession and self-absorption, Clitophon sees in Leucippe what he wants to see.

Clitophon's shortcomings as a narrator not only involve Leucippe. The narrative notice that he accords to enslaved characters has also been shaped by his social position. On several occasions he omits slaves from his narration when one may suspect they were present, either on the basis of either evidence within the

154 Leucippe and Clitophon

text or on social convention. As an elite, Clitophon does not readily perceive the presence of slaves because, it may be possible to say, they are socially dead to him.[16] For this reason, slaves are more present in the novel than they are of narrative interest to Clitophon, who has grown up surrounded by them and who takes their presence for granted.[17] He does, however, reliably note the presence of slaves when their presence is relevant to his affair with Leucippe, either promoting it or impeding it. Clitophon sees, or does not see, slaves in the context of his self-absorption and erotic obsession.

If Clitophon's representation of Leucippe reflects his society's objectification of women, his representation of Satyrus, the most important slave character in the novel, reflects the problematic relationship between masters and slaves. The fiction accords Clitophon as narrator the appearance of authorial power. He cannot, of course, control Fate, but he can try to control his own story. He can decide to act for himself and he can command his slaves to act as instruments of his will. His use of Satyrus in his love affair reveals a tension in their relationship. Masters and slaves were engaged in an ongoing contest in which the master sought to repress the will of the slave and to make of him an obedient extension of his own, the master's, will. But for all his power of domination, the master could not eradicate the slave's sense of autonomy. Slaves struggled to retain their sense of self and to give expression to it, often through acts of resistance, expressions of hostility, running away, theft, and sabotage.[18]

Paradoxically, even obedience to the master gave the slave an opportunity to express his autonomy. The master often depended on the slave to execute his orders with intelligence and judgment. In other words, the more the master used the slave as an instrument of his will, the more likely it was that the slave would need to exercise his own subjectivity, that is, to act less like a slave. The paradox is reflected in the relationship between Clitophon and Satyrus. Clitophon's reliance on Satyrus' assistance, advice, and direction gave the slave the space to express his own autonomy and to destabilize Clitophon's authority as his master. In some instances, it is possible to read resistance, perhaps even hostility, into the assistance that Satyrus renders Clitophon. This natural antagonism between master and slave is reflected in the novel as a contest between the two for control of the story. As slave-owner and narrator, however, Clitophon has the final say. As he is able to use Satyrus as his slave, so may he include or exclude him as a character in the narrative. In fact, well before the novel reaches its conclusion, Clitophon will drop Satyrus from the story for good and without comment.

Preliminaries: noticing and not noticing assorted domestic slaves

Clitophon first mentions slaves when Leucippe and her mother, Panthea, arrive from Byzantium. Leucippe's father, Sostratos, half-brother to Clitophon's father Hippias, had sent the heroine and her mother to Tyre to wait out a war. As the refugees are welcomed, Clitophon notes the large number of slaves that Sostratos had sent with his wife and daughter (1.4.1, πολὺ πλῆθος οἰκετῶν καὶ θεραπαινίδων).

Clitophon's family slaves would have also been present in number. However, he says nothing about them, a narrative silence that reflects the expectation that a wealthy household would be full of slaves. Leucippe's situation is different. She travels with a large retinue of slaves even as a refugee from war, and that draws the narrator's attention.

Clitophon falls in love with Leucippe the moment he sees her, despite that fact that he has been betrothed to his half-sister Calligone (1.4). That night there is a welcoming dinner (1.5). The dining arrangement is that of the Roman triclinium, and Clitophon carefully notes the seating plan couch by couch, as arranged by his father (1.5.1, αὐτὸς κἀγὼ τὴν μέσην, αἱ μητέρες αἱ δύο τὴν ἐν ἀριστερᾷ· τὴν δεξιὰν εἶχον αἱ παρθένοι). The narrator does not take note of the cooks, stewards, and waiters who would have been involved in preparing and serving the dinner. They may well have outnumbered the guests. However, Clitophon does note a slave musician belonging to his father, who entertains the diners (1.5.4, παῖς εἰσέρχεται κιθάραν ἁρμοσάμενος, τοῦ πατρὸς οἰκέτης). His attention is drawn to this slave because his song, about Apollo's pursuit of Daphne, reflects his own freshly conceived passion for Leucippe (1.5.5, τοῦτό μοι μᾶλλον ᾀσθὲν εἰς τέλος τὴν ψυχὴν ἐξέκαυσεν). Clitophon makes the slave a reflection of his own subjectivity. The following morning, he mentions another slave, whose job it was to wake him up, a routine task not worthy of comment. On this occasion, however, the slave interrupts an erotic dream involving Leucippe, and Clitophon rebukes him (1.6.5, ἐπειδή με ἤγειρεν ὁ οἰκέτης, ἐλοιδορούμην αὐτῷ τῆς ἀκαιρίας, ὡς ἀπολέσας ὄνειρον οὕτω γλυκύν).

Clitophon and Satyrus: domination and dependency

This section discusses Clitophon's narration of the slaves who have a role in his attempt to seduce Leucippe and the action that results when the attempt fails. Leading the cast of slaves is Satyrus.[19] Other slaves play significant supporting roles, such as Clio, the heroine's attendant, and Conops, who belongs to Leucippe's mother and who keeps a watchful eye on the heroine. Clitophon also notes the engagement of a wider supporting cast of unnamed slave characters who figure in the action.

Clitophon's narrative interest in these slaves is motivated by the role they play in his erotic scheming. This holds even for Satyrus. However, there is something more at play in Satyrus' case. The narrator and his slave attendant are bound together in a close but twisted master–slave relationship involving domination, resistance, and reciprocal affection and hostility. Clitophon is the master, but he depends on Satyrus for direction in his love affair. Satyrus is the slave, but he takes control of events. In doing his master's bidding, he finds the opportunity to display his intelligence, talent, and verve; in other words, by serving his master, he asserts his own identity.[20] Thus, we see Satyrus take the initiative, even creating the story, as it were, at several key turns: in the first attempt to seduce Leucippe, in his rescue of the heroine from ritual sacrifice, and in his promotion of the match between his master and Melite. As a relationship between a

156 Leucippe and Clitophon

feckless young master and a clever scheming slave, the Clitophon–Satyrus relationship aligns with Plautine examples such as Calidorus and Pseudolus or Mnesilochus and Chrysalus in *Bacchides*. But Achilles is reflecting something darker in the intimate master–slave relationship. From his constant attendance on the master, Satyrus was able not only to meet but also to anticipate the master's needs, desires, thoughts, and commands.[21] In Keith Hopkins's view, such familiarity bred mutual contempt:

> Roman domestic slaves, especially in small "bourgeois" households, were body slaves. To their repeated degradation, they knew their master inside out. They knew him in all his vulnerability, with his trousers down – rather as a wife does, but without the tender feelings or the commitment of a lifetime. The master understandably hated the slaves who knew his weaknesses, and projected the anxiety which that hatred aroused on to the slaves themselves.[22]

Clitophon's authority as master was undermined by his dependence on Satyrus.[23] Satyrus' intimate knowledge of his master's shortcomings further undermined Clitophon's nominal mastery. It is possible to observe an undercurrent of ambivalence and even hostility in their relationship. An early indication of ambivalence is the incidental manner in which Clitophon brings Satyrus into the story. Returning from the funeral of his cousin Clinias' young lover, who had been killed in a riding accident, Clitophon attempts for the first time to make love talk to Leucippe in a garden, which he depicts in an ecphrasis that culminates with a description of a peacock. Taking this bird as a cue, he addresses a lecture to Satyrus about the peacock that Leucippe is meant to overhear (1.16.1). As a master, Clitophon acknowledges the slave as a prop in his attempt at seduction; as a narrator, he brings Satyrus into the story without introduction, as if he were an object, not a person. Leucippe, too, is accompanied by a slave attendant, a character whom Clitophon also notes for the first time, Clio (διαβαδίζουσα γὰρ ἔτυχεν ἅμα τῇ Κλειοῖ).[24] Ancient readers of the novel (and Clitophon's unnamed listener from the opening frame) would have expected a slave to be in attendance on the master. It may be reasonable to infer that Satyrus had been present earlier, when Clitophon first saw Leucippe, when he sat opposite her at the banquet, when he confessed to Clinias that he was in love, and at the funeral of Clinias' lover: *ubi Clitophon, ibi Satyrus*. However, the slave rises to the level of narrative interest only now, when his master assigns him a role in the seduction.

Clitophon seems to have intended to use Satyrus as a passive instrument, casting him as the audience for his speech about the peacock. However, Satyrus does not remain passive. He catches on at once (1.17.1, Καὶ ὁ Σάτυρος συνεὶς τοῦ λόγου μου τὴν ὑπόθεσιν) and encourages his master to continue talking about love, asserting himself by seizing the initiative in serving his master's aims. In addition, Clitophon does not seem to have realized that Satyrus already knew that he was in love. Soon after, when he explicitly asks Satyrus for his assistance, the slave notes that he already had known his master

Leucippe and Clitophon   157

was in love but had kept this knowledge to himself out of consideration for Clitophon's feelings (2.4.1). Now that things are out in the open, Satyrus informs his master that he had seduced Clio, who had been entrusted with the care of her mistress in the bedroom. He would coax his fellow slave into helping as well (2.4.2). Satyrus knew that his master had fallen in love, but Clitophon was unaware of his slave's erotic activity. The slave is a closer observer of the master than the master is of the slave.

Thus, Satyrus becomes his master's erotic advisor, a *praeceptor amoris*, along with Clitophon's cousin Clinias. Satyrus urges Clitophon to be bold. Inspired by this advice (2.5.1, ὑπὸ τοῦ Σατύρου παροξυνθείς), Clitophon finagles a first kiss from Leucippe, seizing an unusual opportunity: The heroine was alone. Even Clio, he comments, was away (2.6.1, μόνη δὲ ἦν καὶ οὐδὲ ἡ Κλειὼ συμπαρῆν). Note the reversal: Clitophon tends to omit mention of slaves who are present but who have no bearing on his love affair; on this occasion, he notes the absence of a slave that makes this kiss possible. Serving as a wine steward at dinner that evening, Satyrus repeatedly switches Clitophon's and Leucippe's wine cups so that they can play the elegiac game of cup-kissing (2.9.1–3).[25] After dinner he contrives to lead Clio off, giving his master another opportunity to get Leucippe alone while she is taking a walk (2.10.1–4). However, a noise interrupts their kissing. Satyrus had been watching and made the noise himself, claiming that he thought someone was coming (2.10.5). Helen Morales argues that Satyrus, having arranged the meeting, contrives to break it up. According to Morales, the slave character is an intrusive presence in his master's love life, who both "encourages and thwarts desire."[26] It may also be possible to frame Satyrus' frustrating interruption in the context of the conflicted relationship between master and slave. Even as he assists Clitophon, Satyrus asserts himself, in this case by sabotaging his master.

After that evening, Clitophon's father, Hippias, hastens the preparations for his son's wedding to Calligone. However, the wedding is averted. Callisthenes, a noble but profligate young man from Byzantium, had also fallen in love with the heroine but was rejected as a suitor by Leucippe's father. He followed Leucippe to Tyre in order to abduct her. However, he mistook Calligone for her cousin Leucippe and kidnapped the wrong girl. Clitophon's reaction to his half-sister's calamity reminds the reader of just how brutally self-interested a narrator he could be (2.18.6 – 19.1):

> The unexpected cancellation of the wedding was a relief. Still, I was pained for my sister's misfortune. I let a few days go by and addressed Leucippe: "How long will we stop at kissing, darling? The prelude is good. Let's give it a sexy coda" (προσθῶμεν ἤδη τι καὶ ἐρωτικόν).

Satyrus steps up to make this possible. He obtains a duplicate key to the wing of the house where Leucippe and her mother have been accommodated. Through Clio, he even secures Leucippe's cooperation. But there is a fly in the ointment, or rather a "Gnat," the slave named Conops (whose name means "gnat"),

158 Leucippe and Clitophon

belonging to Leucippe's mother Panthea. Conops had gotten wind of a plot and was on the alert. Clitophon introduces him as a busybody, a chatterbox, and a glutton (2.20.1, Ἦν δέ τις αὐτῶν οἰκέτης πολυπράγμων καὶ λάλος καὶ λίχνος). From Panthea's point of view, however, Conops would have been an exemplary slave, on the alert night and day to protect his owner's family (2.20.1, ὑποπτεύσας μή τι νύκτωρ ἡμῖν πραχθῇ, διενυκτέρευε μέχρι πόρρω τῆς ἑσπέρας).[27] Panthea will continue to trust Conops after the attempt on Leucippe. He remains on the lookout for threats; his absence while on an errand for his mistress will enable Leucippe to run away (2.31.4, καὶ γὰρ ὁ Κώνωψ, ὅσπερ ἡμῖν ἐφήδρευε, κατὰ τύχην ἐκείνην ἀπεδήμει τὴν ἡμέραν, τῇ δεσποίνῃ διακονησόμενος.).[28] However, as an impediment to Clitophon, Conops is a bad slave, and the narrator tags him with some of the stereotypical tropes: He does not mind his own business. He does not know when to keep his mouth shut. He likes to eat.[29] Clitophon does not see Conops. He sees an impediment who happens to be a slave and draws on the normative social stereotype of the bad slave to describe him.

A contest between Satyrus and Conops ensues, Satyrus' first star turn in the narrative. The contest begins with an exchange of fables between the two slaves. Playing on his own name, Conops tells Satyrus a fable about a gnat whose buzzing bested an elephant. Satyrus responds with a counter-fable, about a gnat who defeated a lion but then flew into a spider's web. He concludes with a warning to Conops (2.22.7): "So, you, too, should watch out for spiders." The contest is decided a few days later, when Satyrus invited Conops to dinner, knowing that the other slave's love of food would overcome his wariness (2.23.1, εἰδὼς αὐτὸν γαστρὸς ἡττώμενον). He poured a sleeping potion into Conops' parting glass and cleared the way for Clitophon. The contest reflects the association between slaves and the fable.[30] Both fables represent a situation in which an apparently insignificant creature, the gnat, is able to conquer a powerful adversary, an elephant and a lion. In Satyrus' version, however, after the gnat triumphs over the lion, it is ensnared by another humble creature, the spider. Corinne Delhay has noted that in literary terms the contest prefigures the victory of Satyrus and Clitophon over Conops and Panthea.[31] We should also consider the ideological potential of these fables. A fable in which a lesser animal defeated a stronger one could have encoded, for a slave, a fantasy of compensatory revenge or an implied warning.[32] In this case, however, the implied antagonists are not master and slave but two slaves, each of whom competes on behalf of his master.[33] Achilles adopts the outward form of the slave-associated genre but ignores (or rejects) its ideological potential.

Clitophon gains entry to Leucippe's bedroom, but then everything goes wrong. Warned in a dream, Panthea wakes up and rushes in. Satyrus helps Clitophon to get away but not before Leucippe's mother realizes that there had been an intruder (2.24.4–6). The events that follow illustrate how the actions and reactions of master and slave characters have been linked together in a web of socially conditioned expectations and practices. Panthea assumes Clio was guilty of complicity and assaults the slave, slapping her and tearing her hair (2.24.1). The mother's worst fear is that her daughter had had an assignation with a slave (2.24.4). More on that detail later.

Meanwhile, Clitophon and Satyrus run away before Clio exposes them under torture (2.25.3, καὶ ἐδόκει κράτιστον εἶναι φεύγειν, πρὶν ἢ ἕως γένηται καὶ τὸ πᾶν ἡ Κλειὼ βασανιζομένη κατείπῃ). Clitophon's lack of concern here for the fate of Clio is significant in two ways. As a self-interested narrator, he has lost interest in Clio because she is no longer an asset in his love affair; as a privileged youth, he is not concerned about the fate of slave who will be tortured.[34] Clitophon and Satyrus leave the house, telling the slave in charge of the door that Clitophon was going to see a mistress (2.26.1). The pretext is plausible. Clitophon's sexual experience before Leucippe, as he will reveal later, had been limited to prostitutes, who may also have been slaves (cf. 2.37.5). The imaginary lover in this case might also be imagined as a slave. In any event, Clio followed close behind them, unwilling to be left behind, that is, to accept Clitophon's loss of narrative interest in her, and forcing her way, as it were, back into the story. She knew what awaited her and preferred death to torture. Clitophon reports the slave's dread of torture through her own words (2.26.3): "Clio said, 'I'm going with you. If I wait for tomorrow, death will be my prize, sweeter than torture.'" Clinias takes over and finds a seemly way to shunt her out of the story, giving her to one of his own slaves to get her shipped safely away (2.27.3, καὶ τὴν μὲν Κλειὼ τῶν οἰκετῶν αὐτοῦ τινι παραδίδωσι). Back at the house, Leucippe is able to defy her mother's questions with greater confidence in Clio's absence (2.28.2–3). When Satyrus arrives to persuade her to join him in flight, she has already decided to run away (2.30.1–2). A few days later, while Conops is away on other business, Satyrus contrives her escape, using the rest of the sleeping potion on Panthea and two of her slaves, Leucippe's new maid, whom he also had pretended to be in love with, and a doorman (2.31.1–4). The protagonists are ready to run off.

As Clitophon tells the story, Satyrus is his master's indispensable agent in the scheme to seduce Leucippe. He stands apart, but he does not stand alone. Clitophon also notes the role played by other slaves in the erotic escapade, Clio and Conops, of course, but also the roles played by bit-part, nameless enslaved characters: the slave doormen who are drugged or lied to, Leucippe's new chambermaid, the slave whom Clinias instructs to put Clio on a boat, and perhaps even the imagined slave who, Panthea fears, had slept with her daughter.[35] Clitophon's detailed narratorial attention to the activities of these slaves, from Satyrus to nameless doormen, may, in part, be read as a reflection of his self-centeredness. They figure in his account because they figure in the seduction, either as aides or obstacles. They count for Clitophon for this reason alone. The possibility that some of these slaves might be tortured in an investigation following Leucippe's disappearance does not concern him.

Beyond carrying out his master's instructions, Satyrus knows his master's will; he advises, exhorts, and enables Clitophon. In other words, Clitophon's passion serves as an opportunity for the slave to express himself, as it were, to display his intelligence, his cunning, and his audacity. Satyrus acts ostensibly on his master's behalf, but the initiative he is allowed also may give him an opportunity

160 Leucippe and Clitophon

to express his hostility to his owners. Had Clitophon been successful and had he had sex with his cousin Leucippe, Satyrus would have, through him, struck a serious blow against his master's household. Satyrus is not a normal *servus callidus*, who gains his young master access to a courtesan; he tries to make it possible for Clitophon to have sex with Leucippe, a member of his master's own extended family.[36] When Panthea first questioned her daughter, in great anxiety she asked if Leucippe had had an assignation with a slave (2.24.4): "οἴμοι τῶν κακῶν· μὴ καὶ δοῦλος ἦν;" In a sense, it was a slave who had – almost – struck a blow against the honor of the family.[37]

* * *

The couple flee, along with Clitophon's cousin Clinias, in the company of three slaves, Satyrus and two unnamed slaves who belong to Clinias (2.31.5, ἦμεν δὲ οἱ πάντες ἕξ, ἡμεῖς καὶ ὁ Κλεινίας καὶ δύο θεράποντες αὐτοῦ). On board they meet Menelaus, an Egyptian who is returning home after a sentence of legal exile. He is, like Clinias, a lover of boys and had, like Clinias, lost his *erōmenos*, having killed him in a hunting accident. Clitophon's description of the introductions at 2.33.3 does not mention the slaves who are present. Nor does he mention any slaves in attendance on Menelaus (2.34). It seems possible, however, that slaves had attended him during his exile. Slaves were known to accompany their masters into exile, and the narrator's silence on this point does not imply that Menelaus was returning home unaccompanied.[38]

During two days of smooth sailing, the young men share food, tell their stories, and debate the merits of heterosexual and homosexual love. On the third day, a sudden storm sinks the ship and throws everyone into the sea. Leucippe and Clitophon cling together to a part of the prow. They see Menelaus and Satyrus holding on to the mast and Clinias holding on to the yardarm (3.5.1). The wind drops, and Clitophon sees Menelaus and others washed ashore. He and Leucippe reach another part of the beach near the mouth of the Nile at Pelusium. They grieve for Clinias and Satyrus (3.5.6). Clitophon makes no reference to Clinias' two slaves or any slave who was attending on Menelaus.

They hire a boat to sail on to Alexandria. But bandits who infest the region, the *boukoloi*, or herdsmen, attack their boat and take them prisoner (3.9). The next morning an emissary from the bandits' leader comes and takes Leucippe away to sacrifice to their god (3.12). Clitophon is rescued soon after when soldiers attack his captors. The commander of the soldiers hears his story and enlists him in the cavalry. Clitophon also notes that the commander gave him an Egyptian slave as his attendant (3.14.4, ἔδωκε δέ μοι καὶ θεράποντα τὸν ἐπιμελησόμενον Αἰγύπτιον), a slave assigned in acknowledgment of his status. The next morning, Clitophon believes he is an eyewitness to Leucippe's sacrifice. He sees the robbers, who were separated from the soldiers by a ditch, appear to disembowel Leucippe on an altar (3.15). He looks on in stunned silence, like Niobe, in tears and unable to move (3.15.6).

That evening, Clitophon goes to kill himself in despair at the very altar on which Leucippe had been murdered when Menelaus and Satyrus suddenly appear. They

Leucippe and Clitophon   161

uncover the coffin that had been left there and reveal the heroine alive. Menelaus tells Clitophon how the bandits had enrolled him, as a native Egyptian, into their ranks and accepted Satyrus as his slave (3.19.3, ἐξαιτοῦμαι δὴ καὶ τὸν Σάτυρον ὡς ἐμόν). Then Menelaus gives the narration over to Satyrus to tell how they managed to save Leucippe. Since it had been the slave's doing, it was his story to tell (3.19.3, "λέγε δὴ τὰ ἐπίλοιπα, Σάτυρε, σὸς γὰρ ἐντεῦθεν ὁ λόγος"). Menelaus' invitation allows Satyrus to enjoy a second star turn, during which he takes over the narration. Satyrus tells his master at length how he devised and, with Menelaus' help, executed the theatrical ruse, involving a blood-filled bladder and a collapsible stage knife, that enabled them to fake the sacrifice and save Leucippe's life (3.20–22). The props reinforce the idea that Satyrus has written, produced, and starred in his own drama.[39] When the slave is finally finished, Clitophon is beside himself with joy (3.23.1):

> After I heard this, I became all confused and did not know what I could do to thank Menelaus adequately. So I made the very common gesture of falling at his feet, embracing him, and bowed before him as to a god. Sudden pleasure suffused my soul.

Clitophon's over-the-top gratitude to Menelaus draws attention to the absence of acknowledgment given to his slave, who, in fact, deserved most of the credit. The narrator's failure to acknowledge Satyrus may be considered in the generic context of a slave's social marginality.[40] Clitophon may care for Satyrus, but Satyrus is still a slave, a person of less social importance.[41] However, another aspect of master–slave relations may be at play here in addition to the slave's social marginality. Satyrus' ingenuity and invention in this episode, though exercised on his master's behalf, destabilizes Clitophon's position as the master, implying an unflattering contrast between the slave's resourcefulness and the master's inability to act. It is possible to read Clitophon's failure to express gratitude to Satyrus as an attempt, after his own feckless conduct, to reassert himself as master by ignoring his slave.

After this incident, Clitophon seems to push Satyrus out of the narrative. Satyrus is present, but his presence is not noted. Clitophon turns instead to Menelaus' guidance to fend off Charmides, the leader of the Egyptian forces, when he falls in love with Leucippe. He turns to Menelaus again when Leucippe goes inexplicably insane. The heroine's illness continues for ten days, during which time Charmides leads his army to a major victory over the *boukoloi*. After the battle, Chaereas, a sailor in the Egyptian forces, told Clitophon how an Egyptian soldier, Gorgias, had fallen in love with Leucippe and suborned a slave to give her a love potion that caused her illness; this Gorgias had been killed in the battle, but his slave, who had survived, would supply the antidote for a price (4.15). Satyrus reenters the narrative for the first time since he described his rescue of Leucippe from ritual sacrifice back at 3.22. Clitophon is able to purchase the antidote because Satyrus had managed to save his master's money during the shipwreck and keep it safe even while among the *boukokloi* (4.17.6, ἦν δὲ τὸ πᾶν ἡμῖν ἐφόδιον σῶον· ὃ γὰρ ὁ Σάτυρος ἔτυχεν ἔχων ἐζωσμένος, ὅτε ἐναυαγήσαμεν,

162 Leucippe and Clitophon

οὐκ ἀφῄρητο ὑπὸ τῶν λῃστῶν). Satyrus' resourcefulness saves the day again, but for a second time, his master fails to thank him.

After a final victory over the *boukoloi,* the protagonists, Satyrus, and Menelaus travel downriver to Alexandria. Chaereas joins them (4.18). Clitophon continues to rely on Menelaus, who finds a house for the protagonists to rent (5.2.3). Then Chaereas tries to kidnap the heroine. He arranges for pirates to seize her and carry her off in a boat. As Clitophon gives chase and gains on the kidnappers, they bring a woman out on deck, behead her, and toss her into the water. Clitophon believes it is Leucippe. He begs the commander of his boat to give up pursuit so that he can retrieve Leucippe's headless torso (5.7.1–4). It is Menelaus, Clitophon notes, who consoles him and enables him to keep on living (5.8.1, θεραπευθεὶς ἄκων τὸ τραῦμα, τοῦ Μενελάου με παρηγοροῦντος, διεκαρτέρησα ζῶν). All this time, Satyrus has been present for the action but absent from the story, displaced by Menelaus. Six months go by and Clitophon's heart is beginning to heal. One day he sees his cousin Clinias in the marketplace. Clinias catches him up on events, how he survived the shipwreck and how, the day after they all had fled, a note arrived from Leucippe's father betrothing her to Clitophon. Clitophon's father, Clinias says, would be coming to bring him and Leucippe home to Tyre. However, having set in motion the events that led to Leucippe's death, Clitophon cannot bear to face his father. He determines to flee farther (5.11.1–3).

As Clitophon and Clinias are talking, Menelaus and Satyrus return. Satyrus tells Clinias about Melite, a wealthy widow of Ephesus, who has fallen in love with Clitophon. This Melite, Satyrus continues, wants to make Clitophon even more than a husband, she wants him to be her master (5.11.6, βούλεται δὲ τοῦτον ἔχειν δεσπότην· οὐ γὰρ ἄνδρα ἐρῶ) and to take him home with her to Ephesus. Satyrus adopts the slavery-to-love metaphor here to impress Clinias with the extent of the woman's passion. The slave may know how slave-owners like to talk about passionate desire as a kind of slavery; he had likely been present back at Tyre when Clinias and his master were teasing one another about being metaphorical slaves of this sort (cf. 1.7.2–3). The speech also reminds the reader that Satyrus has also been present all the time in Alexandria, living in the same house as the protagonists and accompanying his master in the city, possibly even to Pharos the day Leucippe was murdered. In addition, for some four months, Satyrus has apparently been acting on his own initiative, urging his master to take up things with Melite. But Clitophon has been resisting the widow's attentions and entreaties because he is too proud or because, Satyrus notes maliciously to Clinias, he thinks his Leucippe will come back to life (5.11.6, νομίζων αὐτῷ Λευκίππην ἀναβιώσεσθαι).

Clitophon has not noted Satyrus' presence in Alexandria, much less his efforts at matchmaking. Grief explains his lack of interest in Melite. Or perhaps he had been resisting the match because Satyrus was promoting it. He yields instead at the urging of his cousin Clinias (5.12.2, "Ἄγε με," εἶπον, "ὅποι θέλεις, εἰ καὶ Κλεινίᾳ τοῦτο δοκεῖ ...") with the proviso that consummation be deferred until the arrival in Ephesus so that Clitophon can honor an oath he says he

Leucippe and Clitophon   163

took not to have relations with another woman in the city where he had lost Leucippe. Satyrus, more eager than his master, rushes off to arrange things with Melite (5.12.3, ταῦτα ἀκούσας ὁ Σάτυρος, προστρέχει πρὸς τὴν Μελίτην εὐαγγέλια φέρων). Clitophon bids farewell to Menelaus and duly notes the tearful departure of this worthy friend from the narrative (2.15.1, νεανίσκος πάνυ χρηστὸς καὶ θεῶν ἄξιος καὶ ἅμα δακρύων ἐμπεπλησμένος· καὶ ἡμῖν δὲ πᾶσι κατεφέρετο δάκρυα). He notes that Clinias will join him and Melite (2.15.2). He does not mention Satyrus, although he will figure importantly in the events that transpire at Ephesus.

* * *

Leucippe, it turns out, is alive and near Ephesus, sold by the pirates to Sosthenes, the slave foreman of an agricultural estate belonging to Melite. While he and Melite are inspecting the estate, Clitophon fails to recognize her – she was the very image of an abused slave with shorn hair and dressed in rags – but Melite takes the heroine under her care (5.17).[42] Back in town, Satyrus gives Clitophon a letter from Leucippe (5.18). The detail suggests the possibility of Satyrus' unnarrated presence during the visit to the farm and some backstage action after that in town, when Leucippe got in touch with the slave, told him what happened during the kidnapping (5.20.1), and gave him the letter. In any event, when Clitophon learns that Leucippe is alive, he is ready to rush into her arms. Satyrus cautions him not to: They were caught in a trap without resources and dependent on Melite, a powerful woman madly in love (5.19.4, γυναῖκα ὁρᾷς πρώτην Ἐφεσίων μαινομένην ἐπὶ σοί, ἡμᾶς δὲ ἐρήμους ἐν μέσαις ἄρκυσιν). He advises Clitophon to write a propitiatory letter to Leucippe and tells his master that he himself tried to help on that score by swearing to Leucippe that his master had married Melite unwillingly (5.20.2, κἀγὼ γὰρ αὐτῇ διωμοσάμην, ὡς ἄκων αὐτὴν ἔγημας.).

At this juncture, Clitophon surprises Satyrus: He and Melite are not really married because he has not yet had sex with her. The slave is incredulous (5.20.3): "You're joking, sir; you sleep together!" But Clitophon affirms that the marriage is yet unconsummated. He asks Satyrus what he should write. Satyrus tells his master to write the letter himself; Clitophon is cleverer than he (impatience disguised as servile flattery?), and Eros himself will tell him what to say (5.20.4). The exchange reflects the distance that has grown between master and slave. Satyrus has lost the close knowledge of his master that he once had. In any event, Clitophon composes a quick note, gives it to Satyrus, instructing him to supplement the note by saying the right things on his behalf (5.21.1).

At that point, Melite's husband, Thersander, returns (for he had been no more lost at sea than Leucippe had been beheaded) and puts Clitophon under guard as his wife's adulterous lover (5.23.4–7).[43] Melite then learns that the slave who had approached her at the farm was Clitophon's Leucippe. She also learns that Clitophon is still in love with her. Melite accepts this, and after a single consolatory night of love with Clitophon, she arranges his rescue. Her plan to help Clitophon

164   Leucippe and Clitophon

involves Satyrus at several points. He will wait with Clinias for Clitophon and Leucippe at the house of Melite's *syntrophos*, her foster brother (6.1.2). When this plan goes awry and Clitophon is put in jail, Melite informs Satyrus and Clinias, who go to comfort the protagonist in prison (6.14.1). The slave returns the next day to offer further support (6.15.1). Finally, when Clitophon is framed for the purported murder of Leucippe and is ready to confess to the crime in his despairing belief that Leucippe really has been murdered, he notes that both Satyrus and Clinias tried to dissuade him (7.6.6). He also records that Clinias and Satyrus changed houses so as not to be staying with Melite's *syntrophos*, an attempt, it seems, to obscure their collaboration.

That is the last time Clitophon mentions Satyrus. The slave then disappears from the story without comment. Clitophon still has much to tell: his trial and condemnation (7.7–12); the flight of the wicked Sosthenes (7.10); the escape of Leucippe (7.10); the arrival in Ephesus of Leucippe's father, Sostratos (7.12); Clitophon's release on bail and the reunion of Clitophon, Leucippe, and Sostratos (7.16); the dinner hosted by the priest of Artemis in which Clitophon summarizes for Sostratos the couple's adventures (8.4–5); a second courtroom confrontation and the chastity trials of Leucippe and Melite (8.8–14); and, finally, the capture of Sosthenes and his confession (8.14–15) and a second dinner hosted by the priest where Leucippe relates her part of the story and Sostratos informs the couple of the happy fate of Clitophon's sister, Calligone (8.15–18).

The reader, however, should not assume Satyrus' absence from these events from his absence from the narration. After Thersander's return, the slave came to be associated with Clinias, who plays an important role in the events that lead to the denouement. Clinias delivers a spirited speech in Clitophon's defense at the trial (7.9). He is present at the temple of Artemis to celebrate Leucippe's reunion with Clitophon and her father (7.15–16). He is not at the dinner hosted by the priest of Artemis later that night. But Clitophon notes the reason for the absence. His cousin had remained in his lodgings so as not to impose on their host (8.7.2). These were the lodgings that Clinias was sharing with Satyrus. It seems, then, that Satyrus is around. As a slave, he had reason to stay away from his master's trial, where he could have been examined under torture.[44] But no such caution entailed his absence after the trial. It was possible for Satyrus to be in attendance on his master during dinner with the priest; he could also have been present at the final celebratory dinner. Given his association with Clinias, it seems possible that Satyrus would be present at the end of the novel, the day after the final dinner, when Clinias came to report the fate of Thersander (8.19).[45] Clitophon does not remark on Satyrus' presence on any of these occasions, in part, because the novel's erotic intrigue is over. Satyrus steps back into the background as his master's marginalized slave attendant.

But the slave's disappearance may also be read as Clitophon's definitive assertion of control over his resourceful and assertive slave, domination expressed here in the form of exile from the narrative. Behind Clitophon's narrative treatment of Satyrus is an author who was himself keenly aware of the complexities of an intimate master–slave relationship. At the same time, however, Achilles seems

Leucippe and Clitophon   165

more interested in how this relationship may contribute to his characterization of Clitophon as an unreliable narrator than in commenting on the character of masters as a class or nature of the master–slave relations in general.

Melite's slaves

Leucippe's and Clitophon's reunion in Ephesus is played out in a broader company of slaves belonging to Melite and Thersander. When the protagonists first fell in love, the stage had been similarly crowded with slave characters. At Tyre the slaves involved in the erotic plot were all domestic slaves: Satyrus, Clio, Conops, the unnamed doormen, and other domestic functionaries. This is also the case at Ephesus. Melite's house was the largest in Ephesus, with many slaves and expensively furnished (5.17.1, θεραπεία πολλὴ καὶ ἡ ἄλλη παρασκευὴ πολυτελής). However, the enslavement of the heroine also offers a brief look at agricultural slavery. Melite's country estate was a working farm on the villa model, staffed by another body of slaves, supervised by a man who was himself a slave.

Events in Ephesus follow the pattern established in Tyre, in which slave characters are intimately involved in their owners' love lives, both as agents and witnesses. The first such slave agent is the heroine herself. Soon after their arrival in Ephesus, while Melite and Clitophon are inspecting Melite's rural estate, a farm slave approaches them. She is filthy and dressed in rags, with shaved head and fetters around her ankles, bearing a hoe. This slave tells Melite her story. She was once free, a Thessalian named Lacaena; now a slave, she is at the mercy of Sosthenes, the head slave on the farm, who was beating her because of her refusal to sleep with him. Lacaena bares her back and shows her scars. "Lacaena," of course, is Leucippe. Melite is moved. She is able to see through the disfigurement of slavery and to recognize the woman's noble quality. She agrees to rescue Lacaena from the farm and arrange to return her home without ransom (5.17).

Melite has need of Lacaena, who is from Thessaly, where women are famed for witchcraft. The next day she asks her to provide herbs in order to stimulate Clitophon's interest in sex. Night after night, he has lain next to her no more amorous than a eunuch. Happy to learn that Clitophon has not slept with Melite, Leucippe agrees to help her mistress (5.22). Like Callirhoe and Anthia, Achilles' heroine acts like a slave, in allowing Melite to think that she knows something about witchcraft. As narrator, Clitophon expresses discomfort with this deceit, a discomfort similar, perhaps, to the ambivalence that Chariton and Xenophon expressed when their protagonists acted like bad slaves. He expresses the opinion that Leucippe deceived her mistress because "[s]he did not think she would be believed if she denied having knowledge of witchcraft. I think that that is why she promised" (5.22.7, ἀρνουμένη γὰρ οὐκ ᾤετο πίστιν ἕξειν· ὅθεν οἶμαι καὶ ἐπηγγείλατο). In his identification of motive, Clitophon seems not to appreciate Leucippe's sense of vulnerability as a slave. She is wary of the consequences should Melite learn who she really was – Clitophon's lost love. Her caution here aligns with

166 Leucippe and Clitophon

Satyrus' caution when he warns Clitophon not to reveal the heroine's identity after he learns she is alive (5.19.3).

On his unexpected return, Thersander heard about his wife's new lover from Sosthenes and rushes to seize him. He assaults Clitophon, puts him in chains, and locks him up (5.23). In the tumult, Clitophon lets drop the letter from Leucippe, which Melite picks up and reads. That night, after Thersander goes to stay at a friend's house, she visits Clitophon in his cell. She reproaches him for misleading her, convinces him to make love to her this one time, and then, generously, sets him free him to be with Leucippe.

Clitophon notes the actions of the slaves involved in setting him free. Melite first avoided the other slaves in the household (5.25.1, λαθοῦσα τοὺς ἄλλους), the many domestic slaves in her household. She spoke to a guard, who was watching over the cell (τῷ τὴν φυλακὴν τὴν ἐμὴν πεπιστευμένῳ), to gain admission and posted two trusted attendants outside to be on the lookout while she was with him (θεράποντας δύο τοῦ δωματίου προκαθίσασα). After they made love, Melite disguised Clitophon in her clothing and entrusted him to her trusted slave Melantho (6.1.4, θεράπαινα δὲ ἦν αὕτη τῶν πιστῶν), who took Clitophon out of the house and gave him over to one of Melite's freedmen, whom Clitophon knew from the voyage to Ephesus and whom he liked (6.2.2, ἀπελεύθερος δὲ αὐτὸς τῶν συμπεπλευκότων ἦν ἡμῖν καὶ ἄλλως ἐμοὶ κεχαρισμένος). Clitophon only notes the presence of this ex-slave character when he has a role to play in his own story. Clitophon also notes how Melite later revealed the deception to Pasion, the guard responsible for keeping a watch on his cell.[46] Melite explains to Pasion that she deceived him not out of distrust but to protect him from complicity in the plot and the possibility of torture. She then gives him a reward, ten pieces of gold, and advises him to lie low until Thersander's temper has cooled (6.2.4–6).

Melite's generous concern for Pasion and her trusting relationship with Melantho reflect an idealized version of master–slave relations.[47] The involvement of slaves named Melantho and Pasion also point to Achilles' interest in slavery as a literary *topos*. The name of Melite's trusted attendant posits the *Odyssey* as an intertext, where Melantho was the disloyal slave of Odysseus' faithful wife Penelope. In *Leucippe and Clitophon*, Melantho is the loyal slave of Thersander's disloyal wife, Melite. The inversion signals that the moral assessment of a slave in this text depends more on the slave's loyalty to the master rather his or her innate goodness or wickedness. From Thersander's perspective, Melantho would have been the wicked slave of his adulterous wife.[48] A similar situation was present with Conops, a slave loyal to his mistress, Panthea, but an officious busybody as far as Clitophon was concerned. Finally, Pasion's name suggests famous slaves from history as an intertext. A historical Pasion, the fourth-century slave banker became, as a freedman, the wealthiest man in Athens and received Athenian citizenship in return for his benefactions.[49] Achilles may have had this person in mind, a figure who could have been known to his readers through the speeches of Demosthenes. The ten gold pieces that Melite gives the prison guard suggests a learned joke (the start of this Pasion's fortune?) via the reader's knowledge of Athenian history and his reading of Athenian oratory.

Leucippe and Clitophon 167

Leucippe as enslaved protagonist

Leucippe reenters the story as a slave on Melite's farm near Ephesus at 5.17, very much alive. The pirates had, in fact, beheaded another woman. The heroine they sold to a slave dealer who sold her, in turn, to Melite's estate manager. She was there the whole time Clitophon was mourning her in Alexandria. The narration of her enslavement comprises two episodes. The first was her encounter with Melite and Clitophon on the farm. In the second, Leucippe has to fend off the unwanted attentions of Melite's husband Thersander, who will turn up at 5.23. Clitophon's reliability as a narrator is particularly in doubt in the second episode. He is present during her first appearance as a slave on Melite's estate but fails to recognize her. What kind of lover is that? What kind of narrator is that? During the events of the second episode, Clitophon was in jail, charged with adultery. How does he know what happened? In brief, as Achilles engages with Leucippe's enslavement, a key motif, he focuses as much on the unreliability of his narrator as he does on the substance of the heroine's slavery.

Consider Clitophon's description of the heroine's appearance as a slave on Melite's estate (5.17.3):

> As soon as we arrived and were walking through the crop rows, a woman suddenly fell at our knees. She was bound in thick chains about her feet and held a mattock. Her head was shaved. She was filthy and had pulled up her disgusting tunic for work. "Pity me, mistress, woman to woman. I was free, but now I am a slave – so it is pleasing to Fortune." Then she fell silent (καὶ ἅμα ἐσιώπησε).

Melite commands the slave to stand up. Affirming that she can recognize the slave's noble origins (5.17.4, κέκραγε γάρ σου καὶ ἐν κακοῖς ἡ μορφὴ τὴν εὐγένειαν), she asks her who she is and who put her in chains. Leucippe tells her owner that she was Lacaena, a Thessalian; that Sosthenes, the slave foreman of Melite's farm, had punished her for refusing his advances. She begs Melite to allow her to repay her purchase price. Then she displays the full extent of her mistreatment, opening up her tunic and showing the whip marks on her back (5.17.6). Melite rebukes Sosthenes and commands him to tell the truth about how he came to buy Lacaena and then dismisses him as steward (5.17.10, ἡ δὲ τὸν μὲν τῆς διοικήσεως, ἧς εἶχεν, ἀπέπαυσεν). Finally, she orders Lacaena's chains to be removed and gives her over to the care of her slave attendants to clean, clothe, and take to the city (5.17.10, αὐτὴν δὲ παραδίδωσι θεραπαίναις).

Koen De Temmerman has noted parallels between Leucippe and Chariton's heroine Callirhoe. Leucippe appears, like Callirhoe, as a slave on an estate in Asia Minor. On meeting her owner, each heroine asserts her free birth and promises to pay the price of her freedom.[50] In both cases, the slave-owners, Dionysius and Melite, recognize the noble birth of the slave and sharply question the estate manager regarding the purchase. Dionysius and Melite both promise the enslaved heroine her freedom and give her over, for the time being, to the care of their

168   Leucippe and Clitophon

other slaves. Finally, each enslaved heroine misleads her owner by omission. Callirhoe fails to tell Dionysius that she is married. Leucippe does not tell Melite that she was Clitophon's lover, the man at that moment walking at her mistress's side. These parallels suggest that Achilles is engaging with the enslaved-protagonist motif through Chariton's novel.[51]

Achilles reinforces the meta-literary character of the representation of Leucippe's slavery through the perceptions of his ego-narrator. For all his close observation of detail in this episode, Clitophon sees only a generic figure who has been assembled out of attributes that signify a farm slave – fetters, a farming implement, shorn hair, a tattered cloak, filth, the marks of the whip on the slave's back – a generic slave who is not herself an individual. In contrast, Melite sees beneath this surface and recognizes a woman of noble birth. Clitophon says that he was troubled by all this but because the slave reminded him of Leucippe (5.17.7, καὶ γάρ τι ἐδόκει Λευκίππης ἔχειν).[52] The detail confirms earlier observations: Clitophon does not take much note of slaves unless they have some relevance to his desire for Leucippe. But neither is he a particularly close observer of Leucippe. Something about "Lacaena" reminded him of Leucippe, and for this reason, he was moved. Of course, she is Leucippe, but Clitophon cannot quite see that.[53]

At dinner that evening, Satyrus hands Clitophon a letter from Leucippe reproaching him for marrying another woman after all she had suffered for him: she was made a human sacrifice and then died a second death; she was sold as a slave, bound in fetters, forced to work the ground with a hoe; and she was whipped (5.18.4, διὰ σὲ ἱερεῖον γέγονα καὶ καθαρμὸς καὶ τέθνηκα ἤδη δεύτερον· διὰ σὲ πέπραμαι καὶ ἐδέθην σιδήρῳ καὶ δίκελλαν ἐβάστασα καὶ ἔσκαψα γῆν καὶ ἐμαστιγώθην). The letter throws the narrator into emotional confusion (5.19.1, τούτοις ἐντυχὼν πάντα ἐγινόμην ὁμοῦ· ἀνεφλεγόμην, ὠχρίων, ἐθαύμαζον, ἠπίστουν, ἔχαιρον, ἠχθόμην).[54] He is especially moved when he reads Leucippe's description of the punishments she had endured as a slave and notes (5.19.6):

> When I got to the part about the whipping and the torture that Sosthenes had inflicted on her, I cried as if I were actually witnessing it. For my intellect directed the eyes of my soul to the content of the letter and revealed the things they saw as if they were happening.

Leucippe's catalogue of action reprises Clitophon's ecphrasis of her enslavement earlier. Indeed, he had, at the least, witnessed the marks that "the whips and tortures applied by Sosthenes" had left on Lacaena's body. The fact that Clitophon now knows that Lacaena is really Leucippe may be sufficient to explain why he is more affected by reading about the mistreatment of a slave than by seeing the results of the mistreatment. But it may also be the case that Achilles' narrator is more easily engaged by slaves in texts than by actual slaves.[55]

De Temmerman notes additional points of comparison and contrast between Achilles and Chariton in a second episode involving Leucippe's slavery, when

Leucippe and Clitophon   169

Thersander tries to seduce her, using Sosthenes as a go-between.[56] In encouraging his master Thersander, Sosthenes corresponds to Dionysius' steward Leonas. However, Achilles' version of the episode is darker and more violent than Chariton's. In Chariton, Leonas had bought Callirhoe as a consolatory gift for his grieving master. In Achilles, Sosthenes tries to take Leucippe for himself but later sends his master in her direction out of spite, because she had rejected him and because his mistreatment of her resulted in his removal as estate manager. In Chariton, Dionysius never struck the heroine. He rejected Leonas' suggestion that he just assert his rights over Callirhoe as her master, noting at the time that he would not prove worse than the pirates who sold her to him (*Call.* 2.6.1–3). Like Dionysius, Thersander acts with restraint when he first sees Leucippe, struck by her beauty and moved to compassion by her plight (6.7). But he soon shows his true nature.[57] In Chariton, Dionysius had treated Callirhoe with more consideration of her physical comfort after learning she was noble-born. Thersander, in contrast, uses physical force against Leucippe only after he has learned of her noble origin.

The next day, Sosthenes returns to the hut where Leucippe is held captive. There are further parallels to Chariton.[58] Sosthenes boasts to Leucippe that he has managed to make his master fall so in love that he is willing to make her his wife (6.11.3–4). This self-aggrandizement recalls Artaxates' attempt to get credit for making the Great King fall in love with Callirhoe (*Call.,* 6.5.5). Chariton noted that the eunuch, as a barbarian and a slave, could not understand that Callirhoe, a free woman and a Greek, would not want to have the Great King as a lover (*Call.,* 6.4.10). Chariton's heroine deflected Artaxates with irony (*Call.,* 6.5.8, κατειρωνεύσατο): She was unworthy of the Great King, a slave of Dionysius (*Call.,* 6.5.9, Διονυσίου δούλη); Artaxates had mistaken his master's pity for love. Like Callirhoe, Leucippe responds to Sosthenes with irony (6.12.1): "May you receive the same good fortune that you have brought to me." Clitophon comments that Sosthenes does not understand the heroine's irony (τὴν εἰρωνείαν οὐ συνείς) because he cannot understand that she would not want to be his master's lover, the noblest man in all of Ionia (6.12.2, γένει δὲ πρῶτος ἁπάντων τῶν Ἰώνων).[59] The characterization recalls Callirhoe's master, Dionysius (*Call.,* 2.5.4, Μιλησίων πρῶτος, σχεδὸν δὲ καὶ τῆς ὅλης Ἰωνίας). Leucippe remains unmoved and Sosthenes leaves her with a threat about the consequences of incurring Thersander's anger (6.13.3–4). The threat recalls Artaxates' warning to Callirhoe, that Chaereas would die a horrible death should he best the king as a rival in love (*Call.,* 6.7.13).

In the chapter on Chariton, I argued that Callirhoe's consciousness of Dionysius' power was sufficient coercion in itself. Dionysius never resorted to physical violence.[60] In contrast, Achilles realizes Thersander's power to compel in vivid violence. As Artaxates had misled the Great King about the results of his first solicitation of Callirhoe (6.6.6–8), so does Sosthenes mislead Thersander about the prospect of seducing Leucippe. The slave takes his master back to the hut where the heroine is confined. Outside, they overhear Leucippe (who they believe is Lacaena) express her love for Clitophon and boast of her noble

170   Leucippe and Clitophon

family (6.16.6): Her fatherland is Byzantium; Sostratos is her father; Panthea is her mother. Leucippe's soliloquy echoes Callirhoe, who was ever conscious that she was the daughter of Hermocrates, the leading citizen of Syracuse (cf. *Call.*, 2.9.2).

After she finishes, Thersander enters the hut. He forces her head up to kiss him (6.18.3–5). Leucippe rebukes him for acting like Sosthenes, a slave worthy of his master (6.18.6).[61] Her words enrage him. He strikes her (6.20.1, ῥαπίζει δὴ κατὰ κόρρης αὐτὴν) and insults her as a miserable slave (ὦ κακόδαιμον ἀνδράποδον). Sosthenes eggs his master on to torture her so that she will learn not to look down on her master (6.20.4, ὡς ἂν μάθῃ δεσπότου μὴ καταφρονεῖν). Leucippe responds with grandiloquent disdain for torture (6.21.1–2):

> Set up the torture show. Bring on the wheel. Here are my arms, stretch them. Bring on the whips. Here is my back. Strike it. Bring on the fire. Here is my body, burn it. Bring on the ax. Here is my neck, cut it.

Achilles' heroine is ready to submit to all this – but she will die before submitting to Thersander. He can never harm her free soul.

It is also possible to see here an amplification of Callirhoe's response to Artaxates' threat of torture if she rejected the Great King (*Call.*, 6.7.8). Chariton's heroine laughed off the eunuch's threat: She had already been buried alive, kidnapped by pirates, and (worst of all) she now knew that Chaereas was nearby but could not be with him. "Bring it on!" she seemed to say. Her words also recall Habrocomes' defiant assertion that he was ready to undergo any of the tortures used to compel slaves (*Eph.*, 2.4.4). One may also read in Leucippe's disdain for torture the outlines of a textbook Stoic.[62] While precise alignment with another text is uncertain, the general point is clear. Clitophon's account of Leucippe as a slave refers more to the representation of slaves in books rather than to actual slaves, in this case how an enslaved novel heroine acts.[63] She defends her chastity and rejects a man who is trying to seduce or marry her. She fends off the overtures of his go-between with irony. She expresses her love for the hero. Koen De Temmerman has connected Leucippe's heroic behavior with a logical problem concerning the first-person narration. Clitophon describes events that took place in his absence. Bryan Reardon suggests that Achilles has here abandoned the convention of the ego-narrator for the sake of the story.[64] De Temmerman suggests instead that Clitophon is filling in the details of what he does not know with his generic knowledge of how novelistic heroines are expected to behave.[65] In particular, Clitophon is adding in his generic knowledge of how novel heroines act when they have been enslaved.

How an enslaved young woman of noble birth acts is only one of the things Clitophon has learned from his reading. Callow youth that he is, he attempts to assert his narratorial authority by pronouncing on various aspects of human psychology, the nature of love, and the character of women, slaves, and barbarians.[66] The narrator's book knowledge of the world is distilled in a series of *sententiae*, or learned pronouncements. These *sententiae*, uttered by Clitophon himself or attributed by him to other characters, mark the novel in general.[67] Some of the

Leucippe and Clitophon   171

narrator's sententious knowledge concerns the psychology and physical manifestation of strong emotion. He explains why, during the first encounter with Thersander, Leucippe's state of mind could be reflected in her facial expression (6.6.2–3) and how her tears came to evoke the man's pity (6.7.1–7). Later he explains why Thersander took encouragement from Sosthenes about his chances to win over Leucippe in a generalization about the hopefulness of lovers (6.17.5). The longest and most elaborated of all the novel's *sententiae*, on the complex relationship between love and anger (6.19), appears during a second confrontation between Leucippe and Thersander. After Thersander tries forcibly to kiss her, Leucippe lashes out at the villain, accusing him of being as much a slave as Sosthenes (6.18.6, οὔτε ὡς ἐλεύθερος ποιεῖς, οὔτε ὡς εὐγενής· καὶ σὺ ἐμιμήσω Σωσθένην. ἄξιος ὁ δοῦλος τοῦ δεσπότου). On hearing these words, Thersander grows angry (6.19.1, ὠργίζετο), and Clitophon launches into a long digression about the two flames of love and anger.

Helen Morales has analyzed the passage both on a functional and a formal level.[68] The digression shifts the focus away from Thersander himself and represents his emotional conflict in terms of a general truth regarding human physiology and psychology. Paradoxically, by telling us more (about what we do not need to know), the digression tells us less (about Thersander himself). The language is elaborate and full of mixed metaphors. One metaphor describes how, if a lover is rejected, his anger takes control, shackling love as a slave of desire (6.19.4, ὡς δοῦλον τῆς ἐπιθυμίας πεδήσας κρατεῖ). When Clitophon returns to the narration, his description of Thersander enacts the general truth outlined in the digression. So long as he thought she might love him, Thersander was Leucippe's slave (6.20.1, ὅλος Λευκίππης δοῦλος ἦν); rejected by her, he abuses her as a wretched human chattel (Ὦ κακόδαιμον ἀνδράποδον) and strikes her. The *sententia* could function, as Morales notes, to frustrate the reader's desire to know what will happen.[69] A reader who had read Chariton might have been anxious to know, as she plowed through the digression's overwrought rhetoric, if Thersander, an anti-Dionysius, was going to rape Leucippe, in contrast to Dionysius, who had not raped Callirhoe. Only on returning to the plot would she learn how the heroine avoids rape, paradoxically, by challenging Thersander to torture her instead (6.21–22), a challenge that confuses and stymies him (7.1). Leucippe is able soon after to escape (7.13).

The author has used slavery, real and metaphorical, as an organizing idea for the episode and the digression. Leucippe is Thersander's slave in the real world as it has been represented in the fiction. The digression describes how anger is the metaphorical enslaver of love in the struggle taking place in Thersander's soul. The villain himself was Leucippe's metaphorical slave so long as he thought she might love him; when she rejects him, he abuses her as his actual slave. Thus, in the action, Leucippe challenges Thersander to torture her, a master's right, in order to prevent him from raping her, another master's right. But the worst is avoided. Leucippe is neither raped nor tortured. The reader thrills. Achilles' interest, again, is not in slavery *per se* or in the psychology of love and anger but in how these concepts can be exploited for suspense, melodrama and rhetorical display.

172 Leucippe and Clitophon

Clitophon as "enslaved" protagonist

Clitophon is not enslaved. In contrast to the heroine, he is neither sold nor given a new name nor put to work as a slave. However, Achilles associates Clitophon with qualities that were associated with slavery and casts him in the slave role in narrative situations that in other texts represent master–slave relations. Again, the evidence suggests a text that explores narrative possibilities present in slavery rather than an interest in slavery itself.

When Thersander unexpectedly returns home, he bursts in on his wife and Clitophon and attacks Clitophon. The hero does not resist. He asserts that he could have defended himself but was afraid to (5.23.6, ὑποπτεύσας δέ τι κακὸν εἶναι, ἐδεδοίκειν ἀμύνασθαι, καίτοι δυνάμενος). This apologetic passivity potentially aligns with the cowardice that was stereotypically associated with slaves.[70] The author associates the hero's passivity, if not his cowardice, with slavery in a second episode. Having been convicted for Leucippe's murder, Clitophon is led off to execution. But the execution is put off for religious reasons when Leucippe's father, Sostratos, arrives in Ephesus on a sacred embassy. At the same time, Leucippe has miraculously reappeared as a suppliant in the Temple of Artemis after escaping from the hut where Thersander had imprisoned her. The lovers are reunited (7.12–16). Then Thersander bursts in (8.1.1). There is an exchange of insults. Thersander asserts that Leucippe is his slave and a slut (8.1.1, δούλην ἐμήν, γυναῖκα μάχλον); Clitophon calls Thersander a slave through three generations (8.1.3, τρίδουλος); Thersander retorts that Clitophon is bound as a slave and has been condemned to death (8.1.3) and then assaults him (8.1.3–5):

> He struck me across the face really hard and laid on a second one. Streams of blood began to flow from my nostrils, for the blow had channeled all of his rage. But when he struck a third time, carelessly on the mouth, he struck his hand on my teeth. His fingers were wounded; he cried out and could barely pull his hand back. Thus, my teeth avenged the outrage done my nose. For they wounded the striking fingers, and his hand suffered the punishment it had meted out.

The attack on the narrator recalls an aspect of violence in master–slave relationships sufficiently common to move the medical writer Galen, a second-century contemporary of the author, to counsel his slave-owning readers not to strike their slaves with their own hands:

> If a person adheres to this practice, he will one day find himself less prone to anger than before, that he is not angered for trifling or middling reasons but only when the cause is great – and only a little. And later he will be only slightly angry even over the greatest provocations, if he observes what I myself have practiced my whole life, ever since I was a young man, that is, never to strike one of my slaves with my hand. This was also the practice of my father, who reproached many of his friends who had bruised a nerve

Leucippe and Clitophon   173

in striking their slaves on the teeth, saying that they deserved to have a fit and die of their very rage, when it was possible for them a little later to accomplish this end by applying as many blows as they wished with a cane and a whip.[71]

In the novel, Thersander aligns with the sort of angry master whom Galen takes to task; Clitophon aligns with the slave who has been struck in the mouth. The protagonist's failure to defend himself provides more evidence for his cowardice.[72] But Clitophon's cowardice here may also reflect the conditions faced by a slave, for whom passivity in the face of such an attack may have been the best choice.[73] Active resistance, striking back, might provoke an even worse beating. The doctor, of course, was concerned with the well-being of the slave-owner, whose power encouraged a habit of anger that was injurious to his or her own mental and physical well-being. In contrast, a hidden transcript of this violence could have celebrated the master's injury, not deplored it. Clitophon's comic conclusion, that his teeth avenged his nose, could have reflected such a version.

However, Achilles has detached the episode, and possibly a servile version of it, from the context of master–slave relation, transforming it into entertainment for his readers. Clitophon is not a slave and Thersander is not his master. In addition, the author dissipates the violence of the assault through an elaborate rhetorical display in which the victim assigns fingers, nostrils, and teeth a role in a drama involving *hybris* and retribution. The conceit then continues in a literary direction in Clitophon's appeal to the crowd assembled in the temple of Artemis (8.2.3–4): Thersander's bloody hand has done the work of a sword in the human sacrifices performed by the Scythians in their worship of this goddess! Thersander has turned Artemis of Ephesus into the bloodthirsty goddess worshipped by the Taurians! Achilles' focus lies not in the hard punch to the face that Clitophon took, that is, the blunt violence suffered by the slave (or here, the "slave-ish" character), but in how his narrator turns this violence into a form of clever display and learned entertainment.

Another instance in which Achilles has adapted a narrative situation that may have originally involved master–slave relations is the episode in which Clitophon finally has sex with Melite. All the while that Clitophon believed that Leucippe was dead, he had refused to have sex with the widow of Ephesus. Only after he learns that Leucippe is alive does he make love to her. The irony has impressed critics, who tend to consider Clitophon's infidelity in the context of his defective character or his relationship with Leucippe.[74] Leucippe will not learn about Clitophon's infidelity because he does not tell her, the one detail he omits from his account of the time he spent with Melite (8.5.3, ἓν μόνον παρῆκα τῶν ἐμαυτοῦ δραμάτων). Clitophon himself describes his behavior as an act of erotic pity, a sort of medicine for Melite's lovesick heart (5.27.2, φάρμακον ὥσπερ ψυχῆς νοσούσης). A final detail: After they make love, Melite disguises Clitophon in her clothing and arranges for his escape from the house (6.1.1).

A tradition about master–slave relationships in popular narrative, the first-century CE *Life of Aesop*, offers additional perspective on this episode.[75] At

174   Leucippe and Clitophon

one point, Aesop's master Xanthos promises him his freedom if the slave is able to extricate him from a difficult obligation. Aesop accomplishes this, but when he reminds his master of his promise, Xanthos chases the slave away, possibly with a blow (74, ὑβρίσας ἐξεδίωξεν).[76] Aesop vows to avenge himself. When Xanthos is away, Aesop goes outdoors naked and begins to masturbate. Xanthos' wife sees him and is filled with desire at the sight of his large penis. She promises him a cloak if he would have intercourse with her ten times. Aesop agrees, for so he will be able to pay back Xanthos for his mistreatment (75, θέλων δὲ καὶ τῷ δεσπότῃ ἀνταμύνασθαι). The tenth effort proves too much for Aesop, and Xanthos' wife refuses to give him the cloak.[77]

The master's cuckolding is completed in the coda to the story. Aesop asks Xanthos to settle a dispute he has with his master's wife. He complains to Xanthos that the woman had promised him a cloak if he could knock ten plums from a plum tree with a single stone. This, Aesop says, he was able to do; however, one plum landed in dung, and his mistress refused him the cloak. Xanthos' wife acknowledges that she gathered nine plums but argues that the tenth did not count. She offers Aesop a second chance to throw a stone and shake the tenth plum from the tree. Aesop rejects the offer, claiming that his wrist is lame. Xanthos awards him the cloak. This coda adds a significant detail to the slave's cuckolding of his master. The Greek for plum, *kokkymēlon*, evokes the cuckoo (κόκκυξ), ornithology's signifier for cuckolds.[78] Another pun in which Aesop hints at Xanthos' cuckoldry is contained in his excuse for not wanting to throw another stone, that his wrist is no longer up to the job: (76, οὐκέτι μου ὁ καρπὸς εὐγονεῖ). *Karpos* also means "fruit" or "produce," and *eugoneō* means "to be fruitful or productive." Both words suggest the sexual act in their association with productivity and fertility. However, Xanthos' narrow understanding of language prevents him from picking up on these hints; he awards Aesop the cloak that his wife had promised.[79]

In this episode, the slave Aesop avenges his mistreatment by sleeping with his master's wife, who promises to reward the slave with one of her garments. He secures this prize by exploiting his master's obtuseness with language.[80] The same narrative elements are present in Clitophon's cuckolding of Thersander. Clitophon has sex with Melite after Thersander beats him. After they have sex, Melite gives Clitophon her clothing. As was the case with Aesop's master, Thersander's cuckolding is made complete through his deficient understanding of language. However, this happens much later: At the end of the novel Clitophon is still in danger if he can be proved to have been Melite's lover. To prove the accusation false, Melite undergoes a ritual trial in which she denies that Clitophon had been her lover. If she swore a false oath, the ritual would expose both her and Clitophon (8.12.9). Melite is confident because Thersander has required her to swear that she had not had sexual relations with Clitophon during the time that he had been away (8.11.2, παρ' ὃν ἀπεδήμουν χρόνον). It was only after Thersander's return that she had sex with Clitophon. Like Aesop, Clitophon is able to complete his revenge because of his antagonist's linguistic obtuseness. Like Xanthus, Thersander is betrayed by his deficient understanding of language.

Leucippe and Clitophon   175

These parallels raise the possibility that Achilles found inspiration for the episode involving Clitophon's adultery with Melite in a narrative tradition involving master–slave relations that also informed the *Life of Aesop*. Achilles, however, has detached the story from slavery. He may have been more interested in the narrative possibilities of these elements than in the master–slave relations on which they reflect. In particular, he appears to have mitigated the element of hostility between slaves and masters by suppressing the idea that Clitophon was motivated by revenge, the explicit motivation for the slave Aesop. Instead, Clitophon sleeps with Melite as an act of gallantry, a gesture of erotic pity.

Slavery and literary play

After the lovers have been reunited, Thersander's plots against them are close to a complete and final exposure. At a dinner hosted by the priest of Artemis, Clitophon's soon-to-be father-in-law Sostratus asks for a summary of the couple's adventures. It seemed at first that the presence of Leucippe's father would turn the dinner into one long shame-fest for the reckless lovers (4.5.1, καὶ ἦν ὅλον τὸ συμπόσιον αἰδώς). Sostratus, however, encourages Clitophon not to be ashamed (8.4.4, μηδὲν αἰδούμενος) but to tell his story. When one's trials are over, he says, telling about them provides more solace than pain (ἔπειτα τῶν ἔργων παρελθόντων ἡ διήγησις τὸν οὐκέτι πάσχοντα ψυχαγωγεῖ μᾶλλον ἢ λυπεῖ). Sostratus' encouragement and his advice about the therapeutic power of narration point to the conclusion of Chariton's *Callirhoe* as an intertext for this episode. Like Sostratus, so did Chaereas' father-in-law, Hermocrates, urge him not to feel shame in giving an account of his and the heroine's adventures and misadventures to the Syracusan *dēmos*. The brilliant conclusion to his story, its *lampron telos*, would overshadow what happened at the start (*Call*, 8.7.4).

Encouraged, Clitophon tells his story, from the couple's nighttime flight from Tyre up to Sostratus' arrival in Ephesus (8.5). One wonders how much shame Clitophon actually felt and how much encouragement he really needed. He uses Sostratus' exhortation to talk to make himself look good, exaggerating his own continence (8.5.2, ἐξῆρον τὸ πρᾶγμα ἐμαυτοῦ πρὸς τὴν σωφροσύνην μεταποιῶν) and omitting mention of the time that he and Melite did have sex (8.5.3, τὴν μετὰ ταῦτα πρὸς Μελίτην αἰδῶ).[81] Then he turns to the trials that Leucippe had endured, even greater than his own (8.5.4): "She has been sold. She worked as a slave. She dug ditches. She has been robbed of her crowning beauty – you see how her hair has been cropped" (πέπραται, δεδούλευκε, γῆν ἔσκαψε, σεσύληται τῆς κεφαλῆς τὸ κάλλος· τὴν κουρὰν ὁρᾷς). Leucippe still bears the scars of her experience. Clitophon emphasizes not only that she has been a slave but that as a slave she endured physical abuse and degradation (8.5.5):

> I exaggerated her part of the story more than mine (motivated by my love to please her while her father was listening), how she endured every bodily assault and outrage save one, on account of which she withstood the others.

176 Leucippe and Clitophon

The contrast between Clitophon's summary and its intertext, Chaereas' summary, is striking. In contrast to Leucippe, who is present at dinner and still bears the scars of her ordeal, Callirhoe, after a brief appearance before the Syracusan *dēmos*, had returned home to rest after the stress of her journey home (*Call.*, 8.7.3). Chaereas, despite his father-in-law's encouragement, remained a reluctant narrator, who obscured or mitigated the circumstances of Callirhoe's slavery even while the heroine herself was not present to hear it.[82] Clitophon, in contrast, proves a willing narrator of the awful things that had happened to himself and to Leucippe.[83] He hammers home the point that Leucippe had been a slave (cf. πέπραται, δεδούλευκε, γῆν ἔσκαψε) and even calls attention, in her very presence, to her shorn hair, in the dubious expectation that this would please her (cf. χαριούμενος). The recollection of slavery had been so painful for Chaereas that he tried to avoid talking about it; when forced to give an account, he tried his best to obscure or spin what it had been like, even when Callirhoe was not there to listen. For Clitophon, in contrast, the heroine's slavery made for a great story, one that he thought he could tell in a manner that might even please Leucippe and her father. Chaereas' summary reflected the psychological impact of slavery on those who endure it. Clitophon's summary tries to exploit enslavement as material for exciting and interesting storytelling in a manner that exposes his own cluelessness.

In its contrast with Chaereas' hesitant and unwilling summation, Clitophon's breezy account of Leucippe's slavery attaches to the broader pattern of Achilles' exploitation of literary representations of slavery for the experimentation and entertainment. The author has drawn from Callirhoe and other erotic novels, for example, in the case of Leucippe's melodramatic soliloquy (6.16); he has adapted fable, in the confrontation between Satyrus and Conops; he has reapplied popular narrative, in the cuckolding of Thersander; he draws from an anecdotal tradition, in the episode in which Thersander wounds his hand on Clitophon's teeth. Achilles also alludes to famous and infamous slaves from the historical record and other literature, such as Melantho and Pasion.

The author's repeated use of the *Scheintod* motif also belongs to this pattern. Previous scholars have seen a literary send-up of authors such as Chariton.[84] Leucippe dies three false deaths: the first, her fake disembowelment and, the second, her apparent beheading. The third *Scheintod* was the false report Clitophon heard in prison, that Melite had arranged for Leucippe's murder (7.1–5). Parody is indeed the intent, but it is also possible to see Leucippe's three *Scheintode* as another instance in which Achilles has appropriated a motif associated with slavery and detached it from its original context.[85] Only the second false death is followed by the heroine's enslavement, when the pirates sold her to Sosthenes in Ephesus. The first *Scheintod* is followed by the lovers' reunion. The false report of Leucippe's death that Clitophon hears in prison set in motion a chain of events that, one may argue, resulted in the heroine's escape from slavery rather than her entry into it.[86] In contrast to Xenophon, Chariton, and even Longus, in whose novels false death serves as a metaphor for the social death experienced by the protagonist through slavery, Achilles exploits this motif as an occasion for the Grand Guignol rhetorical effect of the heroine's disembowelment and beheading

Leucippe and Clitophon 177

in the first two "deaths" and as an opportunity to emphasizes the narrator's gullibility in the third: "Fool me once, shame on you. Fool me twice, shame on me." But three times, Clitophon?[87] In his repeated use of the *Scheintod* we may see another instance in which Achilles has detached narrative material associated with the experience of slavery from its original context and exploited it for the purpose of narrative experimentation and play.

* * *

In concluding, I shall try to close the frame where Achilles does not. A key element in this author's narrative experimentation is his use of Clitophon as an embedded first-person narrator. Achilles represents not slavery but his narrator's perception, or lack of perception, of slaves. The occasions on which Clitophon notes or does not note slaves align with the social attitudes of his class. However, Achilles is also interested in Clitophon *per se* as a defective and self-centered narrator in general, not only when it comes to slaves. This concern may have a bearing on the novel's introductory frame, where an unnamed narrator arrives after a stormy voyage at Sidon, meets Clitophon, and then hears his story. Achilles neglects to close this frame. Rather, Clitophon ends *in medias res* with a cursory summary: the protagonists' departure to Byzantium and their wedding there; then, their return to Tyre and the wedding of Clitophon's sister Calligone to Callisthenes; and, finally, their intention to winter at Tyre and then return to Byzantium. End of story – no return to Sidon. The reader is left to wonder how Clitophon ended up in Sidon and why he seems to be unhappy and without Leucippe.

Ian Repath's consideration of the puzzle is helpful.[88] Rejecting suggestions that the text is incomplete or that the author was incompetent, Repath argues that Achilles' failure to close the frame was deliberate, the culmination of his subversion of the novel genre and its norms. In his view, the unexplained presence of the unhappy protagonist at the beginning of the novel represents the greatest generic subversion of all, "a Greek novel with a non-happy non-ending."[89] My discussion builds on that. But first it will be useful to note two additional perspectives. Massimo Fusillo saw elements of generic subversion in what he saw as the "the strange and unsatisfactory rapidity" of the novel's ending. Clitophon's cursory summary left no room to celebrate the marriage that should have been the novel's climax and undercut the happy ending. Fusillo saw this unsatisfactory conclusion as a reflection of the author's ironic and ambivalent attitude to the genre.[90] John Morgan noted that Clitophon is characterized by "blindness to himself and others" as a narrator. As a character, he seems incapable of learning from experience.[91] The indeterminacy of the novel's conclusion raises the possibility that Leucippe and Clitophon did not live happily ever after, and Morgan sees a plausible reason for this in Clitophon's inability to learn from experience. The young man's personal shortcomings, Morgan notes, are accentuated just before the conclusion, in Sostratus' account of Callisthenes and how his love of Calligone transformed him from an irresponsible wastrel, that is, someone much like Clitophon, into an upstanding citizen, considerate of the poor,

178 Leucippe and Clitophon

respectful to his elders, generous to his city, and brave in battle.[92] That is, an anti-Clitophon.

The unexplained absence of Leucippe at the conclusion of this novel points to another absence or, perhaps, an unnoted presence, that of Satyrus, Clitophon's slave attendant. Clitophon dropped him from his story well before the conclusion although Satyrus was still in Ephesus in attendance on his master. He could also have been in Sidon with Clitophon in the novel's opening frame, a point after the action of the novel has concluded. Clitophon's neglectful treatment of his slave attendant reflects his own limitations both as a narrator and as a person, perhaps his ingratitude as a master most of all. In the novel's *in medias res* conclusion, Achilles puts a stop to Clitophon's story with the same abruptness and lack of explanation that characterize Satyrus' disappearance from Clitophon's narration, arranging a bit of narrative payback for his amusing but annoyingly self-absorbed narrator.[93] For Achilles, as the author, has the power to control his characters as a perfectly realized master might control his slaves: He names them, defines their identities, directs what they do, and, when he has no further need of their services, sends them off. Thus, when he is finished with his novel, Achilles the author dispenses with Clitophon as Clitophon the narrator earlier dispensed with Satyrus.[94]

Satyrus' disappearance from the story may be related to another aspect of Clitophon's first-person narration. In contrast to Achilles, who has complete control over the narrative as the author, Clitophon is an internal narrator, another character in the novel, with only partial knowledge of events and limited control over his own story. His narration is additionally delimited by his deficiencies of character, his agenda as a lover, and his status as the scion of an elite family. These limiting factors are especially apparent in Clitophon's representation of the novel's slave characters. However, his control over them is no more complete than his control of the story. We saw, for example, how Satyrus transformed service to his master into a form of self-assertion that undermined Clitophon's mastery over his slave and, possibly, over the narrative. Clitophon pushes Satyrus out of the story, but the reader may infer the slave's continuing presence. Satyrus is still there, a presence, an independent subjectivity. In the ongoing conflict between master and slave over mastery, Achilles found a metaphor for his experiment in first-person narration.

Notes

1 Vogliano 1938.
2 Morgan 2004b, 499–502.
3 Achilles' exploitation of slavery as a theme for literary play may imply his own unconscious exercise of the privilege he enjoyed as a slave-owner.
4 Morgan 2004b notes among the key issues in Clitophon's first-person narration the distinction between the narrator and the author, the problematic nature of the non-omniscient narrator's knowledge of events, and the question of Clitophon's obvious biases.
5 Cf. Morales 2004, 55–56; Morgan 2007b, 110–111; De Temmerman 2014, 154–155.

Leucippe and Clitophon   179

6 On μύθοις: cf. Morgan 2007b, 111: "a story which is neither true nor like the truth."

7 See Fowler 2011 on the *logos/mythos* dichotomy; examples of the opposition in Plato: *Grg.* 523a; *Prt.* 324d; *Phd.* 61b.

8 Morgan 2004b, 499–502, 2007b. Morales 2004, 53–55 argues that Clitophon's assertion, that what he has to say is like fiction "acknowledges the far-fetched character of his tale." However, Morales argues, Clitophon only "undermines his credibility by emphasising the incredibility of his material."

9 For Clitophon's narration as both "character-defined" and "character-defining," see Morgan 2007b, 107.

10 Whitmarsh 2011, 90; also, p. 91, "a brutally self-interested narrator." At pp. 85–89, Whitmarsh argues that narrative authority was subject to intensified skepticism during the second century.

11 Morales 2004. Cf. Egger 1994a, 35–40 on the visual economy of *Callirhoe*.

12 Morales 2004.

13 Konstan 1994, 60–64.

14 Morales 2004, 156–165 makes the case for a more complex power dynamic. The heroine's beauty overpowers Clitophon and the other male characters who look at her; however, Leucippe's power is not the sort that gives her freedom of action.

15 De Temmerman 2014, 194–202.

16 Another way in which Clitophon's thinking about slavery reflected his status is reflected in his use of the slavery-to-love metaphor. At 1.7.2–3, Clitophon teases his cousin Clinias, the lover of a younger man in a homoerotic relationship, about being a slave to love (ἔσκωπτον οὖν αὐτὸν ἀεὶ τῆς ἀμεριμνίας, ὅτι σχολάζει φιλεῖν καὶ δοῦλός ἐστιν ἐρωτικῆς ἡδονῆς), and Clinias teases Clitophon in return (ἔσῃ ποτὲ καὶ σύ μοι δοῦλος ταχύ). When first courting Leucippe 2.6.2–3 Clitophon tells her that one of the gods has sold him to be her slave, as Heracles was sold to Queen Omphale (2.6.2–3, καὶ μὴν πέπρακε μέ τίς σοι θεῶν ὥσπερ καὶ τὸν Ἡρακλέα τῇ Ὀμφάλῃ).

17 Or it may be that Clitophon's failure to note the presence of slaves in his narration is an unconscious reflection of the social perspective of the author himself.

18 Cf. the remarks of Bradley 2000, 121–125.

19 Anderson 1988 comments on the importance of Satyrus, his master's *praeceptor amoris* and mover of much of the plot, despite his unannounced entrance ("a curious technical oversight," p. 190) and his abrupt exit. Anderson suggests that Achilles establishes a connection with Petronius' *Satyrica* through Clitophon's busy slave; both novels "share an ethos of self-indulgent rhetoric and sexual opportunism" (p. 192).

20 Cf. Joshel 1992, who examines the funerary epitaphs of slaves and freedmen for evidence of the importance of work in their identity formation. Behind Joshel is Hegel's model of master–slave relations in *Phenomenology of Mind*, in which the dominated slave reconstituted his own subjective identity through the labor he was compelled to do for his master.

21 Cf. the discussion in Fitzgerald 2000, 13–31 on the symbiotic potential of a master–slave relationship; in particular, Fitzgerald cites (p. 16) a poem by Ausonius to a slave secretary with an unsettling ability to anticipate what his master will say ("in Notarium," *Ephemeris* 7): "What is this novel state of affairs / that what my tongue has not yet formed / should reach your ears?"

22 Hopkins 1993, 22–23. Cf. Fitzgerald 2000, 13–17.

23 The model of the master–slave relationship in Hegel 1949, 228–240, esp. 236–237 can describe this aspect of the Clitophon–Satyrus relationship. The master becomes dependent on the slave for his identity as master and "is thus not assured of self-existence of his truth." Cf. Kojève 1969, 3–30 as a guide to Hegel's essay on lordship and bondage.

24 Note Gaselee's 1917, 49 comment, "Satyrus and Clio are rather inartistically introduced without further description."

180 Leucippe and Clitophon

25 Yardley 1991, 192 remarks on the episode, noting that elegy knew cup-kissing from comedy, in which case it is appropriate that Satyrus, as a comic *servus callidus*, makes the game possible.

26 Morales 2004, 124.

27 Morgan 2004b, 500 notes that the reader would realize that Clitophon is bad-mouthing Conops only because Panthea's slave keeps him from Leucippe; thus, the episode invites, "a critical and distanced reading based on the narrator's character."

28 Conops did not share his suspicions about Satyrus and Clitophon with Panthea (2.20.1, ὑποπτεύσας μή τι νύκτωρ ἡμῖν πραχθῇ). Was his mistress's trust in him not merited? Or did Conops realize that his word as a slave would have no standing against that of Clitophon?

29 On these elements of the stereotype, see the previous discussion, p. 6.

30 Cf. Rothwell 1994, on Aristophanes' characterization of Philocleon in *Wasps* as a lower-class citizen through the association of this character with fables.

31 Delhay 1990, 124.

32 Retaliatory violence: see the discussion in Bradley 1987, 152 on the fable of the fox and the eagle.

33 Achilles may have adapted or created these fables. Versions of both appear in the Aesopic corpus. However, as Delhay 1990, 118 notes, Achilles himself could have been the source.

34 Was Satyrus, too, unconcerned about what would happen to Clio, his lover and fellow slave? Clitophon does not tell us.

35 Note that Callisthenes assigns the job of recruiting the brigands who were to seize Leucippe (but who kidnapped Calligone instead) to the most trusted of his slaves (2.16.2, ἑνὶ τῶν οἰκετῶν τὴν κόρην, ὃς ἦν αὐτῷ πιστότατος).

36 In this regard, Satyrus differs from, for example, Pseudolus, who secures Calidorus access to Phoenicium, or from Tranio who secures his young master Philolaches access to Philematium.

37 Cf. Létoublon 1993, 83–84 on Panthea's anxiety about possible damage to the family's reputation.

38 For example, writing to Atticus from exile in October, 58 BCE, Cicero notes his intention to dismiss the better part of a retinue that would have included slaves as well as friends and freedmen (*ad. Att.* 3.19.1, *ero cum paucis, multitudinem dimittam*). An important exile such as Cicero represents an exceptional case; however, it seems plausible that Menelaus was accompanied by at least one attendant.

39 Plautus similarly represents Pseudolus' deception of Ballio as a play that the *servus callidus* has written, casted, costumed, produced, and directed (cf. *Ps.* 720–755).

40 A point noted by Egger 1990, 301–302: "But while this young man finds words of high praise and gratitude for his other comrades, the slave receives no acknowledgement for his unceasing support: his dedication is expected, even taken for granted. Though it is nowhere expressly said, it is subtly implied that as a human being, he does not count much."

41 Although warped by master–slave antagonism, the relationship between Clitophon and Satyrus is not without affection. Clitophon expressed grief for his slave as well as Clinias when he thought they had perished in the shipwreck (3.5.6, εἶτα ὠλοφυρόμεθα τὸν Κλεινίαν καὶ τὸν Σάτυρον). He inquired about the fate of both at the oracle at Pelusium (3.6.2). However, it is also meaningful that this concern did not extend to slaves in general. Clitophon made no mention of the fate of Clinias' two slaves, who presumably had drowned. If Menelaus had slave attendants, Clitophon does not mention their fate; the reference to individuals who were washed ashore with Menelaus after the shipwreck (3.5.5, τοὺς μὲν οὖν ἀμφὶ τὸν Μενέλαον θᾶττον προσάγει τῇ γῇ τὸ κῦμα) could refer either to Menelaus' fellow passengers or his slaves.

Leucippe and Clitophon   181

42 On Clitophon's failure to recognize Leucippe on this occasion, see the later discussion, pp. 167–168.

43 Normative stereotyping may be read in the details of the false report of Thersander's death: His slaves appear to have saved themselves and reported their master's death in error (5.23.4, τῶν γὰρ συνόντων αὐτῷ τινὲς οἰκετῶν, ὡς περιετράπη τὸ σκάφος, σωθέντες καὶ νομίσαντες ἀπολωλέναι, τοῦτο ἀπαγγείλαντες ἔτυχον).

44 Melite had agreed to submit her slave attendants to judicial examination; Thersander had similarly agreed to produce Sosthenes (7.10.2, Μελίτη τὰς θεραπαινίδας ἐδίδου καὶ Θέρσανδρον ἠξίου διδόναι Σωσθένην).

45 Perhaps Satyrus was present with his master in Sidon at the beginning of the novel, when Clitophon meets the unnamed stranger to whom he tells his story (1.2). In this case, it would be the unnamed primary embedded narrator who has elided the presence of the slave.

46 One may assume that Clitophon has learned this detail later or that Achilles has ignored the implications of first-person narration, a characteristic of the second half of the novel, where he increasingly resembles an omniscient third-person narrator: Reardon 1994, 84–86; Morgan 2004b, 499.

47 She was also willing to submit her slave attendants to torture during Clitophon's trial for Leucippe's murder. These attendants may not have mattered to her. Or she may have been maneuvering Thersander to produce Sosthenes (7.10.2, Μελίτη τὰς θεραπαινίδας ἐδίδου καὶ Θέρσανδρον ἠξίου διδόναι Σωσθένην).

48 Cf. Thalmann 1998, 51–52, who argues that in the *Odyssey* personal subjectivity is denied to "good" and "bad" slaves alike: Each kind of slave is defined in respect to the owner.

49 On the wealth and career of Pasion and his son Apollodorus, see Trevett 1992.

50 De Temmerman 2014, 192, notes a linguistic parallel between the two. Both fall silent after addressing their owner: Leucippe, after she declares her free birth (5.17.3, καὶ ἅμα ἐσιώπησε) and Callirhoe, after Dionysius questions her about her origins (2.5.6, ἐσιώπα).

51 De Temmerman 2014, 191. An additional parallel: Each heroine was the subject of a spectacular *Scheintod* immediately before her enslavement. Cf. Lalanne 2006, 169–170 for additional points of reference between Achilles and Chariton.

52 Satyrus later appears to let Clitophon off the hook, consoling him that no one would have recognized Leucippe. Her haircut alone made her look like a boy (5.19.2, καὶ τότε μὲν οὖν οὐδ' ἂν ἄλλος αὐτὴν ἰδὼν γνωρίσειεν, ἔφηβον οὕτω γενομένην· τοῦτο γὰρ ἡ τῶν τριχῶν αὐτῆς κουρὰ μόνον ἐνήλλαξεν); however, if Satyrus had been present on the visit to the estate (as were Melite's attendants), he might have recognized his fellow slave and knew to keep silent. Montiglio 2013, 70–76 emphasizes Clitophon's failure as novelistic lover.

53 Clitophon's description of the enslaved Leucippe aligns with key elements of the description of enslavement in Patterson 1982, 35–76, as a ritual process that renders the slave "socially dead" but incorporates her into society as a dishonored person. The first stage involves the symbolic death of the free person. In Leucippe's case, this was enacted through the *Scheintod*, her apparent beheading by the pirates. This process continues with the acquisition of a new name: Leucippe becomes Lacaena. The new slave then acquires the marks and badges distinctive of slavery: filthy rags to wear as clothes and chains about her ankles; other marks of slavery include her shaved head, the stripes the whip has left on her back, and the farm implement she bears. These marks and badges all indicate Lacaena's new status as a slave on Melite's estate.

54 Fusillo 1999 notes that such asyndetic expressions of conflicting emotions are emblematic of the genre.

55 Morales 2004, 202–203 notes the forceful impact of Leucippe's letter on Clitophon.

182   Leucippe and Clitophon

56 De Temmerman 2014, 191–192.
57 Repath 2007, 73–77 notes the relevance of Platonic psychology to Thersander's characterization.
58 De Temmerman 2014, 192.
59 Cf. the remarks in Richlin 2017, 314–318 on double meaning as a rhetorical strategy adopted by Plautus' slaves to disguise what they are really thinking.
60 This restraint has earned Dionysius a good reputation, perhaps obscuring the extent to which he did coerce Callirhoe: p. 64, n. 26.
61 Leucippe reflects the view that slaves, perhaps in their lack of subjectivity, reflect the moral qualities of their masters. Cf. the discussion in Bradley 1990, 144–146 on the acknowledgment in Roman law that slave criminality was sometimes instigated by the master.
62 Cf. Epictetus 1.1.23–25, "But I will fetter you." What is that you say, man? Fetter me? My leg you will fetter, but my moral purpose not even Zeus himself has power to overcome. "I will throw you into prison." My paltry body, rather! "I will behead you." Well, when did I ever tell you that mine was the only neck that could not be severed? (Oldfather 1925)
63 De Temmerman 2014, 190–193, observes that Leucippe acts like the heroine of a novel for the first time during this episode.
64 Reardon 1994, 84–86. Fundamental is the discussion in Hägg 1971, 127–137, who notes the varieties of strictness in Achilles' ego-narration and his increasing turn to an omniscient perspective; similarly, Fusillo 1989, 168. Morgan 2007b, 108, frames the issue: Clitophon's "documentary authority is weakest when he is furthest from personal participation in the action or from a direct line of information; and when his authority is weakest, the narrator's own personality and invention are most liable to manifest themselves."
65 De Temmerman 2014, 194. Alternatively, De Temmerman notes, one might imagine that Leucippe later told Clitophon what had happened in the confrontation with Thersander and Sosthenes. In that case, it would be Leucippe who presented herself to Clitophon as a typical Greek novel heroine.
66 Useful is the discussion in De Temmerman 2014, 176–187.
67 Scarcella 1987 discusses the *sententiae* collectively, irrespective of speaker, as a reflection of the normative opinions of Achilles' society. Morales 2004, 106–117 reviews how the *sententiae* in the novel pronounce authoritative judgment on women, slaves, and barbarians.
68 Morales 2000, 80–85, 2004, 117–130.
69 Morales 2004, 120.
70 Konstan 1994, 23–24 discusses the episode in the general context of the passivity of the genre's male protagonists. Hunt 1998, 160–164, discusses the stereotype of slave cowardice in the context of the ideology of Greek citizenship, which defined the citizen-soldier in opposition to the cowardly slave, and notes that slave-owning classes throughout history have subscribed to the stereotype. As noted in the introduction to this chapter, Clitophon himself, with his customary lack of self-reflection, endorses the stereotype when Sosthenes runs off in a panic and he observes that all slaves are cowards (7.10.5).
71 Text: W. de Boer, ed., Galeni, *De propriorum animi cuiuslibet affectuum dignotione et curatione*, Corpus medicorum Graecorum 5.4.1.1. Leipzig: Teubner, 1937: 3–37.
72 De Temmerman 2014, 178 notes four passages where Clitophon fails to defend himself from attack because of unheroic passivity: this passage; 3.12.2 (when the *boukoloi* seize the protagonists); 5.23.5–7 (Thersander's first assault on Clitophon); 7.14.3 (Sostratus' attack on Clitophon). From this, views such as that of Heiserman 1977, 126–127, who labels Clitophon a "comic coward" and Anderson 1997, 2283, who calls the narrator "a learned coward" in reference to his inaction during the sacrifice

Leucippe and Clitophon   183

of Leucippe at 3.15. Durham 1938, 4–6 sees a parody of novel heroes, such as Theagenes, who act more heroically. His argument was undercut by Vogliano's 1938 publication of the papyrus showing that Achilles Tatius came before Heliodorus;
nonetheless, Durham's point may be valid in the sense that Achilles is subverting
aspects of the genre.

73 See the discussion in Chapter 3, pp. 107–108 on the servile context for the passivity of
the novel hero.

74 Holzberg 1995, 89 expresses astonishment; Heiserman 1977, 126 sees a comic
triumph of the claims of *erōs* and humanity over the romantic code of chastity;
Reardon 1994, 90–91, suggests that the double standard cuts some slack for men,
allowing Clitophon his dalliance while exacting strict chastity from Leucippe;
Konstan 1994, 53 argues that physical chastity is less important in the genre than
emotional loyalty and that Clitophon's loyalty to Leucippe "is not put to the test in
the arena of physical continence."

75 Hägg 1997 argues that the prototype for the collection may have been composed as
early as the first century BCE to the second century CE. Moreover, Hägg suggests
that the origins of some of the elements in the *Life* may be found even earlier, in
the Hellenistic period or the fifth century.

76 *Life of Aesop* references are from *Vita W* in Perry 1952, 81–107.

77 Konstantakos 2006 discusses the episode in the context of a popular narrative and literary tradition involving adultery tales.

78 Cf. Hough 1970, 95–96, who observes a pattern of sound play in Plautus' *Amphitruo*,
repetition of the *cu* sound, which he argues is an aural evocation of Amphitryon's
cuckolding by Jupiter.

79 The slave's ability to turn his master's own words against him is a repeated motif in
the *Life of Aesop*. At one point, Xanthos tells Aesop to make "a lentil stew." Aesop
obliges by boiling a single lentil bean (39–41). On a subsequent occasion, Xanthos
tells Aesop to give some choice tidbits from a party "to her who loves me" (44, τῇ
εὐνοούσῃ), which Aesop takes as a reference to his master's dog rather than his
master's wife.

80 Konstantakos 2006, 591, identifies a sexual offense (adultery, incest, necrophilia) and
a related riddle as the core elements of the traditional adultery story. He also notes (p.
582) that clothing plays a role in both the Aesopic version and in Herodotus' account
of Periander's intercourse with his wife, Melissa, whom he had murdered (5.92).

81 When Clitophon recounts Leucippe's first *Scheintod*, he again credits Menelaus, not
Satyrus, for inventing the stratagem that saved her life (8.5.1, τὴν Μενελάου τέχνην).
On this, see the earlier discussion, pp. 160–162. Menelaus had remained in Egypt. If
Satyrus was in attendance on his master at the dinner, a possibility, he would experi-
ence his master's ingratitude a second time.

82 On Chaereas' summary, Chapter 3, pp. 77–80.

83 Whitmarsh 2011, 91–93, who also notes Achilles' use of Chariton as an intertext for
this episode, focuses on how Clitophon has slyly shaped his account to reflect well on
himself and Leucippe. However, Chaereas' final summary was no less marked by
omission and spin. In this regard, the actual contrast between Chaereas and Clitophon
may lie in the fact that Clitophon himself directs the reader's attention to his own
omission and spin.

84 Woronoff 2002 discusses the extreme character of Achilles' use of the motif; Anderson 1982, 27–28 notes how the author has self-consciously pointed to his repetition
of the motif. On the occasion of the third *Scheintod*, that is, the false report of the
heroine's death, Clitophon laments "that his beloved's body is subject to a law of
diminishing returns" (7.5.3): "In the case of those sham deaths I always had some
consolation, however small: in the first, your whole body was left me; in the
second, I lacked only your head (as it then seemed) for a proper burial. But now

184   Leucippe and Clitophon

you have died twice over – soul and body both are gone." McGill 2000 notes that Clitophon's lament in the second *Scheintod* reprises a theme from epigram.

85 In the case of the second *Scheintod*, McGill 2000 notes parallels between Clitophon's lament over the headless corpse and an epigrammatic tradition of lament for those lost at sea.

86 Clitophon's confession to the murder was followed by a legal wrangle that led to the possibility that Sosthenes would be tortured. He ran away in a panic, leaving Leucippe's hut unlocked.

87 Whitmarsh 2003, 197–198 frames the narrator's credulity as a failure to understand that the heroine of a novel does not die. Even Clinias betrays his impatience when he tries to console Clitophon (7.6.2): "For who knows if she is alive again or not. Hasn't she already died many times? Hasn't she come back to life many times?"

88 Repath 2005, with bibliography on the question at 250–251, n. 3.

89 Repath 2005, 265.

90 Fusillo 1997, 220.

91 Morgan 1996, 182–186; "blindness": p. 182.

92 Morgan 1996, 186 on the account of Callisthenes' reformation.

93 Still, getting too worked up over deficiencies of Achilles' comic antihero would be as out of place as condemning Bertie Wooster for social parasitism.

94 Most 1989 also considers the ending of the novel with reference to Clitophon's first-person narration in the context of Greek rhetorical and cultural conventions regarding self-revelation to strangers.

6 *Aethiopica*

Love and slavery, philosophy and the novel

Introduction

Heliodorus' *Aethiopica* (or *Ethiopian Tale*) is the latest and the longest of the five surviving Greek novels, having been composed most likely in the fourth century CE.[1] The heroine Charicleia is the daughter of Hydaspes and Persinna, the King and Queen of Ethiopia. At the moment her daughter was conceived, Persinna looked up at a painting of Andromeda. The image of Greek Andromeda imprinted itself on the child-to-be and the baby was born with white skin. Fearing that she would be accused of adultery, Persinna told her husband that her baby had died; in fact, she had given her to the holy man Sisimithres for safekeeping along with tokens of her identity. Sisimithres raised the child in secret until she was seven years old. Then, fearing discovery, he gave her, along with the birth tokens, to Charicles, a priest of Delphi whom he met in the town of Katadoupoi, near the first cataract of the Nile. Charicles took the girl back with him to Delphi, adopted her, and named her Charicleia. Charicleia grows to be a remarkable beauty but is devoted to Artemis and is completely uninterested in men.

It is then that Calasiris, a priest of Isis, appears on the scene, either by accident or design. He had exiled himself from his native Egypt, both to escape the snares of a courtesan whom he knew would lead him into sin and to avoid witnessing the dispute that his prophetic powers had revealed would arise between his sons, Thyamis and Petosiris, over succeeding him in his priesthood. Exile takes him to Delphi, where he is accepted as an exotic celebrity. He becomes friends with Charicles but begins to suspect the true identity of the Delphic priest's foster daughter. Or it may have been that Calasiris arrived in Delphi already suspecting who she was. As he works to confirm his suspicions, the hero, Theagenes, arrives from Thessaly to lead a sacrifice in honor of his ancestor, Neoptolemus. Theagenes is almost as handsome as Charicleia is beautiful. The two fall in love at first sight. Calasiris is a close observer and narrator of all that happens. By his own admission, he keeps Charicleia's foster father in the dark regarding both the young woman's feelings and his own plans for her. Finally, after confirming her identity, he contrives a deception to spirit Charicleia and Theagenes away and to take them to Ethiopia, the heroine's true home, where she and Theagenes can be married.

186   Aethiopica

Adventure follows. The protagonists and their chaperone priest are ship-wrecked on their arrival in Egypt at the mouth of the Nile. They are taken prisoner then by Thyamis, who, it will be revealed, is Calasiris' elder son, now turned bandit after his brother deprived him of the Isis priesthood. Like other novel protagonists, Theagenes and Charicleia maintain their fidelity to one another despite repeated episodes involving capture and separation. They are finally reunited in Memphis. But Calasiris dies and the protagonists become the slaves of the wife of the Persian satrap Oroondates, Arsace, who has fallen in love with the hero. They manage to escape and arrive in Ethiopia after more narrative twists and turns but as prisoners of King Hydaspes, Charicleia's father, who has just defeated Oroondates in battle. A last-minute recognition prevents the king from sacrificing the lovers to the gods as first offerings for his victory. Charicleia is reunited at last with her parents, Hydaspes and Persinna, and proclaimed their legitimate daughter. The novel ends as Charicleia and Theagenes make their way in procession to Meroë to be married.

The author has complicated this eventful tale even more through an intricate narrative scheme.[2] Heliodorus, as external third-person narrator,[3] begins the story *in medias res*; earlier events are related through a dramatic mode of presentation staging two internal first-person narrators.[4] The first, Cnemon, is a young Athenian gentleman who meets up with the protagonists in Egypt and tells them the story of the misfortune brought on him by his lustful stepmother Demaenete and her conniving slave Thisbe (1.9–1.17 and 2.8.4–2.9). Cnemon and Thisbe are then themselves integrated into the protagonists' own story.[5] The second embedded first-person narrator is Calasiris, who tells Cnemon, now acting as an embedded listener, the story of his self-exile to Delphi, how he contrived to bring Charicleia and Theagenes together, and their flight with him to Egypt. Calasiris' narration takes up nearly a third of the novel (2.24–5.1 and 5.17–5.33). After he is finished, Heliodorus, as third-person narrator, takes over until the end (5.34–10). However, the narrative strategy in the first half is even more complicated. Both Cnemon's and Calasiris' narratives contain their own embedded narrators. Cnemon's narrative includes an internal account from his friend Charias (1.14.4–1.17). Calasiris' account is a narrative Matryoshka doll, except with priests. Within the Isis priest's narration is embedded the account of the Delphic priest Charicles (2.29–33) and within Charicles' account a story he heard from Sisimithres (2.31), an Ethiopian gymnosophist, or combination holy man and royal advisor.[6]

Heliodorus filters his representation of slaves and slavery through this complex arrangement of narrative perspectives: Cnemon, a sensual young Athenian; Calasiris, a pious Egyptian priest; finally, Heliodorus himself, who, as author, drew on both philosophical ideas and normative stereotypes about slaves to articulate his conception of ideal love. On a metaphorical level, Heliodorus aligns slavery with ideas about love that are Platonic in inspiration: first, to sharpen a contrast between the carnal love of bodies and the spiritual and transcendent love of the protagonists and, second, to subvert that contrast, when the metaphor of slavery to love is employed to suggest that Theagenes' and Charicleia's feelings for one another, while chaste in practice, are nonetheless carnal in feeling.

Aethiopica   187

The novel observes the generic motif of the enslaved protagonist in Heliodorus' third-person account of Arsace's enslavement of the protagonists in Memphis. This episode alludes to Xenophon's account of the enslavement and torture of Habrocomes. However, in contrast to Xenophon, Heliodorus affirms the transcendence of elite virtue, even during the most severe trials of slavery. This affirmation has been reflected in the social status of the principal narrators. Cnemon is an upper-class Athenian citizen; Calasiris is a high priest and prophet of Isis. Last of all, the author himself, in the final sentence of the novel, as Heliodorus, son of Theodosius, declares his descent from Helios (10.41.4).[7] These elite narrators in different ways all reflect or endorse normative elite opinions regarding slaves.

Erōs, *sophia*, **and slavery**

Charicleia's and Theagenes' love share is exceptionally chaste. The protagonists aspire to a version of *sōphrosynē* more stringent than what is found in the other novels. Their love is a love of souls that marginalizes (while not eliminating) physical love. This notion of love has been inspired by Platonic ideas.[8] Charicleia and Theagenes fall in love at first sight, like the philosophical lovers in *Phaedrus*, whose kindred souls recognize one another (250–255). Ken Dowden has noted that the contrast between the love of the protagonists, the love of two noble souls, and a lesser kind of love, the love of bodies, appears to have been grounded on a distinction outlined in Pausanias' speech in the *Symposium* (180d2–185a), between Uranian (or Heavenly) Love and Pandemic (or Vulgar) Love.[9] The former involves the love between immortal and divine souls. Pandemic Love, on the other hand, is directed toward love of the body more than love of the soul (cf. 183d, ὁ τοῦ σώματος μᾶλλον ἢ τῆς ψυχῆς ἐρῶν).

In an aside to Cnemon, Calasiris associates Pandemic Love with slavery and Uranian Love with what is immortal and divine. The Isis priest was telling about how Theagenes had asked him to use his Egyptian magic to make Charicleia fall in love with him. Calasiris breaks off his account to comment that Theagenes had been mistaken in his belief that Egyptian wisdom, or *sophia*, was all the same; there were, in fact, two varieties (3.16.3–4):

> The one sort of wisdom is vulgar (δημώδης) and one might say that it crawls upon the ground, a personal slave of phantoms (εἰδώλων θεράπαινα) and wraps around dead bodies. It busies itself with herbs and relies on magic spells, bringing no good end either to itself or those who make use of it. It trips itself up in most matters, and its successes are painful and slight, false appearances taken for true that deceive one's hopes. This wisdom is an inventor of lawless deeds and an attendant to unchecked pleasures (ἡδονῶν ἀκολάστων ὑπηρέτις). The other sort of wisdom, my son, the true wisdom, with which the first kind has no right to share its name, is the one that we priests and prophets cultivate since youth. It looks up to the heavens. It associates with the greater gods and shares in their nature.

188   Aethiopica

> It investigates the movements of the stars and acquires knowledge of what is to come. It stands apart from those things of earthly evil, acting in all things for the good and what is beneficial to mankind.

The two wisdoms, one false and one true, reflect broadly the Platonic distinction between the world of appearances and the realm of what is true and eternal. However, as Meriel Jones has noted, the two kinds of wisdom align in particular with the distinction between Uranian and Pandemic love in the *Symposium*.[10] The description of the vulgar form of Egyptian *sophia* as *dēmōdēs* (δημώδης) evokes Vulgar Love, that is, *Eros Pandemos*.[11] Such wisdom "crawls upon the ground" (χαμαὶ ἐρχομένη) in contrast to the true form of wisdom, which "looks up to the heavens" (ἄνω πρὸς τὰ οὐράνια) evoking Uranian, or Heavenly, Love. Heliodorus further expresses the alignment between true wisdom and Heavenly Love, on one hand, and vulgar wisdom and Vulgar Love, on the other, through the narratives that deal with the two different kinds of love. First, there is the chaste and idealistic love of the protagonists. As John Morgan has observed, Charicleia and Theagenes fall in love at first sight but, possessing *sōphrosynē*, defer physical confirmation of their love until after marriage.[12] Their feelings are characterized by mutuality and exclusivity. They are devoted to one another for all time. Heliodorus, Morgan demonstrates, has contrasted the story of this love and these lovers with the Demaenete and Arsace stories. The love there is the opposite of what Charicleia and Theagenes feel. Both women are already married. Neither can control herself. Each seeks to conquer and dominate someone who does not love her in return. As Morgan observes, the contrast between the two loves is reflected in how the two kinds of love story end. Charicleia and Theagenes marry and exit in a triumphal torch-lit procession. In contrast, unchecked and illicit passion brings about the downfall of both Demaenete and Arsace.[13]

Heliodorus also expresses the moral and philosophical distinction between the two kinds of love and wisdom in social terms. The debased form of Egyptian wisdom is associated with servility. It is a kind of personal slave or attendant, a *therapaina* or *hypēretis*, which serves the base desires of those who employ it. In the tales of Vulgar Love, Demaenete and Arsace each attempts to fulfill her desire by enlisting a slave who encourages, aids, and abets the worst instincts of her master. Cnemon's account of the destructive passion of his stepmother Demaenete centers on the web of deceit and destruction wrought by Demaenete's slave Thisbe. The story of Arsace's passion for Theagenes describes how Arsace brings destruction on herself by following the advice of her slave Cybele. The setting of this tale, the palace of the Persian satrap of Egypt, contains an army of ancillary slaves and eunuchs in addition to Cybele. In contrast, Calasiris' complex account of the chaste love of the protagonists is notable for the absence of meaningful participation by slaves. Calasiris, I argue, is distinguished as a non-narrator of slavery. Enslaved characters play no significant role in his account of the events that bring the protagonists together; in fact, he seems to push slave characters out of his narration. In addition, Charicleia and Theagenes themselves have no meaningful interaction with slave characters.

Aethiopica 189

The next three sections contrast Calasiris' account of the chaste love of the protagonists, a narrative remarkable for the absence of slaves, with the two tales of unchaste love involving Demaenete and Arsace, each of which features the activities of a wicked slave agent, Thisbe and Arsace. I argue that through the absence or presence of slave characters Heliodorus has characterized the love featured in each tale as either chaste, idealistic, and noble or carnal, base, and servile.[14]

Calasiris' tale of chaste love: a nonnarration of slaves

As an internal first-person narrator, Calasiris tells Cnemon the story of how Charicleia and Theagenes met and fell in love in Delphi, ran away together with him, and at last arrived in Egypt. The two are guests of the Greek merchant Nausicles, who lives in the fictional Egyptian town of Chemmis. Calasiris tells how he worked to bring Charicleia and Theagenes together, playing the role of a go-between who worked at both ends, consoling, encouraging, and abetting each protagonist. He acted, he says, in response to the oracle (2.26 and 2.35) and in obedience to an epiphany of Artemis and Apollo (3.11).

The protagonists fall in love during a ceremony in honor of Theagenes' ancestor Neoptolemus. When they first look into one another's eyes, it was, Calasiris notes, as if their souls recognized one another as kindred (3.5.4, ὥσπερ τῆς ψυχῆς ἐκ τῆς πρώτης ἐντεύξεως τὸ ὅμοιον ἐπιγνούσης καὶ πρὸς τὸ κατ᾽ ἀξίαν οἰκεῖον προσδραμούσης). They continue to gaze at one another as if they were summoning up a memory, having known or seen the other before (3.5.5, ὥσπερ εἴ που γνωρίζοντες ἢ ἰδόντες πρότερον ταῖς μνήμαις ἀναπεμπάζοντες). They blush and then suddenly turn pale, rapid changes that betray the agitation of their souls (3.5.6, τῆς ψυχῆς τὸν σάλον). This description of the moment draws on ideas in Socrates' discourse on *erōs* in the *Phaedrus*.[15] The eye is love's conduit into the soul (255c), through which the lover is unaware that he is seeing himself as if in a mirror (255d, ὥσπερ δ᾽ ἐν κατόπτρῳ ἐν τῷ ἐρῶντι ἑαυτὸν ὁρῶν λέληθεν); the apprehension of beauty in the beloved inspires the soul with something of the awe it felt long ago when contemplating divine beauty (251a, ὅταν θεοειδὲς πρόσωπον ἴδῃ κάλλος εὖ μεμιμημένον ἤ τινα σώματος ἰδέαν, πρῶτον μὲν ἔφριξεν καί τι τῶν τότε ὑπῆλθεν αὐτὸν δειμάτων); the vision of earthly and the recollection of divine beauty induce a painful physical response in the soul of the lover (251c).[16] The moment Theagenes and Charicleia fall in love is a Platonic moment of pure, transcendent Uranian Eros.

But even Heavenly Love faces earthly challenges. Charicleia has to abandon her own intention to be a priestess of Artemis and never to marry. Theagenes must thwart Charicles' plan to marry her to his nephew Alcamenes. Finally, the match has to be accommodated to Calasiris' divinely ordained mission to reunite Charicleia with her real parents. In order to accomplish all this Calasiris deals underhandedly with all involved.[17] He pretends to Theagenes and Charicles that he was some sort of magician who could manipulate Charicleia to fall in love, in effect, a practitioner of the same debased wisdom he disdains.[18]

190   Aethiopica

When Charicleia does, indeed, fall in love, he encourages both men in their belief that this was the result of his powers. As the heroine exhibits the symptoms of lovesickness and Charicles asks Calasiris to examine her, the Isis priest knows what is happening but tells his worried friend that someone had cast the evil eye on her during the course of the procession. He concludes this diagnosis with a bewildering series of learned digressions involving the evil eye and *erōs*, digressions whose real purpose is to distract Charicles from the matter at hand.[19]

In front of Theagenes, Calasiris puts on a show of being possessed by higher powers that have revealed to him that Theagenes was in love (3.17.2); he assures the hero that through his *sophia* (that is, the base *sophia* he in fact despises) he would make Charicleia submit to his will (3.17.5, οὐχ οὗτος ἐκείνη κρείττων ἔσται τῆς ἡμετέρας σοφίας). Soon after, he tells Theagenes that his skill, indeed, has forced the girl to fall in love (4.6.4, τὴν ἐμὴν τέχνην, ὑφ᾽ ἧς ἥλωκεν ἡδὺ καὶ ἐρᾶν σου κατηνάγκασται). Calasiris has less success, however, in deceiving Charicleia. He put on a similar nonsense show when he was pretending to examine her for the evil eye. But the heroine seems to see through him (4.5.4). He may have more luck in securing the heroine's trust through his claim that by means of his *sophia* he has intensified Theagenes' ardor (4.11.2, ἐπέτεινα δὲ αὐτῷ κἀγὼ σοὶ χαριζόμενος σοφίᾳ τὴν ἐπιθυμίαν).[20] Calasiris may also be lying when he tells Charicleia that he came to Delphi at her mother's behest, to bring her home (4.12–13).[21]

After he has made himself certain of Charicleia's identity and that she and Theagenes are in love, Calasiris contrives and manages a deception worthy of a Plautine *servus callidus*. The protagonists, previously his targets, become his accomplices: the *iuvenis* and *meretrix* whom the successful deception will unite. Poor old Charicles is the *senex*, his mark. Calasiris first buys time to figure out a means of escape. Following his instructions, Charicleia puts her foster father off by pretending to love his nephew Alcamenes (4.13). When Charicles has a dream in which an eagle seized his stepdaughter and carried her off to the end of the earth, Calasiris cozens the old man with a reassuring and dishonest interpretation (4.14). Next, he contrives to get possession of the tokens that will help prove Charicleia's identity to her parents, steering Charicles into giving them to the heroine (4.14). Finally, when all is ready for flight, he instructs Theagenes and his companions to assemble a band of revelers, a *kōmos*, who will carry off a ready and willing Charicleia (4.17).[22]

Others have remarked on the contrast between Calasiris' high status and his assumption of the role of *servus callidus*.[23] More broadly, the contradiction between Calasiris' idealistic ends and his dishonest means has posed an interpretive challenge.[24] Was he forced to adopt deception for a noble end?[25] Or was there truly something shifty about him?[26] Jack Winkler set the contradiction between the priest's idealistic ends and dodgy means at the heart of his reading of the novel.[27] For Winkler the point was not so much that Calasiris uses duplicity toward a noble end; rather, Heliodorus is suggesting that duplicity itself is a proper moral attitude, that is, "duplicity in the sense of carefully weighing alternatives and respecting the

Aethiopica 191

volition of all the characters."[28] Duplicity in this sense would serve as a model for how to read the novel, that is, with openness to ambiguity and respect for it. Winkler's *Aethiopica* is a hermeneutically oriented novel, concerned with the process itself of reading and interpreting complex texts (and life).[29]

As a *servus callidus* in all but name, Calasiris aligns not only with the slaves of New Comedy, but also slave characters in other novels who advise and assist their masters in their erotic affairs. Like Plangon and Artaxates in *Callirhoe*, he functions as a go-between. His deception of Charicles finds a parallel in the machinations of Satyrus, who advises his master how to romance Leucippe, devises a scheme to get him into her bedroom, and finally flees with his master and his master's lover. In Heliodorus' novel, however, a chaste and pious priest has usurped a role and function associated with duplicitous slaves. Through Calasiris, Heliodorus signals that he is telling a story about *erōs*, but a different kind of story (for a different kind of *erōs*), one in which the slave character has been deprived of his generic function as go-between. Thus, the paradox involving this character is related to a paradox concerning *Aethiopica* itself, an erotic novel that extols chastity so highly so that the protagonists remain virgins throughout the novel and have sex only after it has ended.

In fact, Calasiris contrives a deception that has no roles for slaves to play. No slave accompanies him and the protagonists in flight. In contrast, Satyrus' intrigue was slave-labor intensive, involving Leucippe's slave Clio and a servile supporting cast. When the plot failed, Leucippe and Clitophon fled Tyre in a second scheme involving the participation of yet more slaves (*Leucippe and Clitophon*, 2.31.5). Calasiris seems to marginalize other slave characters even as he notes their presence. For example, a slave who interrupts to announce the arrival of Theagenes and the Thessalians is "someone rushing in" (2.34.1, εἰσδραμών τις). As Calasiris is explaining to Charicles how his stepdaughter may have contracted the evil eye, another hurried slave interrupts (3.10.1, ἐφίσταταί τις ἐσπουδασμένος). This particular slave has come to invite them to Theagenes' symposium. His manner is impertinent, especially for a slave addressing free men. John Morgan's translation captures the tone (3.10.1–2):

> Gentlemen, the way you are dawdling anyone would think you had received an order to go into battle rather than an invitation to a banquet thrown by Theagenes, the finest of men, under the patronage of Neoptolemos, the greatest of heroes. Come along! Do not keep the party waiting all day! All the guests are there but you.[30]

Calasiris, as he relates the incident, does not respond to the slave's effrontery. Instead, Charicles whispers in his friend's ear about the inappropriateness of the invitation, which, he implies, reverses the order of master and slave (3.10.2): If they do not obey him, he might beat them (ὡς δέος μὴ καὶ πληγὰς ἡμῖν ἐμφορήσῃ τελευτῶν)! The next day, one of Charicles' slaves interrupts Theagenes' confession to Calasiris of his love (3.15.1, ἥκων τις παρὰ τοῦ Χαρικλέους). These slave messengers are bit players; however, Calasiris has marginalized them

192   Aethiopica

even more through the anonymizing indefinite pronoun. They are εἰσδραμών τις, τις ἐσπουδασμένος, ἥκων τις, a human being who performs an action but lacks a personality – in other words, a slave.[31] When the slave messenger from Theagenes stood outside his lack of personhood with some saucy language, Charicles reacted, not Calasiris, who tends not to note the presence of slaves.

In some instances, the priest seems to prevent the possibility that slaves who are present might take part in the action. For example, when he finds Charicles crying at home with his slaves because of his stepdaughter's lovesickness (4.5.2, ἄλλους τε τῶν οἰκείων καταλαμβάνω δεδακρυμένους καὶ οὐχ ἥκιστα τὸν Χαρικλέα), he tells Charicles to stand up and orders the slaves to go away (4.5.2, ἀνίστω, ἔφην, καὶ οἱ λοιποὶ πάντες ἔξιτε). Then, alone with Charicleia, Calasiris gets her to promise to acknowledge her feelings to him the next day (4.6.1). When that day arrives, Calasiris again clears Charicleia's room of the slaves in attendance, who had been the witnesses to Charicleia's worst night (4.10.1, μεταστησάμενος οὖν τοὺς παρόντας). She thus confesses her love to the priest alone. Calasiris not only narrates what happened; he also managed the action, making sure to minimalize the involvement of slaves.

At other times, Calasiris' narration seems to remind the reader that slaves are not present when they might be. After the fugitives have made their way out of Delphi, Calasiris returns to town to throw off pursuit. The heroine is concerned about her lack of a protector (4.18.5, ἄνευ προμάχου) and makes Theagenes swear an oath to respect her chastity. The reader realizes that the protagonists really are alone, just the two of them, for Charicleia had taken no slave attendant with her when fleeing with the *kōmos* (cf. 4.17.4).[32] The absence of slaves is implied in a second episode, when the three fugitives put in for the winter on the island of Zacynthus (5.18). Calasiris looks for an appropriate accommodation for himself and the protagonists, away from the sailors and their ship. He finds lodgings at the house of Tyrrhenus, an old fisherman, but only after Tyrrhenus ascertains that they not the sort of people who need a big house and travel with a large complement of slaves (5.18.6, εἰ μή τις τυγχάνοις πολυκλίνους οἴκους ἐπιζητούντων ἢ θεραπείαν εἰς πλῆθος ἐπαγομένων).

As was the case with Achilles Tatius' characterization of Clitophon, Calasiris' failure to take note of slaves serves as an aspect of his characterization.[33] Toward the end of his narration, Cnemon, the priest's internal audience, interrupts him to call his attention to a loud commotion from elsewhere in the house (5.1.4, θροῦς τις καὶ βόμβος ὄχλου κατὰ τὴν οἰκίαν περιηχεῖ). Nausicles' many slaves (cf. 6.11.1, ἄλλου τῆς οἰκίας πλήθους) are greeting the return of their master (5.1.4, ὁ τῆς οἰκίας δεσπότης). Calasiris, however, has not heard the commotion, either, as he explains it, because of his old man's hearing or because he was so engrossed in his own storytelling (5.1.5, τάχα μέν που ἢ δι᾽ ἡλικίαν ... ἴσως δὲ καὶ πρὸς τὴν διήγησιν ἠσχολημένος). But it may also be the case that Heliodorus has depicted Calasiris, engrossed in a narration that takes scant notice of slaves, as failing to note (or deliberately neglecting?) the presence of slaves who are then in the house with him.[34] Thus, as Calasiris has taken on a dramatic role associated with slaves, he marginalizes actual slave characters in his narration,

Aethiopica   193

giving them scant notice, failing to note them at all, or pushing them out of the action altogether.

The protagonists align with their priestly mentor in the scant attention he pays to slaves. Charicleia has no significant connection to the slaves around her. When the *kōmos* arrives to take her away, the young men make off with a fair number of household items that the heroine wanted to keep (4.17.4, οὐκ ὀλίγα τῶν ἐπίπλων ὅσα κατὰ βούλησιν ἦν τῇ κόρῃ) but no slave attendant who might have been close to her.[35] Nor does Calasiris note the interaction between Theagenes and any of his slaves.[36] Heliodorus' protagonists thus contrast with Xenophon's Anthia and Habrocomes, whose closest confidants were their slaves Leucon and Rhode; they contrast with Chariton's Callirhoe, who conspired with her fellow slave Plangon; they contrast with Achilles' Clitophon, who was utterly, if conflictedly, dependent on Satyrus. Other novel lovers confide in slaves and depend on them to help bring about the consummation of their love, but not Theagenes and Charicleia.[37]

Calasiris' internal narrative of the protagonists' love story is significant in its non-representation of slaves. The marginalization or absence of enslaved characters, especially in situations where a reader might expect to find them, signals a different kind of erotic novel, indeed, a different kind of *erōs*, a love between kindred souls, a chaste and transcendent form of love, one unmarked by any trace of servility.

Demaenete and Cnemon: the first tale of unchaste love

After Charicleia and Theagenes had been taken prisoner by the bandit leader Thyamis, Cnemon, their fellow prisoner, tells them the story of how Demaenete, his stepmother, fell in love with him (1.9.11–18.1 and 2.8.4–9.5). Cnemon rejected her and Demaenete directed her slave Thisbe to punish him.[38] Demaenete ordered Thisbe to gain Cnemon's trust by pretending to love him. The slave obeyed at once, a case of "love at first command" in contrast to the protagonists' love at first sight (1.11.3, τοῦτο ἐπ᾽ ἐμὲ καθίησιν ἐρᾶν μου δῆθεν προστάξασα, καὶ ἦρα παραχρῆμα ἡ Θίσβη). Thisbe then led Cnemon to believe that he could catch his wicked stepmother in the act of betraying his father. He rushed into her bedroom with a drawn sword. But on seeing not an adulterous lover but his father, Aristippus, he dropped the sword in shame. The Areopagus tried and convicted him of attempted parricide; because of a technicality, he was sentenced to exile instead of death.

The continuation of Cnemon's story comprises an inset narration by his friend Charias, another of Thisbe's lovers. Charias has learned what happened next from Thisbe herself and relayed it to Cnemon in exile on Aegina. He tells how Thisbe and Demaenete became enemies and how the slave concocted an elaborate deception against her mistress culminating in Cnemon's father believing that he had caught his wife in bed with a lover. As Aristippus led his wife off for trial and punishment, Demaenete threw herself into the sacrificial pit by Academe and killed herself. His father, Charias tells Cnemon, was now working for his recall from exile.

194   Aethiopica

There was more to tell, in particular, how Cnemon came to be in Egypt. But it was late and everyone went to sleep. The next day rival bandits attacked Thyamis' camp. Thyamis had Charicleia hidden away in the cave but, despairing of victory, went to kill her. After Thyamis' defeat, Cnemon and Theagenes return to the cave to rescue the heroine. They come upon the body of a woman near the cave entrance, who they first believe is Charicleia. Theagenes is in utter despair. But then the light of a torch reveals the body of Thisbe. Charicleia next emerges from the depths of the cave and the lovers are reunited with lots of hugging and kissing. Cnemon completes his story about Thisbe over her corpse (2.8.4–9.5). He had learned this last part from another friend, Alcimedes. The slave had fallen out with her friend Arsinoe, another courtesan, after stealing Arsinoe's wealthy lover, Nausicrates, a Greek merchant living in Egypt. To get back, Arsinoe informed Demaenete's relatives how Thisbe had plotted against her. They, in turn, brought a suit against Aristippus for murder and demanded that he produce Demaenete's unknown (and nonexistent) lover. Aristippus was preparing to have Thisbe examined under torture when she ran off with Nausicles to Egypt. Without his key witness, Cnemon's father was convicted and forfeited his property. Having learned all this, Cnemon set off for Egypt with Alcimedes to find Thisbe, to bring her back to Athens, to make her testify, and to restore his father's property. That much Cnemon could tell. Thisbe, however, supplies the coda to her own story (2.10.1–3). On her body is found a letter she hoped to get to Cnemon. She, too, had been captured by Thyamis' bandits but was kept out of view by Thermouthis, a bandit who had fallen in love with her. She thus remained true to herself to the very end, flattering Cnemon (cf. 2.10.3, τῷ καλῷ), pretending to care for him, promising her love, and claiming to have avenged him by bringing about the death of Demaenete.

In addition to Demaenete and Thisbe, Cnemon's tale features a whole cast of characters implicated in a network of relations based on sexual desire, Pandemic Eros: Aristippus, who was infatuated with his young wife; Charias, Nausicles, and Thermouthis, all Thisbe's lovers; Arsinoe, the courtesan who lost Nausicles to Thisbe; finally, Cnemon himself, scion of an aristocratic Athenian family and Thisbe's fatuous lover. Cnemon is not, however, without virtues. He rejects Demaenete's advances with appropriate horror. He is a loyal son who tried to defend his father's honor when he thought that Demaenete was with a lover. After the Athenian state confiscated his father's property, he goes to Egypt in search of Thisbe, whose testimony under torture would establish Aristippus' innocence.

It was natural that a well-born Athenian like Cnemon see Thisbe as a duplicitous slave who brings ruin on everyone. At the same time, Cnemon's character has limited his ability to understand his own role in what happened to him. A Pandemic lover telling a story involving multiple instances of Pandemic Eros, misfortune has left him sadder but not, perhaps, wiser. By his own admission to Calasiris, he can never get enough sex and never tires hearing about it (4.4.3):

I find fault even with Homer, Father, when he declares that there is such a thing as too much sex, something of which in my judgment there

Aethiopica   195

can never be enough, neither in enjoying its pleasures or hearing about them.[39]

After Demainete ordered Thisbe to seduce Cnemon, she led him on "with looks, gestures, and lovers' signals" (1.11.3, τότε παντοίως ἐφείλκετο βλέμμασι νεύμασι συνθήμασιν). He was foolish enough to believe that she had suddenly found him attractive after previously rejecting him, something which he himself acknowledges (ἐγὼ δὲ ὁ μάταιος ἀθρόον καλὸς γεγενῆσθαι ἐπεπείσμην). Later in Chemmis, Nausicles ensnares the aristocratic young Athenian as a husband for his daughter Nausicleia, drawing Cnemon's attention to her, "by making her appear more beautiful and adorning her more ornately than usual" (6.6.1, ἁβροτέραν τε τοῦ εἰωθότος ὀφθῆναι τὴν παῖδα καλλωπίσας καὶ πολυτελέστερον κοσμήσας). Thus, Nausicles procures (ἐμπορεύεται) Cnemon as a son-in-law, leading him on as had Thisbe earlier (6.7.8, ποικίλως ἐφελκόμενος, cf. ἐφείλκετο at 1.11.3).[40]

Cnemon's continuing erotic susceptibility may inform Charicleia's judgment that "he was no longer a proper (εὐπρεπῆ) traveling companion nor above suspicion (ἀνύποπτον)" (6.7.8). At any rate, in marrying Nausicleia, Cnemon casts his lot with Nausicles, another of Thisbe's lovers, rather than with the protagonists, from whom he separates. Allusion to the presence of slaves at the wedding ceremony underscores the significance of this choice. Nausicles marries the two in the presence of his household slaves, whom he directs to sing the wedding hymn (6.8.2, τὸν ὑμέναιον ᾄδεσθαι πρὸς τῶν οἰκείων), a contrast with the protagonists' romance, in whose love story slaves play no role. Cnemon exits the novel right after the wedding, so we do not learn about his married life. However, he has fallen in with company better than Thisbe in the person of his wife, who had become attached to Charicleia during the heroine's stay at her father's house (6.11.1). Thus, things may work out well for him, a possibility for Pandemic lovers indicated in the *Symposium*, who might do good or bad depending on fortune (181B, ὅθεν δὴ συμβαίνει αὐτοῖς, ὅ τι ἂν τύχωσι, τοῦτο πράττειν, ὁμοίως μὲν ἀγαθόν, ὁμοίως δὲ τοὐναντίον).

* * *

Cnemon's status as an Athenian gentleman prepared him to see Thisbe for the cunning, amoral slave that she was.[41] His character as a Pandemic lover, on the other hand, prevented him from realizing his own moral slavery to love and, perhaps, learning from this realization. The lesson is available to the reader, but not in Cnemon's account. When Calasiris, Nausicles, and Cnemon are traveling on to retrieve Theagenes, who, they have learned, was being held by the Persian commander Mitranes, events lead Cnemon to recapitulate in short form the Thisbe tale, beginning with his father's remarriage and the illicit lust of Demaenete, then the wicked machinations of Thisbe and her escape to Egypt with a new lover, a merchant from Naucratis, and finally Cnemon's arrival in Egypt, his capture by the bandits, and his meeting with Charicleia and Theagenes.

196   Aethiopica

Cnemon already knows that Nausicles was the merchant from Naucratis (cf. 2.8 and 2.24) but keeps that to himself. As Nausicles wonders whether to reveal himself, the group are met on the road by another traveler, one of the merchant's acquaintances, a man in a desperate hurry. He will inform them that Mitranes' young captive had been seized by Thyamis. First, however, he tells them the reason for his hurry. He had been commanded by his lover, Isias of Chemmis, to fetch a Nile flamingo. This mistress demands much of him (6.3.2):

> For now, everything I do is aimed at one thing, how I may fulfill the commands (τὰ προσταττόμενα ὑπηρετοίμην) of Isias of Chemmis. I work the earth for her. I furnish her with everything. Because of her I am awake night and day, refusing her nothing, whether she orders (ὃ ἄν μοι ἐπιτάττῃ) something large or small – while I incur toil and loss. Just now, I am hurrying to bring this bird, as you see, a Nilotic phoenix, in accord with my dearest's command (ἐπίταγμα).

John Morgan contrasts the mutuality, spirituality, and commitment of the protagonists' love with the materialism of the relationship between Isias and her harassed lover.[42] He notes in particular how, through reference to the elegiac trope of *servitium amoris*, Heliodorus has characterized this fellow as a metaphorical slave of love, an attendant in constant service to his mistress. The language of obedience and command underlines this character's subordination: τὰ προσταττόμενα ὑπηρετοίμην; ὃ ἄν μοι ἐπιτάττῃ; ἐπίταγμα. While Heliodorus has given the metaphorical slave-owner a name, Isias, he has left the harassed lover without one; he is some acquaintance of Nausicles (6.3.1, γνωρίμῳ τινὶ), a metaphorical slave of love, marginalized in a manner similar to the unnamed slave lackeys who hurry in and out of Calasiris' account.[43] Morgan associates the Isias vignette with Cnemon's narrative, an association facilitated by Cnemon's summary of his story right before the encounter with Isias' lover. Both stories provide a similar contrast to the protagonists' noble love. However, the Isias vignette provides an additional comment in ironic mode on Cnemon's story that Cnemon himself is unable to supply. As a Pandemic lover, a lover of bodies, he, too, was a slave of Pandemic Eros.[44]

Arsace and Theagenes: the second tale of unchaste love

The protagonists and Calasiris are finally reunited at Memphis. Thyamis and his bandit troops had earlier freed Theagenes from Mitranes and took him with them to Memphis. Instead of attacking the city, Thyamis meets his brother Petosiris in single combat to settle the issue of the succession to their father's priesthood. Chariclea and Calasiris arrive to stop the contest. Father and sons are reunited after ten years. Thyamis is restored to his priesthood. Chariclea and Theagenes are rejoined with Calasiris. But Arsace, sister of the Great King and wife of the Persian satrap Oroondates, sees Theagenes from the walls of the city and falls in love with him. Calasiris dies, and Arsace contrives to invite the grieving protagonists to move to the palace. She then sets out to seduce Theagenes through the

Aethiopica   197

machinations of her slave Cybele. The hero is able to resist Arsace's advances until she finds a pretext to claim him as her slave. Theagenes cannot refuse Arsace's commands; he continues to resist, however, through a guise of outward deference. Driven by *erōs* and the pernicious advice of her slave, Arsace arranges to have Theagenes tortured as a means of persuading him into bed. She also finds an excuse to have Charicleia tortured in order to put even more pressure on Theagenes. Both protagonists remain firm. In the meantime, news of Arsace's misbehavior reaches her husband, and in anticipation of a reckoning, she kills herself.

John Morgan has noted that the story of Arsace's perverse love for Theagenes, like the account of Demaenete's illicit desire for Cnemon, serves as a dramatic and philosophical foil for the protagonists' love story. Morgan also notes how the two stories of perverse love are aligned. Demaenete and Arsace are both associated with Hippolytus' stepmother Phaedra; both women are assisted and led to ruin by the destructive advice of their slaves.[45] Coming before and after Calasiris' narrative, these stories frame the priest's account of the protagonists' ideal love. The Arsace tale, the frame's closure, assigns an even greater role to slaves as characters and to slavery as a metaphor for perverse love than the Demaenete tale. In Arsace's home, the palace of the Persian governor of Egypt, Heliodorus creates a Persian *doulotopia* much like Chariton's Babylon, where all were slaves to the Great King. In Memphis, it seems, all are slaves to Arsace. Secluded in their room in the palace, Charicleia and Theagenes are surrounded by slaves: the old slave who holds the key to their apartment, the eunuchs who bring the protagonists leftovers from Arsace's table (7.18.1) and who summon Theagenes to Arsace's presence (7.18.2), and the Greek slave boy and slave girl whom Arsace sends to attend on Theagenes and Charicleia (7.19.6); Cybele herself, who, we learn, sleeps in Charicleia's room (7.22.1). The presence of all these slaves serves as a reminder of Arsace's power to dominate and command.[46] Cybele has a greater part than Thisbe in setting events in motion. Heliodorus gives prominence to other enslaved characters in addition to the evil Cybele: Achaemenes, Cybele's son, and the eunuch slaves Euphrates and Bagoas. However, even bit-part slave characters may play an important role in events, such as the unnamed slave girl whose error (an instance of fortuitous servile negligence?) will save Charicleia's life.

The *doulotopia* of the governor's palace in Memphis is a world-turned-upside-down in which the Persian noblewoman Arsace takes direction from Cybele the slave. Cybele, who was born free on Lesbos, believes that her slavery in Memphis is superior to what her free life would have been on Lesbos (7.12.5, ὑπ' αἰχμαλωσίας μὲν ἀχθεῖσα δεῦρο, πράττουσα δὲ τῶν οἴκοι βέλτιον). She even advises Arsace in judging the qualities that distinguish a person of good birth, a *kaloskagathos* (7.12.6):

> I am everything to my mistress. She all but breathes and sees because of me. I am her mind, her ears, her everything. I point out to her the handsome men of good birth (τοὺς καλοὺς αὐτῇ κἀγαθοὺς γνωρίζουσα) and am faithful to her in all of her secret dealings.

198 Aethiopica

Taken to this extreme, the concept that the slave is an extension of the master's will, a human tool lacking her own subjectivity ends in paradox. The master becomes the slave of her slave. Thus, Arsace, in pursuit of her illicit love affair, is guided by Cybele's perceptions and judgments. In particular, her reliance on a slave to decide which young men possess the aristocratic quality of *kalokagathia* signals the debasement of her own nobility.[47] We need not discount what Cybele says here as servile boasting like that of Artaxates to Callirhoe.[48]

This perverse *doulotopia* provides an apt setting for Arsace's destructive passion, a form of love characterized by domination and enslavement. Heliodorus introduces Arsace with language that plays with the contrast between political domination and moral slavery. She was beautiful, tall, intelligent, and, as sister of the Great King, proud of her lineage. But her way of life was open to censure, because she was overmastered (7.2.1, ἐλάττων) by illicit and unrestrained pleasure. After seeing Thyamis outside the walls and then in the city, Arsace returns to the palace where she exhibits the traditional symptoms of lovesickness, tossing and turning on her bed, feverish and groaning deeply, calling for a slave and then sending her away with a command (7.9.2–3). Coming to her mistress' aid, Cybele asks Arsace, who could be so proud or out of his senses, not to be mastered (7.9.5, μὴ ἡττῆσθαι) by her beauty. She assures Arsace that no one is so unbending that he can withstand her spells (7.9.5, ὡς μὴ τοῖς ἡμετέροις ἁλῶναι θελγήτροις). Cybele's comment associates Arsace's *erōs* with the debased Egyptian *sophia* that Calasiris condemned, the *sophia* that worked through spells (3.16.3, ἐπῳδαῖς). The dominated slave thinks of *erōs* as a form of domination.

Arsace tells Cybele the object of her passion, something that the slave seems already to have known (cf. 7.10.4).[49] Cybele promises her mistress that she will make Theagenes love her (7.10). When Cybele goes to make a sacrifice the next morning, she learns that Calasiris had died over the night and that the temple is closed to all outsiders. Theagenes and Charicleia had to stay somewhere else. Cybele seizes the opportunity and invites them to the palace as guests of her mistress. As she takes them there, Heliodorus employs language associated with enslavement to signal their peril (7.12.2): Fortune was taking the protagonists captive (αἰχμαλωτίζουσα) under the guise of kindness, like prisoners who had surrendered themselves of their own will to the enemy (δεσμώτας ὥσπερ αὐθαιρέτους τῇ πολεμίᾳ).

As a slave, Cybele has no understanding of the protagonists' noble character. She tries to seduce Theagenes through reference to Arsace's power to dominate (7.17.3–4):

> Everything will be yours through one person: rank, wealth, luxury, and enjoyment of the flower of your youth. Just acknowledge your fate and prostrate yourself before Arsace (προσκύνει τὴν Ἀρσάκην). Only obey me in how she is to be approached and beheld when she commands you (ὅταν τοῦτο ἐπιτρέψῃ), how you should serve her (ὑπουργητέον) in whatever she commands (τι προστάττῃ). Her spirit, you know, is great and swollen

Aethiopica 199

with pride and kingly, raised yet more by her youth and beauty. She does allow anything she commands (εἴ τι κελεύοι) to be disregarded.

Cybele's speech is marked by the language of obedience and command. To love Arsace is to submit. In particular, the reference to *proskynēsis*, the ritual obeisance performed to the Great King, would have reminded readers of the literary stereotype of Persia in which all the king's subjects were his slaves. Summoned to her presence, Theagenes refuses to perform the gesture and greets her with his head held high (7.19.2). His defiance recalls Greek resistance to Persian enslavement. Almost a week passes. Cybele continues in her cajolery and threats as the hero continues in his resistance (7.20). Cybele even tries to enlist the aid of Charicleia, who, she believes, is Theagenes' sister and who would share in her brother's good fortune as Arsace's lover (7.20.6). Perhaps in consciousness of her own feelings, Charicleia replies that it is only human that Arsace loves Theagenes (7.21.1, ἀνθρώπινον). She, too, sees Arsace as a victim of conquest by love (νενίκηται, ἥττων ἐστὶ τῆς ἐπιθυμίας). Despite her nobility (ἀρίστην Ἀρσάκην), she has been conquered (νενίκηται) and defeated by desire (ἥττων ἐστὶ τῆς ἐπιθυμίας). Charicleia says she will help if Cybele can guarantee that Theagenes will not be in danger of punishment from Arsace's husband. In fact, she will urge Theagenes at least to pretend to yield, to try to deflect Arsace with mild words that would buy them some time. However, Theagenes refuses even to do that, because "saying shameful things is as unseemly as doing them" (7.21.5).

Arsace begins to turn her anger against the overpromising but underdelivering Cybele (7.22.2–3; 23.1), when Cybele's son Achaemenes seizes his opportunity.[50] He had earlier recognized that Theagenes was the young Greek who had been taken prisoner by Mitranes (7.16.2). Now, after arranging through his mother to get Arsace to promise to give him Charicleia, Achaemenes reveals that Theagenes is Arsace's slave (7.24.1, δοῦλος ὤν) since he had been taken prisoner in war (7.24.1, ὡς πολέμου νόμῳ ληφθείη καὶ γένοιτο αἰχμάλωτος). Theagenes, like other protagonists of the novel – Habrocomes and Anthia, Chaereas and Callirhoe, Daphnis, and Leucippe – is enslaved. Arsace summons the resistant lover to her presence. After Theagenes confirmed that he had been taken prisoner and had been placed under Achaemenes' custody, she proclaims (7.24.4):

Then know that you are our slave (δοῦλος)! You will perform the duties of a houseslave (τὰ τῶν οἰκετῶν) and answer to my every command, even if you do not want to (τοῖς ἡμετέροις νεύμασι καὶ ἄκων ἑπόμενος). I betrothe your sister to Achaemenes here, who has our highest regard, in recognition of his mother and his good will towards us.

Theagenes is stunned and drops his posture of proud defiance (7.24.5–6), sidestepping Arsace's attack as one would a wild animal (καθάπερ θηρίου), with flattering words. He thanks the gods to be a slave to her and no one else (τὸ μὴ ἄλλοις σοὶ δὲ δουλεύειν), a mistress who treats foreigners with such gentleness and kindness (ἡμέρως τε καὶ φιλοφρόνως). He tries to prevent his sister, that is,

200   Aethiopica

Charicleia, from sharing in his calamity: She had not been taken as a war captive and was not for that reason a slave (αἰχμαλώτου μὲν οὐκ οὔσης οὐδὲ διὰ τοῦτο δούλης). Even so, Theagenes continues, Charicleia chooses to serve Arsace and to be called whatever it pleases her mistress to call her (αἱρουμένης δέ σε θεραπεύειν καὶ κεκλῆσθαι τὸ σοὶ καθ᾽ ἡδονήν), which Arsace, after having taken due consideration (βουλευσαμένη), should decide.

James Scott observed that dominated individuals tend to adopt a public posture of deference. They may, for example, try to secure kinder treatment by encouraging the humane instincts of their oppressors through flattery.[51] That is the rhetorical approach that Theagenes adopts as soon as he is declared a slave. In response, Arsace says nothing about Charicleia's fate, but she assigns Theagenes to the ranks of her wine pourers, under the supervision of Achaemenes (7.24.6, κατατετάχθω, ἔφη, ἐν τοῖς τραπεζοκόμοις καὶ οἰνοχοεῖν πρὸς Ἀχαιμένους ἐδιδασκέσθω), who holds the servile position of chief wine pourer (7.23.4, ἀρχιοινόχοον), in training for his eventual service to the Great King. Theagenes' appointment as wine pourer recalls the process of enslavement described by Orlando Patterson: He acquires from his owner a new and degraded identity. He will also receive, in Patterson's formulation, the marks and badges of slavery, in this case, the palace livery, a costume embroidered with gold and gems. Nonetheless, behind his flattery and the outward markers of his enslaved identity, Theagenes continues to resist Arsace.

Arsace sends Cybele back to Theagenes. It is time for the slave to obey his mistress' command or suffer the worst of slavery and punishment (7.25.2, δουλείαν μὲν τὴν ἐσχάτην καὶ ἀτιμοτάτην ὑπηρετησόμενος κολάσεως δὲ πᾶν εἶδος ὑποστησόμενος). Arsace's threat establishes *Ephesiaca* as an intertext, specifically the episode in which Manto threatened Habrocomes with torture if he refused her.[52] Here, Charicleia appears to take on the role of Leucon, who had counseled Habrocomes to appease Manto. However, Theagenes rejects the suggestion that he give in to Arsace for Charicleia's sake, to prevent somehow her marriage to Achaemenes (7.25.6–7). He devises a counterstrategy, for "necessity is the mother of invention" (7.25.7, εὑρέτις ἄρα ἐπιλογισμῶν ἡ ἀνάγκη). In a private audience, but with Cybele as a witness, Theagenes tells Arsace that he had rejected her earlier out of a concern for his own safety. Since fortune has done him the good turn of making him her slave (7.26.2, ἐπειδή με καὶ δοῦλον τάχα καλῶς ποιοῦσα ἡ τύχη σὸν ἀπέφηνε), he is ready to yield. He asks only that Arsace cancel the marriage between Charicleia and Achaemenes. It would be an affront to all that is right (ἀθέμιτον) for someone of Charicleia's nobility to be wedded to a lowly house slave (οἰκότριβι) like Achaemenes. If Arsace denied him this, he would kill himself (7.26.3). When Arsace protests to Theagenes that she has sworn an oath to marry Achaemenes to his sister, the hero reveals that Charicleia is not his sister but his betrothed. Arsace is jealous but agrees. Her goal is in sight (7.26.4–6).

In his adoption of rhetorical guile, one of the few resources available to powerless slaves, Theagenes would appear to align with Anthia and Callirhoe, who assumed the behavior of stereotypical slaves, lying and deceiving, to survive as best they could.[53] In contrast, Theagenes manipulates his master not by lying, that is, by acting like a slave but by telling the truth and acting in conformity with his innate nobility. By telling the truth about Charicleia, that she is not his sister but his betrothed, he not only protects the heroine but also sets in motion events that will lead to Arsace's undoing. The enslaved heroines in Xenophon and Chariton acted like slaves in their deceptive manipulation of their masters. Theagenes, in contrast, manipulates his master by means of calculated honesty; the contrast reflects the ideological difference between Heliodorus' novel and Xenophon's *Ephesiaca*.

Theagenes remains aloof from slavery in other respects. He knows, for example, how a real slave like Achaemenes will react to the cancellation of his marriage to Charicleia. Theagenes expects him to plot against Arsace, because (7.26.10) "[h]e was a man fated to be a slave (ἄνδρα δοῦλον μὲν τὴν τύχην) and that which is ruled is, on the whole, opposed to that which rules." Heliodorus indicates Theagenes' aloofness from slavery in another detail, drawing a contrast between servile training and aristocratic nature, which is manifest, paradoxically, even in the performance of servile tasks. Theagenes does not need to be trained, like a real slave, how to serve wine at the satrap's table (7.27.2).[54] Achaemenes, present as the chief wine pourer, can only look on in jealousy as Arsace savors the wine that Theagenes has served her with his innate grace (7.27.3). Finally, Arsace grants Theagenes permission to wear his slave's livery only when serving her at the table (7.27.4). Her concession reinforces the idea that Theagenes' slavery is something external that does not affect his nature, a costume he could take off at will.

Arsace's deference to her love slave set in motion the events that destroy her. As Theagenes anticipated, Achaemenes, jealous as a slave of Arsace's new favorite and jealous as a lover too, sped off to inform Oroondates after learning from his mother that she had broken off the marriage to Charicleia, his fellow slave (7.28.2, οὐκ εἰμὶ ἄξιος γαμεῖν ὁμόδουλον ἐμαυτοῦ). The satrap then dispatched his eunuch Bagoas with a letter for Arsace, commanding her to send him Charicleia and Theagenes. He also sent a letter to Euphrates, the chief eunuch, bidding him to make Arsace comply (8.3). At the same time, Thyamis inquired at the palace after his friends and was appalled to learn that Arsace was claiming that they were her slaves (8.3.8, δούλους τοὺς αἰχμαλώτους). He left but warned Arsace she would regret her behavior (8.4).

The events that follow further associate Arsace's perverted love with servility. Disturbed by Thyamis' warning and suspecting that Achaemenes had run off to inform against her, Arsace turns to Cybele. It would be cruel, Arsace says, to be accused of adultery without actually having had sex with Theagenes (8.5.7). She asks Cybele to do everything she can to bring him around. Cybele chides Arsace for coddling the young man as if she were his slave and not the reverse (8.5.10, οὐ γὰρ ὡς δέσποινα κρατεῖς ἀλλ᾽ ὡς δουλεύουσα θεραπεύεις τὸ μεράκιον). She encourages Arsace to have him tortured. After a show of hesitation, Arsace agrees. The love she felt, the author comments, was the sort that, despairing of its object, turned to vengeance (8.6.1). Theagenes is put in irons,

202 Aethiopica

locked in a dark cell, and given over to the slave eunuch Euphrates for punishment. Starved and tortured, when he asks why he is being punished, the eunuch lays it on even harder than Arsace ordered (8.6.2, πλέον ἢ ἐβούλετο ἡ Ἀρσάκη).

As the torture daily increased in intensity, however, Theagenes grows in his resistance. Torture offers him an opportunity to display his virtue and prove his love. Cybele would check in on him frequently, to see if he was weakening in his resolve, but her hopes are disappointed (8.6.4):

> His body was utterly exhausted, but his soul drew strength from his chaste moderation (τὸ μὲν σῶμα καταπονούμενος τὴν δὲ ψυχὴν ἐπὶ σωφροσύνῃ ῥωννύμενος). Proudly raising his head to fortune, he boasted that although fortune was causing him tremendous torment, it was doing him a favor in what was most important, providing an opportunity for him to display his devotion and faithfulness to Charicleia. He considered it the greatest of all goods if only she could know this. And he continually called Charicleia his life, his light, and his soul.[55]

Heliodorus may again have Xenophon of Ephesus in mind. In his unbending resistance to torture, Theagenes distinguishes himself from Habrocomes, who was broken both physically and mentally by the torture he endured for rejecting Manto.[56] As Theagenes persists in his resistance, Cybele instructs Euphrates to lay it on even harder (8.6.5). Still, the hero remains adamant. Cybele is desperate, fearing punishment either from Oroondates, as Arsace's assistant, or from Arsace herself, because her assistance has come to naught. She decides that her only chance of escape is to kill Charicleia. With her gone, then Theagenes may relent. If not, Cybele thinks, she can murder him too and destroy the evidence of the affair (8.6.7). Arsace agrees that the heroine be poisoned. But the plan backfires. The slave serving the wine mistakenly gives the poisoned cup to Cybele, who drinks it and dies a horrible death.[57] Charicleia is condemned for the murder and sentenced to be burned at the stake.

After the heroine's conviction, the slave who served the wine comes forward and testifies that she, not Charicleia, had served the wine. She is, in fact, the Ionian slave girl whom Arsace had assigned to wait on Charicleia earlier. Heliodorus interjects that she came forward either because she had come to feel affection for Charicleia or because she had been inspired by divinity (8.9.2, εἴτε τι παθὸν εὐνοίᾳ τῇ περὶ τὴν Χαρίκλειαν ὑπὸ συνηθείας τε καὶ συνδιαιτήσεως, εἴτε καὶ δαιμονίᾳ βουλήσει χρησάμενον). What may be significant is that up to this point, Heliodorus had omitted any mention of affectionate feeling between the heroine and her slave attendant. He moots the possibility of such feeling now but at the same time indicates he is uncertain.[58] Surrounded by slaves in the *doulotopia* of Arsace's palace, Charicleia nonetheless remains aloof from them. In this respect, she differs from Anthia and Callirhoe, each of whom survives, in part, because she becomes close to a fellow slave who assists her.

After the heroine is saved from being burned at the stake by the pantarbe, a magical stone that protects the wearer from fire, Arsace arranges for Charicleia

Aethiopica 203

to be tortured together with her lover, believing that each of the lovers would feel the pain of the other more than their own (8.7.21, ᾔδει γὰρ ὡς πάθος τοῦ ἐρωμένου τὸν ἐρῶντα πλέον ἢ τὸ ἴδιον ἀλγύνει). She understands the noble protagonists no better than Cybele did (8.9.22):

> This turned out to be more of a consolation for them. They counted it as a boon to be tested by the same suffering, thinking that if one of them were tormented less, that one was defeated by the other and was falling short as a lover. In addition, there was the opportunity to talk together, and to offer consolation and encouragement in enduring both nobly and heroically (εὐγενῶς τε καὶ γενναίως) their fate and the trial of their mutual chastity and faithfulness (ὑπὲρ σωφροσύνης τε καὶ πίστεως).

The episode signals the ability of Heliodorus' protagonists to withstand the worst that slavery has to offer. Together in the same dank cell, they exhort one another to show their noble virtue, to endure fortune and struggle for virtue. In this regard, they may resemble the philosophical lovers that Socrates describes at *Phaedrus* 256b, who, through the exercise of virtue, prevail over the temptations of physical love. Charicleia and Theagenes, through the exercise of virtue, prevail instead over physical punishment. Torture, thus, for them has become an occasion for the display of virtue, a display that reaches its climax when they are tortured in one another's presence and engage in a bizarre form of erotic competition in which each wants to be tortured more than the other in proof of their greater love. In contrast, a lesser, if more realistic, novel hero, Xenophon's Habrocomes, was broken by torture. Another hero, Chariton's Chaereas, was undone by the brutal conditions of agricultural slavery. Callirhoe's anguish that her unborn child would be born a slave led her to relinquish her *sōphrosynē*, to marry Dionysius, and to lie to him that the child was his. These authors depicted how slavery broke the will of their protagonists. Heliodorus' protagonists do not break. They enact the elite conceit that noble birth transcends circumstances.

Bagoas arrives with the orders to turn the protagonists over to him to take to Oroondates at Thebes (8.13). On the way there, they receive news that Arsace has hanged herself (8.15). The protagonists' adventures will continue, but the Arsace story is over. In this story, Heliodorus draws on metaphors involving slavery and featuring slave characters to indicate the difference between the love of the protagonists and the degraded form of love that Arsace feels, a love characterized as a form of conquest, domination, and enslavement. Arsace tries to bring her degraded love to consummation through the agency of enslaved characters who direct the action. In contrast, Heliodorus' protagonists remain apart from the slaves who surround them in the *doulotopia* of the palace. Unlike novel heroes like Anthia and Habrocomes, they do not act like slaves in order to survive. They remain, even under torture, true to their noble natures and their love for one another. Heliodorus draws on elite ideas about masters and slaves to underline the difference between the protagonists' idealistic love and the debased and unchaste form of love. His affirmation of elite ideology

204   Aethiopica

may even point to a degree of exoneration for Arsace; indeed, slaves turn out to be the tale's chief villains. Cybele pressured her into torturing Theagenes; she also came up with the plan to murder Charicleia. And it was in response to Cybele's command that the slave Euphrates laid the torture on Theagenes more severely than Arsace's instructions that the hero be tortured only gently (8.6.5, παρὰ μὲν τῆς Ἀρσάκης ὡς ἠρέμα βούλοιτο πιέζεσθαι τὸν Θεαγένην).

From philosophy to novel

Charicleia's observation that Arsace had been only human in submitting to the unchaste form of *erōs* can apply to the heroine herself and her lover. The love Heliodorus' protagonists share is chaste in practice but carnal in feeling. This carnality appears to have been grounded in the metaphor of the charioteer of the human soul in the *Phaedrus*. The charioteer guides a two-horse chariot. One of the horses is of good quality and responsive to his commands; the other, not (246b). Over time, the horse of bad quality wears down even the best of drivers. This will happen even to Charicleia and Theagenes but not before they have reached Ethiopia, the limits of this earth, and not before Heliodorus has reached the end of their story. While they are not completely defeated by physical passion like Arsace, they are no less human than she is. They do slip up.[59]

For example, during the attack on Thyamis' robbers' lair, when Theagenes goes to retrieve Charicleia from the cave, he first believes he has come across her corpse. He is close to killing himself; however, the heroine appears in time, and the two forget themselves in their relief, embracing so tightly that they fall down. Heliodorus notes that it was as if they were one person; they seemed little short of dying (2.6.3, ὥσπερ ἡνωμένοι καὶ μικροῦ ἔδει ἀποθνήσκειν αὐτούς). The shock of finding one another alive again has caused them to forget themselves. They reflect, if only for a moment, the honorable but less than philosophically minded lover in the *Phaedrus* who loses control of the lesser horse of his soul because of too much wine or some other form of carelessness (256c, τινι ἄλλῃ ἀμελείᾳ). Fortunately, Cnemon arrives on the scene. This excess of pleasure (2.6.4, τῆς ἡδονῆς τὸ ἄμετρον), Heliodorus observes, was posing a real danger to the protagonists, when their Athenian friend brought them to their senses by splashing water on their faces. Red-faced (not only) with embarrassment at being seen rolling down on the ground together (Charicleia more so than Theagenes), they ask Cnemon for his forgiveness, but he teases them in reply (2.7.2): He had only praise for them, as would anyone who has wrestled with love. Heliodorus thus adapts philosophical allegory to the melodrama and comedy of the erotic novel.

Soon after, Charicleia and Theagenes are left alone in the cave. Later in a flashback, Heliodorus will describe how they took advantage of their solitude (5.4.4–5):

> For the first time they were alone and free of all hindrance. They took their fill of unimpeded and complete embraces and kisses. They were oblivious of

Aethiopica 205

everything else and clung to each other as if their bodies were grown together (οἱονεὶ συμπεφυκότες).[60]

This time, there is no Cnemon to administer cold water. However, the protagonists maintain their self-control. John Morgan's translation captures the erotic element of Heliodorus' comment to the reader (5.4.5):

But the love they consummated (κορεννύμενοι) was sinless and undefiled; their union was one of moist, warm tears; their only intercourse was one of chaste lips. For if ever Charicleia found Theagenes becoming too ardent in the arousal of his manhood, a reminder of his oath was enough to restrain him; and he for his part moderated his conduct without complaint and was quite content to remain within the bounds of chastity (σωφρονεῖν ῥᾳδίως ἠνείχετο), for though he was the slave of love, he was the master of pleasure (ἔρωτος μὲν ἐλάττων ἡδονῆς δὲ κρείττων γινόμενος).[61]

Morgan's translations, "slave of love" and "master of pleasure," may realize what is only potential in Heliodorus' Greek.[62] Nonetheless, the antithesis employs language involving domination and submission to parse a distinction between Pandemic Love (ἔρωτος) and sexual pleasure (ἡδονῆς) that underlines the sexual passion that Theagenes feels and the *sōphrosynē* through which he is able to keep passion under control.

These two episodes are not the only instances in which things appear to have heated up between the protagonists. Earlier in the novel, Charicleia reminded Theagenes of the many times she had repelled his advances (1.25.4, πολλάκις μὲν ἐπιχειροῦντα διασωμένη). Such advances can only have happened when Calasiris was not present, for example, on Zacynthus when Calasiris and Tyrrhenus were talking about the pirate Trachinus' plot to carry the heroine off (3.20).[63] However, after that reminder, Charicleia reassures Theagenes with a physical expression of her love (he had been jealous of Thyamis); she embraces him and kisses him – many, many times (1.26.2, μυρία φιλήσασα). For all that they are different from other lovers, Charicleia and Theagenes feel sexual passion. Where they differ is in their ability to exercise *sōphrosynē*, an exercise in which Charicleia leads and Theagenes follows.[64] In any event, as Rachel Bird observes, *sōphrosynē* is not really *sōphrosynē* if there is no desire present for it to moderate.[65]

The sexual element of Charicleia's and Theagenes' feelings was present in Delphi when they first fell in love. While Calasiris banished slave characters from a significant role in his narration of these events, he describes the protagonists' lovesickness in terms of metaphorical enslavement and domination. In addition to words that refer directly to slavery (e.g., δουλεύω and δοῦλος), Calasiris describes the protagonists using terms that indicate submission (e.g., ὑπήκοος, ἐλάττων, ἁλίσκομαι, ἡττάομαι) and domination (e.g., κρείττων, νικάω). For example, when Theagenes declared his love to Calasiris and asked for his assistance, he breaks down in tears because it seems, Calasiris remarks, he was exposed as someone who had been forcibly conquered by a girl (3.17.3, ὥσπερ

206   Aethiopica

ὅτι πρὸς βίαν ἥττηται κόρης ἐνδεικνύμενος). Heliodorus seems again to have Xenophon's *Ephesiaca* in mind. Theagenes' words align him with Habrocomes, another slave of love.[66] Even Charicleia is enslaved, and Calasiris' observations suggest a parallel with Habrocomes' lover Anthia (3.19.1):

> She was completely enslaved to passion (δεδούλωτο μὲν γὰρ ὁλοσχερῶς τῷ πάθει). The bloom fled from her cheek (τήν τε παρειὰν ἤδη τὸ ἄνθος ἔφευγε) and the brightness of her eyes seemed to be extinguished by her tears (τὸ φλέγον τοῦ βλέμματος καθάπερ ὕδασιν ἐῴκει τοῖς δάκρυσιν ἀποσβεννύμενον) like fire by water.[67]

The next time he saw her after she had crowned Theagenes winner of the foot race, Charicleia seemed even more enslaved to desire than before (4.4.4, δεδούλωτο τῷ πόθῳ πλέον ἢ πρότερον). This language suggests that Heliodorus' protagonists were, in fact, not wholly different from the novel's Pandemic lovers and is distinct from Calasiris' earlier description of the moment of Platonic purity when the protagonists met for the first time. On that occasion, when each looked into the other's eyes, it was "as if the soul was recognizing its like from the first encounter and rushing towards what was properly its own kin" (3.5.4, ὥσπερ τῆς ψυχῆς ἐκ τῆς πρώτης ἐντεύξεως τὸ ὅμοιον ἐπιγνούσης καὶ πρὸς τὸ κατ᾽ ἀξίαν οἰκεῖον προσδραμούσης). The emphasis here is on mutuality and equality (τὸ ὅμοιον, τὸ κατ᾽ ἀξίαν οἰκεῖον), not on the domination that the protagonists experience soon after in their lovesickness.

There are parallels even between Charicleia and Arsace. John Morgan, for example, has noted Charicleia's first bouts of lovesickness in Delphi, when she spends a sleepless night (3.18). In her crazed reaction to the prospect of marrying Alcamenes (4.7), she resembles the lovesick Arsace.[68] Charicleia's feelings continued after the escape from Delphi. Much later, at Nausicles' house in Chemmis, after Cnemon and Nausileia celebrate their wedding (6.8.2), the heroine shuts herself in her room and bewails her continuing separation from Theagenes. The corollary to this separation is the heroine's sexual frustration. She calls herself Theagenes' wife in name only (6.8.4, τοῦ δὲ μέχρις ὀνόματος νυμφίου Θεαγένους) and then, in action that anticipates lust-plagued Arsace, throws herself on her bed and tears her hair and clothes (6.8.6). When he sees her the next morning, her clothes torn, her hair in disarray, and her eyes still swollen with tears, Calasiris understands the erotic cause (6.9.2, συνίησι μὲν τὴν αἰτίαν). He chides her for being mastered by her circumstances (6.9.3, τί δὲ οὕτως ἐκφρόνως ἥττων γίνη τῶν προσπιπτόντων;); he could not recognize the young woman whom he had known in the past to endure fortune with the self-control worthy of her birth (ἀεὶ γενναίαν καὶ σώφρονα τύχας ἐνεγκεῖν τὸ πρόσθεν ἐγνωκώς). Heliodorus suggests a similar parallel between Charicleia and Cnemon, who, the heroine observes, has been conquered by the same passions as she herself (6.7.8, ἀπὸ τῶν ἴσων παθῶν κεκρατημένον), and the pirate Trachinus, who takes Calasiris and the protagonists captive while they are sailing from Zacynthus. Calasiris remarks to Cnemon how Trachinus became

Aethiopica 207

an obedient slave to Charicleia's beauty (5.26.4, ὑπὸ τῶν βλεμμάτων πρὸς τὸ ὑπήκοον ἐδούλουτο).

One would expect such slavery of a pirate. However, Calasiris himself, the ascetic priest, provides an *a fortiori* illustration of the principle that all human beings are susceptible to passion. At the start of his narration, Calasiris describes his own close encounter with the degradation of physical love. One of the two reasons that he left his priesthood and went into exile, he tells Cnemon, was to avoid sin with the beautiful courtesan Rhodopis, second in beauty only to Charicleia. It was inevitable, Calasiris says, that one would be conquered by her (2.25.1, οὐ γὰρ ἦν ἐντυχόντα μὴ ἡλωκέναι), including Calasiris himself (2.25.2):

> Because I saw her often, she conquered me (γίνεται δὴ κἀμοῦ κρείττων), winning a victory (ἐνίκα) over the continence that I had practiced all through my life. Though I greatly tried to see her with the eyes of my soul rather than of my body, in the end I was defeated (ἡττηθεὶς) and sunk by passion of love.[69]

An association of Rhodopis' near conquest of Calasiris with enslavement may also lie behind the tradition connected with the famous courtesan herself. Herodotus (2.134–135) records that Rhodopis was a fellow slave of Aesop. She was brought to Egypt by Xanthos of Samos (Aesop's master in the *Life of Aesop*) and set free there by Sappho's brother Charaxos to work as a prostitute.[70]

Ken Dowden has noted that Heliodorus does not offer a schematic opposition between Uranian and Pandemic Eros. Rather, the author accommodates the Platonic distinction between the two forms of love to an erotic novel, which depicts the actions of fictional but human characters rather than philosophical allegories. Charicleia and Theagenes feel sexual desire because, for all their virtue, they are human after all.

Conclusion

Heliodorus uses slavery as a metaphor to articulate the thematic distinction between Pandemic and Uranian Eros. This metaphor is additionally significant in an ideological context. The association of Pandemic Love with slavery and Uranian Love with nobility rehearses the contrasts in elite thinking between body and soul, physical desire and transcendent ideal, slave and master. This thinking is evident not only in the *Aethiopica*'s organizing metaphor but is also present in the nature of the narrative. The wicked slaves in the Demaenete and Arsace tales, Thisbe and Cybele, not only reflect elite stereotype of slaves as cunning and immoral; they also drive the action of these tales as each leads her mistress to ruin. In contrast, Calasiris manages the protagonists' love affair and prevents the participation of slave characters, pushing them to the margins of his account.

Heliodorus also used the representation of slavery as a point of comparison and contrast with other novels; he turns to *Ephesiaca* in particular for an

208 Aethiopica

intertext. For example, in contrast to novel protagonists such as Habrocomes and Anthia, who have a close relationship with their enslaved *syntrophoi* Leucon and Rhode, Charicleia and Theagenes remain aloof from their own slaves and, it seems, any other slave characters whom they encounter. When they themselves are enslaved, Heliodorus' protagonists remain aloof from slavery itself. In contrast to Xenophon's protagonists, neither acts like a slave in order to survive in slavery. Torture breaks Habrocomes but becomes for Charicleia and Theagenes an opportunity to display aristocratic fortitude. In the character and actions of his protagonists, Heliodorus assumes and, perhaps, affirms the ideology of elite birth. A noble is always noble and never a slave. This suggests an ideological contrast with Xenophon and Chariton, whose protagonists are forced to act like slaves. Heliodorus instead offers the reader a *mythos* featuring two almost perfect protagonists who embody the transcendence of birth and nobility.

To complement these idealized protagonists, in an extreme expression perhaps of this idealizing *mythos*, the author alludes to a wishful alternative to the chaotic world in which nobles can be wrongly enslaved. In one episode, during his activity as an outlaw, Calasiris' son Thyamis ransoms off or releases out of pity alone women who were slaves only because they had been taken prisoner; he enslaved only the women of lesser birth or character, for whom slavery was a way of life (1.19.5, τὰς δὲ ἐλάττους καὶ ἅς δουλεύειν οὐχ ἡ αἰχμαλωσία μᾶλλον ἀλλὰ συνήθεια κατηνάγκαζε). In a second episode near the end of the novel, after his victory over Oroondates, King Hydaspes distributed as slaves the captives who had been slaves; he set free the well-born (9.26.1, τοὺς μὲν δωρούμενος, οὕς δούλους ἐξ ἀρχῆς ἐγνώριζεν ἡ τύχη, τοὺς δὲ εὖ γεγονότας ἐλευθέρους ἀφιείς). In these glimpses of a better world, better than the novel norm, nobles are not enslaved.

At the same time, it must be remembered that Charicleia and Theagenes do feel sexual desire and are described by Calasiris as metaphorical slaves of love. Their metaphorical slavery became a point of intertextual contact with the protagonists of *Ephesiaca*, who similarly succumb to sexual longing. Their sexual desire places Charicleia and Theagenes on the same continuum as Demaenete, an aristocratic citizen wife, and Arsace, a royal Persian, two other metaphorical slaves of love. There is the possibility of ideological critique: If basic human desire can break down the distinction between master and slave, the distinction may be arbitrary. For this reason, possibly, Heliodorus draws a clear line. Slaves to love, Demaenete and Arsace turn themselves over to the direction of cunning, immoral slaves. Slaves to love, Charicleia and Theagenes entrust themselves to a pious, ascetic priest. Metaphorical slavery to love alone does not destroy nobility; reliance on the judgment of a degraded slave does.

Notes

1 For bibliography, Andreadakis 2016, 1, n. 1, who notes for a *terminus post quem* the incorporation of the author's native Emesa within the province of Syria Phoenice in 194 CE and reference to Heliodorus as Bishop of Tricca during the reign of

Aethiopica   209

Theodosius the Great (379–395) for a *terminus ante quem*, if one accepts the identification of the bishop with the author of *Aethiopica*. Morgan 2003, 417–421 accepts the identification of the author with the bishop but suggests the Parthian siege of Nisibis in 350 is the *terminus post quem*, a complex feat of engineering that resembled the siege of Syene described in Book 9 (cf. Julian's account of the Nisibis siege in *Orations* 1 and 3).

2 In the terminology of narratology, the novel's *sujet* is even more complicated than its *fable*.

3 Or "Heliodorus," since narratologists caution against identifying a narrator with the biographical author: cf. De Jong 2014, 17–19.

4 See Morgan 2004c for an overview of the novel's internal and secondary narrators. Morgan 1994b discusses how these narrators regularly challenge the reader into interpretation, speculation, and inference by omitting or postponing important information.

5 Cf. Morgan 1989b, 101–102.

6 The account of Charicleia's birth that her mother Persinna embroidered on the cloth that she left with her infant daughter might be considered an additional embedded narrative within Calasiris' narrative. M. J. Anderson 1997 makes Persinna's story central to a structural and thematic reading of *Aethiopica*.

7 Morgan 2003, 417–421 sees no reason to doubt the authenticity of the sentence and reconstructs "a speculative biography" based on this information and further notice in the fourth-century church historian Socrates.

8 Dowden 1996. Cf. Létoublon 1993, 139, who finds in Heliodorus a deep appreciation of Plato.

9 Dowden 1996, 269.

10 Jones 2004, 82.

11 Jones 2004, 83–88, reviews characters who illustrate different aspects of what it means to be *dēmōdēs*: the old woman who uses necromancy to revive her son's corpse (6.14–15); Cybele, who offers to seduce Theagenes with magic spells (7.9.5); Cnemon, who uses herbs to heal Theagenes' wound (1.8.5).

12 Morgan 1989b, 107–111. Papadimitropoulos 2013 identifies *sōphrosynē* as the most important distinguishing characteristic of the protagonists' love. Keul-Deutscher 1997, follows Morgan in his description and contrast of the two kinds of love; however, she argues that Heliodorus posits a *tertium quid* as best of all, that is, a life without *erōs*, the life of a religious ascetic.

13 Jones 2004, 82–83 notes that Calasiris' division of Egyptian wisdom lends support to Morgan's thesis regarding the two kinds of love. Beyond that, she discusses (pp. 83–88) how the Platonic distinction between Uranian and Pandemic Love provides a framework for the ethical evaluation of the novel's characters.

14 The disparaging association of physical love with slavery here reflects not only the influence of Plato, but the tradition of elite thought to which Plato belonged that associated slavery with the body. Aristotle's comparison in the *Politics* (1254^a) of the master's rule over the slave with that of the soul over the body and the Stoic recognition of individuals whose bodies are enslaved but whose souls are free belong to the same tradition. The practice of slavery aligned with this tradition, reducing slaves to bodies: The bodies of slaves were exploited for their labor and sex; slaves were controlled through physical rewards and punishments.

15 Rattenbury and Lumb 1960 (1935), 106, n. 2, for example, note this passage as an illustration of Platonic doctrine on love. Feuillâtre 1966, 125–127, emphasizes that Heliodorus drew on the best-known (likely vulgarized) aspects of Plato's thought on love, noting parallels in the protagonists' first meeting and their subsequent love-sickness. Winkler 1982, 125 remarks, "the hint of Platonic *anamnēsis* is muted but unmistakable." Montiglio 2013, 117–119 offers a helpful discussion of the episode. Cf. Kövendi 1966, 157–158; Fusillo 1989, 199–200; Morgan 2003, 453.

210 Aethiopica

16 A reason the response causes pain is that the soul begins to regrow the wings it had lost (251b). An allusion to this detail may be present in Theagenes' boast before the armored race that winged Eros has made him swift (4.2.3, Οὐκ οἶσθα ὅτι καὶ τὸν Ἔρωτα πτεροῦσιν οἱ γράφοντες, τὸ εὐκίνητον τῶν ὑπ᾽ αὐτοῦ κεκρατημένων αἰνιττόμενοι;).
17 On Calasiris' deceptions in Delphi, cf. Paulsen 1992, 172–184.
18 Cf. Paulsen 1992, 178–179.
19 Cf. Morales 2004, 129 on digressions in *Leucippe and Clitophon* that provide the reader with "too much knowledge or, more precisely, too much of the wrong sort of knowledge," which has the capacity to hide what is really important.
20 The claim aligns Calasiris with slave characters in other novels: Artaxates claimed to Callirhoe that he had helped make the Great King fall in love with her (*Call.*, 6.5.5), and Sosthenes declared to Leucippe that he had convinced Thersander to marry her (*Leucippe and Clitophon*, 6.11.3–4).
21 This is the view of Baumbach 1997; Bretzigheimer 1998.
22 Heliodorus alludes to the deception's comic associations through this *kōmos*. The reference to the revelers being armed (4.17.3, ἔνοπλος κῶμος) may punningly allude to the phallus-bearing revelers of a comic *kōmos*. Plautine parallels to discrete parts of the deception: In *Miles Glorious*, Acroteleutium pretends to be in love with the rival; Tranio pretends to be in conversation with a spirit to deceive his master in *Mostellaria*. In *Pseudolus*, the title character cozens a vital document, a letter, that enables him to deceive the pimp; cf. M. J. Anderson 1997, 308–309 on how Calasiris tricks Charicles into giving him the fillet on which Persinna had embroidered the story of her daughter's birth. In Menander's *Perikeiromene*, Polemon is ready to lead a mob to storm the house where his estranged lover has taken refuge.
23 Cf. Paulsen 1992, 188–189; Sandy 1982a, 68.
24 Andreadakis 2016, 77–82 surveys interpretations of Calasiris from the eleventh-century Byzantine monk Michael Psellos to the present.
25 Sandy 1982b, 143–154 discussed Calasiris' characterization as both pious priest and charlatan in the context of figures of the imperial period such as Alexander of Abonuteichos and Peregrinus Proteus, who, similarly, were perceived as both sages and charlatans, a complex type which, Sandy argues (pp. 148–149), Heliodorus associated with the justification of lying for a noble end put forward by Neoplatonist philosopher and later Christian bishop Synesius of Cyrene. Andreadakis 2016, 82–101 arrives at a similar conclusion, that Calasiris was a pious man who lies only to achieve divinity's plan for Charicleia.
26 Paulsen 1992, 177 argues that Calasiris' duplicity was an essential element of his character and a means by which he asserted his superiority over others. The Isis priest similarly misleads his listener Cnemon, whom he has no need to deceive (pp. 175–178). Winkler 1982, 140–145, on the other hand, argues that Cnemon, in his sentimentality and naivety, misunderstands Calasiris as had Charicles and Theagenes.
27 Winkler 1982.
28 Winkler 1982, 136.
29 For a critique of Winkler, Morgan 1989b, 104–106, who argues that the omniscient third-person narration in the second half of the novel emphasizes substance over manner and deliberative action rather than the process of interpretation itself.
30 Morgan 1989a, 417.
31 One of Nausicles' slaves coming to summon Calasiris and Cnemon to a sacrifice presided over by his master and is described as "someone arriving from Nausicles" (5.13.1, παρὰ τοῦ Ναυσικλέους ἥκων τις): cf. Fitzgerald 2000, 51–68, on the employment of slaves in literature as a medium of communication between the free.
32 On the detail, see the later discussion, p. 193.
33 The resemblance is on the surface: Clitophon failed to note slaves both because of his social formation as an elite and his egocentrism. Calasiris has also been conditioned

Aethiopica   211

by elite social attitudes; however, a more important motivation for him may be the religious-philosophical orientation that causes him to look beyond slaves, mere bodies, to the divine.

34 Earlier, after agreeing to continue his narration into the night, Calasiris ordered a slave girl to bring a lamp into the room (3.5.1, Ταῦτα εἶπε καὶ λύχνος τε ἡμμένος εἰσεφέρετο, θεραπαινίδι τοῦτο τοῦ πρεσβύτου προστάξαντος). The syntax itself appears to marginalize Calasiris' interaction with the slave, subordinating it in a genitive absolute to the main-clause completion of the command. In any event, the detail reminds the reader that Cnemon was not Heliodorus' only listener. Did Calasiris command the slave to light the lamp in Egyptian? Or did she speak Greek, as a slave of the Greek merchant Nausicles? If so, how did she respond to the tale of Charicleia's enslavement to love?

35 During the winter on Zacynthus, Charicleia shares a room with the nurse who cares for Tyrrhenus' youngest children (5.18, τροφὸς ἡ τῶν παιδίων). The nurse could have been a slave. Such figures often were. However, Calasiris makes no mention of any exchange between the heroine and this nameless character.

36 For example, the cheeky slave whom Theagenes sent to invite Charicles and Calasiris to his symposium. If this slave's impertinence came from some degree of intimacy with his master, Calasiris does not record it.

37 This holds for the rival lovers: Dionysius' steward Leonas bought Callirhoe as consolation for his master, who woos Callirhoe through Plangon; the Great King himself, Artaxerxes, confided in his eunuch Artaxates. In Achilles' novel, Melite, too, depended on the trust and cooperation of her trusted slaves and an ex-slave the night that she and Clitophon finally make love; Sosthenes tries to procure Leucippe for his master Thersander.

38 The parallels to Phaedra and Hippolytus are well known. Donnini 1981, 145–160 examines the tale type as it is treated in Euripides, Seneca, Apuleius, and Heliodorus.

39 When Calasiris resumes the narration after this interruption, he notes that Charicleia was clearly overpowered and more a slave to desire than before (4.4.3, ἡ Χαρίκλεια δὲ ἥττητο λαμπρῶς καὶ δεδούλωτο τῷ πόθῳ πλέον ἢ πρότερον), a comment that may be read both as a concession to his Pandemic listener (and perhaps the reader, cf. Winkler 1982, 144–146) and an oblique characterization of this sort of desire, be it Cnemon's or Charicleia's, as servile.

40 Rattenbury and Lumb 1960 (1935), 92, n. 1 note a parallel between Nausicles' adornment of his daughter and Thisbe's advice earlier to Demaenete, when the latter thought she was preparing herself for a tryst with Cnemon: "Make yourself attractive. You must look your prettiest when you get there (1.17.1, "κόσμει," ἔφη, "σαυτὴν· ἁβρότερον ἔχουσαν ἥκειν προσήκει").

41 Noting that Thisbe is focalized through Cnemon, Hunter 1998, 42–43 suggests that there might be "more than one account of the slave-girl forced by economic and social circumstances to look after her own position before any consideration of 'conventional morals.'"

42 Morgan 1989b, 106–107.

43 Isias' lover aligns in details with the slave of love as described by Cicero in *Paradoxa Stoicorum* 5.36: "Or can I think a man free who is under the command of a woman, who receives laws from her, and such rules and orders and prohibitions as she thinks fit, who when she commands can deny her nothing and dares refuse her nothing? she asks – he must give; she calls – he must come; she throws him out – he must go; she threatens – he must tremble" (Rackham 1942).

44 Nausicles may be no more self-aware than Cnemon. He finds amusement in his flamingo-fetching acquaintance (6.3.3), although he had himself enlisted a contingent of Persian troops to try to retrieve his own Isias, that is, Thisbe.

45 Morgan 1989b, 112.

212   Aethiopica

46 Doody 1996, 99–100, captures the claustrophobic spirit, noting that Arsace's palace was "full of watching, looking, references to eyes." The omnipresence of slaves in the palace, as participants as well as witnesses, contrasts with the narration of events at Delphi, where Calasiris would usher slaves out of the room and deprive them of their role of witnesses to Charicleia's passion.

47 Arsace's reliance on Cybele may echo the trope of bad emperors who were slaves to their slaves and freedmen: cf. MacLean 2018, 116.

48 Cf. Chariton's dismissal of Artaxates' boast to Callirhoe that he had helped secure her the Great King's affection (*Callirhoe*, 6.5.5): "He could not refrain from adding this bit. Indeed every slave, when he speaks to anyone about his master, has to give prominence to himself as well, in the hope of profiting personally from the conversation."

49 Cf. Satyrus, who knew that his master was in love before Clitophon told him.

50 Note the parallel to when Demaenete turned against Thisbe.

51 Scott 1990, 17–44.

52 See Whitmarsh 2011, 117–119 on Heliodorus' engagement with *Ephesiaca*.

53 De Temmerman 2014, 271–275 describes Theagenes' change in tactics as part of a process in which he has learned, if later than Charicleia, to employ rhetoric to assert control over events.

54 Cf. Forbes 1955, 325 on the training of slaves for domestic service with reference to Aristotle's characterization of such menial tasks as "servile forms of knowledge" (*Pol.* 1255b, 31, αἱ μὲν οὖν τοιαῦται πᾶσαι δουλικαὶ ἐπιστῆμαί εἰσι).

55 Rattenbury and Lumb 1960 (1943), 12, n. 1 note a parallel to Habrocomes' bold declaration of disdain for torture (2.4.4, ἔχουσιν ἐξουσίαν μου τοῦ σώματος, τὴν ψυχὴν δὲ ἐλευθέραν ἔχω). However, Habrocomes spoke these bold words before he underwent torture. Theagenes upholds the ideal in the midst of torture.

56 The parallel noted earlier, between Charicleia and Leucon as advocates of appeasement, suggests that comparison with Habrocomes is intended.

57 In the slave's error, Heliodorus may refer to the stereotype of servile incompetence (8.7.7).

58 Morgan 1982, 227–232 argues that Heliodorus used such expressions of authorial uncertainty to lend his fiction a sense of historical authority. In reference to this passage, Morgan also notes (p. 230) that Heliodorus tended to use the εἴτε … εἴτε καί formula to introduce a supernatural explanation as an explanation of last resort. According to Morgan, the naturalistic explanation, that is, the slave's benevolence, is more likely. In contrast, Winkler 1982, 114–137 views these expressions of uncertainty, which he calls amphibolies, in the context of his hermeneutic reading in which duplicity or, here, uncertainty, is recommended as a proper intellectual attitude. In Winkler's view (122–123), the εἴτε … εἴτε καί formula in the case of this amphiboly gives more weight to the second, supernatural, explanation.

59 Cf. Dowden 1996, 269, who concludes that Heliodorus does not offer a schematic opposition between Uranian and Pandemic Love but "develops his thought with richness and human understanding."

60 The lovers' tight embrace here and in the previous passage may allude to Aristophanes' speech in the *Symposium* describing the embrace of the bodies of the sundered lovers (191b, καὶ περιβάλλοντες τὰς χεῖρας καὶ συμπλεκόμενοι ἀλλήλοις, ἐπιθυμοῦντες συμφῦναι). Rattenbury and Lumb 1960 (1935), 53, n.1, 1960 (1938), 43, n. 1 draw attention to the similarity between these two embraces and the erotic (if frustrated) embrace of Daphnis and Chloe at 2.11.2, κατέκειντο πολὺν χρόνον ὥσπερ συνδεδεμένοι and Habrocomes and Anthia on their wedding night, at 1.9.5, συμφύντες ἀλλήλοις.

61 Morgan 1989a, 448.

62 Plato associates the generic inferiority or subordination indicated by ἐλάττων specifically with the debasement of slavery in his discussion (*Rep.* 587c2–3) of the

Aethiopica 213

inferiority (ἐλαττοῦται) of the tyrant who lives surrounded by slavish pleasures (δούλαις τισὶ δορυφόροις ἡδοναῖς συνοικεῖ).

63 Despite his wisdom and insight, Calasiris is, nonetheless, like Clitophon, an embedded first-person narrator whose knowledge is, at least, theoretically limited. There are also some things he chooses not to observe or note (e.g., the quarrel between his sons; the activity of the slaves around him). In any event, he says nothing about protagonists' embraces. Also relevant to this detail is the discussion in Kruchió 2017 on how the author's elliptical narrative style creates gaps to be filled in retrospectively by the reader.

64 Theagenes' attraction to Charicleia's body (as opposed to her soul) may be indicated when he fails to recognize the heroine in her disguise as a beggar outside the walls of Memphis (7.7.6), an episode which Montiglio 2013, 119–123 reads as the protagonist's failure to live up to the Platonic ideal of the lover. Another such lapse may occur when Theagenes appears to be drawn, despite himself, to the specious attractiveness of the Persian finery he is commanded to wear as Arsace's slave (7.27.1, ἑκών τε τὸ μέρος καὶ ἄκων ἐκοσμεῖτο).

65 Bird 2017, 200. Bird contrasts Charicleia's *sōphrosynē*, which she argues is inherent, from that of Theagenes, which is acquired through effort. Keul-Deutscher 1997, 350 similarly remarked that *sōphrosynē* was a matter of the deep commitment for Charicleia but a limitation imposed from without for Theagenes. Bird is correct that Charicleia takes the lead in limiting how far the couple go sexually; nonetheless, she, too, feels sexual desire.

Cf. Hardie 1998, 34–38, who sees tension between eroticism and *sōphrosynē* in Calasiris' ecphrasis of Charicleia in the Delphic procession (3.4.1–6).

66 Habrocomes laments that he has been defeated and forced to be a slave to a girl (*Eph.* 1.4.1, νενίκημαι καὶ παρθένῳ δουλεύειν ἀναγκάζομαι). Up to the moment he saw Charicleia, Theagenes had shown no interest in *erōs*. Rattenbury and Lumb 1960 (1935), 121, n. 1 note a parallel to Habrocomes, who was too proud to love. Charicleia had earlier tried to deflect Thyamis' marriage proposal with a lie that seems to have been inspired by details drawn from *Ephesiaca* (1.21–2), that she and Theagenes were noble Ephesian siblings who met disaster at sea while on a sacred mission to Delos.

67 In a state of distress similar to Charicles', Anthia's parents note that her beauty is fading away (1.5.6, ὁρῶντες αὐτῆς τὸ μὲν κάλλος μαραινόμενον). Heliodorus and Xenophon make more significant use of the slavery-to-love metaphor than the other novelists. Intertexts make strange bedfellows.

68 Morgan 1998, 65–66: After seeing Theagenes outside the walls, Arsace throws herself on her bed (καταβαλοῦσα ἑαυτὴν ἐπὶ τῆς κλίνης) and spends a sleepless night tossing and turning (7.9.2–3); on a later occasion, as Theagenes continued to resist her, Heliodorus describes how she rushed into her bedchamber and lay on her bed clawing at herself (7.22.2, εἰσδραμοῦσά τε εἰς τὸν θάλαμον ἔκειτο ἐπὶ τῆς εὐνῆς ἑαυτὴν σπαράττουσα). Morgan (p. 66) also differentiates between Charicleia and Arsace, the former "the victim of love but sick with shame"; the latter "surrendered to a foul and perverted passion and sick with sexual frustration."

69 Calasiris is aware of the physical dimension of the protagonists' feelings for one another but encourages them in the direction of the higher form of love. This is the context in which he restrains Theagenes from running off to embrace Charicleia (4.6.5): "Our business is not about plundering (οὐ γὰρ ἅρπαγμα τὸ πρᾶγμα) or buying something cheap (οὐδὲ εὔωνον) and easily available." In brief, the heroine is not a slave who can be seized or bought.

70 duBois 2003, 172–173. Herodotus tells the story of Rhodopis in refutation of the belief that the courtesan had dedicated a pyramid; he does, however, allow that she spent a tenth of her fortune to dedicate a great number of iron spits at Delphi.

Afterword
Conclusions summarized and two points of speculation

Conclusions summarized

As Chaereas summarized his own and Callirhoe's exploits before the citizens of Syracuse, a metonymy, perhaps, for the readers of Chariton's novel, so will I here summarize for the readers of this book the principal arguments and conclusions. The impetus for this study was an observation that each of the five surviving Greek novels narrates the enslavement of one or both of the elite protagonists. The narrative motif in which an elite (or a noble or a god) is enslaved was in itself common in antiquity and may well have come into being soon after the first distinctions in status. It appeared as an element in myth and other traditional tales and came to be represented in genres such as epic, comedy, tragedy, and lyric. But only in the novel, a genre that emerged later in Graeco-Roman antiquity, was the enslavement of an elite a constant. The present readings indicate that in addition to the representation of the motif, each novel engages significantly with slavery, representing the social reality of slavery and master–slave relations, or using slavery to think about love and other matters, or, in Achilles' novel, exploiting the discourse about slavery for the purpose of literary experimentation and play.

The present readings examined each novelist's representation of slavery in the context of the slave-owner's social construction of slaves, which, in the analysis of Orlando Patterson, may be understood as part of a process of social degradation of the slave that has characterized a wide range of slaveholding societies. The readings of *Ephesiaca* and *Callirhoe* argue that Xenophon and Chariton pushed back against this degradation. Both authors devote considerable and sympathetic narration to the physical and mental suffering of enslaved elite protagonists whom circumstances force to act like stereotypically bad slaves. In that regard, both authors pose a direct challenge to the normative ideology, which sought to naturalize slavery and understood bad-slave behavior as the result of a malevolent and defective servile nature.[1] Both novels even extend their sympathy to real slave characters, that is, slaves who were not originally members of the elite and who formed bonds of solidarity with the protagonists, their fellow slaves. Finally, both Xenophon and Chariton focus sympathetically on the protagonists' physical and mental suffering as slaves and condemn the cruelty of their owners.

Afterword 215

While Xenophon and Chariton align with one another ideologically, they differ in their method of narration. Xenophon used folktale types, Potiphar's wife, Snow White, and the Unwanted Suitor, to depict important episodes in his protagonists' slavery. This use of traditional materials may derive from (and allude to) the oral traditions from within slavery. In contrast, Chariton's depiction of Callirhoe's enslavement to Dionysius appears to have exploited the potential of the novel to represent both the slave's and master's perspectives, through the use of implicit and explicit narrative or renarration. Xenophon's use of folktales and Chariton's implicit narrative may reflect Scott's notion of the hidden transcript, the version of power relations through which dominated people expressed their own, off-stage views of their oppression, in contrast to the public transcript, a version reflecting the perspective of the oppressor. In terms of content, the sympathetic attitude toward slaves in *Ephesiaca* and *Callirhoe* and the critique in these novels of the way slave-owners thought may have drawn on ideas contained in servile hidden transcripts. The novels of Xenophon and Chariton thus belonged to a tradition of servile protest but now realized (and disguised) in literary form and insinuated into public discourse for a wider audience.

In this connection, I looked at evidence that Xenophon and Chariton were themselves ex-slaves or, at least, present themselves as such, and I advanced the hypothesis that their sympathetic representation of the slave's perspective would have appealed to readers who had been slaves. I argued that certain recurrent motifs, although universal in their appeal, could also have possessed a particular significance for ex-slave readers, who were degraded as slaves and faced continued degradation as ex-slaves. *Scheintod*, for example, could have signified as a metaphor for the social death of the slave. The assertion of the enslaved heroine's *sōphrosynē* was a means of reversing the stereotype of the sexually available and promiscuous female slave. The passivity of the hero acknowledged how slavery deprived a man of the right to self-assertion through direct speech or direct action. The protagonists' nobility countered stereotypes about ignoble slaves and freedmen who could not erase the stain of the servile past. The valuation of reciprocal love consummated in marriage and the importance placed on family had particular meaning for individuals who may have been coerced into sexual relations, who had, as slaves, no right to marriage and legitimate children.

Xenophon and Chariton also had readers whose understanding of slavery was shaped by their education and experience as slave-owners. Such experience prepared these readers to look at the novels' central themes from a perspective distinct from that of ex-slave readers: *Scheintod* could be a trope of narrative surprise; the enslavement of the noble protagonist, an illustration of the unpredictability of fortune; the pusillanimous hero, a comic figure and foil for the heroine; and love consummated in marriage, a celebration of the continuity of elite families. Xenophon and Chariton provided for the sensibilities of these readers by associating the sympathy for mistreated slaves in their novels with a degree of discomfort or reservation, especially when their enslaved protagonists were forced to act like bad slaves. However, these same reservations

216 *Afterword*

may also have reflected conflicting elements in the identity of ex-slave readers who had once been slaves but were now themselves slave-owners.

The social context of the authors and readers of *Ephesiaca* and *Callirhoe* may be associated with the emergence of elite freedmen during the late republic and early principate; the novels themselves might be counted among the cultural achievements of this subgroup within the literate elite. In their narrative push-back against degrading slave stereotypes, their valorization of reciprocal *erōs* consummated in legitimate marriage, and their account of the protagonists' experience of slavery, these novels align with commemorative practices of freedmen that similarly asserted the ex-slave's dignity, stressed the importance of family relationships, and indicated continuity with the servile past.[2] One such continuity in *Ephesiaca* and *Callirhoe* was a rejection of the dominant ideology, a rejection that may have originated in part in the hidden transcripts of slavery. This rejection found expression in these novels' configuration of sympathies and antipathies, their justification of bad-slave behavior, and their representation of solidarity among the elite protagonists and other enslaved characters.

Xenophon and Chariton, perhaps other early novelists, helped associate the new genre with a story that involved the protagonist's enslavement, experience of slavery, and release from slavery, a slave narrative as it were. The genre that they helped to shape was taken over, exploited perhaps, by the traditional elite.[3] The later authors, all of whom created elite authorial personas, adopted the narrative framework of the slave narrative but rejected the ideology that authors such as Xenophon and Chariton attached to it.[4] In a sense, they made slavery a point of ideological debate within the genre.[5] Their novels contain the narrative motif of a protagonist's enslavement, albeit in attenuated form. In Longus, only Daphnis is a slave; in Achilles, only Leucippe. Achilles and Heliodorus confine the enslavement of their protagonists to discrete, if spectacular, episodes. Leucippe is enslaved for a brief period on Melite's estate outside Ephesus; Charicleia and Theagenes are claimed, and tortured, as Arsace's slaves during their confinement in the satrapal palace in Memphis, a mini-*doulotopia*, Persia in Egypt.

While the later novels retain the enslaved-protagonist motif, they all imply views of slaves and slavery closer to the way slave-owners tended to think. There is less focus on the cruel *realia* of slavery noted in Xenophon and Chariton. Daphnis' life is one of material scarcity, but that is because he is an agricultural peasant more than because he is a slave. In any event, for three-quarters of *Daphnis and Chloe* Longus has put the material hardships of Daphnis' life in the background and emphasized the idyllic beauty of the countryside in which he falls in love, seemingly unaware that he is a slave. Achilles depicts the harsh treatment enslaved Leucippe receives as an anomaly: Another slave, in fact, the evil farm foreman Sosthenes, is to blame, not her kind owner Melite. In Heliodorus, Arsace's palace represents another such anomaly. The setting of Charicleia's and Theagenes' unjust enslavement offers a twisted version of domination administered by evil slaves and distinct from the just practice of enslavement managed by Thyamis and Hydaspes, who do not enslave freeborn captives, only those who have known a life of slavery.

Afterword 217

In addition, each of these novelists has used slavery as a means to think about something other than slavery itself. Longus' representation of slavery was part of his construction of the relationship between nature and art, in which slavery was a culturally enhanced expression of domination that exists in nature. In Longus' view, slavery was just because it was based on nature – an ideological riposte to novelists such as Xenophon and Chariton. Achilles seems to have been interested in the narrative potential of slavery. He exploited various narrative motifs associated with slavery but in contexts detached from slavery. In the limited and selective perspective of Clitophon, who only sees slaves when they reflect his own preoccupations, Achilles appears to be less interested in slavery than in the limitations that exist on a first-person narrator in general.[6] Clitophon is just as deficient an observer of his true love Leucippe as he is of his slave Satyrus. In *Aethiopica*, three principal narrators, Heliodorus himself and the embedded first-person narrators Cnemon and Calasiris, were each distinguished by the manner in which they noted and narrated the activity of slaves. Nonetheless, all three reflected elite perspectives on slaves: Calasiris in marginalizing slaves in his narration and Cnemon and Heliodorus in their depictions of the stereotypically wicked Thisbe and Cybele. Throughout the novel, Heliodorus refers to metaphorical slavery as a field to articulate in narrative form his central theme, the distinction between Uranian and Pandemic Love.

First point of speculation: Italy and Magna Graecia in Xenophon and Chariton

Xenophon and Chariton stand apart from the other novelists in their sympathetic perspective toward slaves and critical attitude toward slave-owners. They also stand apart in their inclusion of the western Mediterranean, Sicily and Magna Graecia, in their narratives. In Xenophon, Anthia was sold to a brothel owner in Tarentum and sold again to Hippothoos, who was then living in Tauromenium on Sicily. Habrocomes had earlier left for Italy in search of her. He arrived first in Syracuse and from there sailed on to Nuceria in Campania before giving up and returning to Ephesus. Chariton's novel began and ended in Syracuse. In this section, I moot the possibility that the geographical ambit of these novels is connected with their representation of slavery. This connection would align with Xenophon's and Chariton's representation of aspects of the institution associated with Roman practice. For example, after he was freed, Habrocomes was still bound to his former master Apsyrtus in the manner of a freedman *cliens* who remained under obligation to his *patronus*;[7] Chaereas labored as a slave on an estate that bore characteristics of slave-run villas as described by the agricultural writers, such as chained work teams, specific work quotas, and a slave barracks or *ergastulum*.

Xenophon's inclusion of Sicily and Campania may allude to the tradition of slave resistance. Severe conditions on Sicily led to two major slave rebellions in the 130s BCE and the last decade of that century. Campania was the site of three smaller rebellions that Diodorus Siculus saw almost as a divine warning of

218 *Afterword*

the second rebellion on Sicily (36.2.1, καθάπερ τοῦ δαιμονίου προσημαίνοντος τὸ μέγεθος τῆς ἐσομένης κατὰ τὴν Σικελίαν ἐπαναστάσεως). Nuceria was the site of a small-scale rebellion of about 30 slaves around 104 BCE; soon after, there was a revolt of 200 slaves near Capua; Titus Minucius Vettius raised an army of some 3,000 men at whose core were slaves he had armed. Campania was also the birthplace of Spartacus' rebellion, at the gladiatorial school near Capua. During the first winter of the revolt, in 73–72 BCE, Spartacus and his army were active in the area and looted Nuceria and other Campanian towns.[8] Steven Ostrow suggests that the early growth in this region of the Augustales, whose membership was largely composed of ex-slaves, may have been part of a policy aimed at promoting the peace in an important region that had seen frequent slave unrest.[9]

In this context, a detail from Habrocomes' time in Nuceria may be significant.[10] After looking for Anthia in vain, Habrocomes was forced by lack of resources to work for wages (5.8.2, αὐτὸν ἀπεμίσθωσε) in a quarry (5.8.3):

> It was painful work. For he was not used to intense and hard labor. He was in a bad way and often lamented his fate, saying, "Behold your Habrocomes, Anthia. Like a common laborer, I have submitted my body to slavery" (τὸ σῶμα ὑποτέθεικα δουλείᾳ).

Habrocomes is no longer a slave, but he reconnects himself with slavery when he laments that he is doing the sort of physically punishing work that slaves do. While this protagonist's reference to his slave-like work may function as a reminder of the harsh labor of slaves in general, it may also allude in particular to slaves in Campania. There were many such slaves, former slaves, and their descendants in the region. Xenophon's ex-slave readers could have lived anywhere in the empire, but perhaps some were in the west, in Campania and Sicily, where their cultural impact was significant. For these readers, geographical inclusion of areas associated with the great slave rebellions of the second and first centuries BCE could have served as a reminder that the long history of slavery in the region was for slaves more than the story of their submission.

A consensus has seen in the Greek city-state of Syracuse an allusion to the perspective of the Greek urban elite in the eastern half of the Roman empire; the novel itself reflects on various aspects of freedom, tyranny, and empire from that perspective.[11] However, Chariton may also acknowledge the presence of readers in the west, implied in the citizens of the Syracusan assembly who gathered to hear Chaereas, a projection of the author, give an account of his adventures, a summary of the novel itself.[12] In addition, for readers who were ex-slaves, many of whose ancestors had been transported from east to west, a historical figure such as Hermocrates could have represented an imagined glorious ancestor, more relevant as a western Greek than remote, and possibly forgotten, ancestors originally from the east. For such readers, Chariton's Syracuse could have signaled that the Greek experience in Italy and Sicily was more than a narrative of submission and slavery. These ex-slave readers may have also included individuals in the eastern part of the empire who had been slaves in Italy but later returned home, in some

Afterword 219

cases endowed with power and wealth by virtue of connection to their former masters; for example, C. Julius Zoilus, a native of Aphrodisias, who was possibly enslaved during the civil wars. Zoilus was later freed by Augustus, returned home, and became the Aphrodisias' most prominent citizen. He served for life as a priest of Aphrodite, was acclaimed as a savior and benefactor, and was ten times in succession *stephanēphoros*, or eponymous magistrate, the same position occupied by an Aphrodisian of the next generation named Athenagoras, whom Stefan Tilg identified as Chariton's employer.[13]

Second point of speculation: critical reception of the novel and its association with slavery

Bryan Reardon asked, "What in the genre of romance, invited disregard?"[14] The genre's association with slavery may have been part of the answer. Early novelists such as Xenophon and Chariton may have associated the emerging genre with a narration involving slavery. The later novelists did not share the ideological perspective of their predecessors. Nonetheless, they inherited the representation of slavery as a generic motif and made it a theme for innovation. Still, the genre retained an association with slavery. In this section, I speculate on the possibility of a connection between this association and the lack of critical regard the novel received in antiquity.

References to the genre are few, far between, and negative.[15] Those who accept that Persius was referring to Chariton's novel in the last line of his first satire note the poet's disparagement. Chariton's readers are not Persius' audience.[16] At the end of the second century, the sophist Flavius Philostratus may also have been taking aim at Chariton in a letter belittling him as an author whom no one would remember (*Ep.* 66): "To Chariton: Do you think that the Greeks are going to remember your book when you have died? Those who were of no account when they were alive, what do you think they are when they are dead?"[17] It seems likely that the genre's representation of *erōs* contributed to its poor reputation. This appears to have been the motivation for the emperor Julian to advise pagan priests in Asia Minor to avoid reading fiction in general but especially stories about love, a possible reference to the Greek novels (*Ep.* 89b, ἐρωτικὰς ὑποθέσεις καὶ πάντα ἁπλῶς τὰ τοιαῦτα).[18] While novel readers were of high status, they were also, in the opinion of some, of low taste.

However, disdain for the novel may have been based not just on its erotic content but also its association with slavery, the motif of the enslaved protagonists, perhaps the servile origins of some of the authors and some of their readers. In the fifth century, Macrobius, in his commentary on Cicero's *Somnium Scipionis*, was digressing on the role of literature in philosophical education (2.7–8):

Fables – the very word acknowledges their falsity – serve two purposes: either merely to gratify the ear or to encourage the reader to good works. They delight the ear as do the comedies of Menander and his imitators, or the plots replete with the fictive adventures of lovers (*argumenta fictis*

220 *Afterword*

casibus amatorum referta) in which Petronius Arbiter so freely indulged and with which Apuleius, astonishingly, sometimes amused himself. The philosophical curriculum (*sapientiae tractatus*) banishes this whole genre of fable (*hoc totum fabularum genus*), that promise only to gratify the ear, from its shrine to the nurse and cradle (*in nutricum cunas*).

(Stahl 1952, 84 adapted)

Macrobius takes aim specifically at the Roman novelists Petronius and Apuleius but has the genre as a whole in mind. What is surprising is his characterization of erotic novels as tales of the sort that *nutrices* would have told children. While novels such as those of Petronius and Apuleius or, for that matter, the Greek novels may not have a role in philosophical education, they seem even less appropriate for young children in the care of *nutrices*. The issue here may not involve the nature of the text but the status of the *nutrix*. Ancient child-care workers tended to be slaves.[19] Macrobius articulates his disparagement of erotic fiction by associating it with the insignificant stories that slaves would tell.

The first-century CE rhetorical writer Quintilian anticipated Macrobius in his disdain for erotic fiction as a genre associated with slavery. In a critique of *grammatici*, or teachers of literature, who comment on a text's every detail, Quintilian asserts that such pedants might as well spend their energies on *fabulae aniles*, that is, old wives' tales (1.8.19, *anilibus quoque fabulis*). Luca Graverini surveys the tradition in which *fabula anilis* was used as a polemic against most forms of fiction, including the novel.[20] Graverini argues that term, which Apuleius applies explicitly to the Cupid and Psyche tale (*Met.* 4.27, *narrationibus lepidis anilibusque fabulis*) through an internal first-person narrator (who is herself an old woman), is relevant to the *Metamorphoses* as a whole.[21] By characterizing *fabulae aniles*, fiction, as a category of literature appropriate for the pedantry of the *grammatici*, Quintilian may connect disdain for the novel with prejudice against ex-slaves, in this case, ex-slaves who pretend to learning. The profession of *grammaticus* (like that of *nutrix*) was associated with slavery. As noted earlier, 15 of the 21 *grammatici* whose lives were recorded by Suetonius were ex-slaves.[22] Quintilian's critique of *grammatici*, whose pedantry is best suited to *fabulae aniles*, may thus connect social disparagement of educated slaves with disdain for a genre associated with slavery.

Notes

1 The idea that circumstances rather than nature can cause a slave to act badly is mooted by Odysseus' enslaved swineherd Eumaios, who says that Zeus takes away half of a man's virtue (*Od.* 17. 323–324, ἥμισυ γάρ τ᾽ἀρετῆς ἀποαίνυται εὐρύοπα Ζεὺς/ ἀνέρος) when he becomes a slave. However, Eumaios' biography may undercut his expression of this idea, because he is an enslaved noble who has retained his virtue.
2 Mouritsen 2011, 284–289; MacLean 2018, 136–143.

Afterword 221

3 In this respect, the genre may be another instance in which the imperial elite adopted ideas and cultural forms created by ex-slaves; cf. Patterson 1991, 234–247; the essays in Bell and Ramsby 2012; MacLean 2018.

4 In the creation of an authorial persona, some later novelists may have followed the example of Xenophon and Chariton more closely. The *testimonia* for the second-century novelist Iamblichus are contradictory but suggest an author who fashioned a background in slavery for either himself or his narrative. According to the *Suda*, the author of the lost *Babylonica* was the child of slave parents; according to a scholiast on Photius' summary of the novel, the author had first heard the story from a Babylonian who had been enslaved after Trajan conquered Babylon (115/116). On Iamblichus and the fragments of *Babylonica*: Stephens and Winkler 1995, 179–245.

5 The Roman novels, too, joined in this discussion; however, for reasons noted in the Introduction, the issues they raise are better taken up in a separate book.

6 This critique theoretically could apply to Achilles himself or anyone who undertakes to write a novel: How can any single mind, limited by knowledge and experience, comprehend the multiple perspectives and diversity of human character that mark the genre?

7 While Greek freedmen might similarly be obligated to their masters under the practice of *paramonē*, Apsyrtus' proposal to marry Habrocomes to the daughter of a citizen (*Eph.* 2.10.2, τῶν πολιτῶν τινος θυγατέρα) suggests that Xenophon had Roman manumission practices in mind.

8 Cf. Bradley 1989, 95.

9 Ostrow 1985, 73–85 argues that the Augustales began to achieve prominence and numbers in the Bay of Naples area during the first century CE. He suggests, p. 71, n. 31 and pp. 95–98, that the emperors appreciated whatever contribution the Augustales could make to the stability of Campania, which had been the locus of numerous slave rebellions and was prone to civil unrest.

10 Coleman 2011 identifies Xenophon's Νουκέριον (a correction for the manuscript, reading μουκέριον) with Nuceria Alfaterna in the Campanian coastal plain east of the Bay of Naples (cf. Henderson 2009, 343). Coleman proposes a late Flavian/early Antonine date for the novel, arguing that the reference to Nuceria indicates that Xenophon knew about the destruction of the harbors of Pompeii and Stabiae by Vesuvius but not about the rehabilitation of Stabiae.

11 See the earlier discussion, p. 57, nn. 3 and 4.

12 Persius' reference at the end of *Satire* 1 to a popular work called "Callirhoe" (134) would provide additional evidence that Chariton had readers in Italy, if, indeed, Persius is referring to the novel. Tilg 2010, 69–78 accepts the identification, which was proposed by Weinreich 1962, 13, and provides a review of opinion on the question. Also in favor of the identification: Schmeling 1974, 18; Plepelits 1976, 29–30; Goold 1995, 4–5; Reardon 2003, 315–317; Bowie 2002, 54 (tentative identification).

13 On Zoilus: Reynolds 1982, 156–164; Tilg 2010, 40–41; Athenagoras: Tilg, 52.

14 Reardon 1991, 50; cf. Holzberg 1995, 8–9.

15 Wesseling 1988, 67–69 surveys some of the more important reactions of ancient readers.

16 Plepelits 1976, 29–30 glosses and translates the line (*his mane edictum, post prandia Callirhoen do*) as follows: "To these people (that is, people lacking education who do not know how to value higher literature) I recommend (instead of reading my satires), the praetor's edict in the morning and *Callirhoe* after lunch." According to Schmeling 1974, 18–19, Persius wrote this line with a sneer. Goold 1995, 4–5; Reardon 2003, 316 refer to the satirist's contempt for the readers of Chariton.

17 Tilg 2010, 79–81 argues that Philostratus refers to Chariton the novelist.

18 Cf. the physician Priscianus, who recommended reading Iamblichus' *Babyloniaca* as a form of ancient Viagra on a par with remedies such as procuring attractive slave girls or boys (*Rerum Medicarum Libri Quattuor*, 2.11.34).

222 *Afterword*

19 The survey of epigraphic evidence for *nutrices* in Bradley 1991, 13–35, indicates (pp. 19–20) women "of no more than humble circumstances – slaves, former slaves, and women close to slavery."

20 Graverini 2006. The term designated not all fiction but only those "*fabulae* that are trivial, ludicrous or morally repugnant, and that are not part of the normally agreed-upon corpus of myths treated by renowned authors" (p. 92). Similarly, Macrobius, after condemning the sort of *fabulae* found in Petronius and Apuleius, noted that stories such as Aesop's fables "draw the reader's attention to certain kinds of virtue" (2.9, *quae ad quandam virtutum speciem intellectum legentis hortantur*).

21 Graverini 2006, 105. The designation, of course, is self-ironic in reference to both the tale and the novel.

22 Cf. Seneca, *Ep.* 88.37, a letter disparaging as not truly *liberales* those *artes* associated with practitioners of servile origin: *grammatici, musici, medici*.

Bibliography

Adams, J. N. 2003. *Bilingualism and the Latin Language*. Cambridge; New York: Cambridge University Press.

Adkins, A. W. H. 1973. "Ἀρετή, τέχνη, Democracy, and Sophists. *Protagoras* 316b–328d." *JHS* 93:3–12.

Alston, R. 1998. "Arms and the Man: Soldiers, Masculinity and Power in Republican and Imperial Rome." In *When Men Were Men*, edited by L. Foxhall and J. Salmon, 205–223. London; New York: Routledge.

Alvares, J. 2001–2002. "Some Political and Ideological Dimensions of Chariton's *Chaireas and Callirhoe*." *CJ* 97 (2):113–144.

Anderson, G. 1982. *Eros Sophistes: Ancient Novelists at Play*. Chico, CA: Scholars Press.

Anderson, G. 1984. *Ancient Fiction: The Novel in the Graeco-Roman World*. Totowa, NJ: Barnes & Noble.

Anderson, G. 1988. "Achilles Tatius: A New Interpretation." In *The Greek Novel A.D. 1–1985*, edited by R. Beaton, 190–193. London: Croom Helm.

Anderson, G. 1997. "Perspectives on Achilles Tatius." In *ANRW, 2.34.3*, edited by W. Haase, 2278–2299. Berlin: De Gruyter.

Anderson, G. 2000. *Fairytale in the Ancient World*. London: Routledge.

Anderson, J. K. 1985. *Hunting in the Ancient World*. Berkeley: University of California Press.

Anderson, M. J. 1997. "The Σωφροσύνη of Persinna and the Romantic Strategy of Heliodorus' *Aethiopica*." *CP* 92 (4):303–332.

Andreadakis, Z. 2016. "Reading for Clues: Detective Narratives in Heliodorus' *Aithiopika*." PhD Thesis, Classical Studies, University of Michigan.

Aubert, J.-J. 1994. *Business Managers in Ancient Rome: A Social and Economic Study of Institores, 200 B.C.-A.D. 250*. Leiden: Brill.

Bakhtin, M. M. 1981. *The Dialogic Imagination: Four Essays*. Translated by M. Holquist. Austin: University of Texas Press.

Balot, R. K. 1998. "Foucault, Chariton and the Masculine Self." *Helios* 25 (2):139–162.

Barton, C. A. 2001. *Roman Honor: The Fire in the Bones*. Berkeley: University of California Press.

Baslez, M.-F. 1990. "L'idée de noblesse dans les romans grecs." *Dialogues d'histoire ancienne* 16 (1):115–128.

Baslez, M.-F. 1992. "De l'histoire au roman: la Perse de Chariton." In *Le monde du roman grec*, edited by M.-F. Baslez, P. Hoffmann and M. Trédé-Boulmer, 199–212. Paris: Presses de l'École normale supérieure.

Baumbach, M. 1997. "Die Meroe-Episode in Heliodors *Aithiopika*." *RhM* 140 (3):333–341.

224 *Bibliography*

Bell, S. and T. R. Ramsby, eds. 2012. *Free at Last! The Impact of Freed Slaves on the Roman Empire.* London: Bristol Classical Press.

Berti, M. 1967. "Sulla interpretazione mistica del romanzo di Longo." *Studi Classici e Orientali* 16:343–358.

Billault, A. 1991. *La création romanesque dans la littérature grecque à l'époque impériale.* Paris: Presses Universitaires de France.

Bird, R. 2017. "Virtue Obscured: Theagenes' *Sōphrosynē* in Heliodorus' *Aethiopica.*" *AN* 14:195–208.

Bloomer, W. M. 1997. *Latinity and Literary Society at Rome.* Philadelphia: University of Pennsylvania Press.

Bodel, J. 1994. "Trimalchio's Underworld." In *The Search for the Ancient Novel*, edited by J. Tatum, 237–259. Baltimore; London: Johns Hopkins University Press.

Bodel, J. 2005. "*Caveat Emptor*: Towards a Study of Roman Slave Traders." *Journal of Roman Archaeology* 18 (1):181–195.

Booth, A. D. 1979. "The Schooling of Slaves in First-century Rome." *TAPA* 109:11–19.

Booth, W. C. 1961. *The Rhetoric of Fiction.* Chicago: University of Chicago Press.

Bowersock, G. W. 1965. *Augustus and the Greek World.* Oxford: Clarendon Press.

Bowersock, G. W. 1994. *Fiction as History: From Nero to Julian.* Berkeley: University of California Press.

Bowie, E. L. 1977. "The Novels and the Real World." In *Erotica Antiqua: Acta of the International Conference on the Ancient Novel*, edited by B. P. Reardon, 91–96. Bangor (Wales): University College of North Wales.

Bowie, E. L. 1989. "The Greek Novel." In *The Cambridge History of Classical Literature*, edited by P. E. Easterling and B. M. W. Knox, 123–139. Cambridge: Cambridge University Press.

Bowie, E. L. 2002. "The Chronology of the Earlier Greek Novels Since B. E. Perry: Revisions and Precisions." *AN* 2:47–63.

Bowie, E. L. 2003a. "The Ancient Readers of the Greek Novels." In *The Novel in the Ancient World*, edited by G. L. Schmeling, 87–106. Leiden: Brill Academic Publishers.

Bowie, E. L. 2003b. "The Function of Mythology in Longus' *Daphnis and Chloe.*" In *Mitos en la literatura griega helenística e imperial*, edited by J. A. López Férez, 361–376. Madrid: Ediciones Clásicas.

Bradley, K. R. 1987. *Slaves and Masters in the Roman Empire: A Study in Social Control.* New York: Oxford University Press.

Bradley, K. R. 1989. *Slavery and Rebellion in the Roman World, 140 B.C.–70 B.C.* Bloomington; London: Indiana University Press and B.T. Batsford.

Bradley, K. R. 1990. "*Servus Onerosus*: Roman Law and the Troublesome Slave." *Slavery & Abolition* 11 (2):135–158.

Bradley, K. R. 1991. *Discovering the Roman Family: Studies in Roman Social History.* New York: Oxford University Press.

Bradley, K. R. 1994. *Slavery and Society at Rome, Key Themes in Ancient History.* Cambridge; New York: Cambridge University Press.

Bradley, K. R. 2000. "Animalizing the Slave: The Truth of Fiction." *JRS* 90:110–125.

Bradley, K. R. 2011. "Resisting Slavery at Rome." In *The Cambridge World History of Slavery*, edited by K. R. Bradley and P. Cartledge, 362–384. Cambridge; New York: Cambridge University Press.

Bremmer, J. N. 1998. "The Novel and the Apocryphal Acts: Place, Time and Readership." In *GCN 9*, edited by H. Hofmann and M. Zimmerman, 157–180. Groningen: Forsten.

Bibliography   225

Bretzigheimer, G. 1998. "Die Persinna-Geschichte eine Erfindung des Kalasiris? Überlegungen zu Heliodors *Äthiopika*, 4, 12, 1–13, 1." *Wiener Studien* 111:93–118.

Broekaert, W. 2016. "Freedmen and Agency in Roman Business." In *Urban Craftsmen and Traders in the Roman World*, edited by A. Wilson and M. Flohr, 222–253. Oxford; New York: Oxford University Press.

Brown, V. 2009. "Social Death and Political Life in the Study of Slavery." *The American Historical Review* 114 (5):1231–1249.

Brulé, P. 1987. *La fille d'Athènes. La religion des filles à Athènes à l'époque classique. Mythes, cultes et société*. Paris: Les Belles Lettres.

Bürger, K. 1892. "Zu Xenophon von Ephesus." *Hermes* 27:36–67.

Burke, P. 1978. *Popular Culture in Early Modern Europe*. New York: New York University Press.

Burrus, V. 1987. *Chastity as Autonomy: Women in the Stories of the Apocryphal Acts*. Lewiston: E. Mellen Press.

Cameron, A. 1939. "Θρεπτός and Related Terms in the Inscriptions of Asia Minor." In *Anatolian Studies Presented to W. H. Buckler*, edited by W. M. Calder and J. Keil, 27–62. Manchester: Manchester University Press.

Carlsen, J. 1993. "The *Vilica* and Roman Estate Management." In *De Agricultura: In Memoriam Pieter Willem De Neeve (1945–1990)*, edited by H. Sancisi-Weerdenburg, R. J. Van der Spek, H. C. Teitler and H. T. Wallinga, 197–205. Amsterdam: Gieben.

Chalk, H. H. O. 1960. "Eros and the Lesbian Pastorals of Longos." *JHS* 80:32–51.

Champlin, E. J. 2005. "Phaedrus the Fabulous." *JRS* 95:97–123.

Christenson, D., ed. 2000. *Amphitruo, Plautus*. Cambridge: Cambridge University Press.

Christes, J. 1979a. "Reflexe erlebter Unfreiheit in den Sentenzen des Publilius Syrus und in den Fabeln des Phaedrus. Zur Problematik ihrer Verifizierung." *Hermes* 107:199–220.

Christes, J. 1979b. *Sklaven und Freigelassene als Grammatiker und Philologen im antiken Rom*. Wiesbaden: Steiner.

Coleman, K. M. 2011. "Sailing to Nuceria: Evidence for the Date of Xenophon of Ephesus." *Acta Classica* 54:27–42.

Connors, C. 2002. "Chariton's Syracuse and Its Histories of Empire." In *Space in the Ancient Novel*, edited by M. Paschalis and S. Frangoulidis, 12–26. Eelde: Barkhuis.

Cook, J. G. 2014. *Crucifixion in the Mediterranean World*. Tübingen: Mohr Siebeck.

Cresci, L. R. 1981. "Il romanzo di Longo Sofista e la tradizione bucolica." *Atene e Roma* 26:1–25.

Croally, N. T. 1994. *Euripidean Polemic: The Trojan Women and the Function of Tragedy*. Cambridge; New York: Cambridge University Press.

Crook, J. A. 1967. *Law and Life of Rome*. London: Thames and Hudson.

Cueva, E. P. 1999. "Longus and Thucydides: A New Interpretation." *GRBS* 39 (4):429–440.

Cueva, E. P. 2004. *The Myths of Fiction: Studies in the Canonical Greek Novels*. Ann Arbor: University of Michigan Press.

Curran, L. C. 1978. "Rape and Rape Victims in the *Metamorphoses*." *Arethusa* XI:213–241.

Dalmeyda, G. ed. and trans. 1962 (1926). *Xénophon d'Éphèse: Les Éphesiaques; ou, Le roman d'Habrocomès et d'Anthia*. Paris: Les Belles Lettres.

Damon, C. 1995. "Greek Parasites and Roman Patronage." *HSCP* 97:181–195.

Damon, C. 1997. *The Mask of the Parasite: A Pathology of Roman Patronage*. Ann Arbor: University of Michigan Press.

Daube, D. 1972. *Civil Disobedience in Antiquity*. Edinburgh: Edinburgh University Press.

De Jong, I. J. F. 2014. *Narratology and Classics: A Practical Guide*. Oxford: Oxford University Press.

226   Bibliography

Delhay, C. 1990. "Achille Tatius fabuliste?" *Pallas: Revue d'Études Antiques* 36:117–131.

De Temmerman, K. 2009. "Chaereas Revisited: Rhetorical Control in Chariton's Ideal Novel *Callirhoe*." *CQ* 59 (1):247–262.

De Temmerman, K. 2014. *Crafting Characters: Heroes and Heroines in the Ancient Greek Novel*. Oxford; New York: Oxford University Press.Di Virgilio, Raffaele. 1991. *La narrativa greca d'amore: Dafni e Cloe di Longo*. Vol. 32.4. Rome: Atti della Accademia nazionale dei Lincei.

Dmitriev, S. 2016. "The Protection of Slaves in the Athenian Law Against *Hybris*." *Phoenix* 70 (1–2):64–76.

Donnini, M. 1981. "Apul. Met. X,2–12; analogie e varianti di un racconto." *Materiali e contributi per la storia della narrativa greco-latina* 3:145–160.

Doody, M. A. 1996. *The True Story of the Novel*. New Brunswick, NJ: Rutgers University Press.

Douglass, F. 1845. *Narrative of the Life of Frederick Douglass, an American Slave*. Boston: Anti-Slavery Office.

Doulamis, K. 2007. "Stoic Echoes and Style in Xenophon of Ephesus." In *Philosophical Presences in the Ancient Novel*, edited by J. R. Morgan and M. Jones, 151–175. Groningen: Barkhuis.

Dover, K. J. 1974. *Greek Popular Morality in the Time of Plato and Aristotle*. Berkeley: University of California Press.

Dowden, K. 1996. "Heliodoros: Serious Intentions." *CQ* N. S. 46 (1):267–285.

duBois, P. 2003. *Slaves and Other Objects*. Chicago and London: University of Chicago Press.

Duff, A. M. 1958. *Freedmen in the Early Roman Empire*. New York: Barnes & Noble.

Durham, D. B. 1938. "Parody in Achilles Tatius." *CP* 33 (1):3–19.

Edwards, C. 2009. "Free Yourself! Slavery, Freedom and the Self in Seneca's *Letters*." In *Seneca and the Self*, edited by S. Bartsch and D. L. Wray, 139–159. Cambridge; New York: Cambridge University Press.

Edwards, D. R. 1991. "Surviving the Web of Roman Power: Religion and Politics in the Acts of the Apostles, Josephus, and Chariton's *Chaereas and Callirhoe*." In *Images of Empire*, edited by L. Alexander, 179–201. Sheffield: JSOT Press.

Edwards, D. R. 1994. "Defining the Web of Power in Asia Minor: The Novelist Chariton and His City of Aphrodisias." *Journal of the American Academy of Religion* 62/63:699–718.

Effe, B. 1999. "Longus: Towards a History of Bucolic and Its Function in the Roman Empire." In *Oxford Readings in the Greek Novel*, edited by S. Swain, 189–209. Oxford: Oxford University Press. Original edition, "Longos. zur Funktionsgeschichte der Bukolik in der römischen Kaiserzeit," in *Hermes*, 110 (1982) 65–84.

Egger, B. 1990. "Women in the Greek Novel: Constructing the Feminine." PhD Dissertation, Classics, University of California Irvine.

Egger, B. 1994a. "Looking at Chariton's Callirhoe." In *Greek Fiction: The Greek Novel in Context*, edited by J. R. Morgan and R. Stoneman, 31–48. Routledge.

Egger, B. 1994b. "Women and Marriage in the Greek Novels: The Boundaries of Romance." In *The Search for the Ancient Novel*, edited by J. Tatum, 260–280. Baltimore: Johns Hopkins University Press.

Egger, B. 1999 (1988). "The Role of Women in the Greek Novel: Woman as Heroine and Reader." In *Oxford Readings in the Greek Novel*, edited by S. Swain, 108–136. Oxford: Oxford University Press. Original edition, "Zu den Frauenrollen im griechischen Roman: die Frau as Heldin und Leserin," in *GCN* 1 (1988) 33–66.

Bibliography 227

Eilers, C. F. 2002. *Roman Patrons of Greek Cities*. Oxford: Clarendon Press.

Elsom, H. E. 1992. "Callirhoe: Displaying the Phallic Woman." In *Pornography and Representation in Greece and Rome*, edited by A. Richlin, 212–230. Oxford: Oxford University Press.

Fakas, C. 2005. "Charitons Kallirhoe und Sybaris." *RhM* 148 (3–4):413–417.

Faverty, F. E. 1931. "The Story of Joseph and Potiphar's Wife in Mediaeval Literature." *Harvard Studies and Notes in Philology and Literature* 13:81–127.

Fetterley, J. 1978. *The Resisting Reader: A Feminist Approach to American Fiction*. Bloomington: Indiana University Press.

Feuillâtre, E. 1966. *Études sur les Éthiopiques d'Héliodore, contribution à la connaissance du roman grec*. Paris: Presses Universitaires.

Fisher, N. 1998. "Violence, Masculinity and the Law in Classical Athens." In *When Men Were Men*, edited by L. Foxhall and J. Salmon, 68–97. London; New York: Routledge.

Fitzgerald, W. 2000. *Slavery and the Roman Literary Imagination*. Cambridge; New York: Cambridge University Press.

Flory, M. B. 1978. "Family in Familia: Kinship and Community in Slavery." *American Journal of Ancient History* 3:78–95.

Flusche, M. 1975. "Joel Chandler Harris and the Folklore of American Slavery." *Journal of American Studies* 9:347–363.

Forbes, C. A. 1955. "The Education and Training of Slaves in Antiquity." *TAPA* 86:321–360.

Forehand, W. E. 1976. "Symbolic Gardens in Longus' *Daphnis and Chloe*." *Eranos* 74:103–112.

Forsdyke, S. 2012. *Slaves Tell Tales: And Other Episodes in the Politics of Popular Culture in Ancient Greece*. Princeton: Princeton University Press.

Fowler, R. L. 2011. "*Mythos* and *Logos*." *JHS* 131:45–66.

Freese, J. H., ed. and trans. 2000. *Aristotle: Rhetoric, Loeb Classical Library*. Cambridge, MA: Harvard University Press.

Fusillo, M. 1989. *Il romanzo greco. Polifonia ed eros*. Venezia: Marsilio.

Fusillo, M. 1997. "How Novels End: Some Patterns of Closure in Ancient Narrative." In *Classical Closure*, edited by D. H. Roberts, F. M. Dunn and D. P. Fowler, 209–227. Princeton: Princeton University Press.

Fusillo, M. 1999. "The Conflict of Emotions: A Topos in the Greek Erotic Novel." In *Oxford Readings in the Greek Novel*, edited by S. Swain, 60–82. Oxford: Oxford University Press.

Fusillo, M. 2003. "Modern Critical Theories and the Ancient Novel." In *The Novel in the Ancient World*, edited by G. L. Schmeling, 277–305. Boston: Brill Academic Publishers.

Gamauf, R. 2007. "*Cum aliter nulla domus tuta esse possit ... D.* 29, 5, 1: Fear of Slaves and Roman Law." In *Fear of Slaves, Fear of Enslavement in the Ancient Mediterranean = Peur de l'esclave, peur de l'esclavage en Méditerranée ancienne*, edited by A. Serghidou, 145–164. Besançon: Presses Universitaires de Franche-Comté.

Garlan, Y. 1982. *Slavery in Ancient Greece*. Translated by J. Lloyd. Ithaca, NY: Cornell University Press.

Garnsey, P. D. A. 1996. *Ideas of Slavery From Aristotle to Augustine*. Cambridge; New York: Cambridge University Press.

Gärtner, H. 1967. "Xenophon von Ephesus." In *RE, Suppl. IX, 2*, 2055–2089. Stuttgart: J. B. Metzler.

Gaselee, S. 1917. *Achilles Tatius, Loeb Classical Library*. London; New York: W. Heinemann; G.P. Putnam's Sons.

228 Bibliography

Genovese, E. D. 1974. *Roll, Jordan, Roll: The World the Slaves Made.* New York: Pantheon Books.

George, M. 2005. "Family Imagery and Family Values in Roman Italy." In *The Roman Family in the Empire: Rome, Italy, and Beyond,* edited by M. George, 37–66. Oxford; New York: Oxford University Press.

Goold, G. P., ed. and trans. 1995. *Chariton: Callirhoe, Loeb Classical LIbrary.* Cambridge, MA: Harvard University Press.

Graverini, L. 2006. "An Old Wife's Tale." In *Lectiones Scrupulosae,* edited by W. Keulen, R. Nauta and S. Panayotakis, 86–110. Eelde: Barkhuis.

Green, F. M. 2015. "Witnesses and Participants in the Shadows: The Sexual Lives of Enslaved Women and Boys." *Helios* 42 (1):143–162.

Gutman, H. G. 1976. *The Black Family in Slavery and Freedom, 1750–1925.* New York: Vintage Books.

Hägg, T. 1966. "Die *Ephesiaka* des Xenophon Ephesios. Original oder Epitome?" *Classica et Mediaevalia* 27:118–161.

Hägg, T. 1971. *Narrative Technique in Ancient Greek Romances: Studies of Chariton, Xenophon Ephesius, and Achilles Tatius.* Stockholm: Svenska Institutet i Athen.

Hägg, T. 1983. *The Novel in Antiquity.* Oxford; Malden, MA: Blackwell.

Hägg, T. 1994. "Orality, Literacy, and the Readership of the Early Greek Novel." In *Contexts of Pre-novel Narrative: The European Tradition,* edited by R. Eriksen, 47–81. Berlin: Mouton de Gruyter.

Hägg, T. 1997. "A Professor and His Slave: Conventions and Values in the *Life of Aesop.*" In *Conventional Values of the Hellenistic Greeks: Studies in Hellenistic Civilization,* edited by P. Bilde, T. Engberg-Pedersen, L. Hannestad and J. Zahle, 177–203. Aarhus: Aarhus University Press.

Hardie, P. R. 1998. "A Reading of Heliodorus, *Aithiopika* 3.4.1–5.2." In *Studies in Heliodorus,* edited by R. L. Hunter, 19–39. Cambridge: Cambridge Philological Society.

Harper, K. 2011. *Slavery in the Late Roman World, AD 275–425.* Cambridge; New York: Cambridge University Press.

Harris, W. V. 1980. "Toward a Study of the Roman Slave Trade." In *The Seaborne Commerce of Ancient Rome,* edited by J. H. D'Arms and E. C. Kopff, 117–140. Rome: American Academy.

Harris, W. V. 1989. *Ancient Literacy.* Cambridge, MA: Harvard University Press.

Harris, WW V. 2001. *Restraining Rage: The Ideology of Anger Control in Classical Antiquity.* Cambridge, MA: Harvard University Press.

Haynes, K. 2003. *Fashioning the Feminine in the Greek Novel.* London: Routledge.

Hegel, G. W. F. 1949. *The Phenomenology of Mind.* Translated by J. B. Baille. 2nd ed. New York: Humanities Press Inc.

Heinze, R. 1899. "Petron und der griechische Roman." *Hermes* 34 (494–519).

Heiserman, A. 1977. *The Novel Before the Novel.* Chicago: University of Chicago Press.

Helms, J. 1966. *Character Portrayal in the Romance of Chariton.* Paris: Mouton.

Henderson, J., ed. and trans. 2009. *Longus: Daphnis and Chloe. Xenophon of Ephesus: Anthia and Habrocomes, Loeb Classical Library.* Cambridge, MA: Harvard University Press.

Henderson, J. 2010. "The *Satyrica* and the Greek Novel: Revisions and Some Open Questions." *International Journal of the Classical Tradition* 17 (4):483–496.

Herrmann, F. G. 2007. "'Longus' Imitation: *Mimēsis* in the Education of Daphnis and Chloe." In *Philosophical Presences in the Ancient Novel,* edited by J. R. Morgan and M. Jones, 205–229. Groningen: Barkhuis.

Bibliography 229

Hillard, T. 2013. "Graffiti's Engagement: The Political Graffiti of the Late Roman Republic." In *Written Space in the Latin West, 200 BC to AD 300*, edited by G. Sears, P. Keegan and R. Laurence, 105–122. London: Bloomsbury Academic.

Himmelmann, N. 1971. *Archäologisches zum Problem der griechischen Sklaverei*. Wiesbaden: Steiner.

Hock, R. F. 1997. "An Extraordinary Friend in Chariton's *Callirhoe*: The Importance of Friendship in the Greek Romances." In *Greco-Roman Perspectives on Friendship*, edited by J. T. Fitzgerald, 145–162. Atlanta, GA: Scholars Press.

Holzberg, N. 1995. *The Ancient Novel: An Introduction*. Translated by C. Jackson-Holzberg. London; New York: Routledge.

Hopkins, K. 1965. "Elite Mobility in the Roman Empire." *P&P* 32:12–26.

Hopkins, K. 1993. "Novel Evidence for Roman Slavery." *P&P* 138:3–27.

Hough, J. N. 1970. "Jupiter, Amphitryon, and the Cuckoo." *CP* 65:95–96.

Hunt, P. 1998. *Slaves, Warfare, and Ideology in the Greek Historians*. Cambridge; New York: Cambridge University Press.

Hunter, R. L. 1983. *A Study of Daphnis & Chloe*. Cambridge: Cambridge University Press.

Hunter, R. L. 1985. *The New Comedy of Greece and Rome*. Cambridge: Cambridge University Press.

Hunter, R. L. 1994. "History and Historicity in the Romance of Chariton." In *ANRW, 2.34.2*, edited by W. Haase, 1055–1086. Berlin; New York: de Gruyter.

Hunter, R. L., ed. 1998. *Studies in Heliodorus*. Cambridge: Cambridge Philological Society.

Hunter, R. L. 2008. "Ancient Readers." In *The Cambridge Companion to the Greek and Roman Novel*, edited by T. Whitmarsh, 261–271. Cambridge; New York: Cambridge University Press.

Iser, W. 1978. *The Act of Reading: A Theory of Aesthetic Response*. Baltimore: Johns Hopkins University Press.

Johne, R. 2003. "Women in the Ancient Novel." In *The Novel in the Ancient World*, edited by G. L. Schmeling, 151–208. Boston: Brill Academic Publishers.

Jones, C. P. 1992. "La personnalité de Chariton." In *Le monde du roman grec*, edited by M.-F. Baslez, P. Hoffmann and M. Trédé-Boulmer, 161–167. Paris: Presses de l'École normale supérieure.

Jones, M. 2004. "The Wisdom of Egypt: Base and Heavenly Magic in Heliodoros' *Aithiopika*." *AN* 4:79–98.

Jones, M. 2007. "*Andreia* and Gender in the Greek Novels." In *Philosophical Presences in the Ancient Novel*, edited by J. R. Morgan and M. Jones, 111–135. Groningen: Barkhuis.

Jones, M. 2012. *Playing the Man: Performing Masculinities in the Ancient Greek Novel*. Oxford; New York: Oxford University Press.

Joshel, S. R. 1992. *Work, Identity, and Legal Status at Rome: A Study of the Occupational Inscriptions*. Norman, OK: University of Oklahoma Press.

Joshel, S. R. 2011. "Slavery and Roman Literary Culture." In *The Cambridge World History of Slavery*, edited by K. R. Bradley and P. Cartledge, 214–240. Cambridge; New York: Cambridge University Press.

Kaimio, M. 1995. "How to Manage in the Male World: The Strategies of the Heroine in Chariton's Novel." *Acta Antiqua Academiae Scientiarum Hungaricae* 36:119–132.

Kanavou, N. 2015. "A Husband Is More Important than a Child: The Ending of Chariton's *Callirhoe* Revisited." *Mnemosyne* Ser. 4 68.6:937–955.

230 Bibliography

Kapparis, K. A. 2002. *Abortion in the Ancient World*. London: Duckworth Academic.

Karabélias, E. 1990. "Le roman de Chariton d'Aphrodisias et le droit: renversements de situation et exploitation des ambiguïtés juridiques." In *Symposion 1988: Vorträge zur griechischen und hellenistischen Rechtsgeschichte*, edited by G. Nenci and G. Thür, 369–396. Köln: Böhlau.

Kaster, R. A., ed. and trans. 1995. *C. Suetonius Tranquillus. De Grammaticis et Rhetoribus*. Oxford: Clarendon Press.

Kerényi, K. 1927. *Die griechisch-orientalische Romanliterature in religionsgeschichtlicher Beleuchtung*. Tübingen: Mohr.

Keul-Deutscher, M. 1997. "Heliodorstudien. 2,: Die Liebe in den *Aithiopika*." *RhM* 140 (3–4):341–362.

Kim, K. Y. 2013. "Orality, Folktales and Cross-cultural Transmission." In *The Romance Between Greece and the East*, edited by T. Whitmarsh and S. Thomson, 300–321. Cambridge; New York: Cambridge University Press.

Kirschenbaum, A. 1987. *Sons, Slaves and Freedmen in Roman Commerce*. Jerusalem: The Magnes Press.

Kloft, H. 1989. "Imagination und Realität: Überlegungen zur Wirtschaftsstruktur des Romans *Daphnis und Chloe*." In *GCN 2*, edited by H. Hofmann, 45–61. Groningen: Forsten.

Kojève, A. 1969. *Introduction to the Reading of Hegel: Lectures on the Phenomenology of Spirit*. Translated by J. H. Nichols. New York: London: Basic Books.

Kolendo, J. 1981. "L'esclavage et la vie sexuelle des hommes libres à Rome." *Index: Quaderni Camerti di Studi Romanistici = International Survey of Roman Law* 10:288–297.

König, J. 2007. "Orality and Authority in Xenophon of Ephesus." In *Seeing Tongues, Hearing Scripts: Orality and Representation in the Ancient Novel*, edited by V. Rimell, 1–22. Eelde: Barkhuis.

Konstan, D. 1994. *Sexual Symmetry: Love in the Ancient Novel and Related Genres*. Princeton: Princeton University Press.

Konstan, D. 2007. "Love and Murder: Two Textual Problems in Xenophon's *Ephesiaca*." *AN* 5:31–40.

Konstantakos, I. M. 2006. "Aesop Adulterer and Trickster: A Study of *Vita Aesopi* ch. 75–76." *Athenaeum* 94 (2):563–600.

Kovacs, D., ed. and trans. 1995. *Euripides II*. Cambridge, MA: Harvard University Press.

Kövendi, D. 1966. "Heliodors *Aithiopika*: eine literarische Würdigung." In *Die Araber in der alten Welt, III: Anfänge der Dichtung. Der Sonnengott*, edited by F. Altheim and R. Stiehl, 136–197. Berlin: de Gruyter.

Kraut, R. 2002. *Aristotle: Political Philosophy*. Oxford; New York: Oxford University Press.

Kruchió, B. 2017. "What Charicles Knew: Fragmentary Narration and Ambiguity in Heliodorus' *Aethiopica*." *AN* 14:175–194.

Kudlien, F. 1989. "Kindesaussetzung im antiken Roman: ein Thema zwischen Fiktionalität und Lebenswirklichkeit." In *GCN, 2*, edited by H. Hofmann, 25–44. Groningen: Forsten.

Kurke, L. 2011. *Aesopic Conversations: Popular Tradition, Cultural Dialogue, and the Invention of Greek Prose*. Princeton; Oxford: Princeton University Press.

Lalanne, S. 2006. *Une éducation grecque: rites de passage et construction des genres dans le roman grec ancien*. Paris: Découverte.

Leigh, M. 2016. "Vergil's Second *Eclogue* and the Class Struggle." *CP* 111 (4):406–433.

Lesky, A. 1966. *A History of Greek Literature*. Translated by J. Willis and C. de Heer. 2nd ed. New York: Thomas Y. Crowell Company.

Bibliography 231

Létoublon, F. 1993. *Les lieux communs du roman: stéréotypes grecs d'aventure et d'amour*. Leiden: Brill.

Levin, D. N. 1977. "To Whom Did the Ancient Novelists Address Themselves?" *Rivista di Studi Classici* 25:18–29.

Levine, L. W. 2007. *Black Culture and Black Consciousness: Afro-American Folk Thought From Slavery to Freedom*. Oxford; New York: Oxford University Press.

Lewis, D. M. 2017. "Orlando Patterson, Property, and Ancient Slavery." In *On Human Bondage: After Slavery and Social Death*, edited by J. Bodel and W. Scheidel, 31–54. Chichester, West Sussex; Malden, MA: John Wiley & Sons Inc.

Lichtenstein, A. 1988. "'That Disposition to Theft, with Which They Have Been Branded': Moral Economy, Slave Management, and the Law." *Journal of Social History* 21 (3): 413–440.

Liviabella Furiani, P. 1989. "Di donna in donna. Elementi femministi nel romanzo greco d'amore." In *Piccolo mondo antico: appunti sulle donne, gli amori, i costumi, il mondo reale nel romanzo antico*, edited by P. Liviabella Furiani and A. M. Scarcella, 43–106. Napoli: Ed. Scientifiche Italiane.

Longo, O. 1978. "Paesaggio di Longo Sofista." *Quaderni di Storia* 4 (8):99–120.

Luginbill, R. D. 2002. "A Delightful Possession: Longus' Prologue and Thucydides." *CJ* 97 (3):233–247.

Lussana, S. 2016. *My Brother Slaves: Friendship, Masculinity, and Resistance in the Antebellum South*. Lexington, KY: University of Kentucky Press.

Lyne, R. O. A. M. 1979. "*Seruitium amoris*." *CQ* 29:117–130.

MacDowell, D. M. 1976. "*Hybris* in Athens." *G&R* 23:14–31.

MacLean, Rose. 2018. *Freed Slaves and Roman Imperial Culture: Social Integration and the Transformation of Values*. Cambridge: Cambridge University Press.

MacQueen, B. D. 1990. *Myth, Rhetoric, and Fiction: A Reading of Longus's Daphnis and Chloe*. Lincoln: University of Nebraska Press.

Manning, C. E. 1989. "Stoicism and Slavery in the Roman Empire." In *ANRW, 2.36.3*, edited by W. Haase, 1518–1543. Berlin; New York: de Gruyter.

McCarthy, K. 2000. *Slaves, Masters, and the Art of Authority in Plautine Comedy*. Princeton: Princeton University Press.

McCulloh, W. E. 1970. *Longus*. New York: Twayne.

McGill, S. C. 2000. "The Literary Lives of a *Scheintod*: Clitophon and Leucippe 5.7 and Greek Epigram." *CQ* N. S. 50 (1):323–326.

McKeown, N. 2011. "Resistance Among Chattel Slaves in the Classical Greek World." In *The Cambridge World History of Slavery*, edited by K. R. Bradley and P. Cartledge, 153–175. Cambridge: Cambridge University Press.

Merkelbach, R. 1962. *Roman und Mysterium in der Antike*. München: Beck.

Merkelbach, R. 1988. *Die Hirten des Dionysos: die Dionysos-Mysterien der römischen Kaiserzeit und der bukolische Roman des Longus*. Stuttgart: B. G. Teubner.

Mixon, W. 1990. "The Ultimate Irrelevance of Race: Joel Chandler Harris and Uncle Remus in Their Time." *The Journal of Southern History* 56 (3):457–480.

Mohler, S. L. 1940. "Slave Education in the Roman Empire." *TAPA* 71:262–280.

Montague, H. 1992. "Sweet and Pleasant Passion: Female and Male Fantasy in Ancient Romance Novels." In *Pornography and Representation in Greece and Rome*, edited by A. Richlin, 231–249. Oxford; New York: Oxford University Press.

Montiglio, S. 2005. *Wandering in Ancient Greek Culture*. Chicago: University of Chicago Press.

Montiglio, S. 2013. *Love and Providence: Recognition in the Ancient Novel*. Oxford: Oxford University Press.

232 Bibliography

Morales, H. L. 2000. "Sense and Sententiousness in the Greek Novels." In *Intratextuality: Greek and Roman Textual Relations*, edited by A. R. Sharrock and H. L. Morales, 67–88. Oxford; New York: Oxford University Press.

Morales, H. L. 2004. *Vision and Narrative in Achilles Tatius' Leucippe and Clitophon*. Cambridge; New York: Cambridge University Press.

Morgan, J. R. 1982. "History, Romance, and Realism in the *Aithiopika* of Heliodoros." *CA* I:221–265.

Morgan, J. R., trans. 1989a. "Heliodorus, *An Ethiopian Story*." In *Collected Ancient Greek Novels*, edited by B. P. Reardon, 349–588. Berkeley: University of California Press.

Morgan, J. R. 1989b. "The Story of Knemon in Heliodoros' *Aithiopika*." *JHS* 109:99–113.

Morgan, J. R. 1994a. "Daphnis and Chloe: Love's Own Sweet Story." In *Greek Fiction: The Greek Novel in Context*, edited by J. R. Morgan and R. Stoneman, 64–79. London: Routledge.

Morgan, J. R. 1994b. "The *Aithiopika* of Heliodorus: Narrative as Riddle." In *Greek Fiction: The Novel in Context*, edited by J. R. Morgan and R. Stoneman, 97–113. London: Routledge.

Morgan, J. R. 1995. "The Greek Novel: Towards a Sociology of Production and Reception." In *The Greek World*, edited by A. Powell, 130–152. London: Routledge.

Morgan, J. R. 1996. "*Erotika Mathemata*: Greek Romance as Sentimental Education." In *Education in Greek Fiction*, edited by A. H. Sommerstein and C. Atherton, 163–189. Bari: Levante.

Morgan, J. R. 1997. "Longus, *Daphnis and Chloe*: A Bibliographical Survey, 1950–1995." In *ANRW, 2.34.3*, edited by W. Haase. Berlin; New York: de Gruyter.

Morgan, J. R. 1998. "Narrative Doublets in Heliodorus' *Aithiopika*." In *Studies in Heliodorus*, edited by R. L. Hunter, 60–78. Cambridge: Cambridge Philological Society.

Morgan, J. R. 2003. "Heliodorus." In *The Novel in the Ancient World*, edited by G. L. Schmeling, 417–456. Boston: Brill Academic Publishers.

Morgan, J. R. 2004a. "Chariton." In *Studies in Ancient Greek Narrative. 1, Narrators, Narratees, and Narratives in Ancient Greek Literature*, edited by I. J. F. De Jong, R. Nünlist and A. M. Bowie, 479–487. Leiden: Brill.

Morgan, J. R. 2004b. "Achilles Tatius." In *Studies in Ancient Greek Narrative. 1, Narrators, Narratees, and Narratives in Ancient Greek Literature*, edited by I. J. F. De Jong, R. Nünlist and A. M. Bowie, 493–506. Leiden: Brill.

Morgan, J. R. 2004c. "Heliodorus." In *Studies in Ancient Greek Narrative. 1, Narrators, Narratees, and Narratives in Ancient Greek Literature*, edited by I. J. F. De Jong, R. Nünlist and A. M. Bowie, 523–543. Leiden: Brill.

Morgan, J. R., trans. 2004d. *Daphnis and Chloe*. Warminster: Aris and Phillips.

Morgan, J. R. 2007a. "Xenophon of Ephesus." In *Studies in Ancient Greek Narrative. 2, Time in Ancient Greek Literature*, edited by I. J. F. De Jong and R. Nünlist, 453–466. Leiden: Brill.

Morgan, J. R. 2007b. "Kleitophon and Encolpius: Achilleus Tatius as Hidden Author." In *The Greek and Roman Novel: Parallel Readings*, edited by M. Paschalis, S. A. Frangoulidis and S. J. Harrison, 105–120. Eelde: Barkhuis.

Morley, N. 2011. "Slavery Under the Principate." In *The Cambridge World History of Slavery*, edited by K. R. Bradley and P. Cartledge, 265–286. Cambridge: Cambridge University Press.

Morton, P. 2013. "Eunus: The Cowardly King." *CQ* 63 (1):237–252.

Most, G. W. 1989. "The Stranger's Stratagem: Self-disclosure and Self-sufficiency in Greek Culture." *JHS* 109:114–133.

Bibliography   233

Mouritsen, H. 2011. *The Freedman in the Roman World*. Cambridge; New York: Cambridge University Press.

Mueller, C. W. 1976. "Chariton von Aphrodisias und die Theorie des Romans in der Antike." *Antike und Abendland* 22:115–136.

Oldfather, W. A., ed. and trans. 1925. *Epictetus: Discourses, Loeb Classical Library*. Cambridge, MA: Harvard University Press.

Omitowoju, R., trans. 2011. "*Callirhoe*." In *Greek Fiction. Chariton: Callirhoe, Longus: Daphnis and Chloe, Anonymous: Letters of Chion*, edited by H. Morales. London; New York: Penguin Books.

Ostrow, S. 1985. "Augustales Along the Bay of Naples: A Case for Their Early Growth." *Historia* 34:64–101.

O'Sullivan, J. N. 1995. *Xenophon of Ephesus: His Compositional Technique and the Birth of the Novel*. Berlin; New York: de Gruyter.

O'Sullivan, J. N. 2014. "Xenophon, *The Ephesian Tales*." In *A Companion to the Ancient Novel*, edited by E. P. Cueva and S. N. Byrne, 43–61. Chichester, UK: John Wiley & Sons.

Owens, W. M. forthcoming. "Reading Apuleius' *Cupid and Psyche* as a Slave's Story: The Tale of Psyche *Ancilla*." In *Slavery and Sexuality in Classical Antiquity*, edited by D. Kamen and C. W. Marshall. Madison: University of Wisconsin Press.

Pandiri, T. A. 1985. "*Daphnis and Chloe*. The Art of Pastoral Play." *Ramus* 14:116–141.

Papadimitropoulos, L. 2013. "Love and the Reinstatement of the Self in Heliodorus' *Aethiopica*." *G&R* 60 (1):101–113.

Papanikolaou, A. D., ed. 1973. *Xenophontis Ephesii. Ephesiacorum Libri V.* Leipzig: Teubner.

Parker, H. N. 1989. "Crucially Funny or Tranio on the Couch: The *Servus Callidus* and Jokes About Torture." *TAPA* 119:233–246.

Patterson, O. 1982. *Slavery and Social Death: A Comparative Study*. Cambridge, MA: Harvard University Press.

Patterson, O. 1991. *Freedom in the Making of Western Culture*. New York: Basic Books.

Paulsen, T. 1992. *Inszenierung des Schicksals: Tragödie und Komödie im Roman des Heliodor*. Trier: Wissentschaftlicher Verlag Trier.

Pellegrin, P. 1982. "La théorie aristotélicienne de l'esclavage ; tendances actuelles de l'interprétation." *Revue philosophique de la France et de l'étranger* 172 (2):345–357.

Perry, B. E. 1930. "Chariton and His Romance From a Literary-Historical Point of View." *AJP* 51:93–135.

Perry, B. E., ed. 1952. *Aesopica, I: Greek and Latin Texts*. Champaign, IL: University of Illinois Press.

Perry, B. E., ed. and trans. 1965. *Babrius and Phaedrus, Loeb Classical Library*. Cambridge, MA: Harvard University Press.

Perry, B. E. 1967. *The Ancient Romances: A Literary-Historical Account of Their Origins*. Berkeley: University of California Press.

Perry, M. J. 2011. "Quintus Haterius and the 'Dutiful' Freedman: The Consideration of Sexual Conduct Between Patrons and Freedpersons in Roman Law." *The Ancient History Bulletin* 25 (3–4):133–148.

Perry, M. J. 2014. *Gender, Manumission, and the Roman Freedwoman*. Cambridge: Cambridge University Press.

Petersen, L. H. 2006. *The Freedman in Roman Art and Art History*. Cambridge; New York: Cambridge University Press.

Plepelits, K., ed. and trans. 1976. *Kallirhoe*. Stuttgart: Anton Hiersemann.

234 *Bibliography*

Propp, V. I. A. 1968. *Morphology of the Folktale*. Translated by L. Scott. Austin, TX; London: University of Texas Press.

Purcell, N. 1983. "The *Apparitores*: A Study in Social Mobility." *Papers of the British School at Rome* 51:125–173.

Quet, M.-H. 1992. "Romans grecs, mosaïques romaines." In *Le monde du roman grec*, edited by M.-F. Baslez, P. P. Hoffmann and M. Trédé, 125–160. Paris: Presses de l'École normale supérieure.

Rackham, H., ed. and trans. 1932. *Aristotle: Politics*, Loeb Classical Library. Cambridge, MA: Harvard University Press.

Rackham, H. ed. and trans. 1942. *Cicero IV, Loeb Classical Library*. Cambridge, MA: Harvard University Press.

Rattenbury, R. M., and T. W. Lumb, eds. 1960 (1935). *Les Éthiopiques (Théagène et Chariclée), I*. Paris: Les Belles Lettres.

Rattenbury, R. M., and T. W. Lumb, eds. 1960 (1938). *Les Éthiopiques (Théagène et Chariclée), II*. Paris: Les Belles Lettres.

Rattenbury, R. M., and T. W. Lumb, eds. 1960 (1943). *Les Éthiopiques (Théagène et Chariclée), III*. Paris: Les Belles lettres.

Rawson, B. 2003. *Children and Childhood in Roman Italy*. Oxford; New York: Oxford University Press.

Reardon, B. P. 1982. "Theme, Structure and Narrative in Chariton." *YCS* 27:1–27.

Reardon, B. P., ed. 1989. *Collected Ancient Greek Novels*. Berkeley: University of California Press.

Reardon, B. P. 1991. *The Form of Greek Romance*. Princeton: Princeton University Press.

Reardon, B. P. 1994. "Achilles Tatius and Ego-narrative." In *Greek Fiction: The Greek Novel in Context*, edited by J. R. Morgan and R. Stoneman, 80–96. London: Routledge.

Reardon, B. P. 2003. "Chariton." In *The Novel in the Ancient World*, edited by G. L. Schmeling, 309–335. Boston: Brill Academic Publishing.

Repath, I. D. 2005. "Achilles Tatius' Leucippe and Cleitophon: What Happened Next?" *CQ* N. S. 55 (1):250–265.

Repath, I. D. 2007. "Emotional Conflict and Platonic Psychology in the Greek Novel." In *Philosophical Presences in the Ancient Novel*, edited by J. R. Morgan and M. Jones, 53–84. Groningen: Barkhuis.

Reynolds, J. M. 1982. *Aphrodisias and Rome*. London: Society for the Promotion of Roman Studies.

Richlin, A. 2014. "Talking to Slaves in the Plautine Audience." *Classical Antiquity* 33.1:174–226.

Richlin, A. 2017. *Slave Theater in the Roman Republic: Plautus and Popular Comedy*. Cambridge: Cambridge University Press.

Rife, J. L. 2002. "Officials of the Roman Provinces in Xenophon's *Ephesiaca*." *ZPE* 138:93–108.

Rodríquez Gervás, M. 2007. "Enseigner la peur, reproduire la domination, une approche." In *Fear of Slaves, Fear of Enslavement in the Ancient Mediterranean – Peur de l'esclave, peur de l'esclavage en Méditerranée ancienne*, edited by A. Serghidou, 337–345. Besançon: Presses Universitaires de Franche-Comté.

Rohde, E. 1960 (1876). *Der griechische Roman und seine Vorläufer*. 2. Aufl. ed. Hildesheim: G. Olms.

Romano, D. 1980. "Il '*lascivus lusus*' di Cicerone." *Orpheus* n.s. 1:441–447.

Rossiter, J. J. 1989. "Roman Villas of the Greek East and the Villa in Gregory of Nyssa *Ep*. 20." *Journal of Roman Archaeology* 2:101–110.

Bibliography 235

Roth, U. 2004. "Inscribed Meaning: The *Vilica* and the Villa Economy." *Papers of the British School at Rome* 72:101–124.

Rothwell, K. S. 1994. "Aristophanes' *Wasps* and the Sociopolitics of Aesop's *Fables*." *CJ* 90.3:233–254.

Ruiz-Montero, C. 1981. "The Structural Pattern of the Ancient Greek Romances and the Morphology of the Folktale of V. Propp." *Journal of Folktale Studies* 22:228–238.

Ruiz-Montero, C. 1994. "Chariton von Aphrodisias: Ein Überblick." In *ANRW, 2.34.2*, edited by W. Haase, 1006–1054. Berlin; New York: de Gruyter.

Ruiz-Montero, C. 2003. "Xenophon of Ephesus and Orality in the Roman Empire." *AN* 3:43–62.

Sacks, K. S. 1990. *Diodorus Siculus and the First Century*. Princeton: Princeton University Press.

Saïd, S. 1994. "The City in the Greek Novel." In *The Search for the Ancient Novel*, edited by J. Tatum, 216–236. Baltimore: Johns Hopkins University Press.

Saïd, S. 1999. "Rural Society in the Greek Novel, or The Country Seen From the Town." In *Oxford Readings in the Greek Novel*, edited by S. Swain, 83–107. New York: Oxford University Press.

Ste. Croix, G. E. M. de. 1981. *The Class Struggle in the Ancient Greek World From the Archaic Age to the Arab Conquest*. London: Duckworth.

Sandy, G. N. 1982a. *Heliodorus*. Boston: Twayne.

Sandy, G. N. 1982b. "Characterization and Philosophical Decor in Heliodorus' *Aethiopica*." *TAPA* 112:141–167.

Sandy, G. N. 1994. "New Pages of Greek Fiction." In *Greek Fiction: The Greek Novel in Context*, edited by J. R. Morgan and R. Stoneman, 130–145. London: Routledge.

Scarcella, A. M. 1970. "Realtà e letteratura nel paesaggio sociale ed economico del romanzo di Longo Sofista." *Maia* 22:104–131.

Scarcella, A. M. 1972. "La donna nel romanzo di Longo Sofista." *Giornale italiano di filologia* 24:63–84.

Scarcella, A. M. 1977. "Les structures socio-économiques du roman de Xénophon d'Éphèse." *Revue des études grecques* 90:249–262.

Scarcella, A. M. 1987. "Caratteri e funzione delle *gnōmai* in Achille Tazio." *Euphrosyne: Revista de Filologia Classica* 15:269–280.

Scarcella, A. M. 2003. "The Social and Economic Structures of the Ancient Novels." In *The Novel in the Ancient World*, edited by G. L. Schmeling, 221–276. Boston: Brill Academic Publishers.

Schlam, C. C. 1993. "Cupid and Psyche: Folktale and Literary Narrative." In *GCN, 5*, edited by H. Hofmann, 63–73. Groningen: Forsten.

Schmeling, G. L. 1974. *Chariton*. New York: Twayne Publishers.

Schmeling, G. L. 1980. *Xenophon of Ephesus*. Boston: Twayne Publishers.

Schönberger, O., ed. and trans. 1989. *Hirtengeschichten von Daphnis und Chloe*. Düsseldorf: Artemis & Winkler.

Schtajerman, E. M. 1964. *Die Krise der Sklavenhalterordunung im Westen des römischen Reiches*. Translated by W. Seyfarth. Berlin: Akademie Verlag.

Schumacher, L. 2001. *Sklaverei in der Antike: Alltag und Schicksal der Unfreien*. München: Beck.

Schwartz, S. C. 1999. "Callirhoe's Choice: Biological vs Legal Paternity." *GRBS* 40.1:23–52.

Schwartz, S. C. 2003. "Rome in the Greek Novel? Images and Ideas of Empire in Chariton's Persia." *Arethusa* 36.3:375–394.

236 Bibliography

Scobie, A. 1979. "Storytellers, Storytelling, and the Novel in Graeco-Roman Antiquity." *RhM* 122:229–259.

Scobie, A. 1983. *Apuleius and Folklore*. London: Folklore Society of London.

Scott, J. C. 1990. *Domination and the Arts of Resistance: Hidden Transcripts*. New Haven; London: Yale University Press.

Scourfield, J. H. D. 2003. "Anger and Gender in Chariton's *Chaereas and Callirhoe*." *YCS* 32:163–184.

Smith, N. D. 1983. "Aristotle's Theory of Natural Slavery." *Phoenix* 37:109–122.

Smith, S. D. 2007. *Greek Identity and the Athenian Past in Chariton: The Romance of Empire*. Eelde; Groningen: Barkhuis; Groningen University Library.

Stahl, W. H., trans. 1952. *Macrobius, Commentary on the Dream of Scipio*. New York: Columbia University Press.

Stanzel, F. K. 1984. *A Theory of Narrative*. Cambridge; New York: Cambridge University Press.

Stephens, S. A. 1994. "Who Read Ancient Novels?" In *The Search for the Ancient Novel*, edited by J. Tatum, 405–418. Baltimore: Johns Hopkins University Press.

Stephens, S. A., and J. J. Winkler, eds. 1995. *Ancient Greek Novels: The Fragments: Introduction, Text, Translation, and Commentary*. Princeton: Princeton University Press.

Stewart, R. L. 2012. *Plautus and Roman Slavery*. Oxford; Malden, MA: Wiley-Blackwell.

Swain, S. 1996. *Hellenism and Empire: Language, Classicism, and Power in the Greek World, AD 50–250*. Oxford; New York: Clarendon Press.

Tagliabue, A. 2017. *Xenophon's Ephesiaca: A Paraliterary Love-Story From the Ancient World*. Groningen: Barkhuis.

Teske, D. 1991. *Der Roman des Longos als Werk der Kunst: Untersuchungen zum Verhältnis von Physis und Techne in Daphnis und Chloe*. Münster: Aschendorff.

Thalmann, W. G. 1996. "Versions of Slavery in the *Captivi* of Plautus." *Ramus* 25.2:112–145.

Thalmann, W. G. 1998. *The Swineherd and the Bow: Representations of Class in the Odyssey*. Ithaca: Cornell University Press.

Thompson, S. 1966. *Motif-index of Folk-Literature*. Bloomington: Indiana University Press.

Tilg, S. 2010. *Chariton of Aphrodisias and the Invention of the Greek Love Novel*. Oxford; New York: Oxford University Press.

Tordoff, R. 2013. "Introduction: Slaves and Slavery in Ancient Greek Comedy." In *Slaves and Slavery in Ancient Greek Comic Drama*, edited by B. Akrigg and R. Tordoff, 1–62. Cambridge: Cambridge University Press.

Treggiari, S. 1969. *Roman Freedmen During the Late Republic*. Oxford: Clarendon Press.

Trenkner, S. 1958. *The Greek Novella in the Classical Period*. Cambridge: Cambridge University Press.

Treu, K. 1989a. "Der Realitätsgehalt des antiken Romans." In *Der antike Roman. Untersuchungen zur literarischen Kommunikation und Gattungsgeschichte*, edited by H. Kuch, 107–125. Berlin: Akademie Verlag.

Treu, K. 1989b. "Der antike Roman und sein Publikum." In *Der antike Roman: Untersuchungen zur literarischen Kommunication und Gattungsgeschichte*, edited by H. Kuch, 178–197. Berlin: Akademie Verlag.

Trevett, J. 1992. *Apollodoros, The Son of Pasion*. Oxford; New York: Clarendon Press; Oxford University Press.

Trzaskoma, S. 2005. "A Novelist Writing 'History': Longus' Thucydides Again." *GRBS* 45.1:75–90.

Bibliography 237

Trzaskoma, S. 2010a. "Callirhoe, Concubinage, and a Corruption in Chariton 2.11.5." *Exemplaria Classica* 14:205–209.

Trzaskoma, S., trans. 2010b. *Two Novels From Ancient Greece: Chariton's Callirhoe and Xenophon of Ephesos' An Ephesian Story: Anthia and Habrocomes*. Indianapolis: Hackett.

Tylawsky, E. I. 2002. *Saturio's Inheritance: The Greek Ancestry of the Roman Comic Parasite*. Bern; Frankfurt am Main: Peter Lang.

Uther, H.-J. 2011. *The Types of International Folktales*. Helsinki: Suomalainen Tiedeakatemia, Academia Scientiarum Fennica.

Veyne, P. 1961. "Vie de Trimalcion." *Annales: économies, sociétés, civilisations* 2:213–247.

Vilborg, E., ed. 1955. *Achilles Tatius. Leucippe and Clitophon*. Stockholm: Almqvist & Wiksell.

Vlassopoulos, K. 2011. "Greek Slavery: From Domination to Property and Back Again." *JHS* 131:115–130.

Vogliano, A. 1938. "Un papiro di Achille Tazio." *Studi italiani di filologia classica* 15:121–130.

Watson, A., ed. and trans. 1985. *The Digest of Justinian*. 4 vols. Philadelphia: University of Pennsylvania Press.

Weaver, P. R. C. 1967. "Social Mobility in the Early Roman Empire. The Evidence of the Imperial Freedmen and Slaves." *P&P* 37:3–20.

Weaver, P. R. C. 1972. *Familia Caesaris: A Social Study of the Emperor's Freedmen and Slaves*. Cambridge: Cambridge University Press.

Weiler, I. 2002. "Inverted *kalokagathia*." In *Representing the Body of the Slave*, edited by T. Wiedemann and J. Gardner, 11–28. London: F. Cass.

Weinreich, O. 1962. *Der griechische Liebesroman*. Zürich: Artemis Verlag.

Wesseling, B. 1988. "The Audience of the Ancient Novels." In *GCN, 1*, edited by H. Hofmann, 67–79. Groningen: Forsten.

West, S. 2003. "Κερκίδος παραμύθια? For Whom Did Chariton Write?" *ZPE* 143:63–69.

Whitmarsh, T. 1998. "The Birth of a Prodigy: Heliodorus and the Genealogy of Hellenism." In *Studies in Heliodorus*, edited by R. L. Hunter, 93–124. Cambridge: Cambridge Philological Society.

Whitmarsh, T. 2003. "Reading for Pleasure: Narrative, Irony, and Erotics in Achilles Tatius." In *The Ancient Novel and Beyond*, edited by S. Panayotakis, M. Zimmerman and W. H. Keulen, 191–205. Leiden: Brill.

Whitmarsh, T. 2005a. "The Greek Novel: Titles and Genre." *AJP* 126.4:587–611.

Whitmarsh, T. 2005b. "Dialogues in Love: Bakhtin and His Critics on the Greek Novel." In *The Bakhtin Circle and Ancient Narrative*, edited by R. B. Branham, 107–129. Groningen: Barkhuis and Groningen University Library.

Whitmarsh, T. 2008. "Class." In *The Cambridge Companion to the Greek and Roman Novel*, edited by T. Whitmarsh, 72–87. New York: Cambridge University Press.

Whitmarsh, T. 2011. *Narrative and Identity in the Ancient Greek Novel*. Cambridge; New York: Cambridge University Press.

Wiles, D. 1988. "Greek Theatre and the Legitimation of Slavery." In *Slavery and Other Forms of Unfree Labour*, edited by L. J. Archer, 53–67. London; New York: Routledge.

Williams, B. 1998. "Necessary Identities." In *Subjugation and Bondage: Critical Essays on Slavery and Social Philosophy*, edited by T. L. Lott, 1–28. Lanham, MD: Rowman & Littlefield Publishers.

Winkler, J. J. 1982. "The Mendacity of Kalisiris and the Narrative Strategy of Heliodorus' *Aithiopika*." *YCS* 27:93–157.

238 Bibliography

Winkler, J J. 1990. *The Constraints of Desire: The Anthropology of Sex and Gender in Ancient Greece*. London: Routledge.

Woronoff, M. 2002. "'La nouvelle de ma mort est très exagérée'." *Ktèma* 27:345–351.

Wouters, A. 1994. "Longus, *Daphnis et Chloé*: le prooemion et les histoires enchâssées à la lumière de la critique récente." *Les Études Classiques* 62 (2–3):131–167.

Wrenhaven, K. J. 2012. *Reconstructing the Slave: The Image of the Slave in Ancient Greece*. London: Bristol Classical Press.

Yardley, J. C. 1991. "The Symposium in Roman Elegy." In *Dining in a Classical Context*, edited by W. J. Slater, 149–154. Ann Arbor: Universitiy of Michigan Press.

Youni, M. S. 2008. "Sur le statut juridique de l'affranchi grec dans le monde gréco-romain." In *La fin du statut servile?*, edited by A. Gonzalès, 161–174. Besançon: Presses Universitaires de Franche-Comté.

Youni, M. S. 2010. "Transforming Greek Practice Into Roman Law: Manumissions in Roman Macedonia." *Legal History Review* 78:311–340.

Youtie, H. C. 1975. "ὑπογραφεύς. The Social Impact of Illiteracy in Graeco-Roman Egypt." *ZPE* 17:201–221.

Zanker, P. 1989. *Die trunkene Alte: das Lachen der Verhöhnten*. Frankfurt: Fischer.

Zeitlin, F. I. 1990. "The Poetics of *Erōs*: Nature, Art, and Imitation in Longus' *Daphnis and Chloe*." In *Before Sexuality*, edited by D. M. Halperin, J. J. Winkler and F. I. Zeitlin, 417–464. Princeton: Princeton University Press.

Zeitlin, F. I. 1994. "Gardens of Desire in Longus's *Daphnis and Chloe*: Nature, Art, and Imitation." In *The Search for the Ancient Novel*, edited by J. Tatum, 148–170. Baltimore: Johns Hopkins University Press.

Zelnick-Abramovitz, R. 2005. *Not Wholly Free: The Concept of Manumission and the Status of Manumitted Slaves in the Ancient Greek World*. Leiden; Boston: Brill.

Zimmermann, F. 1957. "Kallirhoes Verkauf durch Theron: eine juristisch-philologische Betrachtung zu Chariton." In *Aus der byzantinistischen Arbeit der Deutschen Demokratischen Republik*, edited by J. Irmscher, 72–81. Berlin: Akademie Verlag.

Zipes, J. 1979. *Breaking the Magic Spell: Radical Theories of Folk and Fairy Tales*. London: Heinemann.

Index

Page numbers in 'bold' indicate passages in the novels.

abortion 63
Aeschylus 17
Aesop and *The Life of Aesop* 14, 15, 17,
36, 173–175, 180n33, 183n79, 183n80,
207, 222n20
Aethiopica: Calasiris as narrator 189, 217;
as *servus callidus* 190–192; duplicity of
190–191; Cnemon as narrator 186–188,
192, 196, 217; date of novel 208–209n1;
doulotopia 202, 203, 216; *Ephesiaca* as
an intertext in 27, 54n70, 200, 207–208;
Heliodorus' authorial persona 187;
marginalization of slave characters
191–193; Platonic themes and 111,
186, 206–207; plot summary 185–186;
sophia 187–189, 190; *servitium
amoris* in 50n9, 195–196, 204–207, 208,
211n39, 213n67
Aethiopica (*loci*) **1.11.3** 193, 195; **2.25.2**
207; **3.5.4** 189, 206; **3.10**.1–2 191;
3.16.3–4 187; **3.19.1** 50n9, 206; **4.4.3**
194, 211n39; **5.1.4–5** 192; **5.4.4–5**
204–205; **6.3.2** 50n9, 196; **6.6.1** 195;
7.12.6 197–198; **7.17.3–4** 198–199;
7.24.4 199; **8.6.4** 202; **8.9.22** 203
alumnus 51n16, 111n3; *see also syntrophos*
American slavery 1, 11; African-American
folktales and folk traditions of 15, 36;
American slavery 1, 11; Brer Rabbit 15,
36; Brer Wolf 15; Brown, William
Wells 12; Douglass, Frederick 11, 12,
107–108; emasculation of male slaves
107–108, 119n116, 119n117; John (in
African-American folklore) 15; parallels
to Roman slavery 11, 21n19; peculiar
institution 1, n. 20n1
Anansi (African-American folklore): 36

anger: at slaves 31, 42, 91, 112n22, 134,
169, 171, 172–173, 199; expressed in
hidden transcript 17, 74, 75
antigraphē 142–143
Aphrodisias 80n3, 92–93, 112n25,
112n27, 219
Apuleius 4, 15, 19–20, 21n16, 116n81,
211n38, 220, 222n20; "Cupid and
Psyche" 26n90
aretē 6, 58, 73, 75; *see also virtus*
Aristotle 8, 17; *Poetics* 59, 77–78, 139;
Politics 8, 21n21, 22n26, 23n39,
23n40, 23–24n45, 64–65, 84n41,
86n63, 92, 209n14, 212n54; *Rhetoric*
139, 141
Athenaeus 14–15
Augustales 218, 221n9

Babylon 72–77
Bird, Rachel 205
Bodel, John, 19
Bradley, Keith 4–5, 11, 19, 133
Brer Rabbit (African-American folklore):
15, 36
Brer Wolf (African-American folklore): 15
Brown, William Wells 12

Callirhoe: abortion and 63, 82n21, 112n16;
aretē of male protagonist 58, 73, 75–76;
and Aristotle, *Poetics* 77–78, 139;
automolia 75, 85n58; Callirhoe as
ancilla callida 62–63; Callirhoe as bad
slave 66–69, 81n9; Chariton's authorial
persona and status 92–93, 99, 216,
221n4; Chariton as *hypographeus*
(secretary) 81n12, 92, 113n30, 120n126;
Chaereas as bad slave 70–72, 77, 81n9,

240 *Index*

88, 109; crucifixion in 71, 79, 80, 86n73, 90; date 56, 80n1; Dionysius 60, 82–83n26; *doulotopia* 73, 197–198; explicit narrative in 58–64; implicit narrative in 64–70; plot summary 49; Roman practice of slavery and 100; Roman *villa* system in 81n10, 81n14, 89–90; *Scheintod* (false-death motif) 104; *sōphrosynē* Callirhoe 58, 62, 63, 67, 69–70, 73–80.

Callirhoe (*loci*) **1.1.1** 92; **2.1.5** 60; **2.6.2** 61–62; **2.10.6–7** 63, 74; **2.11.6** 63–64, 84n38; **4.2.5–6** 70–71, 91; **8.1.4** 77–78; **8.4.4–5** 76–77; **8.7.3–8.11** 78–80

Campania 217–218, 221n10

catharsis (Aristotle): 77, 78

Chalk, H. H. O. 124, 138

Champlin, Edward 16

Chariton, Ulpius Claudius 93

Cicero 23n41, 101–102, 111n5, 114n44, 117n83, 180n38, 211n43, 219

client and *cliens* 10, 101, 135, 217; *see also* patron and *patronus*

Columella 6, 10–11, 23n1, 82n20, 111n6, 111n8, 147n25

comedy and *fabula palliata* (representation of slavery and influence on the novel): 1–2, 6, 17–18, 21n15, 22n24, 38–40, 66, 82n22, 84n33, 95, 110, 114n36, 121, 135, 140, 146n12, 147n23, 180n25, 191, 204, 214

contubernales 106, 111n8

crucifixion 34, 71, 79, 80, 86n73, 90, 112n14, 149n55

Cueva, Edmund 145

Daphnis and Chloe: *agroikia* (countryside) 125–126, 128, 130–132, 140, 143; *antigraphē* 142–143; and Aristotle, *Rhetoric* 139; date of novel 121–122, 146n1, 146n2; *dēmiourgikē technē* 140; distinctiveness within genre 27, 111; and Galen, *de Praecognitione* 133; infant exposure in 142; inserted tales 128; *mimēsis* in 139–141; *logos* and *mythos* in 128, 136, 141, 143, 144–145, 148n40, 150n73; and New Comedy 121, 135, 146n12, 147n23; Pan and Syrinx myth 128, 147n19; *paradeisos* of Dionysophanes 133, 137–138, 141, 144, 148n44, 149n49, 149n52; Philetas' garden 126, 137–139, 148n44, 149n52; *physis* (nature) in 124, 139, 149n52; and

Plato, *Protagoras* 124, 138, 149n47; plot summary 121–123; *politikē technē* 130, 139, 140, 141; and Thucydides 121, 145; torture (threatened) 136

Daphnis and Chloe (*loci*) **Pr. 2** 121; **2.3.3–4** 125–126; **2.7.1–5** 126; **4.8.3–4** 135; **4.15.4** 142; **4.19.5** 136

dēmiourgikē technē 136, 140, 142

De Temmerman, Koen75, 153, 167, 168, 170

Diodorus Siculus 13, 217

dioikētēs (financial steward): 58, 89

dispensator 89

Douglass, Frederick 11, 12, 107–108

doulotopia 73, 197, 198, 202, 203, 216

Dowden, Ken 187, 20

Drimacus of Chios 14–15

duBois, Page 25n76, 25n81, 213n70

Egger, Brigitte 97

elegiac poetry (representation of slavery and influence on the novel): 28–29, 50n8, 95, 157, 180n23, 196

Ephesiaca (*The Ephesian Tale*): Anthia as *ancilla callida* 38–39; Anthia as bad slave 35–40; critical reception of 27–28, 50n2; crucifixion in 34; date of novel 27, 50n1; epitome theory 27; "Escape from an Undesired Suitor" (folktale) 30, 35, 93, 94; folktales in 28, 29, 30–35; good slave stereotype 40–41; Habrocomes as bad slave 33–35; Habrocomes as freedman 43–45; Leucon and Rhode as *syntrophoi* 30–31; Magna Graecia in 217; and paraliterature 28; plot summary 27; "Potiphar's Wife" (folktale) 29, 30–35, 51n23, 93, 215; Roman practice of slavery and 100; *servitium amoris* in 28–29, 47; "Snow White" (folktale) 93; *sōphrosynē* of the heroine 30, 35, 36, 38, 40; torture 29–35, 49; Xenophon of Ephesus' authorial persona 88, 93–94

Ephesiaca (*loci*) **1.14.4–6** 40–41; **2.4.4** 31; **2.5.4** 31; **2.5.6–7** 31–32; **2.6.1** 32; **2.6.3** 32–33; **2.10.2** 44, 221n7; **3.12.4** 33; **5.1.10–11** 104–105; **5.7.2** 38; **5.8.3** 218; **5.15.1–2** 47

ergastulum (slave barracks): 90, 217

erōs: in *Aethiopia* 187–188; marriage as legally sanctioned *erōs* in *Daphnis and Chloe* 137; reciprocal *erōs* and slaves 49, 105–111

"Escape from an Undesired Suitor" (folktale) 30, 35, 93, 94

The Ethiopian Tale see Aethiopica
eunuchs 73, 74, 169–170, 188, 197, 201–202, 211n37
Eunus 13, 14, 25n64, 108
Euripides 1; 21n16, 42, 51n18, 119n121, 211n38
Ex-slaves: ex-slave elite 99–101; *familia Caesaris* 99, 116n70, 116n71, 116n76, 117n88; family relationships 106–107; *grammatici* 9, 99–101, 220; Hermippus of Berytos 102, 117n87; 9, 99, 100, 101, 220; literacy and literary accomplishments 3, 9, 18, 88–89, 94–99, 103, 107, 108, 218, 219; *macula servitutis* 10, 24n51, 72, 101; mentality 98–103; negative stereotypes 101–103, 220; *obsequium* 10, 45, 54n61, 89, 111n5; *operae* 10, 45, 89, 111n4; *paramonē* 45, 111n4, 116n75, 221n7; in Suetonius, *De grammaticis et rhetoribus* 99–100, 119n122, 220
Ex-slaves (represented in the novel): Callirhoe as ex-slave 76–77; Gnathon as freedman 135–136, 141, 148 n. 35; Habrocomes as *liber ingratus* 45, 89; protagonists as ex-slaves in *Ephesiaca* 47–48, 55n76.

fable and folktale (representation of slavery and influence on the novel): 18, 113n34; in *Ephesiaca* 28, 30–35; 35–40, 42, 143, 215; in *Leucippe and Clitophon* 158, 176, 180n33; as medium for slave's point of view 4, 13–17, 25n76, 25n79, 115n66
fabulae aniles 220
fabula palliata see comedy and *fabula palliata* (representation of slavery and influence on the novel)
familia Caesaris 24n48, 99, 116n70, 116n71, 117n76, 117n88
familia rustica 90
fear (owners' fear of slaves): 6, 16, 22n28, 34, 52n26
Fetterley, Judith 144, 145
Fitzgerald, William 4
Florentinus (Roman jurisprudent) 103
Foley, Helene 144
folktales see fable and folktale (representation of slavery and influence on the novel)
Forsdyke, Sara 15, 17, 110
"The Fox and the Eagle" (fable): 16

Fraenkel, Eduard 17
freedmen and freedwomen see ex-slaves
Fusillo, Massimo 177

Garden of Philetas 125–126, 137–139, 148n44, 149n52
Genesis 29
geography in the novel see Italy, Magna Graecia, Sicily
George, Michele 106–107
Goold, George 69
grammatici 9, 99, 100, 101, 220, 222n22
Graverini, Luca 220
Greek law 22n23, 59, 81n11, 83n29, 113n31, 115n61; *see also* Roman law

Harris, William 91, 95
Hermippus of Berytos 102, 117n87
Hesiod 17
hidden transcript 12, 13–18, 24n58, 25n62, 31, 43–45, 53n41, 57, 89, 93, 105, 109, 110, 119n125, 173, 215–216; *see also* public transcript
Herodotus 73, 85n52, 93, 112n120, 113n29, 183n80, 207, 213n70
Homer 7, 17, 21n16, 36, 65, 75, 95, 97, 121, 144, 194
Hopkins, Keith 156
Hunt, Peter 6
hybris (against slaves): 62, 65, 83n29, 116n75, 173
hypographeus (secretary): 81, n12, 93, 113n30, 120n126

Iamblichus 20n3, 95, 221n4, 221n18
impudicitia (sexual impurity): 6, 35, 101, 107
infrapolitics 13, 25n60
instrumentum vocale 64–65, 92
intertext see under *Aethiopica* and *Leucippe and Clitophon*
Iser, Wolfgang 97
Italy 20, 43, 59, 106, 217–219

John (African-American folklore): 15
Jones, Meriel 188

kalokagathia 6, 22n26, 198
katagraphē 59, 81n11
katharsion 77, 78
Konstan, David 105, 153
Kurke, Leslie 14

242 *Index*

Leucippe and Clitophon: *Callirhoe* as intertext in 168–171; Clitophon as deficient narrator 153; Clitophon as "enslaved" protagonist 172–175; Clitophon's final summary 175–177; Clitophon's relationship with Satyrus 154, 155–165, 180n41, 183n81; date of novel 151, 178n1; and Galen 172–173; and *Life of Aesop* 173–175; Melantho 166, 176; plot summary 151–152; problematic conclusion 177–178; Pasion 166; *Scheintod* in 151, 153, 176–177, 181n53, 183n84; *sententiae* 170–171; torture of Leucippe 168

Leucippe and Clitophon (*loci*): **1.5** 155; **2.18.6–19.1** 157; **3.20–22** 161; **3.23.1** 161; **4.17.6** 161; **5.17.3** 167, 181n50; **5.19.1** 168; **5.19.6** 168; **6.21.1–2** 170; **7.10.5** 153, 182n70; **8.1.3–5** 172; **8.5.5** 175–176

Levine, Lawrence 15

libertus ingratus 45, 89, 111n5

logos 8, 9; opposed to *mythos* 136, 145, 148n40, 150n73, 153, 179n7

MacLean, Rose 106

Macrobius 219–220

macula servitutis 10, 24, n51, 72, 101

Magna Graecia 20, 217–219

manumission 6, 10, 22n23, 45, 54n53, 69, 101, 105, 107, 111n5, 116n75, 118n100, 221n7

Menander 1, 146n12, 148n35, 210n22, 219

metaphorical slavery vs actual slavery see under slaves and slavery (as represented in the novel)

mime 13–14, 17, 99, 110

mimesis 139, 140–141

Morales, Helen 153, 157, 171

Morgan, John 106, 123, 142, 145, 153, 177, 188, 191, 196, 197, 205, 206

Mouritsen, Henrik 106

novel motifs see under slaves and slavery (as represented in the novel)

novel and oral literature 15, 94, 113n35, 114n47, 119n125, 215; *see also* fable and folktale

obsequium and *operae* 10, 45, 54n61, 89, 111n4, 111n5

Ostrow, Steven 218

paideia (as a characteristic of slave-owners): 60, 88, 92, 110, 112n21

Pallas 108

Pan and Syrinx 127–128, 147n19

Pandemic *Erōs* see Uranian and Pandemic *Erōs* (Heavenly and Vulgar Love)

paradeisos (Garden of Dionysophanes): 133, 137–141, 144, 148n44, 149n49, 149n52

paramonē 45, 54n60, 111n4, 116n75, 221n7; *see also* Greek law

paterfamilias 45, 91

patron and *patronus* 9, 10, 24n50, 44, 45, 76, 86n66, 89, 93, 99, 100, 101, 102, 106, 111n7, 117n82, 117n85, 117n87, 118n107, 135, 148n38, 217; *see also* client and *cliens*

Patterson, Orlando 5, 7, 103, 200

Perry, Ben Edwin 96

Petronius 19–20, 55n76, 116n81, 119n122, 179n19, 220, 222n20

Phaedrus 15–16, 25n80, 25n81, 55n76, 116n74, 116n79, 116n81, 119n122, 179n1

Philostratus 219, 221n17

Plato 148n44, 179n7, 209n8; *Phaedrus* 187; *Protagoras* 124, 138–139, 149n47; *Republic* 81n18, 212n62; *Symposium* 187

Plautus 2, 17–18, 21n16, 23n35, 51n22, 53n41, 53n47, 53n48, 54n52, 54n53, 54n58, 87n80, 147n23, 180n39, 182n59, 183n78

Plutarch 14, 112n10

politikē technē 124–125, 128, 130, 138–139, 140–142, 152

"Potiphar's wife" (foktale): 29–30, 33–35, 51n23, 52n25, 93, 215

Priscianus 95, 221n18

public transcript 12, 14, 16, 24n58, 43–45, 57, 59, 64, 215; *see also* hidden transcript

pudicitia (sexual chasteness): 6, 20, 107; *see also sōphrosynē*

Quintilian 220

reader-response critics 94, 97, 115n60

readers: ex-slaves 3, 9–10, 18, 20–21n7, 34, 88–89, 94–110, 215–216, 218–219; middle-class 96, 114n51; slave-owning elite 18, 21n12, 34, 36, 40, 69–70, 114n43, 115n53, 115n64, 115n66; women 97, 115n58, 115n59, 115n63; young people 115n52

Reardon, Bryan 170, 219

Repath, Ian 177

Index 243

Richlin, Amy 17
Rohde, Erwin 27
Roman law 10, 23n32, 35, 38, 45, 54n65,
  83n27, 84n40, 182n61; *Digest* 24n50,
  34, 52n27, 53n43, 53n44, 54n64,
  103–104; *see also* Greek law
Rothwell, Kenneth 16

Sappho 121, 207
Schmeling, Gareth 41
Scott, James 12, 13, 14, 32, 36, 43, 57,
  200, 215
scriba 93, 113n32
senatus consultum Silanianum 34, 52n26;
  see also fear
Seneca 8, 22n27, 23n43, 23n45, 51n20,
  53n42, 83n28, 111n1, 148n30, 211n38,
  222n22
Seneca the Elder 101
servitium amoris (slavery-to-love):
  28-29, 47, 50n7, 50n9 162, 179n16,
  186, 195-196, 204-207, 208, 211n39,
  213n67
sexual impurity (*impudicitia*): 6, 35,
  101, 107
Sicilian slave wars 13, 14, 25n64, 108,
  217–218
Sicily 5, 14, 20, 39, 48, 104, 108,
  217–218
slave: as living possession (*empsychon
  ktēma*) 8; as possession (*ktēma*) 145,
  147n26
slavery (as practiced): hard work in 14, 17;
  Greek slavery 89; *paramonē* 45, 111n4,
  116n75, 221n7; sexual exploitation
  106–107, 118n111; Roman practice of
  45, 88, 90, 100, 217; torture 187, 202;
  see also Greek law, Roman law
slaves: hidden transcripts of 18;
  infrapolitics 13; intellectual resistance
  13, 110; protest, resistance, and rebellion
  11, 18, 72–75; solidarity 14
slaves and slavery (elite views): Aristotle
  and the natural slave 8–9, 22n26, 23n39,
  84n41; Columella, *De re rustica* 6, 10,
  11, 111n8; denial of subjectivity 7;
  Eumaios as good slave 7, 23n35, 40,
  220n1; fear of slaves 6; good slave
  stereotype 4, 6–7; sexual impurity
  (*impudicitia*) 6, 35, 101, 107;
  stereotypes 11–12, 207–208; Stoic views
  8–9; Varro, slave as *instrumentum
  vocale* 64, 65, 92
slaves and slavery (as represented in the
  novel): actual and metaphorical 2, 4,

28–29, 89, 152; *ancilla callida* 39, 62,
  66; enslaved secondary characters 3, 30;
  fables and folktales 15–16; as metaphor
  28–29, 196; motif of ambivalence to
  bad-slave behavior 3, 72, 98, 109–110;
  motif of antipathy to slave owners in
  novel 89–92, 94; motif of false death
  or *Scheintod* 51n11, 103–105, 117n91,
  142, 151, 153, 176–177, 181n51,
  151n53, 183n81, 183–184n84, 185n85,
  215; motif of nobility of enslaved
  protagonists 103; motif of passivity of
  male novel protagonist 107, 172–173,
  182n70, 182n72, 215; motif of sympathy
  for slaves 3, 49, 88, 90–91, 97–98; motif
  of solidarity among enslaved novel
  characters 41–43, 68, 77, 134, 214, 216;
  realistic representation of 89–92; *servus
  callidus* 6, 17, 18, 39, 160, 180n25,
  180n39, 190–191; sexual exploitation
  and rape 3, 17, 22n25, 27, 35–40, 47,
  49, 53n38, 53n43, 62, 69, 84n44,
  118n111, 171; slave owners criticized
  91–92, 217; slavery as social death
  103–104
slaves and slavery (as represented in other
  genres): see under comedy, elegiac
  poetry, fable and folktale, Homer,
  mime, tragedy
"Snow White" (folktale) 42, 54n55, 54n56,
  93, 215
social death 5, 7, 21n21, 103–105, 154,
  176, 181n53, 215
Sophocles 115n59, 144
sōphrosynē 6, 20, 30, 35, 36, 37, 38, 40,
  47, 54n70, 58, 62, 63, 67, 69, 70, 73, 74,
  80, 81n9, 82–83n26, 94, 105–107,
  118n112, 119n120, 149n59, 187, 188,
  203, 205, 209n12, 213n65, 215
Spartacus 14, 112n14, 218
Stephens, Susan 95
Stoics and Stoicism 8–9, 13, 23n41, 23n44,
  25n64, 31, 32, 51n21, 60, 144, 170,
  182n62, 209n14, 211n43
Suda 27, 102, 113n33, 221n4
Suetonius 99–100, 117n85, 119n22, 220
Swain, Simon 96
syntrophos 30, 47, 48, 51n16, 55n74,
  89, 91, 97, 11n3, 148n34, 164, 208;
  see also alumnus

Tagliabue, Aldo 27–28, 46, 48
Terence 1, 26n88, 53n48, 116n74, 117n85,
  148n35
Thalmann, W. G. 7

244 *Index*

Theocritus 115n59, 121, 123, 146n3
Thompson, Stith 30, 35
Thucydides 6, 93, 113n29, 121, 145
Tilg, Stephan 56, 78, 93, 219
tragedy (representation of slavery and influence on the novel): 1–2, 26n84, 38–39, 77–78, 84n33, 95, 103, 110, 214
Trzaskoma, Stephen 145

Uranian and Pandemic *Erōs* (Heavenly and Vulgar Love) 187–188, 194, 196, 205–207, 209n13, 21n39, 212n59, 217

Valerius Maximus 10, 24n52
Varro 64–65, 92
verna 100, 119–120n126

Vettius (slave-revolt leader) 218
Veyne, Paul 19
vilicus and vilica 10, 81n13, 82n20, 90, 111n8, 148n30
villa 10, 81n10, 81n14, 82n20, 85n46, 89–90, 165, 217
virtus 6; *see also aretē*

Weiler, Ingomar 6
Whitmarsh, Tim 35, 48, 57, 92, 95, 153
Williams, Bernard 144
Winkler, Jack 128, 144, 190–191

Xenophon of Athens 6

Zeitlin, Froma 124, 139–140
Zipes, Jack 15

Printed in Great Britain
by Amazon